Geographic Locations map showing:

150°W · 120°W · 90°W · 60°W · 30°W

75°N

Inuit

Beaver

60°N

Gitksan

Naskapi

Cree

Nootka

Itwakwaka'kawa

45°N

England

Cheyenne

Crow

Paiute

Navaho

Iroquois

Lakota

30°N

Kiowa

Aztec

Hopi

Haiti

Apache

Mexico

ATLANTIC

15°N

Carib

PACIFIC

OCEAN

Senegal

Equator

0°

OCEAN

Yanomamo

Xinguano

15°S

Kuikuru

30°S

45°S

Ona

0   1000 miles

0   1000 kilometers

60°S

75°S

150°W · 120°W · 90°W · 60°W · 30°W

of Peoples Referred to in the Text

CULTURAL ANTHROPOLOGY

CULTURAL ANTHROPOLOGY
A Problem-Based Approach

Sixth Edition

Richard H. Robbins
State University of New York at Plattsburgh

WADSWORTH
CENGAGE Learning™

Australia • Brazil • Japan • Korea • Mexico • Singapore • Spain • United Kingdom • United States

WADSWORTH
CENGAGE Learning™

Cultural Anthropology: A Problem-Based Approach, Sixth Edition

Richard H. Robbins

Senior Publisher: Linda Schreiber-Ganster

Acquiring Sponsoring Editor: Erin Mitchell

Senior Development Editor: Lin Marshall Gaylord

Development Editor: Liana Sarkisian

Assistant Editor: Linda Stewart

Editorial Assistant: Mallory Ortberg

Media Editor: Bessie Weiss

Technology Project Manager: Melanie Cregger

Marketing Manager: Andrew Keay

Marketing Coordinator: Jack Ward

Marketing Communications Manager: Laura Localio

Manufacturing Manager: Marcia Locke

Project Management: PreMediaGlobal

Senior Art Director: Caryl Gorska

Senior Print Buyer: Judy Inouye

Senior Rights Specialist: Roberta Broyer

Cover Design and Illustration: Gia Giasullo

Compositor: PreMediaGlobal

For product information and technology assistance, contact us at **Cengage Learning Customer & Sales Support, 1-800-354-9706**

For permission to use material from this text or product, submit all requests online at **cengage.com/permissions**
Further permissions questions can be e-mailed to **permissionrequest@cengage.com**

Library of Congress Control Number: 2011933537

ISBN-13: 978-1-111-83394-7

ISBN-10: 1-111-83394-X

Wadsworth
20 Davis Drive
Belmont, CA 94002-3098
USA

Cengage Learning is a leading provider of customized learning solutions with office locations around the globe, including Singapore, the United Kingdom, Australia, Mexico, Brazil, and Japan. Locate your local office at: **www.cengage.com/global**

Cengage Learning products are represented in Canada by Nelson Education, Ltd.

For your course and learning solutions, visit **www.cengage.com**

Purchase any of our products at your local college store or at our preferred online store **www.cengagebrain.com**

Printed in Canada
1 2 3 4 5 6 7 15 14 13 12 11

CONTENTS

v

Chapter 4
The Social and Cultural Construction of Reality   131

PROBLEM 4: Why do people believe different things, and why are they so
certain their view of the world is correct and other views are wrong?   131

Chapter 5

Patterns of Family Relations   179

Chapter 6

The Cultural Construction of Identity   217

PREFACE

Anthropologists enjoy a unique perspective on education. For us, learning and teaching form part of a cultural process affected by a host of social, cultural, individual, and situational factors. A classroom constitutes but one of many learning environments and, like other environments, influences the kind of learning that occurs within its boundaries. For the anthropologist, classrooms have their own unique cultures—some of which may be more or less conducive to the kinds of learning to which teachers and students aspire.

I designed *Cultural Anthropology: A Problem-Based Approach* to help instructors and students in introductory courses in cultural anthropology to foster a classroom culture that, regardless of class size and instructional technique, actively involves students in the learning process, promotes critical thinking, and impresses on students that they, along with other peoples and cultures of the world, are cultural animals worthy of anthropological study. The case studies in doing anthropology included at the end of each chapter are designed to illustrate the uses of an anthropological perspective and its applications to various career paths.

How can the use of this book and the instructor's resources contribute to active learning? I think in at least three ways. First, the material is organized by problems and questions rather than topics. Each of the eight chapters of the book focuses on a specific problem of anthropological as well as a general concern:

- How can people begin to understand beliefs and behaviors that are different from their own?
- How do we explain the transformation of human societies over the past 10,000 years from small-scale nomadic bands of hunters and gatherers to large-scale urban-industrial states?
- What is globalization, and what does it have to do with me?
- Why do people believe different things, and why are they so certain that their view of the world is correct and others are wrong?
- What do we need to know before we can understand the dynamics of family life in other societies?
- How do people determine who they are, and how do they communicate who they think they are to others?

- Why are modern societies characterized by social, political, and economic inequalities?
- How do societies give meaning to and justify collective violence?

From these problems are derived specific questions, each of which is amenable to study and research and from which it is possible to come to a more or less definitive conclusion. These include:

- Is modern medicine more effective than traditional curing techniques?
- How do we define happiness and well-being?
- How do people come to accept social hierarchies as natural?
- What are the characteristics of peaceful societies?

The selection of specific problems and questions for the text was a difficult one. It is impossible in an introductory-level textbook to present all the problems and questions of relevance to cultural anthropologists. However, I have tried to select problems and questions that are central to anthropological concerns, that allow discussion of anthropological subjects and works typically covered in introductory courses in cultural anthropology, and that are, in addition, meaningful to today's students. The Topic–Question Correspondence chart below links topics in cultural anthropology to questions considered in the text and can be used in guiding discussion.

TOPIC–QUESTION CORRESPONDENCE	
Topic	**Corresponding Chapter or Question**
Applied anthropology	Case Studies 1–8
Art	Question 4.2
Belief	Chapter 4
Caste	Question 7.1
Colonialism	Questions 2.3, 2.5
Corporations	Questions 3.3, 3.4; Case Study 3
Cultural bias	Question 4.4
Cultural evolution	Question 2.1
Cultural relativism	Question 1.2
Culture change	Chapter 2; Case Studies 2, 3
Culture concept	Chapter 1
Ecology	Questions 1.5, 2.3; Case Study 2
Economic anthropology	Chapters 2, 3; Questions 7.1, 7.2
Education	Questions 3.3, 4.2, 6.3, 7.1; Case Studies 6, 8
Family organization	Chapter 5
Feud	Questions 8.1, 8.3

Fieldwork	Question 1.3; Case Studies 1–8
Financial crisis	Question 3.5
Food production	Questions 2.2, 2.3; Case Study 3
Gender roles	Chapter 5; Case Study 5; Questions 6.2, 6.3, 7.3
Gift giving	Questions 5.3, 6.4, 6.5
Globalization	Questions 2.2, 2.3, 2.5; Chapter 3
Hunters and gatherers	Questions 2.1, 2.5, 8.2
Identity	Chapter 6
Industrialization	Questions 2.2, 2.3, 3.3
Inequality	Questions 7.1, 7.2, 7.3
Kinship	Chapter 5; Questions 6.2, 7.4
Language and culture	Questions 1.4, 4.1, 4.3, 6.2, 6.3, 7.4, 8.2, 8.5
Marriage rules	Chapter 5
Medical anthropology	Question 2.4; Case Study 7
Money	Question 3.1
Nation-state	Question 3.4
Neoliberalism	Chapter 3
Peasants	Questions 2.1, 2.3, 2.5; Chapter 5
Political organization and control	Questions 3.4, 7.5, 8.2, 8.3, 8.4, 8.5; Case Study 4
Religion	Questions 1.1, 1.2, 6.4; Chapter 4
Revolution	Questions 7.2, 8.4
Ritual	Questions 1.4, 1.5, 2.4, 4.2, 4.3, 6.2, 6.3, 6.4, 6.5
Sexual stratification	Questions 5.1, 5.2, 5.3; Chapter 7
Sexuality	Questions 1.5, 4.2, 4.4, 6.2, 6.3; Case Study 5
Social stratification	Chapter 7
Status and rank	Chapter 7
Subsistence techniques	Questions 2.1, 2.2
Symbolism	Questions 1.1, 1.4, 1.5, 4.1, 4.2, 4.3, 6.3, 6.4; Case Study 4
Systems of exchange	Questions 3.1, 6.5
Urbanism	Question 7.4
War	Question 3.4; Chapter 8
Wealth	Questions 3.1, 7.1, 7.2

In providing material to explore answers to the questions posed in the text, I have tried to present a balanced approach and to invite readers to form their own informed responses. I have also tried to select studies and writings that represent those classical studies typically found in introductory-level courses and newer or less well-known works that bear on contemporary concerns.

A second way that *Cultural Anthropology: A Problem-Based Approach* contributes to active learning is through exercises, case studies, and simulations—some of which are included in the textbook and others in the instructor's manual available online. These are designed to help students realize some of the implications of the problems or questions for their own lives as well as for others. Students and instructors can use them in various ways: as discussion questions, writing exercises, or topics for group inquiry or cooperative learning. As topics for group work, I have used them in classes as large as 75 students, and I believe they can be used effectively in even larger classes. If used as group inquiry topics, the exercises are designed to take no more than 15 to 20 minutes. As writing exercises, they can be used to prime classroom discussion; students can prepare brief responses prior to class, and these responses can be used as a starting point for discussion. My own experience is that the use of these exercises conveys to students the positive value, the enjoyment, and the necessity of intellectual exchange. The exercises also allow students to bring to the class and contribute their own informed responses to the questions discussed in the textbook. The instructor's manual includes suggestions on using the exercises as well as information on what to expect in the way of student responses. In addition, it includes a guide to articles in introductory readers and film and video material to accompany each question raised in the book, along with suggestions on how the films or videos can be used to stimulate discussion.

The third feature that contributes to active learning stems from my conviction that people learning about the cultures of others cannot fully appreciate them without first understanding something of their own cultural perspectives. That is, to appreciate the fact that people construct their "worlds," students must appreciate the fact that they, as cultural animals, do the same. For that reason, the textbook contains numerous comparisons of world cultures with American cultures, and many of the exercises in the textbook and instructor's manual invite students to apply what they have learned to the analysis of their own behaviors and beliefs.

CHANGES IN THE SIXTH EDITION

There are a number of significant changes in this sixth edition.

There is a new discussion in Chapter 2 regarding the economic, social, and political impact of debt and International Monetary Fund (IMF) structural adjustment programs (SAPs) on emerging economies.

There is a discussion of the role of the automobile as a market externality in Chapter 3. Given the importance of the automobile and its impact on national economies, environments, and health, it seems a major consideration. Also included

in Chapter 3 is an extended description and discussion of the economic crisis that
began in 2007 and continues today. Because that crisis has had global consequences and likely affects students using this book, it is a necessary addition.

There is an extended discussion in Chapter 4 describing grid/group or cultural
bias theory as developed by Mary Douglas and her associates. This is an addition
that I had wanted to make over many editions, but I was concerned about how
useful it would be in an introductory-level anthropology class. However, given the
need to try to understand how different people construe their world so differently,
particularly when there is so much public debate over crucial economic, social, and
environmental issues, I believe Douglas's framework now has special relevance.

I have added in Chapter 7 a new section on the persistence of inequality—
nationally and globally. Again, given the rising gaps between rich and poor, it is
more important than ever for students to understand why inequality persists.

Finally, in Chapter 8, I have added a case study regarding the role of anthropologists in military intelligence in Iraq and Afghanistan. Because this is an issue
taken up by the American Anthropological Association, it will make for lively
discussion in an introductory course.

In addition to these changes, data tables and other information have been
updated when appropriate.

Implicit in the textbook and the instructional materials is the conviction that the
culture of the classroom should foster cooperation. However, cooperation does not
preclude conflict and critique. In fact, it assumes it. I would be grateful for comments
from instructors and students about the book, the questions, and the general approach
as well as suggestions for additional exercises, videos or films, or other materials that
would enhance the use of *Cultural Anthropology: A Problem-Based Approach*. I also
would be happy to distribute those suggestions to others who are using the book. I can
be contacted at the Department of Anthropology, SUNY at Plattsburgh, Plattsburgh,
NY 12901, or by e-mail at richard.robbins@plattsburgh.edu.

SUPPLEMENTS

Instructor Resources

- *Online Instructor's Manual and Test Bank*. This instructor resource provides
  detailed chapter outlines, lecture suggestions, key terms, student activities
  such as exercises from the Anthropology Resource Center, PowerPoint
  slides, and test questions that include multiple choice, true/false, fill in the
  blank, short answer, and essay types.
- *ExamView®*. Create, deliver, and customize tests and study guides, printed
  and online, in minutes with this easy-to-use assessment and tutorial system.
  ExamView® guides you step-by-step through the process. You can build tests
  of up to 250 questions using as many as 12 types of questions. ExamView®
  is available for Windows or Macintosh.

- *BBC Anthropology Video Series.* This exclusive video series was created jointly by Wadsworth and BBC for the anthropology course. Each video contains approximately 60 minutes of footage originally broadcast on BBC.
- *CourseReader: Anthropology. CourseReader: Cultural Anthropology* allows you to create a fully customized online reader in minutes. Access a rich collection of thousands of primary and secondary sources, readings, and audio and video selections from multiple disciplines. Each selection includes a descriptive introduction that puts it into context, and every selection is further supported by both critical-thinking and multiple-choice questions designed to reinforce key points. This easy to use solution allows you to select exactly the content you need for your courses, and is loaded with convenient pedagogical features like highlighting, printing, note taking, and downloadable MP3 audio files for each reading. You have the freedom to assign and customize individualized content at an affordable price. *CourseReader: Cultural Anthropology* is the perfect complement to any class.

Student Resources

- *Anthropology Resource Center for Cultural Anthropology: A Problem-Based Approach, 6e.* This hands-on online center offers a wealth of information and useful tools for both instructors and students in all four fields of anthropology: cultural anthropology, physical anthropology, archaeology, and linguistics. It includes interactive maps, learning modules, video exercises, and breaking news in anthropology.

Additional Student Resources

- *Case Studies in Cultural Anthropology*, edited by George Spindler and Janice E. Stockard, offers a diverse array of case studies that emphasize culture change and the factors influencing change in the peoples depicted. New topics include five genders in Indonesia and Hawaiian fishermen.
- *Case Studies on Contemporary Social Issues*, edited by John A. Young, offers a variety of case studies that explore how anthropology is used today in understanding and addressing problems faced by human societies around the world. Topics range from the cultural practices and politics affecting the spread of Ebola to homelessness in New York City and water resource management in Mexico City.
- *Modules for Cultural Anthropology,* including new Careers in Anthropology by Sunil Khana.

ACKNOWLEDGMENTS

A book such as this is truly a collaborative effort. Among the many whose contributions have made this book possible are the late James Clifton, Leo Weigman, Dan Spinella, Gloria Reardon, Janet Tilden, Rachel Dowty, Ali Pomponio, Jon McGee, Pat Hoffmann, Elvin Hatch, Rosemary Gianno, James Armstrong, Mark Cohen, Philip Devita, Tracy Hopkins, Jeffrey Hopkins, Pat Higgins, Deborah Altamirano, Ted Peacock, Tom Moran, Joyce Waite, Deborah Light, Tina Charland, Christine L. Fry, Susan Abbott-Jamieson, Anne Bolin, Carolyn Epple, Charles O. Ellenbaum, Stanley M. Newman, Myrdene Anderson, Thomas Hakansson, Cheryl Kucharzak, Kim Vander Steen, John Beasley, Elaine B. David, Richard Deutsch, Bonnie Glass-Coffin, Erik Gooding, Nelson Graburn, Krishnakali Majumdar, Cindy Dunn, Julie Pelletier, R. J. Shepherd, Michael Trujillo, Christian Zlonlniski, Jacqueline Fewkes, Christopher Wolf, Linda Davis-Stephens, Gaelan Lee Benway, Richard Deutsch, William Jankowiak, Pamela A. Maack, Karl F. Rambo, Penn Reeve, Lisa J. Rodriguez, and Tiantian Zheng, as well as those integral to the publication of this sixth edition, including Lin (Marshall) Gaylord, Liana Sarkisian, Erin Mitchell, Mallory Ortberg, Rathi Thirumalai, Rebecca Roby, and Christopher Stolle. The students in my introductory anthropology course, who have used and commented on the text, also contributed significantly to its development. Other contributors include the researchers whose studies of human behavior and belief provided the substance for the text and the peoples of cultures around the world whose cooperation has helped enrich our understanding of them, ourselves, and our common humanity. Finally, I wish to acknowledge the patience and help of my family—Amy, Rebecca, Michael, and Rachel—and my parents, Alfred and Yetta Robbins, to whom the book is dedicated.

ABOUT THE AUTHOR

Richard Robbins is SUNY University Distinguished Teaching Professor of Anthropology at the State University of New York, College at Plattsburgh. His research interests include the anthropological study of religion and belief, the social and cultural consequences of globalization, the anthropology of economic growth, technology and culture, and the culture of the classroom. His recent books include *Global Problems and the Culture of Capitalism, Talking Points on Global Issues: A Reader, Darwin and the Bible: The Cultural Confrontation* (with Mark Nathan Cohen), and *Globalization and the Environment* (with Gary Kroll). He is the editor of the series Creative Teaching and Learning in Anthropology and the Anthropology of Stuff published by Routledge Press. He is also the recipient of the 2005 American Anthropological Association's Teacher of the Year award. In his spare time, he enjoys reading, biking, sailing, skiing with his family, and long walks with his labradoodle Zoey.

Gerry Charm/SuperStock/Getty Images

1   CULTURE AND MEANING

PROBLEM 1: HOW CAN PEOPLE BEGIN TO UNDERSTAND BELIEFS AND BEHAVIORS THAT ARE DIFFERENT FROM THEIR OWN?

> We have come to think of our social and cultural world as a series of sign systems, comparable to languages. What we live among and relate to are not physical objects and events; they are objects and events with meaning; not just complicated wooden constructions but chairs and tables; not just physical gestures but acts of courtesy or hostility. If we are able to understand our social and cultural world, we must think not of independent objects but of symbolic structures, systems of relations which by enabling objects and actions to have meaning, create a human universe.
>
> —Jonathan Culler

INTRODUCTION

The World Behind Everyday Appearances

In **cultural anthropology**, as in every science, we strive to look beyond the world of everyday experiences to discover the patterns and meanings that lie behind that world. For example, take the typical classroom chair with attached desk.

In our taken-for-granted, everyday world, this piece of furniture is a utilitarian object: something to sit on, or write on, or even put our feet on. But for the cultural anthropologist, the classroom chair tells some interesting tales and poses some interesting questions. For example, why do we have chairs at all? Many societies do not; people sit or squat on the ground or the floor or sit on stools or benches. Historically, the chair probably first appeared in Europe or the Near East, but it was not even common in Europe until the 18th century. And why does the classroom chair take the form it does? Why do not we sit on stools? One feature of the chair that anthropologists might explore as they try to decipher the meaning of the classroom chair and desk is the erect position into which it forces the body, compelling it, in effect, to "pay attention." We might take a clue from French philosopher Michel Foucault; he refers to the shaping of the human body as a "political anatomy"—a way that people's bodies are controlled by others to operate with the necessary speed and efficiency. Political anatomy produces, Foucault says, "docile bodies."

An anthropologist might suggest that the classroom chair and desk are part of the political anatomy of educational settings—part of the system of relations that gives meaning to the classroom; that is, this piece of furniture forms the body into a shape that prepares it (or forces it) to attend to a teacher and not to others in the same room. Moreover, it is appropriate to its unique setting in the classroom, as are other objects of furniture. For example, imagine replacing classroom chairs with bar stools, whose main purpose is to promote bodily mobility and conversation with others.

Once alert to the idea that the classroom chair might serve as an instrument of control, we might notice other ways in which classroom design serves as a mode of discipline. The distribution of people in space, with each person in a particular

Cultural anthropologists find patterns of meaning even in objects as simple as a classroom chair.

"spot" in ordered rows, serves to discipline people to "pay attention" to the classroom center and not to others around them. We might also notice the distinctive ordering of time and the use of clocks, bells, and whistles to control the movement and activities of people in school settings. One can even take our analysis a step further and examine the discipline of the school setting sequentially—from kindergarten through high school; for example, contrast the wide-open space of the kindergarten classroom with its movable chairs and tables and the teacher's desk set off to the side with the partitioned space of a second- or third-grade classroom with its neatly arranged desks facing the centered desk of the teacher. This is the evolution of classroom discipline.

Students, of course, do not always obey the subtle commands that direct their bodies to do certain things at certain times. Simply examine the strange bodily contortions of students as they resist the form into which the classroom chair tries to force them. They also occasionally try to resist the isolation imposed by the arrangement of classroom furniture or the timetables set by clocks, bells, and whistles.

The way that specific societies order behavior through the arrangement of space and time is but one small area examined by cultural anthropology, but it can serve as an example of how from an anthropological perspective we cannot take anything about even our own beliefs and behavior for granted—let alone the behavior and beliefs of those whose backgrounds and histories differ from our own. This book is about how cultural anthropology can help us see beyond our taken-for-granted world. We will examine how cultural anthropology helps us to understand others and, in the process, to better understand ourselves. In addition, each chapter contains case studies in doing anthropology that illustrate how the concepts and perspectives discussed in the chapter can be applied in various career paths to solve real-life problems, such as preventing HIV/AIDS, designing public policy, designing shopping environments, helping adolescent girls deal with negative body images, and much more.

Because any area of inquiry always begins with certain basic issues or questions, this book is organized around eight general problems that arise from the human condition—problems such as how to understand people with different beliefs and behaviors, reasons why ways of life change, how people justify violence, whether there is any solution to problems of social inequality, and so on. These are problems that concern everyone, not just cultural anthropologists. None of these problems have a definitive answer. The best we can do is reach a greater understanding of why the problem exists and what we might do about it. However, there are some specific questions that we can ask concerning these problems for which anthropologists have sought answers. We will focus on these questions. At various points, we will ask you to supply your own answers to questions and, perhaps, to discuss your solutions to questions with others. Understanding others requires you to recognize that your behaviors and beliefs as well as those of people in other societies are socially patterned and constructed. For that reason, you will find many comparisons between American life and life in other societies.

In considering the principal problem of how we can begin to understand beliefs and behaviors that are different from our own, in this first chapter, we explore five questions along with one case study. The first and most basic is why human beings differ in their beliefs and behaviors; that is, what is it about human nature that produces such a variety of ways of believing and behaving? The second question involves values. More often than not, people react to different ways of life with shock, scorn, or disapproval. Are such reactions warranted, and if they are not, how do we judge the beliefs and behaviors of others? The third question is critical to anthropological inquiry. Is it possible to set aside the meanings that we ascribe to experience and see the world through the eyes of others? Fourth, assuming that it is possible to come to some understanding of how others see the world, how can the meanings that others find in experience be interpreted and described? The fifth question concerns what learning about other people can tell us about ourselves. Finally, we examine what anthropology can tell retailers and manufacturers about why people shop.

QUESTIONS

1.1   Why do human beings differ in their beliefs and behaviors?
1.2   How do people judge the beliefs and behaviors of others?
1.3   Is it possible to see the world through the eyes of others?
1.4   How can the meanings that others find in experience be interpreted and described?
1.5   What can learning about other peoples tell Americans about themselves?

Case Study in Doing Anthropology #1: Shopping and Selling

QUESTION 1.1   *Why Do Human Beings Differ in Their Beliefs and Behaviors?*

From an anthropological perspective, members of a society view the world in a similar way because they share the same **culture**; people differ in how they view the world because their cultures differ. A good place to start to understand the concept of culture is with the fact that members of all human societies experience specific life events, such as birth, death, and the quest for food, water, and shelter. All societies have what are for them appropriate rules for courtship, ideas about child rearing, procedures for exchanging goods, methods of food production, techniques for building shelters, and so on. But from society to society, the meanings people give to such events differ.

Attitudes toward death provide one example. For some people, death marks the passage of a person from one world to another. For others, death is an ending—the final event of a life span—whereas still others consider death a part of a never-ending cycle of birth, death, and rebirth. The Kwakwaka'wakw of British Columbia for example, believe that when a person dies that the soul leaves the body and enters the body of a salmon. When a salmon is caught and eaten, a soul is released and is free to enter the body of another person.

Some societies fear the dead; others revere them. In traditional China, each household contained a shrine to the family ancestors. Before any major family decision, the head of the household addressed the shrine to ask the ancestors' advice, thus making the dead part of the world of the living. However, in southern Italy, funeral customs were designed to discourage the dead from returning. Relatives placed such useful objects as matches and small change near the body to placate the soul of the deceased and ensure that it did not return to disturb the living.

Members of some societies accept death as a natural and inevitable occurrence, whereas others always attribute death to the malevolent act of some person—often through sorcery. In these societies, every death elicits suspicion and a demand for vengeance. Members of other societies require great demonstrations of grief and mourning for a deceased. Some, such as the Dani of New Guinea, require a close female relative of a recently deceased person to sacrifice a part of a finger. It was the practice of the Wari of western Brazil—when they still lived independent of Western civilization—to dispose of the bodies of their dead by eating the roasted flesh, certain internal organs, and sometimes the ground bones. They ate the dead out of respect and compassion for the dead person and the dead person's family, not because they needed the meat or because they liked the taste of human flesh. In southern Europe, widows were required to shave their heads, whereas in traditional India, widows were cremated at their husbands' funerals. In the United States, survivors of the deceased are expected to restrain their grief almost as if it were a contagious disease. To Americans, the sight of southern Italian women pulling their hair and being restrained from flinging themselves into an open grave is as bewildering as their own restraint of grief would be to traditional southern Italians.

Or take the area of food. No society accepts all items in their edible universe as "good to eat." Only a relatively few items are so designated. Such insects as grubs, beetles,

Grief is suppressed in some cultures and openly displayed in others. Here, bereaved relatives weep over the body of a 40-year-old kinsman slain in clashes between police and armed civilians in Moldova in 1990.

© Reuters/Corbis

and ants are acceptable fare in some societies, whereas people in others regard eating insects with horror. Americans generally do not define insects as food (although federal regulations do allow a certain percentage of insect matter to be included in processed food). Most Americans like and are encouraged to drink milk, although some people in China consider milk undrinkable, whereas the Chinese practice of raising dogs for meat is repulsive to most Americans. American children who have raised pet guinea pigs would have a hard time accepting the Peruvian practice of raising guinea pigs for food. Many American tastes in food originate in biblical definitions of what is considered edible and inedible. Thus, of edible land animals, the book of Leviticus says that they must chew their cud and have split hoofs, consequently eliminating not only pig but also camel and rock badger. Of animals of the water, edible things must have scales and fins, removing from a biblical diet such things as clams, lobster, and sea urchins. And of animals of the air, only things that have wings and fly are legitimate dining fare, eliminating the penguin, ostrich, and cassowary. Thus, human beings create and define for themselves what they may eat and what they may not eat independent of what is or is not truly edible.

Of all the some two million species of living organisms that inhabit Earth, only humans dwell largely in worlds that they themselves create by giving meanings to things, events, activities, and people. This creation is what anthropologists mean by the term *culture*. Human beings are cultural animals; they ascribe meanings of their own creation to objects, persons, behaviors, emotions, and events and then act as though those meanings are real. All facets of their lives—birth, courtship, mating, food acquisition and consumption, and death—are suffused with meaning.

Clifford Geertz suggest that human beings are compelled to impose meaning on their experiences because without these meanings to help them comprehend experience and impose order on the universe, the world would seem a jumble—"a chaos of pointless acts and exploding emotions." Geertz (1973, p. 49) says that human beings are "incomplete or unfinished animals who complete themselves through culture—not culture in general, but specific forms of it: Balinese, Italian, Ilongot, Chinese, Kwakwaka'wakw, American, and so on." When people share the meanings they give to experiences, they share and participate in the same culture.

Differences in culture arise in part from the fact that different groups of human beings—for various reasons—create, share, and participate in different realities, assigning different meanings to birth, marriage, death, and food. Objects, persons, behaviors, emotions, and events in a human world have meanings ascribed to them by those who share, use, or experience them. The clothes people wear, the way they wear them, the food they eat (or refuse to eat), and even their gender are defined through the meanings that different groups of people give them.

One of the problems that cultural anthropologists address is understanding why different groups of human beings have different cultures. Why does one group assign one set of meanings to what they experience, whereas another group assigns it another set of meanings? Many of the questions to be addressed

Exercise 1.1 ➤

Food is a cultural creation; that is, human beings define what is and what is not food. For example, consider the items listed here—all of which serve as food for one group of people or another. Which of these would you eat, and which would you not eat? If there are any you would not eat, explain why.

	Yes	No
Eel		
Kangaroo tail		
Dog		
Guinea pig		
Raw squid		
Sea urchin (sea slugs)		
Ants		
Monkey brains		
Grubs		
Opossum		
Rattlesnake		
Iguana		
Horse		
Dolphin		
Pickled pig's feet		
Haggis (stuffed intestines)		
Cow brains		
Blood sausage		
Raw steak		
Rotten meat		
Armadillo		

in later chapters concern how these differences can be explained. We may be able to overcome our initial shock or bewilderment upon confronting different cultures if we understand something of why cultural differences exist. But how should we react if the meanings that others ascribe to experiences differ from our own? It is difficult enough to look beyond everyday appearances at our own beliefs and behaviors, but it is far more difficult when we confront beliefs and behaviors of others that we initially consider wrong, horrible, or bizarre.

QUESTION 1.2   *How Do People Judge the Beliefs and Behaviors of Others?*

Richard Scaglion is fond of telling the story of his friend, a member of the Abelam tribe of Papua New Guinea, who was looking through an issue of *Sports Illustrated* magazine. The friend, dressed in full ceremonial regalia

The ceremonial attire worn by this Hove villager in Papua New Guinea conveys beauty and meaning to the members of this tribe, to whom modern American fashions might seem odd.

with a feather through his nose, was laughing uncontrollably at a woman shown in a liquor advertisement. When he managed to stop laughing long enough to explain what he thought was so funny, he said, "This white woman has made holes in her ears and stuck things in them." When Scaglion pointed out that his friend had an ornament in his nose, the reply was: "That's different. That's for beauty and has ceremonial significance. But I didn't know that white people mutilated themselves."

Scaglion's friend confronted a problem that many people do when they encounter behavior or beliefs that seem to differ from their own, and his response was not unusual. He was shocked and mystified at the strange behavior. And this poses a dilemma: Because there are so many versions of what the world is like, how do we try to understand each of them without making positive or negative judgments? Which version is correct? Are there any we can reject or condemn? Can we say, as so many have, that one culture is superior to another?

In the catalog of human behaviors and beliefs, it is not difficult to find practices or ideas that may seem bizarre or shocking—even to trained anthropologists. Cultural anthropologists have described the beliefs of the Ilongots of the Philippines, who must kill an enemy to obtain a head they can throw away in order to diminish the grief and rage they feel at the death of a kinsman or kinswoman. They have studied the historical records of the Aztecs of Mexico, who when contacted by Cortes in 1519 believed that the universe underwent periodic destruction and that the only way to ward off disaster was to pluck the hearts from live sacrificial victims to offer to the gods. They have reported on the circumcision practices of the people in the Nile Valley of the Sudan, where in order to ensure a young girl's chastity and virginity, her genitalia are mutilated to close the vaginal opening so completely that additional surgery is often required to allow intercourse and childbirth later in life. They have also studied modern states that routinely engage in or sanction torture, terror, and genocide. The question is, how should we react to practices and beliefs such as these?

The Ethnocentric Fallacy and the Relativist Fallacy

If we do condemn or reject the beliefs or behaviors of others, we may be committing the **ethnocentric fallacy**—the idea that our beliefs and behaviors are right and true, whereas those of other peoples are wrong or misguided. Cultural anthropologists have long fought against **ethnocentrism**. They try to show that what often appears on the surface to be an odd belief or a bizarre bit of behavior is functional and logical in the context of a particular culture. They

Human Sacrifice, 1579 (vellum), Duran, Diego (16th century)/Biblioteca Nacional, Madrid, Spain/Giraudon/The Bridgeman Art Library International

To protect their world from potential destruction, Aztecs in the 1500s offered blood to the gods through rituals of human sacrifice and self-mutilation.

find the ethnocentric fallacy *intellectually* intolerable; if all people everywhere think that they are right and others must be wrong, they can only reach an intellectual and social dead end. Furthermore, if we assume that we have all the right answers, our study of other cultures becomes simply the study of other people's mistakes.

Because of the intellectual implications of ethnocentrism, cultural anthropologists emphatically reject this position. But the alternative to ethnocentrism—**relativism**—is equally problematic. Simply stated, relativism holds that no behavior or belief can be judged to be odd or wrong simply because it is different from our own. Instead, we must try to understand a culture in its own terms and to understand behaviors or beliefs in terms of the purpose, function, or meaning they have for people in the societies in which we find them. In other words, relativism holds that a specific belief or behavior can be understood only in relation to the culture—the system of meanings—in which it is embedded.

For example, according to Renato Rosaldo, the ceremonies and rituals accompanying a successful headhunting expedition psychologically help the Ilongot manage their grief over the death of a kinsperson. Rose Oldfield-Hayes

Exercise 1.2a ⊳

After the class has been divided into groups of four to six, *individually* record whether you agree or disagree with each statement that follows. Then, go over each statement in order. See if anyone in your group disagrees with each statement being considered. If even one person disagrees, the group should change the wording so the statement is acceptable to *all* the members of the group. You may not simply agree to disagree. Choose one member to record the revised statements.

Statements:
1. The fact that the United States was able to place people on the moon proves its technological superiority.
2. Foreigners coming to live here should give up their foreign ways and adapt to the new country as quickly as possible.
3. Many of the world's populations do not take enough initiative to develop themselves; therefore, they remain "underdeveloped."
4. Minority members of any population should be expected to conform to the customs and values of the majority.

explains that even to the women of the northern Sudan, the genital mutilation of young girls makes perfect sense. Because family honor is determined in part by the sexual modesty of female family members, by preventing intercourse, the operation protects the honor of the family, protects girls from sexual assault, and protects the honor and reputation of the girl herself. Moreover, says Oldfield-Hayes, the practice serves as a means of population control.

However, relativism poses a *moral* predicament. We may concede that it is permissible to rip hearts out of living human beings, provided you believe this is necessary in order to save the world, or that it is permissible to subject young girls to painful mutilation to protect family reputations or control population growth. But this quickly leads us into the **relativistic fallacy**—the idea that it is impossible to make moral judgments about the beliefs and behaviors of others. Of course, this seems morally intolerable because it implies that there is no belief or behavior that can be condemned as wrong. Thus, we are left with two untenable positions: the ethnocentric alternative, which is intellectually unsatisfactory, and the relativist alternative, which is morally unsatisfactory. How do we solve this problem?

Virginity Testing in Turkey and Cannibalism Among the Wari

To further illustrate the dilemma of relativism and the difficulty of appreciating the cultures of others without making moral judgments, a few years ago, an American-based human rights group issued a report condemning the practice of virginity testing in Turkey. Traditionally, young women in Turkey, as in some other cultures, are expected to avoid sexual relations prior to marriage, although the same rule does not apply to men. The morning after the wedding, the bride's virginity is revealed by displaying the sheet that was spread on the couple's wedding bed with the telltale hymeneal blood stain. The human rights report condemns the traditional testing as well as the reported practice of forcing tests on hospital patients, students, and applicants for government jobs. Here is the question: Is the human rights group being ethnocentric in judging Turkish customs by American cultural norms or is it correctly identifying abuses of women that must be corrected? And does it help if we further understand the so-called logic behind the belief?

In her book on Turkish village society—*The Seed and the Soil*—anthropologist Carol Delaney describes how virginity testing is related to the way that Turkish villagers conceptualize and explain the reproductive process. They see producing children as analogous to the planting and growing of crops: The man provides the "seed" with his semen, and the woman serves as the "soil" in which the seed germinates and grows. As a metaphor for reproduction, the idea of the seed and the soil provides villagers with a way of thinking about and understanding reproduction. However, the metaphor of seed and soil has at least one very important implication: Because seeds do not have a limited life span, as we know semen to have, villagers believe that once planted, the seed (semen) may grow at any time. Consequently, if a woman has had sexual relations with a man other than her husband at any time prior to her marriage, the paternity of the child will be in doubt. Because descent in traditional Turkish villages is closely tied to many things, including property rights, uncertainty about the identity of the true father can have major implications. Thus, in the context of Turkish beliefs about procreation, virginity testing may be said to make sense. Furthermore, Turkish beliefs about conception are not that far removed from our own because our language draws from the same agricultural metaphors as that of Turkish villagers to explain reproduction. We talk about women being "fertile" or "barren" and semen "fertilizing" "eggs." "Sowing one's oats" as an expression of sexual activity is still heard in parts of the United States and Canada. Furthermore, these views are reinforced by religious proscription, legitimized in the Koran and the Old Testament. Thus, before we either condemn or accept the Turkish villagers for their treatment of women, we need to examine what their beliefs tell us about our own. Ours may be equally problematic.

But what of cannibalism, such as the Wari practice of roasting and eating the dead? Surely there is no way of justifying that. As Beth Conklin points out in her study of Wari cannibalism—*Consuming Grief*—cannibalism pushes the limits of cultural relativism, guaranteeing reactions of revulsion and fascination. But in addition to the emotional reactions, it also has political implications. For centuries, cannibalism was the ultimate smear tactic; to accuse one's enemies or people one wished to degrade or dominate of cannibalism was the ultimate justification for conquest, domination, and exploitation. In 1503, Queen Isabella of Spain decreed that Spaniards could legally enslave specifically those American Indians who were cannibals. In 1510, Pope Innocent IV ruled that Christians could punish by force of arms the sin of cannibalism. Thus, by claiming moral superiority, they were claiming the right to decide ultimately what is right and what is wrong. Armed with that kind of power, they felt justified in imposing their own views and way of life. What Queen Isabella and Pope Innocent IV conveniently overlooked, however, was the fact that Europeans at the time themselves practiced cannibalism. As Conklin notes, medicinal cannibalism— the consumption of human body parts for curing purposes—had a long tradition in Europe. Up until two centuries ago, European physicians prescribed the consumption of human flesh, heart, bones, and other body parts as cures for such afflictions as arthritis, reproductive disorders, sciatica, warts, and skin blemishes. Human blood was thought to be a cure for epilepsy, with physicians recommending that it be drunk immediately after the supplier died. Physicians also thought that the blood of someone who died violently was particularly effective. Thus, in Denmark, epileptics would stand around the scaffolds, cups in hand, waiting to catch the blood of executed criminals. And almost every apothecary kept dried and powdered human body parts on hand for anxious customers.

In their ethnocentric justifications for conquest and racism, people of medieval Europe managed to accept in their own lives the same types of practices they condemned in others. Furthermore, they failed to understand those practices from others' points of view. For example, the Wari ate their dead because they believed it was the compassionate thing to do. As Conklin puts it, "More painful

Execution of the Despencers, from the St Alban's Chronicle (vellum), English School, (15th century)/© Lambeth Palace Library, London, UK/The Bridgeman Art Library International

While early modern Europeans condemned cannibalism and justified enslaving people who they claimed practiced it, Europeans themselves prescribed the consumption of human body parts and blood, particularly of those who died violently, as a cure for various afflictions.

than having the corpse eaten would have been to have it *not* eaten." For the Wari, a corpse left intact was a painful reminder of the deceased; people unrelated to the deceased ate the corpse—in spite of the fact that the smell or taste sometimes repulsed them—because it was believed it would help family members come to terms with their loss. Furthermore, the Western practice of burying the dead (which missionaries and government officials forced the Wari to do after contact) was almost as horrific to the Wari as their cannibalism might have been for us. "It's cold in the earth," a father who had recently lost a two-year-old son explained to Beth Conklin. "We keep remembering our child, lying there, cold. We remember and we are sad," he continued. "It was better in the old days, when the others ate the body. Then we did not think about our child's body much. We did not remember our child as much, and we were not so sad."

Burying the body also violated many Wari fundamental values. For the Wari, the ground was considered "dirty" and "polluting." People never sit directly on the dirt, and discarding things on the ground is considered disrespectful. Special ritual objects are never supposed to touch the ground.

Furthermore, if we did not have a deeper understanding of Wari culture, we would not know how consuming the dead fits in with dealing with their emotions and with the meaning that they impose on their world. By consuming the dead, the Wari are trying to obliterate the painful memories of their loss. Not only is the memory of the body painful, but equally painful are the material objects associated with the deceased as well as mention of the deceased's name. Thus, they not only consume the body, but they also burn the house and personal possessions of the deceased. For months, they also make trips into the forest to find places associated with the person, such as a place where a hunter made a kill or a woman felled a fruit tree or a favorite log on which the deceased liked to sit, cut the vegetation around it, and, after it has dried, burn the spot, changing the appearance of the last earthly places to which memories of the deceased might cling. As they "sweep," as the Wari call it, they cry over the memories. Once done, however, "it is different. . . . [T]here is not much sadness there." For us, a dead body is only a shell—its soul or spiritual essence gone. Thus, some societies, such as our own, can prepare the dead to look as they did in life and think of them buried in that way. On the other hand, the Wari—as well as other groups—want to separate the dead from the living, so obliterating their memories is perfectly logical.

Exercise 1.2b ➤ | The Wari attempt to obliterate the memory of the dead in their funeral practices, as do many other societies. Others, however—such as ours—memorialize the dead; forgetting them would be an act of disrespect. Try to list the ways that we try to keep the memory of deceased persons alive, and speculate why we do that rather than trying to forget them.

There are others aspects to Wari beliefs about consuming the dead, such as their belief that the spirits of the dead ultimately enter into the bodies of animals that the Wari depend on for food, thus creating a cycle of eating and being eaten, but the main point is that by imposing the meanings we have adopted for something, such as cannibalism, and failing to see it as others may, we miss the point.

But does this mean that once we understand any practice or belief from "the native's point of view" that it is acceptable? Does understanding the cultures of others require that we accept and justify all beliefs and practices?

Objectivity and Morality

The conflict between ethnocentrism and relativism is not just a theoretical one for anthropologists. In their choice of research subject, anthropologists may face the dilemma of either maintaining a "moral distance" from the objects of their studies and remaining "objective" or becoming actively involved in criticizing behavior or beliefs they encounter (such as genital mutilation).

The contradiction between "objective" anthropology and a politically committed anthropology became apparent to Nancy Scheper-Hughes when she returned as an anthropologist to a shantytown in Brazil where she had previously worked as a community organizer. The women with whom she worked became angry, asking why, when as a community organizer she had helped them organize to fight for clean water, decent wages, and protection from police brutality, was she now, as an anthropologist, so passive and so indifferent to the destruction around her? She tried to explain that as an anthropologist her work was different—that she was there now to observe, document, and write about their lives as truthfully as she could. The women refused to accept that and insisted that if they were to work with her, she had to also work with them to fight for better lives. "What," they said, "is anthropology to us?"

As a consequence of her experience, Scheper-Hughes (1995, p. 416) argues for a politically committed, morally engaged, and ethically grounded anthropology. "Those of us who make our living observing and recording the misery of the world," she says, "have a particular obligation to reflect critically on the impact of the harsh images of human suffering that we foist upon the public."

Scheper-Hughes proposes a more humanitarian anthropology—one that is concerned with how people treat one another. Moral relativism, she says, is no longer appropriate to the world in which we live, and if anthropology is to be worth anything at all, it must be, as she puts it, "critically grounded." Anthropologists cannot ignore the massacres and disappearances of vulnerable people that often occur in communities in which anthropologists work. Anthropologists must, she insists, serve as witnesses and reporters of human rights abuses and the suffering of the poor and the oppressed.

But even serving as a witness for the poor and oppressed can lead to still other moral dilemmas for the anthropologist when the people with whom the anthropologist works engage in behavior that may appear morally questionable. Scheper-Hughes confronted this question when she discovered and reported that impoverished women in the Brazilian shantytowns would sometimes allow their starving infants to die in the belief that they were doomed anyway. When Philippe Bourgois studied the world of crack dealers on the upper east side of New York City, he worried about the negative images he would convey if he reported the personal violence, sexual abuse, addiction, and alienation he witnessed. He recalled the advice of anthropologist Laura Nader, who advised others not to study the poor and powerless because whatever one says will be used against them.

Human rights activists are particularly skeptical about the idea of cultural relativity. If, they say, we must tolerate the beliefs and practices of other cultures because to do otherwise would be ethnocentric, how can we ever criticize what seem to be violations of basic human rights, such the right to bodily integrity, or the right to be free from torture, arbitrary imprisonment, slavery, or genocide? Cultural relativism, say human rights advocates, makes arguments about human rights meaningless by legitimizing almost any behavior.

Consider the case of the practice in some areas of India of *sati*, the burning of a widow on her husband's funeral pyre. The last fully documented case of sati in India occurred in 1987° when Roon Kanwar, an 18-year-old girl, was burned alive on her husband's pyre. Women's rights groups protested, but relatives claimed that it is an ancient Indian custom and accused protestors of being Western imperialists imposing their own cultural standards on them. Although the practice is outlawed, prosecutors rarely enforce the law because of the difficulty of obtaining evidence. Does it matter if Roon Kanwar committed *sati* voluntarily? What would happen if she objected? Does it matter that it is only women who are burned? Is *sati* a practice to deny a widow the inheritance of her husband's family's land? Elizabeth Zechenter, who makes the argument for the establishment of some universal principles for human rights, says that cultural relativists are right to claim that the endorsement or rejection of some foreign custom risks imposing one's own cultural prejudices on others. But the idea that we can make no judgments without being ethnocentric is illusory:

> One simply cannot avoid making judgments when faced with oppression and brutality masquerading under the guise of cultural tradition. Such a nonjudgmental tolerance of brutality is actually an ultimate form of ethnocentrism, if not an outright ethical surrender. (Zechenter, 1997, p. 336)

°Another alleged case was reported in 2002 (see http://www.boloji.com/wfs/wfs091.htm)

Exercise 1.2c ➤

You have been doing anthropological research in the United States with a group of people who believe they must live the life described in the Bible—particularly the book of Acts. They live communally, sharing all property; they believe that women should be subservient to their husbands; they enforce rules against drinking alcoholic beverages and smoking. The group has lately come under attack by a group in the local community as being a "dangerous cult." You know that although their beliefs and practices differ from those of the larger society around them, they are not dangerous and in fact lead lives of harmony. They have asked you to speak in their defense. Can you do this without sacrificing your objectivity?

There is obviously no easy answer to the question of when or if it is proper to judge the beliefs and practices of others to be right or wrong or when to actively work to change behaviors or beliefs judged to be wrong. Ideally, our attempts to understand what at first seems puzzling in some cultures and our arrival at some solution to that puzzle should result in questioning what it was about us that made the behavior or belief seem puzzling in the first place. In addition, we need to understand that if each culture orders the world in a certain way for its members, it also blocks off or masks other ways of viewing things. We need to appreciate that there are perspectives different from our own and that our ethnocentric biases may blind us to those alternatives. In other words, although culture provides us with certain meanings to give to objects, persons, behaviors, emotions, and events, it also shields us from alternative meanings. What our culture hides from us may be more important than what it reveals.

QUESTION 1.3   *Is It Possible to See the World Through the Eyes of Others?*

This question lies at the heart of the anthropological enterprise. The anthropologist must be able to look beyond everyday appearances to decipher the often hidden meanings of beliefs, objects, and behaviors while at the same time setting aside his or her preconceptions of what is normal or proper. The anthropologist must also learn one culture and then relate what he or she learns to members of another culture to translate the meanings of one world into the meanings of another.

Like other social scientists, anthropologists use surveys, written documents, historical accounts, and questionnaires as part of their research toolbox. But the unique feature of cultural anthropology is the application of the **ethnographic method**—the immersion of investigators in the lives of the people they are trying to understand and, through that experience, the attainment of some level of understanding of the meanings those people ascribe to their existence. This immersion process utilizes the techniques of **anthropological fieldwork**, which requires **participant observation**—the active participation of observers in the lives of their subjects.

The ethnographic method is only part of the anthropological enterprise. The anthropologist also seeks to explain why people view the world as they do and to contribute to the understanding of human behavior in general. But fieldwork is the beginning of the enterprise. Fieldwork involves the meeting of at least two cultures: that of the researcher and that of the culture and people the researcher is trying to understand. Anthropological researchers must set aside their own views of things and attempt to see the world in a new way. In many respects, they must assume the demeanor and status of children who must be taught by their elders the proper view of the world. And like children making their way in a world they do not fully comprehend, anthropologists often find themselves in awkward, embarrassing, or dangerous situations and must be prepared to learn from these moments.

The Embarrassed Anthropologist

Awkwardness and embarrassment are a part of fieldwork as well as a part of the process through which the fieldworker learns about another culture. Richard Scaglion spent more than a year with the Abelam of Papua New Guinea. Shortly after he arrived in the field, he observed and photographed an Abelam pig hunt in which the men set out nets and waited while the women and children made lots of noise to drive the pigs into the nets. Soon after, he was invited by the Abelam to participate in a pig hunt, and he took this as a sign of acceptance—that the people "liked him." He started to go with the men, but they told him they wanted him to go with the women and children to beat the bush, explaining, "We've never seen anyone who makes as much noise in the jungle as you." Later, wanting to redeem himself, Scaglion offered to help an Abelam who was planting crops with a digging stick. A crowd gathered to watch as Scaglion used a shovel to try to dig a demonstration hole. After he had struggled for several minutes to get the shovel into the hard-packed soil, someone handed him a digging stick, and he was amazed at how easy it was to use. Later, he found out that several Abelam had shovels but rarely used them because they did not work.

After months of answering Scaglion's questions about their view of the natural world, such as the moon, sun, and stars, some Abelam asked him about his views of the universe. Feeling on safe ground, he gave the usual grade-school lecture about the shape of Earth, its daily rotation, and its travels around the sun. Using a coconut, he showed them the relative positions on Earth of New Guinea, Australia, Europe, and the United States. Everyone listened intently, and Scaglion thought it went well until about a week later—when he overheard some elders wondering how it was that Americans walked upside down!

Beginning again, Scaglion used the coconut to explain how, as Earth rotates, sometimes the United States would be upright and New Guinea would be on the bottom. The Abelam rejected this because they could see that they were *not* upside down, and no one—not even some of the old people in the community—remembered ever having walked upside down. Scaglion began to draw on the physics he had in college, and as he tried to explain Newton's

Exercise 1.3 ➤

> Think of some awkward or embarrassing situation created by something
> you did or did not do or say. What was inappropriate about your behavior,
> and why did it lead to misunderstanding or embarrassment? What did you
> learn from the experience about the meaning of your or others' behavior?

law of gravity (or "grabity," as his friends pronounced it), he suddenly realized
that he did not understand "grabity" either. It was something he had accepted
since third grade—a concept that even physicists simply take for granted as a
convenient theoretical concept.

Confronting Witchcraft in Mexico

Awkward or embarrassing moments in the field may help anthropologists understand a culture or even to question their own view of the world. But the
possibility of seeing the world through the eyes of others remains a subject
of contention among anthropologists. To communicate with anyone—even
members of their own society—people must share some of the meanings they
ascribe to objects, persons, behaviors, emotions, and events. But what happens when views of the world are completely different?

   When Michael Kearney traveled to the town of Santa Catarina Ixtepeji in the
valley of Oaxaca, Mexico, he intended to study the relationship between the people's view of the world and their social arrangements and environment. He began
his work secure in his knowledge of the scientific and materialist view of the world
in which he was reared, but he was often fascinated by the differences between
his view and that of the people of Santa Catarina Ixtepeji. Theirs was a world controlled by mystic notions of "fate," the will of God, and malevolent witches and
other harmful and sometimes lethal spiritual forces. He became familiar with the
Ixtepejanos view of the world—never doubting that it was "unscientific" but perhaps justified by a life in which suffering, disease, and death were common.

   Kearney's faith in his own view of the world was momentarily shattered
by an incident that began innocently enough. Walking to an appointment, he
came upon an obviously distressed woman, Doña Delfina. She was known as a
witch, and Kearney had been trying unsuccessfully to interview her. When they
met, she explained that her sister-in-law had a "very bad disease in her arms,"
and she wanted him to help. Kearney accompanied Doña Delfina to her house,
where he found that the sister-in-law's arms were ulcerated with deep, oozing
lesions that looked to him like infected burns. They rejected his offer to take
the sick woman to a doctor for medical treatment, so Kearney said he had some
ointment that might help, and they eagerly agreed that he should use it. He got
the ointment, which contained an anesthetic, and daubed it on the woman's
sores. Much to the amazement of Doña Delfina, her sister-in-law immediately
felt better. By that afternoon, her arms had greatly improved, the next morning
scabs had formed, and by the day after, she had completely recovered.

Kearney was credited with a "miraculous cure." But the same day, a Ixtepejanos friend asked Kearney what he had done, and he proudly explained.
The friend replied, "Why did you do that? It was not a good thing to do."
The sick woman, he said, had been the victim of black magic; another woman,
Gregoria, was trying to take Delfina's brother away from his wife and was using
black magic to make Delfina's sister-in-law sick. Delfina was using *her* magic to
keep her brother in the household, but Gregoria was winning. Now, the friend
explained to Kearney, he had intervened, tipping the balance of power back to
Delfina but creating a powerful enemy in Gregoria. "Maybe you should leave
town for a while until Gregoria calms down," Kearney's friend suggested. But
Kearney did not take the danger seriously and might never have done so were
it not for two incidents that occurred soon afterward.

A young doctor in town asked Kearney, who had medical training, to assist
in an autopsy of a man who had died in a fall off a truck. It was a particularly
long and gory autopsy, accomplished only with rusty carpenter's tools in a dimly
lit room; images of the scene and the cadaver disturbed Kearney's sleep over
the next few days. One night, about a week later, as the wind beat cornstalks
against his house, Kearney felt an itching on his arm. Rolling up his sleeve, he
discovered several angry welts that seemed to be growing as he watched them.
Immediately, he thought of the chancrous arms of Delfina's sister-in-law, realizing at the same time that Gregoria's house was only 50 yards from his and
she could be trying to kill him. "She got me!" he thought. The image of the
cadaver on the table jumped into his mind, followed by a wish that he had gotten out of town while there was still time. As Kearney put it, he was witnessing
the disintegration of his scientific, materialist view of the world and grappling
with forces with which he was unprepared to deal.

Kearney is not sure how long his initial terror lasted—seconds or perhaps
minutes. As he struggled against it, he realized that he was suspended between
two worlds: that of the Ixtepejanos and his own. He was questioning a world
of meanings that he had until then taken for granted. Kearney is not sure how
long he was able to truly believe that the world was as the Ixtepejanos saw it,
but as he retrieved his own view of the world, the Ixtepejano's worldview—
filled with witchcraft and magic—ceased to be only intellectually interesting.
It acquired a reality and a sense of legitimacy for him that it did not have before he experienced the real fear that he had been bewitched. Kearney came
to realize through his experience that systems of belief are eminently reasonable when viewed from within or, as we will see in a later chapter, when we
participate in the lives of people who hold those beliefs.

The Endangered Anthropologist

The risk of injury, disease, or hostile reactions has always been a feature of
anthropological fieldwork. But as anthropologists increasingly work in areas
where human rights violations are common, these risks are intensified. When
the work of anthropologists such as Nancy Scheper-Hughes threatens the power,
authority, or prerogatives of powerful groups, these anthropologists often expose

themselves to violent retaliation. Working with crack dealers in New York City, Philippe Bourgois feared violent retaliation when he embarrassed a gang leader by accidentally calling attention to others that the leader could not read.

At least four anthropologists have been murdered as a consequence of their fieldwork: In 1982, South African anthropologist and anti-apartheid activist Ruth First was killed by a mail bomb in her office at Maputo University in Mozambique. In 1984, Melanesian anthropologist Arnold Ap was tortured and killed by the Indonesian army and his body dumped by helicopter into the sea. In 1989, South African anthropologist David Webster was shot and killed by members of a pro-apartheid death squad. And in 1990, Guatemalan anthropologist Myrna Mack was stabbed to death by a soldier, ostensibly for her work with Mayan refugees and their experiences in the government's counterinsurgency war of the early 1980s that killed hundreds of thousands of people. In addition, at least two anthropologists—Ricardo Falla and George Aditjondro—went into exile under threat of assassination because of their work. These real dangers that anthropologists face may serve to provide insights into how the people with whom they are working experience the threat of violence.

In 1989 and 1990, Linda Green was doing fieldwork in the Guatemalan community of Xe'caj. As with many similar communities, Xe'caj was only beginning to recover from some 35 years of violence. Beginning with a military coup orchestrated largely by the U.S. CIA against a democratically elected government in 1954, Guatemala experienced regular violence as the militarized state tried to suppress attempts to overthrow the military regime. Hundreds of thousands of Guatemalans were killed—mostly by the government—in an attempt to suppress the revolt. The late 1970s and early 1980s were particularly brutal as the government embarked on a campaign to destroy peasant villages and relocate people to government-controlled towns. In addition, paramilitary groups—largely supplied and supported by the regular military—embarked on campaigns of terror and torture in an attempt to control the largely peasant population.

The people of Xe'caj lived in a state of constant surveillance from the military encampment located above the town. Many of the residents had husbands, fathers, or sons taken away by the military. There were rumors of death lists. They had difficulty sleeping and reported nightmares of recurring death and violence. Soon, said Green, "I, too, started to experience nighttime hysteria, dreams of death, disappearances, and torture."

Green interviewed women who were widowed by the conflict. Without prompting, the women recounted in vivid detail their stories of horror—the deaths and disappearances of husbands, fathers, sons, and brothers as if they had happened last week or last month rather than six to eight years ago.

Then, one day, when Green arrived to continue the interviews, the women were anxious and agitated. When she asked what had happened, they told her that the military commissioner was looking for her and that people were saying that she was helping the widows and talking against other people in the community. When Green told the women that she was going to go see the commissioner, they pleaded with her not to go, explaining that they knew of people who had gone to the military garrison and never returned. Green decided to visit the garrison alone—a visit that would provide a vivid experience of the kinds of fears confronted by the villagers. As she approached the garrison, she writes (1995, p. 116):

> I saw several soldiers sitting in a small guardhouse with a machine gun perched on a three-foot stanchion pointed downward and directly at me. The plight of Joseph K. in Kafka's *Trial* flashed through my mind, accused of a crime for which he must defend himself but about which he could get no information. I didn't do anything wrong, I must not look guilty, I repeated to myself like a mantra. I must calm myself, as my stomach churned, my nerves frayed. I arrived breathless and terrified. Immediately I knew I was guilty because I was against the system of violence and terror that surrounded me.

Fortunately, the comandante said he knew nothing about why she was being harassed and assured her that she could continue with her work; everything went smoothly from there, but Green gained a fuller understanding of the experiences of people who live under the constant threat of violence.

The experiences of these three anthropologists—Linda Green, Michael Kearney, and Richard Scaglion—highlight certain features of the ethnographic method. They especially illustrate the attempt of anthropologists to appreciate the views of others while questioning their own views of the world. They also illustrate what makes the ethnographic method unique. By participating in the lives of others and in their cultural practices, the anthropologist can take him or herself as a subject of investigation. If one can succeed in seeing the world as others do—even if for a brief moment—then it becomes far easier to understand and describe that world. It also helps the anthropologist to understand how others can believe what they do. Tanya M. Lehrmann learned this when she studied contemporary witchcraft in England. After reading materials surrounding the practice of contemporary witchcraft and attending ceremonies, she found herself interpreting events in the world in much the same way as the people she was working with. We will return to her experiences in a later chapter.

Claude Levi-Strauss, one of the leading anthropologists of the 20th century, says that fieldwork and the attempts of anthropologists to immerse themselves in the world of others makes them "marginal" men or women. They are never completely native because they cannot totally shed their own cultural perceptions, but they are never the same again after having glimpsed alternative visions of the world. Anthropologists are, as Roger Keesing put it, outsiders who know something of what it is to be insiders.

QUESTION 1.4   *How Can the Meanings That Others Find in Experience Be Interpreted and Described?*

Sir Arthur Conan Doyle first introduced his now famous detective hero, Sherlock Holmes, in 1887. In his adventures, Holmes had the unique ability to apply deductive reasoning to solve the most baffling of mysteries. In one

Sherlock Holmes detective story, Dr. Watson, Holmes's assistant, decides to teach the great detective a lesson in humility. He hands Holmes a pocket watch owned by Watson's late brother and challenges Holmes to infer from the watch the character of its owner. Holmes's interpretation: "[Your brother] was a man of untidy habits—very untidy and careless. He was left with good prospects, but he threw away his chances and finally, taking to drink, he died."

Watson, astounded at the accuracy of Holmes's description of his late brother, asks if it was guesswork. "I never guess," replies Holmes:

> I began by stating that your brother was careless. When you observe the lower part of the watch case, you notice that it is not only dented in two places, but it is cut and marked all over from the habit of keeping other hard objects, such as coins or keys, in the same pocket. Surely it is no great feat to assume that a man who treats [an expensive] watch so cavalierly must be a careless man. Neither is it a very far-fetched inference that a man who inherits one article of such value is pretty well provided for in other respects.

"But what about his drinking habits?" asks Watson. Holmes responds:

> Look at the innerplate which contains the keyhole [where the watch is wound]. Look at the thousands of scratches all around the hole-marks where the key has slipped. What sober man's key could have scored those grooves? But you will never see a drunkard's watch without them. He winds it at night, and he leaves these traces of his unsteady hand. Where is the mystery in all this?

Had Sherlock Holmes been an anthropologist, he might have also been tempted to draw some inferences about the society in which the watch was manufactured—particularly about their conceptions of time. For example, in some societies, time is task oriented, not clock oriented; time might be measured by how long it takes to cook rice, as in Madagascar. In other societies, time patterns depend on natural events, such as the rising of the sun or the ebb and flow of tides. In his classic account of the life of the Nuer of the Sudan, British anthropologist E. E. Evans-Pritchard noted (1940, p. 103):

> The Nuer have no expression equivalent to "time" in our language, and they cannot, therefore, as we can, speak of time as though it were something actual, which passes, can be wasted, can be saved, and so forth. I don't think they ever experience the same feeling of fighting against time because their points of reference are mainly the activities themselves, which are generally of a leisurely character. Events follow a logical order, but they are not controlled by an abstract system, there being no autonomous points of reference to which activities have to conform with precision. Nuer are fortunate.

An anthropologist might also infer that clocks are instruments of discipline; they tell us when to get up, when to go to bed, when to eat, when to start work, and when to stop work. Clocks define our work patterns themselves, and our wages may depend on the constant repetition over time of a particular task. Historian E. P. Thompson notes that until the institution of modern notions of time and the need to measure it with clocks, work patterns were characterized by alternating bouts of intense labor and idleness—at least whenever people were in control of their own working lives. He even suggests that this pattern persists today but only among a few self-employed professionals, such as artists, writers, small farmers, and, he suggests, college students.

Watson's brother's watch was a product of Western society—part of its culture. Holmes "read" the watch as if it were a collection of symbols or words—a **cultural text** that revealed the character of its owner. He could just as easily have viewed it as a text inscribed with the symbols that revealed the ideas about time and work that characterized the civilization that produced it.

One way to think about culture is as a text of significant symbols: words, gestures, drawings, natural objects—anything, in fact, that carries meaning. To understand another culture, we must be able, as Holmes was with a pocket watch, to decipher the meaning of the symbols that comprise a cultural text. We must be able to interpret the meaning embedded in the language, objects, gestures, and activities that are shared by members of a society. Fortunately, the ability to decipher a cultural text is part of being human; in our everyday lives, we both read and maintain the text that makes up our own culture. We have learned the meanings behind the symbols that frame our lives, and we share those meanings with others. Our task in understanding another culture is to take the abilities that have enabled us to dwell in our own culture and use them to understand the cultures of others.

Deciphering the Balinese Cockfight

To illustrate how an anthropologist might decipher a cultural text, imagine yourself coming upon a cockfight on the island of Bali. You see a ring in which two roosters with sharpened metal spurs attached to their legs are set at each other until one kills the other. Surrounding the fighting cocks are men shouting encouragement to their favorites, each having placed a wager that his favorite will kill its opponent.

What do you make of this? Your first reaction might be shock or disgust at the spectacle of the crowd urging the cocks to bloody combat. After a while, you might begin to find similarities to events that are meaningful to you, such as some American sports. But what if, like Sherlock Holmes (or like Geertz, from whom this example is taken), you want to understand the meaning of what is happening and what that meaning tells you about how Balinese view their world? If you assume that the cockfight is a feature of Balinese culture—a Balinese text filled with symbols that carry meaning about what it is to be Balinese—how might you read and/or interpret this text?

You might begin by finding out the language the Balinese use to talk about the cockfight. You would no doubt discover that the double entendre of cock as a synonym for rooster and as a euphemism for penis is the same for the Balinese as it is for Americans. The double entendre even produces, says Geertz, the same jokes, puns, and obscenities in Bali as it does in the United States. You would discover that *sabung*, the Balinese word for cock, has numerous other meanings and is used metaphorically to mean hero, warrior, champion, political

In Balinese society, cockfighting is a major sporting event that is closely tied to cultural interpretations of manhood, competition, and status.

candidate, bachelor, dandy, lady-killer, or tough guy. Court trials, wars, political contests, inheritance disputes, and street arguments are compared with cockfights. Even the island of Bali is thought of as being cock shaped. You would also find that men give their fowls inordinate attention, spending most of their time grooming them and even feeding them a special diet. As one of Geertz's Balinese informants put it, "We're all cock crazy."

Having discovered the importance of cockfights to the Balinese and the connection they make between cocks and men, you next examine the cockfight itself. You learn that cockfights are public events held in arenas of about 50 square feet from late afternoon until after sundown. Handlers—expert in the task—attach sharp spurs to the cock's legs; for a cock thought to be superior to an opponent, the spurs are adjusted in a slightly disadvantageous position. The cocks are released in the center of the ring and fly at each other, fighting until one kills the other. The owner of the winning cock takes the carcass of the loser home to eat, and the losing owner is sometimes driven in despair to wreck family shrines. You discover that the Balinese contrast heaven and hell by comparing them to the mood of a man whose cock has just won and the mood of a man whose cock has just lost.

You find out that although the Balinese place odds on cockfights, there are strict social conventions that dictate the wagering. For example, a man will never bet against a cock that is owned by someone of his family group or village or a friend's family group or village, but he will place large bets against a cock owned by an enemy or the friend of an enemy. Rarely is a cockfight without social significance (e.g., between two outsiders), and rarely do cocks owned by members of the same family or village fight each other. Moreover, the owners of the cocks—especially in important matches—are usually among the leaders of their communities. You might learn that cockfights come close to encouraging an open expression of aggression between village and kin group rivals—but not quite because the cockfight is, as the Balinese put it, "only a cockfight."

Given the social rules for betting and the ways odds are set, you might reason, as Geertz did, that the Balinese rarely make a profit betting on cockfights. Geertz says in fact, that most bettors just want to break even. Consequently, the meaning of the cockfight for a Balinese has little to do with economics. The question is, what meaning does the cockfight have for the Balinese? What is the cockfight really about if it is not about money?

Geertz concludes that the Balinese cockfight is above all about status—about the ranking of people vis-à-vis one another. The Balinese cockfight is a text filled with meaning about status as the Balinese see it. Cocks represent men or, more specifically, their owners; the fate of the cock in the ring is linked—even if only temporarily—to the social fate of its owner. Each cock has a following consisting of the owner, the owner's family, and members of the owner's village, and these followers "risk" their status by betting on the cockfight. Furthermore, Geertz maintains, the more a match is between near equals, personal enemies, or high-status individuals, the more the match is about status. And the more the match is about status, the closer the identification of cock and man, the finer the cocks, and the more exactly they will be matched. The match will inspire greater emotion and absorption, and the gambling will be more about status and less about economic gain.

For Geertz, the cockfight is like any art form; it takes a highly abstract and difficult concept—status—and depicts it in a way that makes it comprehensible to the participants. The cockfight is meaningful to the Balinese because it tells them something real about their own lives in a way that does not directly affect their lives. They see the struggle for status that is part of everyday life vividly portrayed—even though, in the cockfight itself, no one really gains or loses status in any permanent sense.

A few words of caution are necessary concerning what you might learn about the Balinese from this particular cultural text. First, it would probably be a mistake to assume that the people gain status by being on the winning side or lose it by being on the side of the loser. The status outcomes of the cockfight do not translate into real life any more than the victory of your favorite sports team increases your status. Instead, says Geertz, the cockfight illustrates what status is about for the Balinese. The cockfight is a story the Balinese tell themselves about themselves. It would also be a mistake to assume that the character of the Balinese could be read directly from the cockfight; a conclusion that the cockfight is indicative of an aggressive, competitive, violent national character would quickly be dispelled. The Balinese are shy about competition and avoid open conflict. The slaughter in the cockfight is not how things are literally but how they could be. Finally, the cockfight reveals only a segment of the Balinese character, as Watson's brother's watch revealed only a segment of its owner's character. The culture of a people, like the possessions of a person, is an ensemble of texts—collections of symbols and meanings—that must be viewed together to provide a full understanding.

QUESTION 1.5   *What Can Learning About Other Peoples Tell Americans About Themselves?*

Anthropologists do not limit themselves to the study of cultures that are different from their own. Rather, they often apply concepts and techniques that are useful in understanding and interpreting other cultures to understand and interpret their own.

One of the objectives of studying other cultures is to help us recognize the meanings we impose on our experiences. When Renato Rosaldo asked the Ilongots why they cut off human heads, they replied that rage born of grief drives them to kill others; by severing the heads of their victims, they are able to throw away the anger born of bereavement. Rosaldo found it difficult to accept the ideas that the death of a kinsperson could cause anger or rage and that such rage in itself could drive a person to kill another. He questioned the Ilongots further but could obtain no other reason for their headhunting; he devised other theories to explain it, but none were satisfactory. Only his own experience of grief and anger at the accidental death of his wife Michelle while both were doing fieldwork among the Ilongots helped him realize how grief can generate rage and how grief drove the Ilongots to hunt the heads of their enemies. At the same time that he began to understand the Ilongots, he began to understand his own grief and reaction to death.

A Balinese Anthropologist Studies Football

Whether we approach other cultures as anthropologists, as travelers, or as professionals who need to communicate with people of other cultures, the confrontation with other ways of believing and behaving should cause us to reflect on our own way of viewing the world. To illustrate, let us try to step outside ourselves and objectify an experience whose meaning we take for granted. Pretend you are a Balinese anthropologist who suddenly comes upon a spectacle as important in its way to Americans as the cockfight is to the Balinese: a football game.

As a Balinese, your first reaction to this American text might be one of horror and revulsion to see men violently attacking one other while thousands cheer them on to even more violent conflict. However, as you settle in, you soon find some obvious similarities between the football game and the cockfight with which you are familiar at home. Both are spectator sports in which the spectators sort themselves into supporters of one side or the other. In fact, in football, the sorting is even more carefully arranged because supporters of one team are generally seated on one side of the arena and fans of the other team are seated opposite them.

Your next step (as in interpreting the cockfight) is to examine the language Americans use to refer to the football game. You discover that they use similar expressions in talking about football and war: *defensive line*, *blitz*, *bomb*. Coaches talk about getting "revenge" for defeats, as generals might talk about getting revenge on the battlefield. You conclude that Americans seem to feel the same way about football as they do about war.

A highly popular North American spectator sport, football conveys cultural messages about how to achieve success in the business world.

© Corbis

One of the words Americans use to refer to players is *jock*, a term also applied to an athletic supporter worn only by men. Because you see only men attacking one another, you might assume that the gender meanings of cockfights and football games are also similar. *Cocks* stand for men; football players are men. Moreover, football players dress to emphasize their maleness: large shoulders, narrow hips, big heads, and pronounced genitals. You might test your interpretation with an American spectator, who would argue that football gear is simply protective but, if pressed, would have to admit that it is used offensively as much as defensively. Furthermore, you see young women participating in the spectacle as cheerleaders, dressed to highlight their femininity in the same way the players dress to accent their masculinity. This contrast between male and female in American society leads you to conclude that football is also a story about the meanings that Americans ascribe to gender differences.

You soon discover that winning and losing football games is as important to Americans as winning and losing cockfights is to Balinese. Winners engage in frenzied celebrations called *victory parties*, and losers are often despondent in defeat. As anthropologists know, this is not always the case in other societies. When the Gahuku-Gama of the Highlands of New Guinea started playing soccer, they always played until a committee of elders decided that the score was tied and then the match was considered completed. So, you speculate that football is also about the meanings that Americans give to the idea of success. You learn that success in America (like status in Bali) is a highly abstract idea; because it is abstract, its meaning is embedded in activities whose meanings are shared by members of the society. You need to find answers to certain questions about the meaning of success in American society: How is success defined? How is it obtained? Why does everyone who follows all the rules for gaining success not attain it?

Through your fieldwork, you find that Americans believe that "all men are created equal" and every person has (or at least should have) an equal opportunity to succeed. People compete for success, and they ought to compete on an equal footing—on a "level playing field," as some put it. Success, Americans believe, comes from hard work, sacrifice, and self-denial. But you wonder how Americans know that hard work, sacrifice, and denial bring success. Are there not instances where they do not? How do Americans explain why women and minorities succeed less often than white males do? And why do some people achieve more success than others? You conclude that it is, in fact, impossible to prove directly in real life the correctness of this American success model, which maintains that hard work and sacrifice lead to success. Faith in the value of work and self-denial must be generated in other ways. As a Balinese anthropologist studying the American custom of football, you thus conclude that in addition to its meanings relative to war and gender, the meaning of American football also lies in its demonstration of the American success model as it is supposed to work.

Anthropologists have found that football, like the Balinese cockfight, is carefully controlled by fixed rules so there is only one outcome: Almost always, there is a winner and a loser. As a text that carries meaning about success, *who* wins is unimportant; it is only important that *someone* wins. ("A tie," it has been said, "is like kissing your sister.") But more than that, football tells Americans what it takes to win or lose. Success in football not only takes hard work and sacrifice, but as American anthropologist William Arens points out, it requires teamwork, specialization, mechanization, and submission to a dominant authority: the coach. Two other American anthropologists—Susan P. Montague and Robert Morais—note that the football team looks very much like one of the most important settings in which Americans seek success: business corporations. Football teams and corporations are compartmentalized, hierarchical, and highly sophisticated in the coordinated application of a differentiated, specialized technology, and they both try to turn out a winning product in a competitive market. Football coaches are sometimes hired to deliver inspirational lectures to corporate groups on "winning"; they may draw analogies between football and corporate life or portray the sport as a means of preparing for life in the business world.

Anthropologists therefore can conclude (as did Montague and Morais) that football provides for Americans, as the cockfight does for the Balinese, a small-scale rendering of a concept (status in the case of the Balinese; success in the American case) that is too complex to be directly comprehended. Football is compelling because it is a vivid demonstration of the validity of the value of success as well as a dramatic set of instructions on how to attain it. Consequently, the audience for a football game is led to believe that if the rules that govern the world of football are equated with those of the business world, then the principles that govern success on the football field must also apply in the world of work. That is, if hard work, dedication, submission to authority, and teamwork lead to success in a game, they will lead to success in real life. The rules by which success is won in football can also be applied to win success in the real world.

Of course, football is also a game that people enjoy. Analyzing it should not reduce our enjoyment of it but rather heighten our fascination with it. By looking at football from the same perspective as Geertz viewed the cockfight, we should gain an understanding of why the meaning carried by the game is important. Although understanding the cockfight heightens our appreciation of the football game, it also helps us to see similarities between Americans and Balinese. If you were shocked by the cockfight, seeing the similarities to football should lessen that shock while also making football seem just a bit more exotic.

An Anthropologist Looks at a "Happy Meal"

Nothing is too mundane to provide some insights into the culture of which it is a part. Take the Happy Meal advertised by one of the many fast-food establishments in the United States. It usually consists of a hamburger, French fries, a cola drink, and a plastic toy—often a Barbie doll or a Hot Wheels car or something related to a current popular movie. What can we learn about the culture of the United States by looking beyond the taken-for-granted quality of this meal? Among other things, we can get some idea of American demographic and ecological patterns, agricultural and industrial history, and gender roles.

Why, for example, is meat the center of the meal? Most cultures have diets centered on some complex carbohydrate—rice, wheat, manioc, yams, taro—or something made from these—bread, pasta, tortillas, and so on. It is the spice, vegetables, meat, or fish that when added to these foods give cuisine its distinctive taste. But meat and fish are generally at the edge, not the center, of the meal. Why is beef the main ingredient rather than some other meat, such as pork?

Anthropologists Marvin Harris and Eric Ross note that one advantage of beef was its suitability for the outdoor grill, which became more popular as people moved from cities into suburbs. Suburban cooks soon discovered that pork patties crumbled and fell through the grill, whereas beef patties held together better. In addition, to reduce the risk of trichinosis, pork had to be cooked until it was gray, which makes it very tough.

Beef farmers as well as the farmers who grew the corn fed to beef to achieve a desirable fat content benefitted from the definition of a hamburger set by the U.S. Department of Agriculture:

> "Hamburger" shall consist of chopped fresh and/or frozen beef with or without the addition of beef fat as such and/or seasonings, shall not contain more than 30 percent fat, and shall not contain added water, phosphates, binders, or extenders. Beef cheek (trimmed Beef cheeks) may be used in the preparation of hamburgers only in accordance with the conditions prescribed in paragraph (a) of this section. (quoted in Harris, 1987, p. 125)

As Harris notes, we can eat ground pork and ground beef, but we can't combine them and still call it a hamburger. Even when lean, grass-fed beef is used for hamburger and fat must be added as a binder, the fat must come from beef scraps, not from vegetables or a different animal. This definition of the hamburger protects both the beef industry and the corn farmer, whose income is linked to cattle production. Moreover, it helps the fast-food industry because the definition of hamburger permits the use of inexpensive scraps of fat from slaughtered beef to make up to 30% of its hamburger. Thus, an international beef patty was created that overcame what Harris calls the "pig's natural superiority as a converter of grain to flesh."

The cola drink that accompanies our hamburger is the second part of the fat- and sugar-centered diet that has come to characterize our culture. People in the United States consume, on average, about 60 pounds of sugar a year. Why so much? Sugar, as anthropologist Sidney Mintz suggests, has no nutritional properties, but it provides a quick and inexpensive energy boost for hardworking laborers with little time for a more nutritious meal. Sugar also serves as an excellent complement to the fat in hamburgers because it has what nutritionists call *go-away qualities* that remove the fat coating and the beef aftertaste from the mouth.

We can also learn from the Happy Meal that the fat and sugar diet is highly environmentally destructive. Raising beef is among the most environmentally inefficient and destructive forms of raising food. For example, half the water consumed in the United States is used to grow grain to feed cattle, and the amount of water used to produce 10 pounds of steak equals the household consumption of a family for an entire year. Fifteen times more water is needed to produce a pound of beef protein than an equivalent amount of plant protein.

Cattle raising plays a major role in the destruction of tropical forests in Brazil, Guatemala, Costa Rica, and Honduras, where forests have been leveled to create pasture for cattle. Because burning is used to clear most of the forest, the creation of cattle pasture also creates carbon dioxide and, according to some environmentalists, contributes significantly to global warming.

Sugar is no less destructive a crop. Sugar production alters the environment in a number of ways. Forests must be cleared to plant sugar; wood or fossil fuel must be burned in the evaporation process; wastewater is produced in extracting sucrose from the sugarcane; and more fuel is burned in the refining process. Contemporary sugar production in Hawaii not only has destroyed forests, but waste products from processing have severely damaged marine environments. "Big sugar," as the sugar industry is called in Florida, is largely responsible for the pollution, degradation, and virtual destruction of the Everglades.

Thus, one of the "texts" anthropologists can read from a Happy Meal relates to the extent to which consumption patterns associated with our culture create waste and environmental damage. Because of these consumption patterns, the average child born in the United States will in the course of his or her lifetime do twice the environmental damage of a Swedish child, three times that of an Italian child, 13 times that of a Brazilian child, 35 times that of an Indian child, and 280 times that of a Chadian or Haitian child.

And what about Barbie dolls and Hot Wheels? Clearly, there is a message about the definition of gender roles because girls are expected to choose dolls and boys cars. But one can deduce, if one looks closely enough, even more about our culture from this meal.

Exercise 1.5 ➤

THE HAPPY MEAL

We have examined some of the lessons we can learn about our culture from the Happy Meal. But there are obviously others. See what you might deduce about the following dimensions of life in the United States from the Happy Meal.

1. What can you say about gender roles in the United States?
2. What can you deduce about race relations?
3. What can you say about the physical attributes of people favored in the United States?

CASE STUDY IN DOING ANTHROPOLOGY #1:
SHOPPING AND SELLING

Students taking anthropology classes often say, "I like anthropology, but what can I do with it?" A more or less typical response is, "Anything that you can do with any liberal arts major." But that does not get us very far. Being a professional anthropologist—teacher, researcher, consultant—generally requires an advanced degree. However, an anthropological perspective and methodology can be invaluable in all sorts of career areas—so much so that one national newspaper recently labeled anthropology a "hot major."

Like any discipline, anthropology deals with problems and questions, which is what any career or profession does. People in management must address the problem of how to structure relationships among staff; people in government must address problems involved in designing public policy initiatives, such as reducing juvenile crime. Someone in a medical field may face the problem of how to educate the young regarding sexually transmitted diseases, whereas someone employed in the tourist industry must address the problem of how to minimize the negative consequences of tourism for local populations. The solution to all these and other problems can benefit from an anthropological perspective because all involve ways that people give meaning to their experiences. For example, in a consumer-dominated culture such as ours, people who want to sell goods have a vested interest in finding out how people experience their goods and services. That is what advertisements are all about—defining for the consumer the experience of driving a Porsche, wearing Nikes, or eating at a luxury restaurant.

Paco Underhill is a retail anthropologist. For 20 years, he's been studying people shopping. He watches them move through stores, restaurants, banks, fast-food places, car dealerships, post offices, and so on, to examine the interaction between people and products and people and spaces. The company he founded, Envirosell, works with merchants, marketers, and retail bankers to discover whether retailers and manufacturers meet or fail to meet their customers' needs and how people experience the act of shopping.

Underhill's ideas about retail anthropology originated when he was a student of William H. Whyte, whose research focused on how people used public spaces—streets, parks, plazas, and such. Whyte and his researchers would film people's behavior or stake out some urban plaza for days—often following up on their observations with interviews. They would measure everything: the ideal width of a ledge for sitting; how sunlight, shade, and wind affect park use; and how a public space's surroundings determined the quality of life there. Underhill simply adapted many of the methods and ideas developed by Whyte and his associates to the study of shopping spaces and how they affect consumer behavior. Underhill and his associates watch people shop, trace the paths they take in stores, and observe how they interact with merchandise or how they react to waiting in line. They study how shopping patterns differ by gender or by

© James Leynse/Corbis

Retail anthropologist Paco Underhill founded Envirosell to work with merchants and retailers on meeting customers' shopping needs.

age or how much time shoppers spend in individual stores or on individual aisles or displays. The information then helps retailers and manufacturers design an experience for shoppers that they hope will increase sales.

Underhill found for example that the amount of time a shopper spends in a store is directly related to how much money he or she will spend. Knowing what determines how long people spend shopping and being able to do something about it are invaluable. By observing with whom people shop in one store, Underhill found that the amount of time a woman spent in the store had a lot to do with whom she was shopping: Women shopping with a female companion spent on average 8 minutes and 15 seconds in the store; women with children spent 7 minutes and 19 seconds; women alone spent 5 minutes and 2 seconds; and a woman with a man spent only 4 minutes and 41 seconds. Retailers cannot readily influence with whom people shop, but they can try to make it a little more pleasant for people who might not want to shop. Seating, says Underhill, is critical, and he has advised many clients that having seating is invaluable.

Store organization is also critical. For example, when people enter a store, they need a period to adjust. Almost anything placed near the entrance—shopping baskets, flyers, merchandise—will go unnoticed. Move them 10 feet into the store, though, and they get noticed, used, or bought. Stores encourage shoppers to traverse the whole store by putting commonly purchased items in the back. Thus, dairy cases are in the back of supermarkets, and video rental stores get their customers to the back of the store by putting the new releases on the back wall. It also helps for shoppers to have contact with employees—the "interception rate"—because the higher the interception rate, the more people buy. Greeting a customer with a simple hello works and apparently discourages shoplift-·ing. As Sam Walton, the founder of Walmart observed, "If you hire a sweet old lady just to say hello to incoming customers, none of them will dare steal."

As we see in more detail in later chapters, gender is culturally defined. It is an anthropologist's job to know how different cultures define gender and to determine which behaviors and values are typical of men and which are typical of women. And although there are certainly exceptions, there are some patterns of behavior that differentiate men from women shoppers. For example, men tend to·shop faster, look for what they want, grab it, and run to the cashier. In one study that Underhill did for Dockers, they captured men on video. What they found was that men find a pair of trousers in their size and head directly for the checkout counter without browsing or trying anything else on. "The time spent in the section," says Underhill, "was roughly identical to what men devote to shopping for beer in convenience stores." Men shop the way they drive; they are much less likely to ask for help from store employees and, if they cannot find what they want, will wheel about and leave the store. They are also less likely to look at price tags (72% of men will look compared to 86% of women). But for that reason, men will spend more. Men act as providers, says Underhill; although shopping is not their thing, paying is. When men and women are together in the supermarket checkout line, the men almost always pay. Women often go to the supermarket with lists; men rarely do, and consequently, they buy more. As Underhill (1999, p. 100) puts it:

> Any wife who's watching the family budget knows better that to send her husband to the supermarket unchaperoned. Giving him a vehicle to commandeer, even if it is just a shopping cart, only emphasizes the potential for guyness in the experience. Throw in a couple of kids with Dad and you've got a lethal combination; he's notoriously bad at saying no when there's grocery acquisitioning to be done. Part of being Daddy is being the provider, after all. It goes to the heart of a man's self image.

By watching shoppers examine merchandise, Underhill found that women coolly weigh their purchases, considering the pros and cons, and carefully examine the purchase price. Men breeze through the supermarket, picking up the first head of lettuce and never noting the brown spots or wilted leaves—and never even looking at the price. Men do spend more time examining some merchandise, such as cars, boats, barbecue grills, and computers. Nevertheless, Underhill concludes that women demand more of shopping environments than men. Men want to find what they want and get out fast; women are more patient and inquisitive. And you can't crowd her. One of Underhill's main findings has to do with what he calls the "butt-brush effect": Touch someone, especially a woman, from behind, and she'll immediately move away from the merchandise and often leave the store. At cosmetics counters, women required to stand for a while tend to seek out the corners of counters and buy more than women a few feet away along the main stretch of counter. Some cosmetic counters have little cul-de-sac recesses to allow shoppers to stand clear. Women tend to seek the cul-de-sacs, such as the areas in airport gift shops, away from the grab-and-run counter where they have the newspapers and gum. Thus, the narrower the quarters, the less time women will spend there. Women like to read labels before they buy, and that takes time and space.

However, as Underhill notes, as gender roles have changed, retailers must keep up. Men stay single longer, and as more and more women enter the workforce and become family providers, men are shopping more. And as more and more women have entered the job market, shopping is now something that has to be crammed into lunch hours or predinner routines. To some extent, this is what accounts for the rapid growth of convenience stores. Thus, retailers have to address the decline in shopping time of their best customers.

Retailers also need to address the aging of the population in most industrialized countries. For example, in the United States, by 2025, there will be an 80% increase in the number of people over 65 years of age, when they will make up one-fifth of the population. How will or should retailers adapt to the aging of the population?

Children today are a major segment of the consumer market. Marketing researchers estimate that in the United States, children ages 2–14 directly influence $188 billion of parental spending, indirectly influence another $300 billion, and themselves spend some $25 billion. If a store is unwelcoming to children, parents with children will stay away. Simple things help. For example, aisles need to be wide enough to accommodate baby strollers. But in one department store that Underhill studied, the babies' and children's clothing section was more cluttered with fixtures and racks than any in the store. It was the most difficult to navigate with a stroller and, hence, the least visited part of the store.

Underhill also notes that if you want to sell things to kids, you have to put them where they can be seen and reached. In one study of a supermarket, he found that kids and the elderly most frequently purchased dog snacks, but the snacks were on the top shelves, where they were difficult to reach. When snacks were moved to the bottom shelves, sales immediately increased. Supermarkets have become particularly clever at placing things that kids want at kid level so

Exercise 1.6 ➢

RESEARCHING A STORE

Paco Underhill has what he calls a self-exam in which he asks the owner or CEO of a store to just stand with him for 30 minutes and observe. Inevitably, they see things they never even thought about. In this exercise, you are going to play CEO, owner, or manager of a store. You pick the store and then do the following:

1. As you approach the store, what do you see? Do you know from a distance what is sold in there?
2. Stand right outside the store. What do you see in the windows? Can you see anything? Are the windows clear?
3. Go into the store. Are there baskets to put things in? Are they positioned near the door (a bad idea) or are they scattered around the store (better)?
4. What strikes you as you transition into the store? What attracts your attention? Are there signs? How does the merchandise appear to you?
5. What is the register setup? Do people have to wait, and if so, are there any distractions to help time go faster?
6. Are there any opportunities to touch, feel, or try the merchandise?
7. How is the merchandise grouped? Are things that are adjacent to each other arranged so the sale of one might prompt the sale of the other? Are they arranged in ways that would appeal to women, men, kids, the elderly?
8. How are nonpublic spaces designed? What are the restrooms like? If it is a clothing store, are the dressing rooms likely to add to or detract from the likelihood of a sale?

The single most important determinant of shoppers' opinions of service they receive is waiting time.

they can just grab the items and toss them in the shopping cart. Of course, that can also backfire if parents adapt and begin to avoid the cookie aisle all together.

Underhill notes that retailers must become adept at controlling the experience of time. Bad time is when customers have to wait, but they will up to a point. In study after study, Underhill discovered that the single most important determinant of shoppers' opinions of service they receive is waiting time. If they think the wait was not too bad, they will feel fairly treated; if it goes on too long, they think that the service was poor and inept. If you ask people how long they waited, they are fairly accurate up to 90 seconds. After that, estimates vary widely. Two minutes is acceptable; three is bad. But it is possible to make time seem shorter. Waiting time goes faster after interaction with an employee. Just acknowledging the shopper helps time go faster. Telling people how long they can expect to wait also alleviates time anxiety. Maintaining orderly lines is important; although Europeans can line up in what seems to be an undifferentiated mass, Americans and Britons like an orderly line in which they know where their place is and that they will be served in the order in which they arrived. Time goes faster if people have someone to talk to. At Disney World, the engineers organized lines to wind back and forth, which not only allows the lines to appear shorter than they are but also encourages people to talk to one another, making the time seem to go faster. Diversions also help time go faster. Almost anything will do, says Underhill—short videos, stacks of stuff, the sleazy tabloids at supermarket checkout counters. People experience lines as shorter if they have something to read.

Finally, although Underhill makes his living as a retail anthropologist advising stores and manufacturers how to better serve their clientele, he is often critical of the services they provide. Bathrooms are a major example. For example, in spite of the fact that women use them more than men, store and mall planners are rigidly symmetrical when it comes to bathrooms. Women not only use them more frequently, but they also spend more time in them. That is why you are more likely to see lines outside of women's restrooms than men's restrooms. Retailers do not even take advantage of the time spent in restrooms by putting ads over the urinals. Why not, he says, turn the bathrooms in department stores over to some of the shops that deal in soap, skin creams, fragrance, hair care, or even cosmetics and allow them to run them. Underhill once toured a Lowe's, a home improvement chain, with some of the senior marketing people. He asked to see the ladies' room, which none of the men had ever seen. It was bland and featureless, but one of the major marketing goals of Lowe's is to sell people on modern luxurious bathrooms. Another marketing opportunity is lost.

The point of our discussion on anthropology and shopping is not to imply that every anthropology student should work toward accelerating consumption but rather to illustrate what can be done with knowledge of human beings by people ingenious enough to apply their imagination. Paco Underhill started a whole new field and a lucrative business. But there are few if any careers that cannot benefit by applying the knowledge and perspective of anthropology. In later chapters, for example, we will examine how an anthropological perspective can be applied to—among other things—economic development and community building, public policy, tourism, medicine, and conflict resolution. All these applications are based on looking behind the obvious to see how culture influences the meanings people give things, how they experience events, and the interactions between them.

Conclusions

This chapter considered five questions—some having to do with the problem of how to understand ways of life that are different from our own and others with how to better understand our own lives. Why do human beings differ in what they believe and how they behave? One answer is that human beings— unlike other animals (or, at least, to a greater extent than other animals)— create their own worlds and ascribe meanings to objects, persons, behaviors, emotions, and events—meanings that together constitute a culture. As Geertz suggests, human beings are compelled to create meanings if only to create some sense of order in their lives.

The judgments we make about the beliefs and behaviors of other people create a dilemma. On the one hand, if we assume the meanings that others give to their experiences are wrong, silly, or absurd simply because they are different from ours, we are committing the ethnocentric fallacy. Ethnocentrism is intellectually awkward because it allows everyone to believe that his or her views are correct and that the views of others are wrong. This would make any kind of intercultural understanding virtually impossible. On the other hand, if we conclude that the beliefs and behaviors of others can be judged only in the context of their cultures, we are confronted with the relativistic fallacy, which implies that any belief or behavior is acceptable, provided it makes sense to the people of the society in which it occurs. This places us in a moral dilemma because we must then accept virtually any belief or behavior.

Whether it is possible to set aside the meanings we ascribe to experience and see the world through the eyes of others is another question. Anthropologists conclude that the understandings they reach of other cultures can be at best limited. Furthermore, in many ways, the ethnographic method transforms the fieldworker into a "marginal" person—an outsider who knows only something of what it is to be an insider.

One way we describe and interpret the meanings other people find in their experiences is to consider a culture as a text inscribed with symbols whose meaning can be deciphered. We can examine virtually any cultural activity this way and find in it a portion of the overall view of the world of a people. If we approach our own culture in the same way we approach other cultures, we should gain a better understanding of the meanings we give objects, persons, and events. If we objectify our own beliefs and behaviors in the same way we objectify the beliefs and behaviors of others, our own culture should become more exotic while the cultures of others should become less strange, shocking, or bizarre.

Finally, we examined how an anthropological perspective can be used to understand how people shop and how that information can be applied in a person's choice of career.

REFERENCES AND SUGGESTED READINGS

Introduction: The World Behind Everyday Appearances
The epigraph comes from Jonathan Culler's article "In Pursuit of Signs," in *Daedalus*, vol. 106 (1977), pp. 95–112. The discussion of the meaning of the classroom chair derives from some of the ideas of Michel Foucault in *Discipline and Punishment: The Birth of the Prison* (Vintage Books, 1979). An excellent anthropological study of American education is Norris Brock Johnson's *Westhaven: Classroom Culture and Society in a Rural Elementary School* (University of North Carolina Press, 1985).

Why Do Human Beings Differ in Their Beliefs and Behaviors?
The descriptions of concepts of death come from Stanley Walens's account of Kwakiutl ritual and belief, *Feasting With Cannibals: An Essay on Kwakiutl Cosmology* (Princeton University Press, 1981); Beth Conklin's book *Consuming Grief: Compassionate Cannibalism in an Amazonian Society* (University of Texas Press, 2001); Daniel David Cowell's article "Funerals, Family, and Forefathers: A View of Italian-American Funeral Practices," *Omega*, vol. 16 (1985–1986), pp. 69–85; and Renato Rosaldo, *Culture and Truth: The Remaking of Social Analysis* (Beacon Press, 1989). A comprehensive review of beliefs about death can be found in "Death: A Cross-Cultural Perspective" by Phyllis Palgi and Henry Abramovitch, in *Annual Review of Anthropology*, vol. 13 (1984), pp. 385–417. Clifford Geertz's treatment of the concept of culture is from his essay "The Impact of Culture on the Concept of Man," in *The Interpretation of Cultures* (Basic Books, 1973).

How Do People Judge the Beliefs and Behaviors of Others?
Richard Scaglion's tale of his experiences among the Abelam is told in his article "Ethnocentrism and the Abelam," in *The Humbled Anthropologist: Tales from the Pacific*, edited by Philip Devita (Wadsworth, 1990), pp. 29–34. The example of headhunting among the Ilongot comes from Rosaldo's *Culture and Truth*, cited previously. A description of Aztec ritual sacrifice is found in Marvin Harris's *Cannibals and Kings: The Origins of Culture* (Vintage Books, 1977). The account of female circumcision comes from Rose Oldfield-Hayes's article "Female Genital Mutilation, Fertility

Control, Women's Roles, and the Patrilineage in Modern Sudan: A Functional Analysis," *American Ethnologist*, vol. 2 (1975), pp. 617–33. The material on Turkey comes from Carol Delany's *The Seed and the Soil: Gender and Cosmology in a Turkish Village Society* (University of California Press, 1991), and the material on Wari cannibalism is from *Consuming Grief*, cited previously. The debate between Nancy Scheper-Hughes and Roy D'Andrade about whether anthropology should be more morally committed appeared in *Current Anthropology*, vol. 36 (1995). Scheper-Hughes's dilemma concerning the treatment of infants in the shantytowns of Brazil is described in *Death Without Weeping: The Violence of Everyday Life in Brazil* (University of California Press, 1992). You can read about the experiences of Philippe Bourgois in *In Search of Respect: Selling Crack in El Barrio* (Cambridge University Press, 1995). An excellent critique of cultural relativism is Elizabeth Zechenter's article "In the Name of Culture: Cultural Relativism and the Abuse of the Individual," in a special issue of the *Journal of Anthropological Research—Universal Human Rights Versus Cultural Relativity*, vol. 53 (1997), pp. 319–48.

Is It Possible to See the World Through the Eyes of Others?

Michael Kearney describes his brush with witchcraft in "A Very Bad Disease of the Arms," in *The Naked Anthropologist* (Wadsworth, 1991), pp. 47–57. Nancy Green's account of her fieldwork in Guatemala comes from her article "Living in a State of Fear," in *Fieldwork Under Fire: Contemporary Studies of Violence and Survival*, edited by Carolyn Nordstrom and Antonius C. G. Robben (University of California Press, 1995). Claude Levi-Strauss's observations about the role of the anthropologist are from *Tristes Tropiques* (Atheneum, 1974). Roger Keesing's observations come from his article "Not a Real Fish: The Ethnographer as Inside Outsider," in *The Naked Anthropologist*, pp. 73–78. Three classic accounts of fieldwork experiences are Richard Lee's paper "Eating Christmas in the Kalihari," first published in *Natural History Magazine*, December 1969; Jean L. Briggs's account of her fieldwork among the Eskimo in *Never in Anger* (Harvard University Press, 1970); and Laura Bohannan's account of her experience translating *Hamlet* to the Tiv, "Shakespeare in the Bush," originally published in *Natural History Magazine*, August/September 1966.

How Can the Meanings That Others Find in Experience Be Interpreted and Described?

The use of Sir Arthur Conan Doyle's Sherlock Holmes story "The Sign of the Four," from *The Complete Sherlock Holmes*, vol. 1 (Doubleday, 1930), to illustrate the deciphering of a cultural text was inspired by Manfred F. R. Kets de Vries and Danny Miller in "Interpreting Organizational Texts," *Journal of Management Studies*, vol. 24 (1987), pp. 233–47. The description of the Nuer conception of time comes from E. E. Evans-Pritchard's book *The Nuer: A Description of the Modes of Livelihood and Political Institutions of a Nilotic People* (Clarendon Press, 1940). The discussion about time and discipline appears in E. P. Thompson's article "Time, Work-Discipline and Industrial Capitalism," in *Past and Present*, vol. 38 (1967), pp. 56–97. The approach to culture as a text is best formulated by Clifford Geertz in his 1973 book *The Interpretation of Cultures*. Geertz's analysis of the Balinese cockfight, "Deep Play: Notes on the Balinese Cockfight," first appeared in *Daedalus*, vol. 101 (1972), pp. 1–37.

What Can Learning About Other Peoples Tell Americans About Themselves?

Renato Rosaldo speaks candidly about his struggle to come to grips with his wife's death in *Culture and Truth*, cited previously, which also explores the issues of how we learn about other cultures and what we can expect to understand about them. The analysis of the meaning of American football comes from William Arens's article "Professional Football: An American Symbol and Ritual" and Susan P. Montague and William Morais's article "Football Games and Rock Concerts: The Ritual Enactment of American Success Models"—both in *The American Dimension: Cultural Myths and Social Realities*, edited by Arens and Montague (Alfred Publishing, 1976). A more recent view of the importance of football to American communities in the Southwest can be found in Douglas E. Foley's *Learning Capitalist Culture: Deep in the Heart of Tejas* (University of Pennsylvania Press, 1990). The account of how the Gahuku-Gama of the New Guinea Highlands adapted soccer to their own needs is found in Kenneth E. Read's *The High Valley*, originally published in 1965 by Columbia University Press and reprinted in 1980, pp. 150–52. A look at the role of meat in the American diet is provided in *Food and Evolution: Toward a Theory of Human Food Habits* by Marvin Harris and Eric Ross (Temple University Press, 1987) and Harris's book *Sacred Cow and the Abominable Pig* (Touchstone, 1987). Sidney W. Mintz provides an anthropological analysis of the history of sugar in *Sweetness and Power: The Place of Sugar in World History* (Viking Press, 1985). For another treatment of the creation of the American diet, see *Global Problems and the Culture of Capitalism* (4th ed.) by Richard H. Robbins (Allyn & Bacon, 2008). An excellent, although somewhat dated, review of anthropological studies of American culture can be found in George and Louise Spindler's "Anthropologists View American Culture," in *Annual Review of Anthropology*, vol. 12 (1983), pp. 49–78.

Case Study in How Can an Anthropological Perspective on Shopping Relate to Career Opportunities?

Two excellent resources for finding out about how anthropology can be applied are Alexander M. Ervin's book *Applied Anthropology: Tools and Perspectives for Contemporary Practice* (Allyn & Bacon, 2005) and Margaret A. Gwynne's *Applied Anthropology: A Career-Oriented Approach* (Allyn & Bacon, 2003). Paco Underhill describes his work in two books: *Why We Shop: The Science of Shopping* (Simon & Schuster, 1999) and *Call of the Mall* (Simon & Schuster, 2004). A wonderful book for those interested in careers in anthropology is John T. Omohundro's *Careers in Anthropology* (Mayfield, 2001).

THE MEANING OF PROGRESS AND DEVELOPMENT

PROBLEM 2: HOW DO WE EXPLAIN THE TRANSFORMATION OF HUMAN SOCIETIES OVER THE PAST 10,000 YEARS FROM SMALL-SCALE NOMADIC BANDS OF HUNTERS AND GATHERERS TO LARGE-SCALE URBAN-INDUSTRIAL STATES?

> *Development fostered a way of conceiving of social life as a technical problem, as a matter of rational decision and management to be entrusted to that group of people—the development professionals—whose specialized knowledge allegedly qualified them for the task. Instead of seeing change as a process rooted in the interpretation of each society's history and cultural tradition . . . these professionals sought to devise mechanisms and procedures to make societies fit a preexisting model that embodied the structures and functions of modernity. Like sorcerers' apprentices, the development professionals awakened once again the dream of reason that, in their hands, as in earlier instances, produced a troubling reality.*
>
> —**Arturo Escobar**

INTRODUCTION

The Death of a Way of Life

We live in an era in which we will witness (if we have not already) the extinction of a way of life that is more than 100,000 years old. We know that 10,000 years ago, virtually all human beings lived in small-scale nomadic groups of 30 to 100 people, gathering wild vegetable foods and hunting large and small game as they had for thousands of years. Today, virtually no human beings anywhere in the world live by hunting and gathering, although every society in existence is descended from such people. Hunters and gatherers are the common ancestors of us all.

We have also witnessed the creation of a world that is radically divided into wealthy nations and poor nations. Although some enjoy a standard of living that gives them abundant food, comfortable shelters, and a plethora of consumer goods, more than a billion people worldwide suffer from hunger and poverty, live in urban and rural slums, and lack even the basics of health care.

The gradual extinction of a type of society that had flourished for at least 100,000 years and the creation of a world ill divided into the wealthy and the poor pose both a riddle and a moral predicament. The riddle is why, approximately 10,000 years ago, after thousands of years of living as hunters and gatherers, some of these societies begin to abandon their way of life. Why did they begin to domesticate plants and animals and exchange their nomadic existence for **sedentary** dwelling in villages and towns? And how, over the next 10,000 years, did these villages and towns come to be divided into rich and poor nations? The moral predicament involves our perceptions of the few remaining small-scale tribal societies that exist in the world today, along with the millions of others who go hungry each day. Do we assume, as many have and still do, that human beings chose to abandon a nomadic hunting and gathering life because they discovered better ways of living? Do we assume that the few existing small-scale tribal societies are remnants of an inferior way of life and that, given the opportunity, their members also will choose to adopt modern farming, wage labor, or urban life? Do we assume that we can explain the division of wealth in the world by saying that some nations have progressed, whereas others have not? Or is the concept of **progress**—the idea that human history is the story of a steady advance from a life dependent on the whims of nature to a life of control and domination over natural forces—a fabrication of contemporary societies based on ethnocentric notions of technological superiority?

A thumbnail sketch of what we know about the course of cultural history and evolution will be useful before we examine this problem. Combining what we have learned about human history from the work of archaeologists and historians with information provided by cultural anthropologists who have worked among hunting-gathering and tribal societies creates a relatively clear picture of **culture change**. As stated previously, until approximately 10,000 years ago, Earth's inhabitants were scattered in small-scale nomadic bands of 30 to 100 people who lived by gathering wild plants and hunting small and large game. Because the search for food required mobility, it was probably not unusual for them to move every few days. With groups that were small and mobile, simple economic, social, and political arrangements sufficed; there were no formal leaders and little occupational specialization. If there was a specialist, it was likely to be a person who was believed to have special spiritual powers that could be used to cure illness or (if used malevolently) to cause illness or death. Kinship served as the main organizing principle of these societies, and social differences among people were based largely on age and gender. Because there was little occupational specialization and little difference in individual wealth or possessions, relations among persons likely were of an egalitarian nature.

At some point in history, some hunters and gatherers began to plant crops and domesticate wild animals. These groups became sedentary, living in permanent or semipermanent settlements of 200 to 2,000 people. They practiced **slash-and-burn**, or **swidden**, **agriculture**; they cleared forests by burning the trees and brush and planted crops among the ashes of the cleared ground. They would cultivate this land from one to three years and then they would burn and plant another plot of land. Because larger, more sedentary groups required more formal leadership, certain members assumed the roles of chief or elder, with the authority to make decisions or resolve disputes. Simple occupational roles developed. Villages consisted of extended family groups, and people organized themselves into clans—groups of 200 to 500 people who claimed descent from a common ancestor. As a result of the development of leadership roles, members of some groups were ranked in importance.

Later in history—perhaps because of a need for defense against other groups—settlements combined under common leaders to form **states** consisting of many thousands of persons. The development of agriculture intensified, and plow or **irrigation agriculture** replaced slash-and-burn techniques. Leaders organized labor for the purpose of constructing public works—roads, defensive fortifications, irrigation networks, or religious structures—such as the pyramids in Mexico or the churches of medieval Europe. Competition between groups over available resources contributed to the development of standing armies; hereditary leaders emerged; settlements grew into cities. As technological complexity increased, people began to develop specific skills and to specialize in occupational tasks (such as herder, baker, butcher, warrior, or potter), and occupational specialization led to increased trade and the evolution of a class of merchants. Some 300 years ago, some of these ranked, state societies began to develop into large-scale industrialized states that now are found all over the world—of which the United States is one. Table 2.1 provides a summary of this brief sketch of human social and cultural history.

One simple explanation for the transformation of societies from nomadic bands to industrial states is that human inventions created better ways of doing things; in other words, human culture progressed. In the past forty years, however, anthropologists have begun to question the idea that the life of hunters and gatherers was harsh and difficult. They propose instead that in many ways, this way of life was superior to that of groups maintained by sedentary agriculture.

Some have proposed further that slash-and-burn agriculture was more efficient and less wasteful than modern methods of food production. If that

 TABLE 2.1 SUMMARY OF THE DEVELOPMENT OF SOCIETIES FROM GATHERERS AND HUNTERS TO AGRICULTURAL STATES

	Hunters and Gatherers	Horticulturalists	State Societies
Population Density	Approximately one person per square mile.	Approximately 10 to 15 people per square mile.	Approximately 300 people per square mile.
Subsistence	Hunting, gathering, and fishing.	Slash-and-burn agriculture with mixed livestock herding.	Plow or irrigation agriculture.
Work, Labor, and Production	Very high yield relative to labor expended.	High yield relative to labor expended.	High labor needs relative to yield. High degree of occupational specialization.
Political Organization	Informal political organization. Few if any formal leaders. Conflict controlled by limiting group size, mobility, and flexibility of group membership. Little intergroup conflict.	More formalized political organization, often with well-established leaders or chiefs. Increased population density and wealth result in increased potential for conflict. Intergroup warfare, motivated by desire for wealth, prestige, or women, is common.	Highly developed state organization, with a clear hierarchy of authority. Often a two-class society with rulers (landowners) and peasants. Authority of the elite backed by organized use of force (police or army). Warfare for purpose of conquest is common. Well-established mechanisms for resolving conflict (e.g., courts) exist side by side with informal mechanisms.
Social Organization	Small family groups, whose major purpose is economic cooperation. Few status distinctions other than those of sex and age. Marriage for economic partnership and interfamily alliance.	Emphasis on extended family groups. Descent important for the distribution of wealth and property. Status distinctions based on wealth are common, but status mobility is usually possible.	Emphasis on nuclear family. Family is strongly patriarchal, with women holding low status. Strong bonds of intergenerational dependence are built on inheritance needs. Social distinctions between people are emphasized—sometimes based on occupations. Little or no status mobility.

is true, what other explanations are there for why groups abandoned hunting and gathering for sedentary agriculture and later developed industrialized societies? Moreover, if life in small-scale tribal societies is not inferior to modern life, why are people in societies without advanced agriculture and industry starving and dying of disease? And why are small-scale tribal societies disappearing?

QUESTIONS

2.1   Why did hunter-gatherer societies switch to sedentary agriculture?
2.2   Why are some societies more industrially advanced than others?
2.3   Why do poor countries not modernize and develop in the same way as wealthier countries?
2.4   How do modern standards of health and medical treatment compare with those of traditional societies?
2.5   Why are simpler societies disappearing?

Case Study in Doing Anthropology #2: Doing Development

QUESTION 2.1   *Why Did Hunter-Gatherer Societies Switch to Sedentary Agriculture?*

The simplest explanation of why hunters and gatherers chose at some point to settle down and domesticate plants and animals is that sedentary agriculture was an easier, less dangerous, and more productive way to get food. People who discovered they could plant and harvest crops and domesticate animals rather than having to search for their food began to do so. They had progressed.

The idea that change occurs because of a desire to progress is well entrenched in Western society, and beginning in the 19th century, anthropologists contributed significantly to this view. Lewis Henry Morgan, a Rochester, New York, attorney who took great interest in the evolution of culture, offered his own idea of how humankind had progressed. Morgan first became fascinated with the Iroquois of New York and later sent out questionnaires to travelers and missionaries all over the world asking them about the family organization and kinship terminology of cultures they visited. In his book *Ancient Society*, first published in 1877, Morgan postulated a theory of human development in which human societies evolved through three stages: that he labeled savagery, barbarism, and civilization. He further divided savagery and barbarism into early, middle, and late stages. Some societies, notably our own, had evolved completely to civilization; others had yet to complete their transformation and remained in the stages of savagery or barbarism. The passage of societies from one stage to the next, Morgan reasoned, required some major technological invention. Thus, the advance from early to middle savagery was marked by the invention of fire; from middle to late savagery by the invention of the bow and arrow; from late savagery through late barbarism by the invention of pottery, agriculture, animal domestication, and so on, until certain societies had progressed to civilization. Other writers (including many anthropologists) have elaborated on the scheme developed by Morgan, assuming, as Morgan did, that humankind was progressing and would continue to do so.

For example, in the mid-20th century, Leslie White formulated what was one of the more influential evolutionary schemes to explain the historical development of culture. Like Morgan, White saw technology as the driving force of cultural evolution. From White's perspective, human beings seek to harness energy through technology and to transform that energy into things that are required for survival, such as food, clothing, and shelter. By means of technology, energy is put to work, and the amount of food, clothing, or other goods produced by the expenditure of energy will be proportional to the efficiency of the technology available. Because hunters and gatherers had only their own muscle power to work with, the amount of energy that could be applied to production was limited. As such technological advances as the plow, the waterwheel, and the windmill enabled people to grow more crops and domesticate animals, they became able to transform more and more energy to their use. Later, when new forms of energy in the form of coal, oil, and gas were harnessed by means of steam engines and internal combustion engines, the amount of energy human beings could harness again leaped forward.

Cultural development, from White's perspective, varies directly with the efficiency of the tools employed. More efficient technology allows human societies to transform more energy to fulfill their needs, and these societies can then produce more food and support larger populations. At some point, the increased efficiency in food production allowed a few people to produce enough food for everyone, freeing others to develop other skills and thereby promoting occupational specialization. Specialization then produced widespread trade and led to the development of commerce. The increase in population, along with the increase in contact between groups, required the development of the state to coordinate group activities and organize armies to protect the growing wealth of its members from other groups.

White's view of technology as the driving force in cultural evolution was highly influential in the development of anthropological theory in the 20th century. But more relevant for us, his theories represent the coalescence of a point of view that is prevalent among many people today: that technology is the true measure of progress and that the more energy human societies can

---

Exercise 2.1a ≫ | Make a list of what you think are the advantages and disadvantages of civilization and the advantages and disadvantages of life 10,000 years ago.

harness through the development of new power sources, the more social, economic, and political problems they will solve.

The benefits of technological progress remain a popular explanation for the transformation of societies, and many people view the application of technology as the solution to continuing world problems. Nevertheless, the progress theory of cultural transformation began to be seriously questioned by anthropologists during the 20th century. These questions were raised in part by studies of hunting and gathering societies that suggested that life as a nomadic hunter and gatherer was not nearly as harsh and dangerous as had been supposed. In fact, some anthropologists suggested that hunting and gathering represented something of a lost paradise.

One of the first suppositions about life in hunting and gathering societies to be challenged had to do with the roles of males and females. Contrary to common belief, studies found that the gathering activities of women produced by far the greater share of food in these societies; men hunted, but except in such areas as the arctic and subarctic regions, meat and fish constituted only about one-quarter of the diet. A second supposition—that hunters and gatherers often went hungry—proved to be unfounded. Apparently, they had plenty of food. And contrary to popular opinion, they did not have to work very hard to get it.

Life Among Hunter-Gatherers: The Hadza and the Ju/wasi*

When James Woodburn studied them in the 1960s, the Hadza were a small group of nomadic hunters and gatherers in Tanzania, eastern Africa. Woodburn described their territory as dry, rocky savanna, characterized by one traveler as "barren land" and "desert." Hunters and gatherers are often depicted as living on the verge of starvation, but Woodburn found the Hadza area rich in food and resources. Such wild game as elephant, giraffe, zebra, and gazelle was plentiful. Plant foods—roots, berries, and fruit—were also abundant for those who knew where to look and constituted about 80% of the Hadza diet. The Hadza spent about two hours a day obtaining food.

Hadza women were responsible for almost all the plant food gathered, whereas hunting was exclusively a male activity. The men hunted with bow and poisoned arrows, and when Woodburn lived among them, they used no guns, spears, or traps. Although the Hadza considered only meat as proper food and may have said they were hungry when there was no meat, there was, in fact, plenty of food available. For a Hadza to go hungry, said Woodburn, was almost inconceivable. Plant food was so plentiful that the Hadza made no attempt to preserve it. Physicians who examined Hadza children in the 1960s found them in good health by tropical standards, and Woodburn says that from a nutritional viewpoint, the Hadza were better off than their agricultural neighbors.

---

*The terms that societies use to refer to themselves are often different from those assigned by others. Unfortunately, the latter sometimes become more widely accepted than the former. For example, the Ju/wasi were referred to as Bushmen by Europeans and later as !Kung by anthropologists.

The Ju/wasi peoples of the Kalahari Desert, in Namibia in southwest Africa, are another hunting and gathering society that has contributed extensively to what anthropologists have learned about small-scale societies. Lorna Marshall, assisted by her children Elizabeth and John, began research among the Ju/wasi in the 1950s. Their work, along with later studies by Richard Lee and others, has provided us with a good description of Ju/wasi hunting and gathering activities. There is some controversy in anthropology over whether the Ju/wasi have always been hunters and gatherers, but that was the way they lived when they were visited by the Marshalls and Lee through the 1960s.

Ju/wasi groups lived around waterholes, from which they would wander as far as six miles in search of plant and animal foods. Their groups numbered from 30 to 40 people during the rainy season, when waterholes were full and plentiful, and increased to 100 to 200 during the dry season, when only the larger holes retained water. Lee found that the food quest was constant among the Ju/wasi, as it was among the Hadza. They did little food processing, so they had to get food supplies every third or fourth day. Vegetable foods constituted 60 to 80% of the diet, and women gathered most of it, producing two to three times as much food as men.

Lee reports that the Ju/wasi never exhausted their food supply. The major food source was the mongongo nut, which is far more nourishing than our own breakfast cereals and contains five times the calories and 10 times the protein of cooked cereals. Mongongo nuts provided more than 50% of the Ju/wasi caloric intake; there are 1,260 calories and 56 grams of protein in 300 nuts. Ju/wasi territory contained more than 80 other species of edible plants—most of which they did not even use—although they did eat about 20 species of roots, melons, gums, bulbs, and dried fruits. In addition, an occasional giraffe, antelope, or other large game and the more usual porcupine, hare, or other small game provided meat. Their meat intake was between 175 and 200 pounds per person per year—an amount comparable to the meat consumption in developed countries.

In other words, Lee found that the environment of the Ju/wasi provided ample readily accessible food. Their diet consisted of some 2,300 calories a day, with a proper balance of protein, vitamins, and minerals. If the Ju/wasi diet was deficient, it was in carbohydrates because there was no equivalent to our white bread, pasta, rice, or sugar.

Readily available plant foods, such as the nutrient-rich mongongo nut, were the mainstay of the Ju/wasi diet. Here, Ju/wasi women return to camp after foraging for mongongo nuts to feed their families.

© M. Shostak/Anthro-Photo

The Ju/wasi did not spend much time getting food. Lee conducted a careful study of Ju/wasi work habits. During the first week in which he recorded the amount of time spent getting food, he found that individuals averaged 2.3 days at this work, with a typical working day of six hours. Overall, the average time spent getting food was 2.4 days, or less than 20 hours of work per week. The most active person Lee observed worked at getting food an average of 32 hours a week. Other time was spent doing housework or mending tools.

Lee concludes that contrary to the stereotype that hunters and gatherers must struggle with limited technology to obtain the food they need for survival, they do not have to work very hard to make a living. He says that the idea that hunting and gathering societies struggle for existence is an ethnocentric notion that assumes that our own technologically oriented society represents the pinnacle of development. But if Lee and others are correct about the ease of survival of hunters and gatherers and if their life is not harsh and dangerous, why did those hunters and gatherers of 10,000 years ago abandon hunting and gathering, begin to domesticate crops and animals, and settle in permanent villages and towns?

The Transition to Agriculture

There is a perspective on cultural evolution that views the change from hunting and gathering to modern industrial society less as development or progress and more as a necessary evil. This perspective emphasizes the influences of population growth and **population density**, which is the number of people living in a given area. To understand this point of view, we need to examine the transition from hunting and gathering to agriculture and also explore the reasons for the eventual change from relatively simple slash-and-burn agriculture to more complex labor-intensive irrigation agriculture.

Anthropologist Mark Cohen set out to explain why individuals or groups abandoned hunting and gathering for agriculture and why so many did so in a relatively short period of time. First, he examined the reported food-gathering strategies of hunting and gathering societies. Hunters and gatherers settle in a given area to collect food, and as food resources decline in one spot, they enlarge the area within which they travel in search of them. Imagine this area as a series of concentric circles; as the outer circles are approached from the center, the group may decide to move to another area where food is more plentiful in order to reduce the distance members travel. Cohen suggests that when population density in a given geographical area reached a point at which different groups began to bump into each other or when groups found they had to travel farther and farther to get enough food to feed a growing population, they began to cultivate their own crops. Cohen points out that anthropological and archaeological evidence suggests they knew how to do this all along but chose instead to gather crops until the labor involved in traveling to new food sources surpassed the labor involved in growing their own crops. In other words, the historical transition from hunting and gathering to simple agriculture was a necessary consequence of population growth rather than a consequence of a discovery or invention that was adopted because it made life better. In a limited way, of course, this transition from gathering to cultivating did make life easier; when people began to harvest crops in a limited area and remained in villages, groups no longer needed to travel as much. However, Cohen and others argue that agriculture did not make life better at all; in fact, it made life worse. (We explore that claim a little later in this chapter.)

In most parts of the world, when societies abandoned gathering and hunting, they likely began to utilize slash-and-burn agricultural techniques. Relatively small kinship-based groups can practice slash-and-burn, or swidden, agriculture. As a form of growing crops, it is highly efficient and productive. The Kuikuru, who inhabit the tropical rainforest of central Brazil, annually produce about two

Exercise 2.1b ➤

Here is the situation: The year is approximately 10,000 B.C. You are a group of elders of a hunting and gathering group similar to the Ju/wasi. Your band includes some 80 people. For as long as you can remember, you have lived by gathering nuts, roots, fruit, and other foodstuffs and by hunting wild game. Your territory has always been adequate to supply the necessary food for members of the group, but recently, people have noticed that they have had to travel greater distances to collect food or to find game. Moreover, the territory that you consider your own now overlaps with that of other hunting and gathering groups.

As do most hunting and gathering peoples, you know how to plant crops and harvest them, and you have come to the realization that there is sufficient wild wheat, yams, maize, or other vegetable foodstuff to support your group as long as you cultivate it (plant it, save seeds for replanting, etc.), harvest it when it is ripe, store it, and settle down next to the stored food.

A group of younger members of the band, tired of traveling greater distances in search of food and fearful of conflict with neighboring bands whose territory overlaps yours, advocates settling down and taking advantage of wild crops.

The problem: Should you take the advice of the younger members of the group, begin to harvest and store wild foods, and settle down in relatively permanent villages?

If you say yes, you need to give reasons why this is necessary in order to convince others in the group who are against the move. You must tell them what the consequences of not settling down would be.

If you say no, you need to be able to defend your decision to the younger members of the group and explain to them the consequences of settling down. You also need to tell them the conditions under which you would take their advice.

million calories per acre of land farmed, or enough to feed two people for a year. Moreover, the Kuikuru work only about two hours a day.

However, swidden agriculture requires large tracts of available land because after a plot is farmed for a couple of years, it must lie fallow for 20 to 30 years to allow the brush and trees to grow back so it can be used again. If the population and the amount of land needed to feed it both increase, plots must be used more frequently—perhaps every five or 10 years. But when land is cultivated more frequently, the yield per acre declines. Thus, swidden agriculture is efficient only as long as the population and the amount of land available remain constant.

Farmland may become scarce not only because of increasing population but also because of environmental changes or the encroachment of other groups. Then, new agricultural techniques must be developed to increase the yield on the available land. The digging stick may be replaced with the plow or irrigation systems may be devised, and each of these developments requires a great deal of labor. In other words, the more food the group needs to produce, the more complex is the technology needed to produce it; and the more complex the technology, the greater is the amount of work involved.

Relationships among land, labor, population, and methods of agriculture are suggested in Tables 2.2 and 2.3. Table 2.2 indicates that the amount of labor required to produce a harvest increases with the complexity of agricultural techniques. For example, it requires up to 10 times more labor to produce a

DAYS OF LABOR PER ACRE PER HARVEST
TABLE 2.2 **BY TYPE OF AGRICULTURE**

Type of Agriculture	Days of Labor per Acre
Advanced swidden	18–25
Plow cultivation	20
Hoe cultivation	58
Irrigation agriculture	90–178

Source: Data from Eric R. Wolf, *Peasants* (Englewood Cliffs, NJ: Prentice Hall, 1966).

LAND NEEDED TO FEED 100 FAMILIES BY USING DIFFERENT
TABLE 2.3 **AGRICULTURAL METHODS**

Agricultural Method	Number of Acres Needed to Feed 100 Families
Swidden agriculture	3,000*
Swidden with garden plots	1,600*
Irrigation agriculture	90–200

*Includes unworked land that must be allowed to lie fallow to regain fertility.
Source: Data from Eric R. Wolf, *Peasants* (Englewood Cliffs, NJ: Prentice Hall, 1966).

harvest with irrigation agriculture than it does to produce one with swidden agriculture.

Then, why abandon swidden agriculture? Because there is not enough land to support the population. Table 2.3 lists the amount of land needed to feed 100 families using different agricultural methods. For example, as little as 90 acres of land are required to feed 100 families if irrigation agriculture is used, whereas 3,000 acres are needed if swidden agriculture is used. If a group has enough land, it might as well keep its farming methods simple, changing them only if population increases or the supply of land decreases. However, the history of humankind has in fact been marked by an increase in population and an increase in the ratio of people to land.

Robert L. Carneiro outlines the consequences of population density for cultural development. The increase in the number of people relative to the available land creates two problems. First, if there are more people than there is available land to feed them, conflict may arise between people vying for the available resources. Second, if a growing population decides to intensify methods of growing crops, there is a need for greater societal organization. For example, irrigation agriculture requires the digging of ditches, the building of pumps to bring water to the fields and to drain water from them, and the coordination of one and sometimes two harvests a year. Thus, whether a society deals with an increasing ratio between land and people by intensifying efforts to produce more food or it addresses the problem by denying some people access to the necessary resources, the groundwork is laid for the emergence of a stratified society and the need for a state organization.

The views of such anthropologists as Cohen and Carneiro suggest that the historical change of societies from gathering and hunting to gradually more labor-intensive methods of agriculture was not a matter of choice. Slash-and-burn agriculture was not easier than gathering and hunting, and plow-and-irrigation agriculture was not more efficient than slash-and-burn agriculture. Instead, the changes in food production techniques represented necessities brought about by population increase or an increase in population density, and they created the need for more formal, more elaborate political and social institutions—to organize labor and to maintain order among more and more people.

If we conclude (and not all anthropologists do) that the transition from hunting and gathering to complex agriculture, along with the associated transformations in social, political, and economic institutions, does not represent progress, is not it safe to say, at the very least, that Western society—particularly within the United States—has agricultural techniques that are vastly superior to those of small-scale tribal societies? Those who claim that modern food-producing techniques are far more efficient than any other point out that in American society, only one calorie of human energy is needed to produce 210 calories for human consumption, whereas hunter-gatherers produce fewer than 10 calories of food for every calorie they use collecting the food. But others argue that these figures are deceptive. At the same time we vastly decreased the amount of human labor required to produce food, they say, we vastly increased the amount of nonhuman energy required for food production. From that perspective, we expend one calorie of nonhuman energy in the form of nonrenewable fossil fuels (e.g., oil and coal) for every eight calories we produce.

Producing Potato Calories

To make this point about energy, John H. Bodley compares the production of sweet potatoes in New Guinea with potato production in the United States. In New Guinea, people cultivate sweet potatoes by slash-and-burn agriculture; plots of land are burned, cleared, and planted with digging sticks. When the crops are ready, sweet potatoes are cooked in pits and eaten. In one New Guinea community, sweet potatoes account for 21% of the diet of 204 people. Some of the sweet potatoes are fed to pigs, thus producing protein and accounting for an even larger proportion of the diet. The people use only 10% of the arable land, and there is no danger of resource depletion. With their agricultural techniques, the New Guinea farmers can produce about five million calories per acre.

American potato farms produce more than twice as many calories per acre as New Guinea farmers—about 12 million calories per acre. However, as Bodley points out, in addition to the human energy that goes into American farming, vast amounts of nonhuman energy are expended. Chemicals must be applied to maintain soil conditions and to control insects and fungus. For example, in the state of Washington in the 1960s, 60% of potato acreage was airplane-sprayed five to nine times each season to control insects; another 40% was treated for weeds. American potato farmers need specialized machines to cut, seed, harvest, dig, and plant. In 1969, 36,000 tons of fertilizer were applied to 62,500 acres—more than 1,000 pounds per acre. Thus, although the American system produced more potatoes, the actual energy costs per calorie were lower in New Guinea. Moreover, the United States incurred all kinds of hidden costs from such consequences as soil erosion and pollution.

Americans must also deal with distribution costs, which are minimal in traditional cultures, where most households consume what they produce. In modern industrial societies, where 95% of the population is concentrated in or around urban centers, the energy expended in distributing the food now exceeds the energy expended in producing it. Taking the food-producing process as a whole—the manufacture and distribution of farm machinery, trucks, and fertilizer; irrigation projects; food processing; packaging; transportation; manufacturing of trucks; industrial and domestic food preparation; and refrigeration—Americans expend eight to 12 calories of energy to produce a single calorie of food!

Bodley suggests that the reason Americans expend so much energy to produce food is to make money. He maintains that Western agricultural techniques are wasteful and inefficient. To illustrate his point, consider the potato chip. About half of the potatoes grown in the United States are sold as raw potatoes; the rest are processed into such products as instant mashed potatoes and potato chips. On the average, each American consumes 4.6 pounds of potato chips per year. All potatoes undergo significant processing after being harvested. They are mechanically washed, chemically sprayed to inhibit sprouting, colored and waxed to increase consumer appeal, and transported and stored under controlled conditions. Potatoes sold for potato chips must also be chemically sprayed weeks prior to planting to kill the stems; otherwise, the starch buildup would produce unappealing (but otherwise nutritious) dark potato chips. These potatoes also are chemically treated to prevent darkening after they are peeled and sliced; oils, salts, and preservatives are added in the cooking; and, finally, the end product is packaged in special containers and shipped. Manufacturers expend additional marketing costs and energy to convince consumers to buy the chips.

Thus, the human and nonhuman energy required to convert a potato into potato chips is far greater than the energy expended in New Guinea to produce a more nutritious sweet potato! Moreover, we do not fully appreciate the health risks of our practice of adding some 2,500 substances to our foods to color them, flavor them, or preserve them.

QUESTION 2.2   *Why Are Some Societies More Industrially Advanced Than Others?*

Even if we agree that hunters and gatherers do not have it that bad and that simpler forms of agriculture are more energy-efficient than modern techniques for growing crops and delivering food, we still have not explained the vast divisions in the modern world between rich nations and poor nations. If progress is not the reason, why then do most people in the industrial world enjoy a standard of living superior to those in the so-called nonindustrial or underdeveloped countries of the world? Why, in 1995, did more than a billion people live in absolute poverty, earning the equivalent of less than $1 a day, while, according to the Maryland-based Bread for the World Institute, 358 billionaires listed by *Forbes* magazine have a combined net worth equal to the combined income of the bottom 45% of the world's population? And why, from 2000 to 2007, did the number of individuals with net assets of $1 million rise from some 7.5 million to 9.5 million, representing only 0.01% of the world's population? (See Lysandrou, 2011.)

Trying to answer these questions requires an excursion into world economic history of the past 300 years, but rather than try to pack three centuries of history into the next few pages, let us see what we can learn from the story of the expansion of one industry, in one country, during one phase of its development: the textile industry in England in the last half of the 18th century and the first half of the 19th century.

Prior to the beginning of the **Industrial Revolution** in Europe, the world was significantly different in its distribution of wealth. China was arguably the richest country in the world during the 16th and 17th centuries as gold and silver taken from the mines of South America by the Spanish and Portuguese were funneled into China to pay for Chinese silks, spices, teas, and luxury goods; India was developing a thriving cotton textile industry as Indian calicoes flooded into Europe. Wealthy states had developed in western Africa, and Islamic traders thrived from Africa into Southeast Asia. Seventeenth-century England was a largely rural and agricultural country; even by 1700, only 13% of the population lived in towns of 5,000 or more people. However, England had long enjoyed a thriving trade in textile goods—most notably, raw wool and inexpensive wool textiles.

Early in its development, textile production was largely a handicraft industry, and most steps in the production of wool cloth—from cutting and degreasing the wool to dyeing and spinning the thread to weaving the cloth—were in the hands of rural families or small cooperatives. The finished cloth or wool product might be sold at a local market or fair or, more often, sold to urban-based merchants or traders for resale at fairs or shipment overseas.

But although the trade in home-produced textiles was profitable for all, traders and merchants discovered they needed to better control the type, quantity, and quality of cloth produced by spinners and weavers. The merchants' first solution to this problem was the **"putting out" system**, in which merchants supplied weavers with materials and required them to produce cloth of the desired type. Some merchants supplied only the wool, cotton, or linen, whereas others supplied everything, including the looms. The merchants delivered the supplies and tools and picked up the finished products, generally paying the producers for each piece produced. Putting out had numerous advantages for textile merchants; it gave them more control over the production process, it provided a source of cheap labor as it brought women and children into the production process, and if demand for their products slackened, the merchant could easily control how much was produced by limiting the materials they put out.

Increasingly, however, beginning in the 18th century, English merchants found it expedient to transform the putting-out system into a **factory system** by bringing the spinners, weavers, and others together in one location to produce the cloth. Factories were neither new nor unique to England. Factories employing more than 15,000 workers existed in France in 1685. Furthermore, merchants were not particularly anxious to invest in factories. Profits from manufacture were not nearly as great as profits from trade, especially long-distance exchange. Moreover, removing people from the home-based family to urban-based factories required new mechanisms of discipline and control—a fact that explains why early factories were modeled on penal workhouses and prisons. Finally, the entrepreneur, who previously could halt putting out when demand slackened, now had to keep the factories busy to pay for the investment

This cartoon is one of a series by Robert Cruikshank decrying the exploitation of child labor by British industrialists. Prior to 1833, there were no restrictions on ages or hours worked by children in factory jobs.

in buildings and technology and, consequently, had to create demands for products.

The only things that made manufacturing investments attractive were various kinds of government subsidies or laws (e.g., vagrancy laws that required people to have jobs) that ensured the flow of cheap labor. Textile manufacturers were able to draw on workers who had been forced off their land by enclosure legislation that pushed peasant farmers off common land at the behest of landowners wishing to grow crops for sale to the increasing population of England. Because there were no minimum wage laws or laws restricting the use of child labor, factory owners could also make even more use of the cheap labor of women and children; thus, by 1834, children under 13 represented 13% of the British cotton industry, and by 1838, only 23% of textile factory workers in England were adult men. In addition, government also played a major role in creating and defending overseas markets as well as sources of raw materials, such as cotton.

The growth of the textile industry had numerous effects. For example, it fueled the growth of cities; by 1800, a quarter of the English population lived in towns of 5,000 or more and Manchester, a center of textile manufacture, grew from 24,000 inhabitants in 1773 to more than 250,000 by 1851. Moreover, factories spurred the development of technologies. Mechanization of the textile industry began in earnest with John Kay's flying shuttle in 1733, which doubled the weavers' output. But because spinners could not keep up with the need for thread for the new looms, bottlenecks developed. To meet this need, James Hargreaves introduced the spinning jenny in 1765. In 1769, Richard Arkwright invented the water frame, and then in 1779, Samuel Crompton developed a spinning mule, which combined features of the water frame and the spinning jenny. Finally, in 1790, steam power was added to the production process. These inventions produced a staggering increase in textile production. A hand spinner in India in the 18th century took more than 50,000 hours to process 100 pounds of cotton into thread; in England, Crompton's spinning mule reduced that to 2,000 hours, and power-assisted spinning mules around 1795 reduced this time still further to 300 hours. By 1825, it took only 135 hours to process 100 pounds of cotton.

The growth of the textile industry obviously produced great wealth and employed millions of workers. In economic terms, it transformed England into the wealthiest country in the world. And textiles were not, of course, the only industry that expanded; the trade and manufacture of iron and the agricultural production of food commodities further increased the wealth of the growing British Empire. But the increase in technology and production created two problems: Where was the market for all these textile products to be found, and where were the raw materials—notably the cotton—to come from?

Some historians point to the large domestic market available to English textile producers in the wake of the growth of the English population from six million in 1700 to nine million in 1800. Moreover, English textile manufacturers were able to sell much of their product to markets in Europe and the growing markets of the Americas. But there was still competition for these markets. England was not the only textile producer; Holland, France, and Spain were busy competing (and often fighting each other) for overseas markets as well as sources of raw materials. This competition, along with the growing military superiority of Western Europe, often had dire consequences for once-prosperous industries in other parts of the world. The story of textiles in India is instructive.

The British in India

Mughal India of the 17th century was an empire created by Turks from Turkestan, who made their chief, Babur, the first Mughal emperor in 1527. India was a major trading country, and centuries-old trade networks linked India to the rest of Europe, the Islamic world, and China. In 1690, the British government granted a monopoly in East Asian trade to the British East India Company. A relative latecomer to trade in India, it established a trade center in Bengal, in the city of Calcutta. The British East India Company soon had some 150 posts trading in India for fine silks, cotton, sugar, rice, saltpeter, indigo, and opium.

In the 1750s, the British provoked the rulers of Bengal into war, defeating them conclusively in 1757. As an aftermath to their victory in Bengal, the English plundered the state treasury for some five million pounds and gained control of 10,000 Bengali weavers. By 1765, the British East India Company became the civil administration of Bengal. It promptly increased the tax burden on peasants and artisans, leading to major famines in 1770 and 1783. From its base in Bengal, the company gradually began to extend its control over much of the Indian subcontinent.

Prior to the British military takeover, India produced cloth that was cheaper and better than English textiles; in fact, Indian cotton and calicoes— named after the city of Calicut—were the craze of Europe. To meet this challenge, the British government prohibited the British East India Company from importing calicoes into England. To take advantage of the import restriction, English factories began to produce copies of popular Indian textiles for sale in England and abroad. In addition, India was required to admit English manufacturers free of tariffs. These actions effectively destroyed what had been a thriving Indian textile industry.

India was still a major producer of raw cotton, although it was not a variety favored by English or American manufacturers; instead, it was produced for export to China. However, it was primarily opium that led the trade into China.

The British—and Western European nations in general—had a problem with trade into China; Chinese products—notably tea—were in high demand, but there was little produced in England or the rest of Europe for that matter that the Chinese wanted or needed. However, there was a market in China for opium, and by 1773, the British East India Company had a monopoly over opium sales. Opium was illegal in China, but the Chinese state seemed incapable of cutting off supplies, and smuggling opium into China was hugely profitable for British as well as American and French merchants. When the Chinese government tried to enforce the laws against opium sales in 1839 by seizing opium held by British merchants in warehouses in Canton, the British government intervened militarily and effectively forced the Chinese government to stop enforcing opium laws. An analogy today might be the government of Colombia sending troops to the United States to force acceptance of Colombian cocaine shipments. Moreover, the British demanded and received additional trading rights into China, further opening a market not only for opium but also for textiles.

The British-led opium trade from India to China had three results. First, it reversed the flow of money between China and the rest of the world; during the first decade of the 19th century, China still took in a surplus of 26 million silver dollars; by the third decade, 34 million dollars left China to pay for opium. Second, it is estimated that by the end of the 19th century, one out of every 10 people in China was addicted to opium. Finally, cotton textile exports from England to India and China increased from 6% of total British exports in 1815 to 22% in 1840, 31% in 1850, and more than 50% after 1873.

Cotton, Slavery, and the Cherokee Removal

Cotton and the growth of the textile industry in England figure not only in the story of the economic decline and British colonization of India and China but also in the story of slavery and the removal of thousands of Native Americans from their homeland. The British were able to sell raw Indian cotton to China, but Indian cotton was not acceptable to European and American markets. Indian cotton produced a shorter fiber, whereas cotton produced elsewhere—notably in Egypt and the American South—produced a longer, more desirable fiber. But cotton production in the Americas was labor-intensive and, to be profitable, required slave labor.

Slavery was not created by the need for cotton. As an institution, it extends well back into antiquity. It was not uncommon for nations at war to use captives as slaves. But the slave trade grew from the 15th century to the 19th century in response to the economic expansion and demands of European trade, including Spanish demand for labor in the silver mines; Spanish, Portuguese,

British, and French demands for cane cutters and millers for the sugar plantations of Brazil and the Caribbean; and American demands for workers on the cotton plantations of Georgia, Alabama, Louisiana, Texas, and Mississippi. From 1451 to 1600, some 275,000 slaves were sent from Africa to Europe and America. During the 17th century, some 1,341,000 slaves were sent, and from 1701 to 1810, some six million people were forcibly exported from Africa. Another two million were sold out of Africa between 1810 and 1870—many destined for Cuba.

The production of cotton with slave labor might be said to have fueled the Industrial Revolution in the United States. Although England imported raw cotton from its possessions in the West Indies and from Turkey, by 1807, half was coming from the United States. In fact, between 1815 and 1860, raw cotton constituted half the value of domestic exports from the United States.

Part of the reason for the growth of the American cotton industry was Eli Whitney's cotton gin, an invention that easily separated the seeds from the raw cotton fiber. It allowed a person to clean 50 pounds of cotton in the time it had previously taken to clean one pound. As a consequence, American cotton production increased enormously—from 3,000 bales in 1790 to 178,000 bales in 1810, 732,000 in 1830, and 4.5 million in 1860. But to be competitive, American cotton production required cheap labor, and slave labor cost half the price of wage labor. Each plantation required at least 50 to 200 slaves depending on the quality of the soil.

The British demand for American cotton was obviously not the cause of slavery, but it ensured its continuance in the United States into the second half of the 19th century. Between 1790 and 1860, some 835,000 slaves were moved from Maryland, Virginia, and the Carolinas to Alabama, Louisiana, Mississippi, and Texas in one of the greatest forced migrations of all time. But it was not the only forced migration instigated by the world demand for and profitability of cotton. It was also a driving force behind the forced removal in the 1830s of 125,000 Native Americans from their homes in Georgia, Alabama, and Mississippi to the Oklahoma territory.

The story of the forced removal of the Cherokees is most instructive in supplying an answer to why some people of the world enjoy higher levels of wealth than others. The Cherokees had always been considered one of the more so-called advanced Native American groups—being counted by early American settlers as one of the

Reliance on slave labor in the United States was closely tied to the rise of the British textile industry. Here, a slave family picks cotton on a plantation near Savannah, Georgia, during the early 1860s.

© Bettmann/Corbis

"civilized tribes" of North America. They were horticulturists, living in large autonomous villages and, in the aftermath of the American Revolution, occupying large tracts of fertile land from North Carolina into Georgia. In 1802, in order to persuade southeastern states to give up claims to territory in the West, Thomas Jefferson instituted what became known as the Georgia Compact of 1802. The compact called for Georgia and the Carolinas to give up claims to western territories in exchange for land held by southeastern tribes, such as the Cherokees. But the tribes fought the removal, embarking on a modernization plan; within decades, the Cherokees had constructed plantations, held slaves, and had their own newspaper, schools, and alphabet. They were also among the soldiers under Andrew Jackson that defeated the British in the War of 1812.

The Cherokee lobbied Congress extensively to repeal the Georgia Compact but to no avail. Andrew Jackson, who had made Indian removal one of the cornerstones of his presidential campaign in 1828, signed the final order, and the Army was sent in to forcibly move the population as land speculators flooded onto what had been prosperous Cherokee farms and plantations. White farmers using black slaves took over thousands of additional acres of what had been Indian land and converted much of them to cotton production. Thus, white farmers using Native American land and African labor to produce cotton for the English and American textile industries created much of the future wealth of the young American republic.

In sum, the growth of the textile industry in England produced great wealth for some people but in the process destroyed textile manufacturing in India, led to the colonization of India and China, extended slavery in the United States while it drained Africa of productive labor, and enhanced the wealth of the United States while leading to the forced removal of indigenous people from their lands. The mass production of textiles in England and elsewhere in Europe also destroyed textile manufacture by artisans in areas of the world where British textiles were sold. Because women were often the main textile producers in many societies, we might also speculate that the textile trade may have led to decline of the status of women in these societies.

We must also consider that England was not the only producer of textiles or the only country seeking to open and control overseas markets; France, Germany, Holland, and, later, the United States also had thriving textile industries. We must also remember that textiles represented only one of many industries of Western Europe that required raw materials and new markets. The new demands for sugar, cocoa, palm oil, tobacco, and coffee also led to the conversion of millions of acres of land around the world from subsistence farms to cash crops—further turning self-sufficient peasant farmers into dependent wage laborers or unemployed poor. And, finally, we must remember that we have examined only a brief period of time. In fact, the heyday of European colonial expansion did not occur until the last quarter of the 19th century and the first decades of the 20th. Looking at the bigger picture, we begin to understand why the problems of the so-called nonindustrial nations are due less to their own shortcomings than to the exploitative activities of others and why peasant farmers in India in 1400 were significantly better off economically than their Indian counterparts in 1960.

QUESTION 2.3   *Why Do Poor Countries Not Modernize and Develop in the Same Way as Wealthier Countries?*

The Industrial Revolution radically transformed the lives of people in Western Europe and the United States as the vast majority of the population went from being farmers to laborers. In most cases, this was not a matter of choice; people began to sell their labor—not because wage labor offered a better life but because they no longer possessed land on which to secure a livelihood. Moreover, the availability of jobs was subject to the whims of the market and the rise and fall in the demand for products. As long as there was a demand for products, jobs were secure; when demand slackened, people were thrown out of work. Consequently, the development of industry in the 19th century was marked by periodic downturns in economic growth and the occurrence of economic depressions, such as those of 1840 and 1873.

Overall, however, the rate of economic growth and technological advancement was astounding, resulting in a dramatic improvement in the standard of living of most people in Western countries, although many in the industrialized world did not enjoy increased wealth, and people in the Third World often saw their standard of living decline as their countries fell under the influence of European powers.

Regardless, as countries began to gain independence from their colonial dominators, they wished to emulate the lifestyle and standard of living of the industrial powers; the way to do this, they reasoned, was to imitate the colonizer and industrializer. Hence, the push for what became known as **economic development**.

President Harry S. Truman first propounded the idea of economic development in his inaugural address in 1949. The assumption was that nonindustrial countries of the world were backward and needed to develop—*development* being largely a code word for "westernized." This was going to be done to "improve" people's lives. As one United Nations report (1951, p. 15) put it:

> There is a sense in which rapid economic progress is impossible without painful adjustments. Ancient philosophies have to be scrapped; old social institutions have to disintegrate; bonds of caste, creed and race have to burst; and large numbers of persons who cannot keep up with progress have to have their expectations of comfortable life frustrated. Very few communities are willing to pay the full price of economic progress.

An unprecedented will to know everything about the Third World flourished, and the Third World witnessed a massive landing of experts, each in charge of investigating, measuring, and theorizing about this or that little aspect of Third World societies. In his book *Encountering Development: The Making and Unmaking of the Third World*, Arturo Escobar suggests that these experts conceived of social life as a technical problem that could be entrusted to development professionals, consisting largely of economists and agricultural experts allegedly qualified for the task.

The idea of economic development that emerged was based on three key assumptions: (1) Economic growth and development are the solution to national as well as global problems; (2) global economic integration will contribute to solving global ecological and social problems; and (3) foreign assistance to undeveloped countries will make things better. Thus, countries that wished to develop sought foreign loans and investments to create an industrial infrastructure: dams for hydroelectric power, coal-fired generators, or nuclear power plants; transportation systems, including ports, roads, and railways; and loans to train and educate workers. The loans would allow

Exercise 2.3 ➤

It is 1960. You have been hired as a consultant by the World Bank to evaluate a loan application that seeks to help Brazil industrialize. The country is predominantly agricultural, with some 70% of the population living in rural areas. Most farms consist of subsistence plots worked by small family groups producing crops such as tomatoes, sweet potatoes, and corn. Per capita income is very low—equivalent to about $200 a year in today's currency. Sugar is a major export crop grown largely in the arid northeast region of the country. Virtually all settlement is along the Atlantic coast, while the vast tropical forests of the Amazon are mainly undeveloped—inhabited largely by indigenous peoples and itinerant rubber tappers.

The country is run by a democratically elected legislature whose members are seeking to make Brazil a modern economic and industrial power. Their loan application proposes the following:

1. The building of hydroelectric projects (dams and irrigation facilities) to supply power to attract industry and modernize agriculture
2. Building of roads into the Amazon to encourage settlement and population redistribution
3. Funds to resettle people into areas in which roads will be built
4. Funds to develop new crops for export and expand sugar production

Your task is to evaluate each proposal, consider the impact it will have on the people of Brazil, and recommend whether to fund the proposal. If a proposal is unacceptable, you may propose conditions under which it would be acceptable.

undeveloped countries to produce things that developed countries did not produce themselves—such cash crops as cotton, sugar, palm oil, tobacco, coffee, and cocoa and such natural resources as oil, metal ores, and lumber. This theory of economic development was not new to the second half of the 20th century; what was different was the degree of apparent support offered by the wealthy nations of the world themselves. One major Western institution that was to promote economic development was the **World Bank.**

The World Bank was established in 1944 in Bretton Woods, New Hampshire, at a meeting of the representatives of the major industrial nations allied against the Germans, Japanese, and Italians. Their task was to plan for the economic reconstruction of countries devastated by World War II and develop a postwar plan for worldwide economic and monetary stability. Out of that meeting came the plan for the **International Monetary Fund (IMF)** and the International Bank for Reconstruction and Development (the World Bank). Funds for the bank were to be donated by member nations—largely in the form of loan guarantees. The bank would lend money to governments for specific projects—highways, dams, power plants, factories, and the like—and the governments would agree to pay back the loans over a set period of time. The charter also specified that loans must be made without any regard for political or noneconomic factors, and the bank must not interfere in the political affairs of any member or debtor nation.

The World Bank began operating in 1946, with the initial loans going to European countries to rebuild their economies after World War II. But soon, the World Bank was making huge loans to such countries as Brazil, India, and Indonesia—loans that were supposed to transform their economies, bring wealth, and alleviate poverty. Moreover, once the World Bank approved loans, other banks would often follow. But in spite of the growth of foreign loans to undeveloped countries, many argue that they not only increased poverty but also led to rampant environmental devastation. In spite of apparently good intentions, how could this happen?

Debt, SAPs, and Vultures

Debt proved to be the burden that initiated a period of what is called *neocolonialism*. Accepting the idea that economic development was the key to bettering people's lives, poorer countries—often with the encouragement of agencies such as the World Bank—began to borrow heavily to build roads, power facilities, telecommunication systems, industrial infrastructure, and energy-intensive agricultural systems. They were advised to attract investment money with which to grow economically. The rapid rise in the 1970s of energy costs, the decline in the value of raw materials exported by poorer countries, and the rise in interest payments on loans left most emerging economies unable to pay back the loans that they had gotten from the World Bank as well as from private lending agencies and foreign investors. Unable to pay their debts, and, consequently, unable to borrow more to meet the needs of their citizens, these countries turned to the International Monetary Fund (IMF) (which had been established at Bretton Woods to ensure global financial stability) to somehow restructure their debt to avoid defaulting on their loans. Unlike individuals, countries cannot declare bankruptcy and start all over again. They can default and refuse to repay what they owe (and historically, many countries have done that) or they can repay only a portion of what they owe (and many countries, including European powers, have done that). The problem with default is that it can prevent future borrowing, raise the interest rates charged for loans, or can prompt military confiscation or invasion by more powerful countries seeking to recoup the loans of their citizens.

In the 1980s, the IMF, with the support of member countries, devised agreements, called **Structural Adjustment Programs (SAPs)**, with debtor countries to restructure their economies and their international debts. In exchange, debtor countries agreed to reduce their government workforce (thus throwing thousands out of work), lower remaining government salaries, sell and/or privatize state-owned businesses and services (e.g., utility companies, railroads, health facilities, etc.), end government subsidies (e.g., help to farmers, food programs for the poor, etc.), reduce taxes on foreign investors, weaken state environmental and labor regulations, and devalue local currency—often cutting its worth by half and seriously depleting the buying power of citizens. This economic "shock treatment" imposed by the IMF would, economists believe, ultimately return the country to a sound economic footing and help resume economic growth. However, critics claim that the goal of SAPs is less to help poor countries than it is to help investors, businesses, and corporations profit from the plight of the poor. The IMF and World Bank have responded with various programs to restructure, lower, or forgive the debt of some countries who can never repay the loans plus the interest on the loans. But even those efforts have sometimes been thwarted by investors—in what have been termed *vulture funds*—who buy up the debt of poor countries from private lending agencies for a fraction of what is owed and then sue the debtor countries for repayment of the full debt plus interest. In effect, money that might go for education, health services, or aid to the poor flows back to rich investors.

The consequences of debt, SAPs, and vulture funds on these countries and its citizens can be devastating and helps explain why so many today still live in poverty, with inadequate diets, slum housing, little or no education, and virtually no medical care.

In Senegal, for example, the government instituted a series of reforms in the 1980s and 1990s as part of an IMF-sponsored structural adjustment program, and while economic growth increased, so did the number of people living in poverty. State-sponsored medical programs were replaced with an initiative that purported to promote individual responsibility for health care; user fees were charged for basic health services, and individuals were charged for drugs. But the changes made it impossible for most rural dwellers to participate, and many did not have the money or could not obtain it from household heads—generally men. And a shift away from subsistence agriculture to commercial agriculture further disenfranchised women and increased their difficulty in paying for ·

medical services. Accordingly, women have suffered disproportionately—a fact made evident globally by the almost 600,000 deaths per year of women in childbirth, 99% of which occur in developing countries and most of which have cut government-sponsored maternal services in line with IMF-sponsored SAPs.

Whether the price of progress through industrialization must be increased poverty, hunger, and environmental devastation is, for many, an open question. Many argue that the process of economic and industrial development takes time and that countries such as Brazil and India are now beginning to see a marked improvement in their economic situation. Some point to the cases of the so-called newly industrialized countries, such as Korea and Taiwan, as examples of what can be done. But the non-Western countries that have succeeded in emulating the West (and Japan is foremost among these) were never colonized by the West, as were the poor countries of Africa and South America. And the country that has emerged as the second-largest economy in the world—China—emerged almost totally independent of Western multilateral institutions.

In sum, then, are the people of the world better off now than they were before the industrial revolution? Obviously, the answer depends on who you are. If you are fortunate enough to be a laborer, merchant/businessperson, or professional in one of the wealthy countries of the world, you are likely to be materially better off than your counterpart of five centuries ago, provided the price you pay in health risks because of a damaged environment does not offset your material gains. If you are a laborer or small farmer in one of the poor countries of the world, it is hard to see how you are actually better off than your peasant counterpart of centuries past. And if you are among the landless, unemployed, or underemployed of the world—one of the billion without enough food—one is hard pressed to see how your life could be an improvement over those of people in centuries past.

QUESTION 2.4	**How Do Modern Standards of Health and Medical Treatment Compare with Those of Traditional Societies?**

Even if the economic changes of the past two centuries have not improved the lives of many of Earth's inhabitants, can we not at least assume that some technologies—notably medical technologies—have improved the lives of virtually everyone? To answer this question, we need to examine two things: First, we have to ask whether we have progressed in our ability to treat disease; and second, we have to ask whether we have fully understood the traditional medical techniques that modern medicine has sought to replace.

Illness and Inequality

One of the supposed triumphs of modern society is the treatment and cure of disease. Life expectancy has more than doubled in the 20th century: In 1900, world life expectancy was approximately 30 years; in 2000, it was 63 years. Antibiotics save millions each year from death, and modern diagnostic methods and equipment allow medical practitioners to more easily identify the onset of disease. But the progress that we often take for granted is not available to all. In fact, the single most important determinant of a country's ability to protect its citizens from disease is the degree of economic equality. Worldwide, 32% of all deaths are caused by infectious diseases, but in the poorer countries of the world, infectious diseases are responsible for 42% of all deaths, compared to 1.2% in industrial countries. Another 40% of all deaths are caused by environmental factors—particularly organic and chemical pollutants. These pollutants are far more deadly in poorer countries, where, for example, 1.2 billion people lack clean, safe water and where industrial wastes are dumped untreated into rivers and lakes. Thus, your income determines your chances of coming into contact with a deadly pollutant. This is true even in the United States, where three out of four off-site commercial hazardous landfills in southern states were located primarily in African American communities, although African Americans represent only 20% of the population. Industrialized countries already ship 20 million tons of waste annually to the poor countries of the world.

We can perhaps better judge the extent to which we have "progressed" to the degree to which we are protected from infectious diseases by examining what it takes for us to die of an infectious disease. At least four things have to happen: First, we have to come into contact with some **pathogen** or **vector**—such as a mosquito, tick, flea, or snail—that carries it. Second, the pathogen must be virulent; that is, it must be able to kill us. Third, if we come into contact with a deadly pathogen, it must evade our body's immune system. Finally, the pathogen must be able to circumvent whatever measures our society has developed to prevent it from doing harm. As we will see, our chances of dying are affected at every step by social and cultural patterns—particularly by the degree of economic and social inequality.

First, what actions of human beings increase their likelihood of coming into contact with an infectious pathogen? One feature of cultural history is that cultural complexity has served to increase our exposure to infectious agents. Large permanent settlements attract and sustain such vermin as rats and fleas, which serve as hosts to microorganisms and ensure their survival and spread. Permanent settlements also result in the buildup of human wastes. Sedentary agriculture requires altering the landscape in ways that can increase the incidence of disease. For example, schistosomiasis is a disease caused by worms or snails that thrive in the irrigation ditches constructed to support agriculture. The domestication of such animals as dogs, cats, cattle, and pigs—another characteristic of advanced societies—increases contact between people and disease-causing microorganisms. The requirements of large populations for the storage and processing of food also increase the likelihood of the survival and spread of disease-causing agents. In the modern world, the poorer you are, the more likely you are to be exposed to infectious pathogens.

Coming into contact with an infectious pathogen need not be enough to kill you; the pathogen must be deadly. But this can also depend on your social and cultural situation and your income. In fact, human actions can make a pathogen more or less harmful. Generally, it is not to the advantage of pathogens—viruses, bacteria, parasites—to kill their hosts; it is better for the pathogen to allow its host to live and supply its nutrients. However, if the pathogen does not need its host in order to survive, it can evolve into a more deadly form. This is the case with waterborne infections. For example, diarrheal diseases tend to be more virulent if they are spread by water systems and do not require person-to-person contact. Disease pathogens that spread by contaminated water can survive regardless of how sick their host becomes, and by reproducing extensively in their host, they make it more likely that they can contaminate water supplies through the washing of sheets or clothing or through bodily wastes. Thus, you are far more likely to contact a more deadly disease if you do not have access to clean and treated water.

Even if you come into contact with a deadly pathogen, your immune system is designed to prevent it from killing you. However, the ability of your immune system to function is clearly a function of your diet, and diet is largely determined by income level. In this respect, we have not progressed. In 1950, 20% of the world's population (500 million people) was malnourished; today, some 50% (three billion) of the people in the world are malnourished. Insufficient food is one of the main factors that increases the likelihood of immune system failure.

Finally, even if our immune system fails to repel an infectious pathogen, societies do develop methods to cure whatever illnesses afflict them. And there is little doubt that the discovery of methods to cure infectious disease marks one of the great success stories of modern culture. Unfortunately, citizens' access to these cures is determined largely by the degree of economic inequality in their country, not by their country's absolute wealth. For example, the United States—the wealthiest country in the world—ranks 25th in the world (well behind all the other rich countries, and even behind a few poor ones) in life expectancy. Not coincidentally, the United States has the largest income gap of any industrialized country; Japan, with the lowest income gap between rich and poor, has the highest life expectancy, despite having triple the cigarette usage of the United States.

The relationship between wealth and access to cures is most evident with HIV/AIDS. Some 40 to 50 million people in the world are presently infected with HIV, with more than three-quarters living in African countries. Medicines exist to prevent HIV from developing into full-blown AIDS, but they are prohibitively expensive and completely out of reach of victims living in poor countries whose health care systems have been decimated by World Bank and IMF policies.

In sum, although we have indeed made dramatic progress in understanding and curing infectious disease, we have made no progress and, in fact, have regressed and continue to regress in our ability to provide access to these cures. At the same time, we have increased global exposure to environmental pollutants and infectious pathogens. .

The Meaning of Illness

Even if we conclude that modern societies are more susceptible to contagious disease, have they not at least improved the techniques for curing illness? To answer this question, it is important to realize that the meanings members of different societies give to illness vary as much as the meanings they give to other aspects of their lives. In American society, illness is most often viewed as an intrusion by microorganisms: germs, bacteria, or viruses. Our curing techniques emphasize the destruction or elimination of these agents. Death can occur, we believe, when we have failed to eliminate them. In many other societies, the interpretation of illness is different. Illness may be attributed to witchcraft, sorcery, soul loss, or spirit possession. Belief in witchcraft or sorcery involves a claim that a witch or sorcerer can use mystical or magical power to inflict illness on another person. Belief in soul loss assumes that illness results from the souls leaving the body. Spirit intrusion or possession is based on the idea that a foreign spirit enters the patient and causes illness. These explanations are not mutually exclusive; for example, the soul may flee the body as the result of witchcraft or sorcery.

Americans sometimes have difficulty appreciating the meanings others place on events, and the meaning of illness is no exception. We fail to recognize that belief in illness or death by witchcraft, sorcery, soul loss, or spirit possession involves an additional belief that illness has social as well as supernatural causes. Members of societies that believe in spiritual or magical causes for illness do not believe that the witch or sorcerer strikes at random, that the soul leaves the body without cause, or that the spirit possesses just anyone. They believe that there also must be a social reason for the witch to act or the soul to flee. Witchcraft involves relationships between people; the witch voluntarily or involuntarily afflicts someone who has offended him or her or who has breached a rule of conduct. Likewise, in cases of soul loss or spirit possession, the soul leaves the body of a person who is having difficulty with others or the spirit possesses a person who has created social problems or who has not honored social obligations.

The Chewa of Malawi in southeast Africa claim that illness and death are caused by sorcery. Max Marwick points out that sorcery-induced illness or death does not strike randomly; it occurs when there is a conflict over judicial rights and claims or when someone fails to observe some social norm. Whereas we react to illness or death by seeking the disease or accident responsible, the Chewa ask what wrong the victim has committed, with whom the victim has quarreled, or who is jealous of the victim. The Chewa explicitly recognize the connection between sorcery and social tension; they say that people who have quarreled are likely to practice sorcery against each other.

A Chewa who becomes ill consults a diviner to discover the cause of the illness. During the consultation, the patient and the diviner discuss the social

In a healing ceremony designed to restore the patient to his proper place in the world, a traditional Navajo doctor paints an image of the universe with colored sand on an earthen floor.

roots of the illness. The diviner needs to know about the patient's relationships with kin and, if ancestral spirits may be responsible, the genealogy of the patient. Thus, Chewa medical theory, although couched in the idiom of sorcery, is a social theory of illness, not simply a supernatural one. Someone gets ill because of a breach in social relations, not solely because of some magical act.

There is a disease syndrome in Latin America called *susto*. There are other terms for it—*pasmo, espanto, perdida de la somba*—but all are based on the belief that the soul has detached itself from the body. Symptoms of *susto* include restlessness, listlessness, loss of appetite, disinterest in dress or bodily appearance, loss of strength, and introversion. The onset of the illness is said to follow a fright brought on by a sudden encounter or accident, and the cure begins with a diagnostic session between the patient and a healer. After deciding what brought on the disorder, the healer coaxes the soul back into the body. The patient is then sweated, massaged, and rubbed with some object to remove the illness.

Anthropologist Arthur Rubel, who analyzed specific cases of *susto*, found that all the cases share two characteristics: *Susto* occurs only when the patient perceives some situation as stressful, and the stress results from difficulties in social relations with specific persons. In one case of *susto*, a father was afflicted when he discovered he could no longer provide for his family, and in another, a mother was stricken when she was not able to take proper care of her child. A wife lost her soul as a result of not honoring her obligations to her husband, and a young boy lost his after he refused to act in a way thought to be appropriate by his peers. In every case, according to Rubel, *susto* resulted when a person did not or could not fulfill an expected social obligation. In other words, *susto*, like witchcraft or sorcery, is a statement about social tensions, not simply a description of a magical event.

These traditional theories of illness—soul loss, spirit possession, sorcery, and witchcraft—all have one thing in common. They are all expressions of an **interpersonal theory of disease**. Simply stated, in the interpersonal theory of disease, it is assumed that illness is caused not by microorganisms but by tensions or conflicts in social relations. So-called natural explanations for illness fail to take into account that witches, spirits, and souls are mediating concepts; they are theoretical entities that, like germs, provide a link between a social cause—tension and conflict—and a physical result—illness or death.

If giving meaning to an instance of illness involves the attribution of illness to social causes, then it follows that the cure must also be, at least in part, social. Therefore, a curer attempts to not only remove a spell, return the soul to the body, or remove a spiritual object that is causing the symptoms of illness but to also repair the social problem that initiated the episode of illness. To illustrate, Victor Turner provides a look at one society: the Ndembu, an agricultural society in northwestern Zambia.

The Ndembu believe that a persistent or severe illness is caused either by the punitive action of some ancestral ghost or the secret malevolence of a sorcerer or witch. The ghosts punish people when they forget to make a ritual offering to their ancestors or because, as the Ndembu put it, "kin are not living well together." Explicit in Ndembu interpretations of illness is the idea that illness results either from personal failure to fulfill social obligations or from social conflict.

To effect a cure, the Ndembu patient consults a native doctor. The doctor first inquires about the patient's social relations: Has he or she quarreled with anyone? What is the state of the patient's marital relations? Is anyone jealous of the patient? The doctor asks those with whom the patient has quarreled or insulted to participate in the ceremony—a dramatic affair with chanting and drumming that sometimes lasts for hours. People who have complaints about the patient's social behavior may come forward, and the patient may report grudges against neighbors. At the climax, the doctor may dramatically extract from the patient's body some object that could have been causing the illness. In one case Turner followed closely, the doctor did indeed succeed in patching up a patient's social relations, along with his physical complaints.

The Ndembu recognize, at least implicitly, that social strain and stress may produce physical illness, and one way to treat illness is to treat the sources of social strain. Western medical practice has been slow to recognize the impact

Exercise 2.4 ➤

CONTACTING ALIEN WORLDS

In an issue of *Parade* magazine, the "Ask Marilyn" column features a letter from a man who recommends that we stop trying to contact alien worlds. "It is very likely," he writes, "that any civilization we find will be far more advanced than our own. History has shown that whenever a more advanced civilization comes into contact with a less advanced one, it leads to the destruction of the latter, even if the intent of the former is not hostile." In her response, Ms. vos Savant says: "In my opinion we should continue the search. . . . While it may be true that less advanced civilizations are absorbed into advanced ones, we usually call this progress, not destruction. Few of us would wish to return to our ancestors' way of living, unless we've romanticized them beyond reality."

Continue the exchange with Ms. vos Savant. What might you say to her in response?

of stress on physical health, but there is significant evidence that certain life events can significantly increase the likelihood of becoming ill. Such events as the death of a spouse, the loss of a job, relocation to a new home, and even holidays such as Christmas can increase the chances of illness. These are the same kinds of events that can trigger the need for ceremonial cures in traditional societies. Thus, rather than viewing the traditional healing practices of traditional societies as somehow inferior, it makes far more sense to recognize that they focus on real causes of illness—social stress—that their curing techniques are well equipped to address.

Furthermore, traditional cures can be not only beneficial but also affordable. One of the consequences of medical advances is our increasing dependence on expensive technology. Consequently, although significant advances have been made in medicine, the cost to the patient of many such advances has made them unavailable to all but a small percentage of the world's population. Indeed, they are unavailable to many Americans. But in traditional societies, when healing arts are lost or·discouraged by Western-educated government officials who consider them backward, members are left with virtually no medical treatment.

QUESTION 2.5   *Why Are Simpler Societies Disappearing?*

Modern societies have not been kind to traditional groups that have retained or tried to retain a way of life that is thousands of years old. Societies such as the Ju/wasi, the Inuit of Alaska and the Canadian Arctic (the proper term for the people we call Eskimos), and the people of the New Guinea highlands have not fared well when contacted by more complex civilizations. Living in small scattered groups with little need for complex political structures or technology, they were no match for the well-armed, organized, acquisitive people and governments who coveted their land or labor. Even hunting and gathering peoples in isolated, seemingly inhospitable locations have proven susceptible to cultural extermination or genocide.

For example, the Ona inhabited the island of Tierra del Fuego just off the southern tip of South America, whose climate was described by an early settler as 65 days of unpleasant weather and 300 days of rain and storms. After their first encounters with Europeans in the 1870s and 1880s, the Ona were exposed to deadly European diseases to which they had no resistance, such as syphilis, measles, and tuberculosis; were systematically hunted and killed by European sheepherders and miners; and were captured by Argentine soldiers and

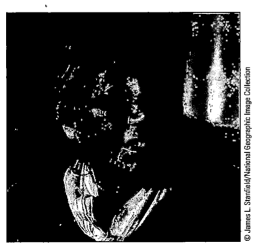

Through disease, starvation, and outright killing, European settlers completely exterminated the Ona tribe of Tierra del Fuego, just off the southern tip of South America. The last full-blooded Ona died in 1973.

© James L. Stanfield/National Geographic Image Collection

Exercise 2.5 ➤

It is the year 1967. You are members of a task force of the Botswana government that has been asked to evaluate the living conditions of the Ju/wasi. Another group of government officials, distressed over the primitive ways of the Ju/wasi, had recommended that they should begin to enjoy the benefits of civilization. Specifically, the group recommended that the government should settle the Ju/wasi in permanent villages, dig wells to ensure a steady water supply, distribute domesticated animals to ensure a ready food supply, and introduce modern health services. The group had also recommended that jobs be found for the Ju/wasi.

You have toured the area and spoken to some of the Ju/wasi. Your specific job is to evaluate the recommendations of the previous government task force and then make your own recommendations to the government on how the lives of the Ju/wasi could be improved. You may agree or disagree with the previous panel, but you must give reasons for your recommendations.

sent to mission stations or kept by the soldiers as servants. Those who survived on the island were pushed farther inland, and European hunters systematically depleted the animals on which they depended for food. Having little food on which to survive, they began to raid sheep ranches and were shot by hunters or ranchers who were paid a bounty for every Ona killed. At the turn of the century, Europeans built lumber camps in the last forests in which the Ona could live without being in permanent contact with Europeans. Finally, in 1973, 100 years after the first European settlement was built on Tierra del Fuego, the last full-blooded Ona died.

The extermination of the Ona was not an isolated event. Representatives of modern societies all over the world systematically exterminated native groups. For example, the Spanish totally exterminated the natives of the Florida peninsula. The indigenous peoples of the American plains, who lived by gathering and hunting as late as the 1860s, were first decimated by disease and then systematically driven from their land by miners and ranchers. Today, Native American populations that were isolated by government decree on reservations face unemployment rates approaching 90% and an infant mortality rate that is five times the national average. In areas of Brazil that are now being entered by Europeans, members of the native population—many of whom still live by hunting and gathering or small-scale agriculture—are being hunted and killed much as the Ona were some 100 years ago.

Cultural Devastation and Radical Hope

The experiences of peoples such as the Ona raise an important question: What does it mean to experience cultural devastation? The question is important not only for what it tells us of the experiences of other people but for how we understand what culture is and what culture change can mean. Clearly all cultures are vulnerable; that is, the way that people view the world, what counts as important, what is valued, and what the good life means are all subject to sudden upheaval. Such cultural upheavals are constantly in the news.

One of the best examples is what happened to indigenous peoples in the United States. At the time of Columbus's arrival in the New World, there were hundreds of thriving societies that were quickly devastated by disease that wiped out probably 90% of the existing population. The devastation continued well into the 19th century as the remnants of these populations struggled to adapt to the westward expansion of settlers. The indigenous peoples of the Plains, such as the Lakota (Sioux), Blackfeet, Cheyenne, Kiowa, and Crow, had adapted by organizing their societies around the horse and the buffalo— often competing against each other for control of territory on which to hunt. But from the period of roughly 1850 to 1880, these cultures were forced by the U.S. government onto reservations to depend on government rations— that were often undelivered or inedible—to replace the buffalo that had been virtually exterminated to make way for cattle ranchers supplying beef to satisfy the demand for meat coming largely from Great Britain. But what did it mean to go from a culture built on buffalo hunting and horse raiding to one on a government reservation?

Plenty-coups, chief of the Crow, told his life story to Frank Linderman but ended the story when his people were forced onto a reservation, explaining "after this, nothing happened."

In 1930, Plenty-coups, the chief of the Crow, dictated his life story to rancher Frank B. Linderman. Linderman's book *Plenty-coup: Chief of the Crows* (originally titled *American: The Life Story of a Great Indian*) became an anthropological classic. In the book, Plenty-coups told of his life as a Crow hunter and warrior, but he refused to talk about his life after the buffalo were gone and after the Crow were restricted to their reservation. "I have not told you half of what happened when I was young," he told Linderman. "I can think back and tell you much more of war and horse stealing. But when the buffalo went away," he said, "the hearts of my people fell to the ground and they could not lift them up again. *After this, nothing happened.*"

Philosopher Jonathan Lear devotes his book on Plenty-coups, *Radical Hope: Ethics in the Face of Cultural Devastation*, to trying to explain what it means to say "After this, nothing happened." In so doing, he helps us understand what it means to experience cultural devastation and live through it.

In the early 19th century, the Crow lived, as did many Plains Indian groups, by hunting buffalo, raising horses, and raiding rival groups, particularly the Lakota, Blackfeet, and Cheyenne. War and raiding were a concern not only of men but of the whole tribe. Girls as well

National Anthropological Archives, Smithsonian Institution. BAE GN 3404 A

as boys derived their names from the exploits of warriors; wives publicly displayed their husbands' war trophies, such as scalps and weapons; and a woman grieving the loss of a husband or son was a goad to retaliatory raids. Religion was suffused with the symbolism and rituals of war, and visions, dreams, and prayers inspired military undertakings. Child rearing was training for war, and boys counted coup on animals while girls danced with the hair of a wolf or coyote in place of a scalp.

Counting coup was the ultimate sign of courage. In battle, counting coup involved planting one's coup stick in the ground and defending it against an enemy until death. As Lear put it, it "marked a boundary across which a non-Crow enemy must not pass" (2006, 13). Plenty-coups described it as follows:

> To count coup a warrior had to strike an armed and fighting enemy with his coup stick, quirt, or bow before otherwise harming him, or take his weapons while he was yet alive, or strike the first enemy falling in battle, no matter who killed him, or strike the enemy's breastworks while under fire, or steal a horse tied to a lodge in an enemy's camp. (Linderman, 1962, pp. 55–56)

Such was the value of courage and daring in war that a common adage was that "old age is a thing of evil, it is well for a young man to die in battle" (Lowie, 1983, p. 218). If we had to compare the Crow pursuit of war honors with an activity of our society, we could probably compare it to the pursuit of money or wealth on which virtually our entire society is built.

The Crow concern for war was built on a real need to defend the territory on which they depended for sustenance. The westward advance of Europeans had forced such groups as the Lakota and Crow to struggle for what territory remained. These struggles ended only with the cultural devastation that accompanied U.S. military action against indigenous groups and the virtual extermination of the buffalo.

For the Crow, the end began when they signed the Fort Laramie Treaty in 1851, giving the tribe rights to some 33 million acres and $50,000 worth of supplies a year—although these supplies were only delivered once. In 1867, the treaty was renegotiated, giving the Crow 25% of the land recognized in the first treaty, and in 1882, the land was further reduced to about two million acres. Then, disease struck as they moved to a reservation in 1882–1884. In this life imposed on them by the United States, nothing that had meaning to them any longer existed. If things that counted as events, such as planting a coup stick, counting coup, going on a raid, or hunting buffalo were no longer possible, it would make sense to say that "after this, nothing happened."

If money were somehow removed from our life, what would be the point of life? All our activities—going to school, getting a job, preparing to buy a house—would cease to have any meaning. The context for living would be destroyed, as it was for the Crow. There would no longer be a conception of happiness—the good life. The problem for the Crow, says Lear (2006, p. 56), "was not simply that they could not pursue happiness in the traditional ways. Rather, their conception of *what happiness is* could no longer be lived. The characteristic activities that used to constitute the good life ceased to be intelligible acts."

How can one survive such devastation? One option is to fight to restore the life lost. Many North American tribes did but ultimately were defeated. One can flee, as did the Nez Perce, but after an epic military campaign, they were captured and returned to a reservation. Or one can give in to despair. The Crow chose another option—one that was revealed to Plenty-coups in a dream vision when he was nine years old.

The Crow believed that dreams provided access to a world beyond anything available to ordinary consciousness. There were different kinds of dreams: Some were "no account" dreams, in which the dreamer merely witnessed some common incident. Then, there were "wish dreams," in which the dreamer saw some hoped for outcome. Finally, there were "medicine dreams," which the Crow believed provided insights into the future.

When he was 10 years old, Plenty-coups went on a vision quest, a spiritual journey in which young Crow men sought a vision that would reveal their future destiny. He went to a mountaintop, cut off one of his fingers to elicit pity from the spirits, and, on the second night, had his dream. He saw a buffalo bull, which turned into a man-person wearing a buffalo robe. He was led to a hole in the ground. Man-person shook his red rattle, and Plenty-coups saw endless numbers of buffalo emerging from a hole in the ground and covering the plains. But then, they disappeared, and strange spotted animals emerged from the hole to replace them, lying around and eating the grass on the plains. "Do you understand what I have shown you?" asked Man-person. "No," Plenty-coups replied. "I was only 10 years old."

Then, Man-person showed Plenty-coups an old man sitting under a tree and asked "Do you know him, Plenty-coups?" "No," he said. "This old man is yourself," said Man-person. At this point, a tremendous storm arose and, as Plenty-coups related it, the Four Winds began a war against the forest, knocking down all the trees but one. Man-person said that that sole standing tree was the lodge of the chickadee. The chickadee, for the Crow, represented a good listener; nothing escaped his ears, he never missed a chance to learn from others, and he gained success from learning how others succeeded. Only the lodge of Chickadee-person was left standing by the Four Winds, and Man-person told Plenty-coups: "Develop your body, but do not neglect your mind. . . . It is the mind that leads a man to power, not strength of body" (Lear, 2006, p. 71).

When he returned from his vision quest, Plenty-coups related the story to Yellow Bear, a tribal elder considered the "wisest man in the lodge," who interpreted the dream as follows: Plenty-coups had been told that in his lifetime, the buffalo would go away forever and that in their place on the plains would come the bulls and calves of the white man. "I have myself seen these Spotted-Buffalo drawing loads of the white man's goods," said Yellow Bear.

> And once at a big fort . . . I saw cows and calves of the same tribe as the bulls that drew the loads. The dream of Plenty-coups means that the white man

will take and hold this country and that their Spotted-buffalo will cover the
plains. He was told to think for himself, to listen, to learn to avoid disaster
by the experience of others. He was advised to develop his body but not to
forget his mind. The meaning of this dream is plain to me. I see its warning.
The tribes who have fought the white man have all been beaten, wiped out.
By listening as the Chickadee listens we may escape this and keep our lands.
(quoted in Lear, 2006, p. 72)

Become a chickadee, then, is the advice of the dream.

Lear imagines Plenty-coups's reasoning as follows:

- Traditional life will end.
- The conception of the good intrinsic in a hunting life must end.
- Things will change in unexpected ways.
- There is more to hope for than mere physical survival—a dignified passage "across the abyss."
- My commitment to God and goodness is involved in the idea that something good will emerge, even if I do not know what it could be.
- I am thus committed to the idea that since we Crow must abandon the goods associated with our way of life, we must abandon the conception of the good life that our tribe has worked out over the centuries.
- We shall get the good back, although at the moment, we can have no more than a glimmer of what that might mean.

We do not, of course, know the depth of Plenty-coups's thought—whether he was simply being practical in the face of overwhelming power, whether he may have had profound insights into history, or whether he was expressing some religious conviction. We may even be disappointed that he did not face up to the evil inflicted on his people. But, as Lear emphasizes, Plenty-coups responded to the devastation of his culture with *radical hope*. It is radical because there is no understanding of what one is hoping for—only a conviction that some other good will somehow emerge. And it is radical because it avoided despair.

On the basis of his dream, the tribe elected to ally itself with the United States, joining with them to fight the tribe's traditional enemies: the Sioux, Blackfoot, and Cheyenne. Although the United States nevertheless kept revising its treaties with the Crow, the Crow were never displaced from the land, and they could say that they had never been defeated. They listened, as the chickadee listens, sent their children to school, built a college, and, surviving a period of cultural devastation, adopted many cultural traits of white culture. And Plenty-coups in old age could feel that the dream had been confirmed by his experiences. In fact, he related his story to Linderman sitting in the same spot under the same tree revealed to him in his dream: "And here I am, an old man, sitting under this tree just where that old man sat seventy years ago when it was a different world." He had, says Lear (2006, p. 143),

brought himself to the spot where the dream told him he would be. And
the recitation of the dream to Linderman was in its own way the triumphal

counting of coup: he was telling the story of how he successfully went to "battle" to protect his land. He was now sitting under the tree that the dream told him he would if he adopted the virtue of the chickadee.

CASE STUDY IN DOING ANTHROPOLOGY #2: DOING DEVELOPMENT

Efforts by countries to "progress" and modernize have often undermined the lives of indigenous peoples as well as the lives of craftspeople and small farmers. The idea of progress clearly contains some ethnocentric assumptions about what constitutes the "good life." Very often, the idea of "development" means simply the export of Western culture to sometimes willing but often unwilling recipients. That does not mean, however, that efforts to address economic, social, and human rights problems should be ignored. Around the world, 24,000 people die every day from hunger or hunger-related causes. Many women around the world have little or no access to education or job opportunities but are responsible for the health and livelihood of their children. These and other problems need to be addressed by those with the power and money to do so.

Governments, international organizations such as the World Bank, United Nations, and USAID, and such nongovernmental organizations (NGOs) as Oxfam, Amnesty International, and Doctors Without Borders/Médecins Sans Frontières (MSF) recognize that anthropological perspectives are critical to addressing these problems, thus creating career opportunities for professional anthropologists and people with a background in anthropology. To illustrate, let us examine three of the many areas of development that require some anthropological background: (1) the interaction between development programs and local culture and society, (2) the use of indigenous knowledge, and (3) the role of women in development.

Culture and Development

A failure of development professionals to understand the cultures and values of the people they are trying to help has, in the past, had disastrous consequences. A case in point is that of the indigenous people of the Mackenzie Delta, an area in the western Canadian Arctic near the Alaska and Yukon border. It has been the home of Inuit, Metis, and Dene peoples, living for centuries by hunting, fishing, and, later, trapping. After World War II, the Canadian government wanted to develop the area in order to extract oil, gas, and mineral reserves. The government also wanted to bring services to indigenous peoples to prepare them for "modern" life through schooling and wage labor. However, planning was top down, with little or no participation from the people themselves.

A failure of development professionals to understand cultures and values of people has, in the past, had disastrous consequences. A good example is the construction of the town of Inuvik in the Canadian Arctic.

© Staffan Widstrand/Corbis

The centerpiece of the modernization plan was the construction of a large-scale "science town" that was to house a school, a commercial and service center, and a hospital to serve the indigenous peoples of the entire region. The government planners encouraged the establishment in the town of oil companies, commercial airlines, hotels, restaurants, stores, and construction companies. By the late 1950s and early 1960s, the town was completed. As Alexander M. Ervin describes it, the impact on the people of the Mackenzie Delta was profound. Of the 5,000 people who inhabited the town, including Euro-Canadians, only about 150 lived off the land. Half the population were "southerners"—transient workers from southern Canada—including doctors, nurses, and government officials who were paid generous salaries and allowances to encourage them to resettle—if only for a short time—in the Arctic. Few of the people of the Delta were employed after the initial building phase, and they were overwhelmed by the social and economic advantages of the southerners. Southerners rarely interacted with the native northerners, and relations became hostile and full of tension. Rather than being designed for northern youth, school curricula were modeled after programs in southern urban schools. Dropout rates were very high, and the alienation of the young was marked by petty crimes and assaults—crimes that had not existed in indigenous settings. Native women who had children with transient whites were stigmatized, and conflict arose between families that had a steady income and the material possessions they could buy and families dependent on government payments. Men could not return to their traplines because they had given up their equipment and because the fur trade was uncertain. The high stress was also evident in high rates of alcohol consumption and such crimes as assault, theft, and wife battering—all associated with alcohol. Clearly, the optimism of the government that the new town would better the lives of the native peoples was misplaced.

Various things—typical of large-scale development projects—clearly went wrong. There was no consultation with the people themselves regarding the changes; everything was planned and implemented by outsiders with their own pre-existing notions about the native communities and what would be good for them. Nobody considered the complex interactions among family structure, cultural values, economics, education, and new residents. No one attempted to integrate local knowledge into the planning process. And no one considered the unintended consequences of the changes.

However, more recently in Canada, development projects have integrated the work of trained anthropologists. Beginning in the 1970s, the Quebec government initiated a huge hydroelectric project in northern Quebec that had severe impacts on the native Cree and Naskapi populations and required agreements with the Cree to compensate them for the loss of hunting territories. One program was an annual income program in lieu of welfare that resulted in an increase in commercial trapping among men. The annual income enabled the men to upgrade their equipment and hence engage in a culturally valued activity. A study done by anthropologist Richard Salisbury and his associates on behalf of the Canadian Department of Indian Affairs on programs regarding health, education, and social services discovered that although there were benefits to these programs, they had also created conflicts between Cree bureaucrats and villagers as well as between Cree and Euro-Canadian bureaucrats. Salisbury's findings and recommendations were implemented to resolve these conflicts.

Using Indigenous Knowledge

Another development to which anthropologists have contributed is the use of indigenous knowledge. Generally, development projects involve "experts" who, because of their own preconceptions about cultures other than their own, assume that the people whom they are trying to help have little to contribute. Time and again, this has led to development disasters. For example, James Scott describes the *ujamaa* village campaign in Tanzania from 1973 to 1976. The project aimed to permanently resettle most of the country's population into villages planned—partly or wholly—by officials of the central government. There was virtually no consultation with local people themselves to take into consideration their economic needs or the knowledge and techniques for growing crops and herding animals that had sustained them over generations.

The project, which succeeded in moving more than 13 million people into 7,684 villages, was to transform the citizenry into producers of exportable crops, strung out along paved roads, where state services could be easily delivered and where the population could be easily monitored. Project designers and supporters assumed that African cultivators and pastoralists were backward, unscientific, and inefficient. They assumed that only through supervision or, if necessary, coercion by specialists in scientific agriculture could they contribute to a modern Tanzania.

As might be expected, the results of villagization were disastrous. Huge imports of food were necessary from 1973 to 1975 because of the immediate decline of agricultural production—the cost of which would have bought a cow for every Tanzanian family. Some 60% of the new villages were built on semiarid land that required long walks to reach farm plots. Peasants were moved from fertile farmlands to poor lands or land whose soil was unsuitable for the crops the government demanded farmers grow. Villages were located at a distance from crops that left the crops open to theft and pests. The concentration of people and livestock encouraged cholera and livestock epidemics, while herding cattle in concentrated areas devastated rangeland and livelihoods. Instead of achieving legitimacy, the villagization campaign created an alienated and uncooperative peasantry, for which Tanzania would pay a huge financial and political price.

Contrast this with an agricultural project designed by anthropologist Ronald Nigh in Mexico, in which indigenous methods of agriculture and stock raising are being applied not only to raise crops but to regenerate rainforests destroyed by stock breeding.

Along with most Central American countries, Mexico has lost vast amounts of its rainforests. At the beginning of the 20th century, Mexico had 13 million hectares (31 million acres) of rainforest. Today, less than 2.4 million hectares remain. Of the total destroyed, 5.5 million hectares were converted to pasture, and more than half of that is in an advanced stage of degradation and erosion. Furthermore, although 60% of Mexico's productive land is devoted to pasture or forage for animals, more than 50% of its population never consumes animal products.

Nigh argues that the destruction of the rainforest by cattle grazing is largely the result of the imposition of a **factory model** of agricultural production common in large-scale industrial societies. The factory model produces a single product (such as corn, soy, beef, or pork) in as short a time as possible. It tends to be technology-intensive and environmentally damaging. Furthermore, it tends to convert whole regions to a single type of agricultural production—cattle in one area, corn in another, wheat in another, and so on. In Central America, the factory model of cattle raising has required clearing large tracts of land with fire and herbicides and reseeding with grasses that are not well suited to the environment. The result is degradation of the land by uncontrolled grazing and its eventual abandonment and return to secondary vegetation.

Nigh suggested that it is far more productive and far less damaging to the environment to look at agriculture as an ecological rather than a manufacturing process. He suggests that we need to combine an **agroecological approach** that incorporates indigenous practices that have produced food but preserved the environment with contemporary agricultural research. The major difference between a factory approach and an agroecological approach is that the latter creates a polyculture—the production of multiple crops and animals—rather than a monoculture—the growth or production of a single crop or animal. Indigenous methods of production in the rainforest create a system that enhances regeneration of land, flora, and fauna.

For example, there are sites of secondary vegetation in the Mexican rainforest left by Mayan farmers who practice swidden agriculture. The farmers clear a site, use it to grow corn for five to eight years, and then move on. These sites may soon look like the land abandoned by cattle ranchers, but Mayan farmers do not abandon the sites. Instead, they continue to work the garden, perhaps planting fruit trees, and use the site to attract mammals and birds to hunt. In fact, the area is designed to attract an animal crop; the Maya refer to it as "garden hunting." Because, unlike the factory model, no herbicides are used to clear the land, plant and animal life can regenerate. Thus, traditional agriculture creates an environment that mixes fields, forests, and brushlands. The idea is to create productive modules—each a mosaic of productive spaces. The agroecological model, drawing as it does on indigenous systems developed over centuries, creates an ecologically sustainable system of production modeled after natural systems instead of a system that displaces natural ones.

Rather than demonizing cattle, Nigh said, it is possible to design an agricultural system modeled after indigenous systems in which cattle are integrated into an agroecological model—one in which diversity rather than uniformity is emphasized. For example, one area would be used for such annual crops as corn, squash, root crops, spices, and legumes. Secondary areas, including those previously degraded by overgrazing, can be used for fruit trees, forage, and so on. Other secondary areas, using specially selected animal breeds and grasses, can be devoted to intensive grazing. For example, in his project, they selected a breed developed in New Zealand that is small but a high milk producer. Intensive grazing frees up tropical rainforest land that should never have been converted to pasture to begin with. Nigh maintains that by using only organic fertilizers and controlled grazing, it is possible to recover aquatic areas (ponds, rivers, and lakes) and take advantage of such water resources as fish, mollusks, turtles, and birds.

Thus, studying and using rather than ignoring or dismissing indigenous knowledge can contribute to the success of development initiatives.

Women in Development

One of the areas involved in development that has been given special emphasis by anthropologists is referred to as *women in development* (WID). A high proportion of development workers are women (partly because in some areas of the world, women work best with women on development projects). The importance of WID has to do with the need to involve women in development projects, particularly those having to do with education, health, and child care. Women's growing place in the labor market and their importance in supplementing household budgets in many areas of the world make them central in development planning. And anthropologists bring a special orientation to development projects. For example, a project intended to benefit Indonesian rice farmers was targeted primarily at men; however, as anthropologist Margaret Casey pointed out, women were involved in agricultural activities and decision making, thus opening extension services to women and enhancing the project. In Kenya, the Kenya Water for Health Organization (KWAHO) is charged with bringing clean water to rural Kenyans. When communities approach KWAHO for help, they supply anthropological consultants who encourage community representatives to take charge. Thus, when wells are dug and pumps are supplied, a coalition of small women's groups is organized to monitor the pumps.

CONCLUSIONS

We began this chapter by noting that in a period of 10,000 years, human societies have abandoned a way of life that had survived for some 100,000 years. How do we explain why societies of hunters and gatherers changed into societies of sedentary agriculturists? The need to progress and develop better ways of living might explain the change. However, studies of hunter-gatherer societies reveal that they live quite comfortably and with a minimum amount of effort. If we reject the idea of progress, how do we explain the transformation of human societies over the past 10,000 years? An increase in population or population density may have fueled the transition of societies from hunting and gathering to swidden agriculture and then to plow or irrigation agriculture. But although the transition to more labor-intensive forms of agriculture may have been the result of population pressure, modern agricultural technology may simply be better and more efficient. However, John Bodley's analysis of the energy expenditures of modern agriculture suggests that it is difficult to conclude that it is in fact simply better.

When we try to understand the gap between the wealthy and poor nations of the world, we find that we must consider the history of the economic expansion of Europe and the military, political, and social exploitation of the countries of Asia, Africa, and the Americas. We find that hunger is not so much due to a lack of modern agriculture as it is a consequence of poverty and attempts to industrialize. The need to repay bank loans secured for industrialization has led countries to encourage the development of large farms primarily growing cash crops for export. People are dispossessed of their land and left without enough money to buy food. Furthermore, burdened by debt, poor countries are forced to accept financial restructuring by multilateral organizations, such as the International Monetary Fund (IMF), that reduces citizens' access to jobs, food, education, and health facilities and reduces the value of local currencies. Under these conditions, it is hard to see how people in the developing world are better off than their predecessors.

But modern societies may have an advantage in health care and methods of medical treatment. Are Western standards not higher than those of less modern societies? In fact, researchers have concluded that infectious disease is more common in modern societies and that human behaviors associated with industrialization, modernization, and the unequal distribution of wealth often promote the spread and incidence of contagious disease. Moreover, traditional theories of illness and curing ceremonies can be effective in the diagnosis and treatment of illness or disease.

Then, why, in spite of all they have to offer, are simpler societies disappearing? The answer is that most are disappearing not because of the choice of their members but rather because of the actions of so-called civilized countries. The idea of progress may simply be a convenient rationale for one society to impose its economic and political will on others.

Finally, we examined how an anthropological background or an anthropological perspective can aid in planning development projects and how knowledge of local concerns, the use of local knowledge, and the involvement of segments of the population that are sometimes ignored can mean the difference between assisting people or disrupting their lives.

REFERENCES AND SUGGESTED READINGS

Introduction: The Death of a Way of Life

The epigraph comes from Arturo Escobar's study of economic development programs: *Encountering Development: The Making and Unmaking of the Third World* (Princeton University Press, 1995). A general discussion of the issues of cultural evolution and a comprehensive bibliography are provided in William H. Durham's article "Advances in Evolutionary Culture Theory" in the *Annual Review of Anthropology*, vol. 19 (1990), pp. 187–210. A classic account of cultural history is Alfred L. Kroeber's *Anthropology* (Harcourt, Brace, 1948). A more recent comprehensive work is Eric R. Wolf's *Europe and the People Without History* (University of California Press, 1982).

Why Did Hunter-Gatherer Societies Switch to Sedentary Agriculture?

An excellent account of the history of anthropological theory is John J. Honigmann's *The Development of Anthropological Ideas* (Dorsey Press, 1976). Lewis Henry Morgan's book *Ancient Society* was originally published in 1877 and was reissued by the Belknap Press in 1964. Leslie White's theories of cultural evolution are summarized in *The Science of Culture* (Farrar, Straus and Giroux, 1949) and elaborated in *The Evolution of Culture* (McGraw-Hill, 1959). The description of the Hadza comes from James Woodburn's "An Introduction to Hadza Ecology" in *Man the Hunter*, edited by Richard Lee and Irven DeVore (Aldine, 1968). Elizabeth Thomas's most noted work among the Ju/wasi is found in her book *The Harmless People* (Alfred A. Knopf, 1959). Lorna Marshall's work is represented in *The !Kung of Nyae Nyae* (Harvard University Press, 1976). John Marshall is best known for his films about the Ju/wasi, including *The Hunters, Bushmen of the Kalahari*, and *Ni: Story of a !Kung Woman*. The description of the Ju/wasi by Richard Lee is found in *The Dobe !Kung* (Holt, Rinehart and Winston, 1984). For some dissenting views on the lives of gatherers and hunters, see Carmel Schrire's article "Wild Surmises on Savage Thoughts" in *Past and Present in Hunter Gatherer Studies*, edited by Carmel Schrire (Academic Press, 1984). See also Edwin N. Wilmsen and James R. Denbow's "Paradigmatic History of San-Speaking Peoples and Current Attempts at Revision" in *Current Anthropology*, vol. 31 (1990), pp. 489–512. A comprehensive review of the literature on hunter-gatherers is available in Fred R. Myers's "Critical Trends in the Study of Hunters-Gatherers" in the *Annual Review of Anthropology*, vol. 17 (1988), pp. 261–82. Mark Cohen's *The Food Crisis in Prehistory* (Yale

University Press, 1977) contains one of the best explanations of the reasons for the adoption of agriculture. Another view is provided by David Rindos in *The Origins of Agriculture* (Academic Press, 1984). Marvin Harris also provides an account in *Cannibals and Kings* (Vintage Books, 1977). The analysis of slash-and-burn (swidden) agriculture comes from Robert L. Carneiro's "Slash-and-Burn Cultivation Among the Kuikuru and Its Implications for Cultural Development in the Amazon Basin" in *The Evolution of Horticultural Systems in Native South America: Causes and Consequences, Anthropologica* (supplement 2) (1979), edited by J. Wilbert. Information in the tables on land, labor, and agriculture was adapted from Eric Wolf's *Peasants* (Prentice Hall, 1966). The material on modern potato farming and the potato chip comes from John Bodley's *Anthropology and Contemporary Problems* (2nd edition) (Mayfield, 1985). *The Statistical Abstract of the United States* (1990) provided the information on how many potato chips Americans consume.

Why Are Some Societies More Industrially Advanced Than Others?

A recent account of global inequality can be found in Photis Lysandrou's article "Global Inequality, Wealth Concentration and the Subprime Crisis: A Marxian Commodity Theory Analysis" in *Development and Change*, 42(2011), pp. 183–208. A brilliant anthropological account of the Industrial Revolution and its impact on the non-Western world is contained in Eric Wolf's *Europe and the People Without History*, cited earlier, but the historical material available is vast. Good general sources include the third volume of Immanuel Wallerstein's three-volume account of the expansion of the capitalist world-system: *The Modern World-System III: The Second Era of Great Expansion of the Capitalist World-Economy, 1730–1840s* (Academic Press, 1989); the second volume of Fernand Braudel's three-volume work: *Civilization and Capitalism 15th-18th Century: Vol. II, The Wheels of Commerce* (Harper & Row, 1982); and Michel Beaud's *A History of Capitalism, 1500–1980* (Monthly Review Press, 1983). John Bodley also supplies an excellent account in Chapter 11 of his textbook *Cultural Anthropology: Tribes, States, and the Global System* (Mayfield, 1994). *Global Problems and the Culture of Capitalism* (Pearson 2011) by Richard H. Robbins gives a comprehensive answer to this question. Ashok V. Desai's article "Population and Standards of Living in Akbar's Time" in the *Indian Economic and Social History Review*, vol. 9 (1972), pp. 42–62, provides a comparison of the life of Indian peasants in the 15th century and the 1960s.

Why Do Poor Countries Not Modernize and Develop in the Same Way as Wealthier Countries?

The material on the early assumptions of economic development comes from Arturo Escobar's critical account of development in *Encountering Development: The Making and Unmaking of the Third World*, cited earlier. The United Nations Report's *Measures for the Economic Development of Under-Developed Countries* (United Nations, 1951) provides the ideological blueprint for undermining traditional societies as a way to modernize them. Excellent accounts of the history of the Bretton Woods institutions (IMF and World Bank) and the impact of World Bank policy on developing nations are given in *Mortgaging the Earth: The World Bank, Environmental Impoverishment, and the Crisis of Development* by Bruce Rich (Beacon Press, 1994) and in *Faith and Credit: The World Bank's Secular Empire* by Susan George and Fabrizio Sabelli (Westview Press, 1994). In *Food First: Beyond the Myth of Scarcity* (Random House, 1977), Frances Moore Lappé and Joseph

Collins give additional information on the impacts of the introduction of cash crops and industrialization. See also Parker Shipton's review "African Famines and Food Security" in the *Annual Review of Anthropology*, vol. 19 (1990), pp. 353–95. *Hunger and Public Action* by Jean Drèze and Amartya Sen (Cambridge University Press, 1991) provides an excellent overview of the problem of and reasons for world hunger. An attempt to explain why the Third World has failed to develop (although without considering their colonial past) is given in Paul Kennedy's *Preparing for the Twenty-First Century* (Random House, 1993). See also *Global Problems and the Culture of Capitalism* by Richard H. Robbins, cited earlier. The impacts of structural adjustment programs is described and reviewed by James Pfeiffer and Rachel Chapman in "Anthropological Perspectives on Structural Adjustment and Public Health" in the *Annual Review of Anthropology*, 39, pp. 19–65, and a case study of the health implications can be found in *Your Pocket Is What Cures You: The Politics of Health in Senegal* by Ellen E. Foley (Rutgers University Press, 2010). A exploration of the effects of SAPs on maternal mortality can be found in "Free Markets and Dead Mothers: The Social Ecology of Maternal Mortality in Post-Socialist Mongolia" by Craig Janes and Oyuntsetseg in *Medical Anthropological Quarterly*, 18, pp. 230–257.

How Do Modern Standards of Health and Medical Treatment Compare with Those of Traditional Societies?

The discussion of infectious disease is based largely on Mark Cohen's *Health and the Rise of Civilization* (Yale University Press, 1989) and the chapter on disease in *Global Problems and the Culture of Capitalism* by Richard H. Robbins, cited earlier. Additional material can be found in Ann McElroy and Patricia Townsend's *Medical Anthropology* (Duxbury Press, 1979) and Marcia C. Inhorn and Peter J. Brown's "The Anthropology of Infectious Disease" in the *Annual Review of Anthropology*, vol. 19 (1990), pp. 89–117. Information on traditional curing techniques can be found in Peter Worsley's article "Non-Western Medical Systems" and Allan Young's article "The Anthropology of Illness and Sickness"—both in the *Annual Review of Anthropology*, vol. 11 (1982), pp. 315–48 and 257–85, respectively. The account of Chewa beliefs about illness and curing comes from *Sorcery in Its Social Setting* by Max Marwick (University of Manchester Press, 1965). The analysis of *susto* is found in Arthur Rubel's "The Epidemiology of a Folk Illness: Susto in Hispanic America" in *Ethnology*, vol. 3 (1964), pp. 268–83. Victor Turner provides a brilliant analysis of Ndembu cures in *The Forest of Symbols: Aspects of Ndembu Ritual* (Cornell University Press, 1967). A review of the role of stress in illness can be found in James S. House, Karl R. Landis, and Debra Umberson's "Social Relationships and Health" in *Science*, vol. 241 (1988), pp. 540–45.

Why Are Simpler Societies Disappearing?

The account of the Ona comes from Jason W. Clay's "Yahgan and Ona—The Road to Extinction" *Cultural Survival Quarterly*, vol. 8 (1984), pp. 5–8. Material on the plight of peasant farmers in Chiapas can be found in Volume 18 of *Cultural Survival Quarterly* (1994). Cultural Survival, Inc., is an organization whose purpose is to assist tribal societies to resist extinction and exploitation. Information about the services, products, and publications of Cultural Survival can be obtained by writing to 53-A Church St., Cambridge, MA 02138. Frank B. Linderman's account of Plenty-coups's life is *Plenty-coups: Chief of the Crows* (University of Nebraska Press, 1962), and the best ethnography of traditional Crow life is Robert H. Lowie's *The Crow Indians* (University of Nebraska Press, 1983). The examination of the

Crow adaptation to the destruction of their culture comes from Jonathan Lear's book *Radical Hope: Ethics in the Face of Cultural Devastation* (Harvard University Press, 2006). For a full discussion of the plight of indigenous peoples, see John Bodley's book *The Victims of Progress* (Mayfield, 1999) and *Indigenous Peoples, Ethnic Groups, and the State* by David Maybury-Lewis (Allyn & Bacon, 1997).

Case Study in Doing Anthropology #2: Doing Development

In addition to material from Alexander M. Ervin's book *Applied Anthropology: Tools and Perspectives for Contemporary Practice* (Allyn & Bacon, 2005) and Margaret A. Gwynne's book *Applied Anthropology: A Career-Oriented Approach* (Allyn & Bacon, 2003), this section draws on Ronald Nigh's article "Animal Agriculture for the Reforestation of Degraded Tropical Rainforests" in *Culture and Agriculture*, vol. 51/52 (1995), pp. 2–5, and James C. Scott's superb critical analysis of large-scale state projects in *Seeing Like a State: How Human Schemes to Improve the Human Condition Have Failed* (Yale University Press, 1998).

3

GLOBALIZATION, NEOLIBERALISM, AND THE NATION-STATE

PROBLEM 3: WHAT IS GLOBALIZATION, AND WHAT DOES IT HAVE TO DO WITH ME?

> *The incredible concentration of wealth and power that now exists in the upper echelons of capitalism have not been seen since the 1920s. The flows of tribute into the world's major financial centres have been astonishing. What, however, is even more astonishing is the habit of treating all of this as a mere and in some instances even unfortunate byproduct of neoliberalization. The very idea that this might be—just might be—the fundamental core of what neoliberalism has been about all along appears unthinkable.*
>
> —**David Harvey**

INTRODUCTION

My T-Shirt

In 2006, economist Pietra Rivoli walked into a Walgreens drugstore in Fort Lauderdale, Florida, and bought a T-shirt. That year, she had attended a student demonstration at Georgetown University, where she taught. Students had occupied administrative offices to protest what they thought were unfair policies by such multilateral institutions as the World Trade Organization (WTO), the International Monetary Fund (IMF), and the World Bank and their impact on workers and the environment all over the world. They were protesting what is commonly termed *globalization*.

As an economist, Rivoli assumed that globalization was a good thing—that the increased manufacture and sale of commodities, such as T-shirts, were helping create jobs in poor countries as well as supplying inexpensive goods to consumers. To satisfy herself of the benefits of trade, she wanted to trace the chain of production and distribution of her T-shirt from the growing of the cotton to its delivery at Walgreens. In other words, she wanted to examine what Igor Kopytoff calls the biography of a commodity and discover its social, economic, and political impacts.

She began by locating the company that printed and distributed the T-shirt—Sherry Manufacturing of Fort Lauderdale—which, she found, had purchased it from China—one of about 25 million cotton T-shirts shipped from China that year. Rivoli then traveled to China to visit the factory that assembled the T-shirt, then the place where the fabric was knit, and finally the factory where the yarn was spun out of raw cotton. The cotton itself, she discovered to her surprise, was grown in Lubbock County, Texas. The question Rivoli asked is, what can a cotton T-shirt purchased in a Fort Lauderdale drugstore, printed and distributed by a Florida textile manufacturer, assembled, sewn, and spun in Chinese factories out of cotton grown in Texas tell us about globalization and our role in it?

The T-shirt purchased by Rivoli was an infinitesimal fraction of what people all over the world consumed on that day or any other day. All over

College students at SUNY at Plattsburgh model their distinctive T-Shirts.

the world each year, people spend more than $20 trillion on goods and services—up from $4.8 trillion in 1960. Almost a billion and a half households in the world have a TV, and each year, some 41 billion passenger vehicles roll off the assembly lines, adding to the already 531 million vehicles on the road. Consumers spend some $35 billion a year on bottled water. Of course, this consumption is highly skewed toward the well off. Some 20% of the population, living in the richest countries of the world, account for 86% of total private consumption; the poorest 20% of the world's population account for only 1.3% of consumption. Two obvious questions are "Why do we spend so much, and what impact does this have on our lives?" We obviously enjoy buying stuff; shopping has become a major leisure time activity and even a form of therapy. Some people suggest that wanting things is natural, although as anthropologists, we know of many societies in which the accumulation of goods is discouraged rather than encouraged. If surveys are accurate, people—at least in the United States—were happier in the 1950s consuming about one-quarter of what they consume today. In 1946, the United States topped the list of the four wealthiest countries in the world as the happiest. By 1976, the United States ranked 8th among 11 nations, and by 1986, it ranked 10th among 23 nations—some of them from the Third World. There has also been a steady decrease in the percentage of Americans who say that their marriages are happy, that they enjoy their jobs, and that they take pleasure in where they live.

But we seem to take for granted that more is better and that it is somehow "natural" for people to want more and more stuff. The question is also important because, as research suggests, we are literally consuming our planet and ourselves to death: global warming, industrial pollution, the rapid decrease of clean water, and the piling up of waste are clearly major problems linked to our consumption habits.

To begin to understand how and why human beings have reached levels of consumption that threaten their existence, we need to ask at least five questions. First, how do we define happiness and well-being? All societies have conceptions of the good life; as we mentioned in Chapter 2, for the Crow, it was being able to hunt for buffalo and raid their enemies for horses. For other societies, it was the successful growing of certain crops; in others, it was the ability to give gifts to others. In contemporary society, it is the ability to make and spend money. How did this happen, and what are its consequences?

Second, to attain this good life means that the amount of goods and services into which we convert our money must continually grow. Where does this growth come from?

Third, few societies in the history of the world have been as successful at economic growth as contemporary market economies. What sort of policies and philosophies have made them so successful at maintaining perpetual economic growth?

Fourth, the modern nation-state is instrumental in the workings of the modern economy. What is the role of the nation-state, and how does it assist the growth of the economy?

Finally, we need to ask why do economies occasionally collapse?

QUESTIONS

3.1   How do we define happiness and well-being?
3.2   Where does the wealth needed to sustain growth come from?
3.3   What kind of economic system is necessary to sustain growth?
3.4   What is the role of the nation-state in sustaining growth?
3.5   Why do economies collapse?

Case Study in Doing Anthropology #3: Anthropology and Public Policy

QUESTION 3.1   *How Do We Define Happiness and Well-Being?*

Money, Wealth, and Well-Being

Every culture has its distinct material symbol or activity that defines for its members what is most important in life and what is needed for well-being and happiness. The Trobriand Islanders engaged in the accumulation of yams and the ritual exchange of shell necklaces and bracelets and the ancient Aztecs of Mexico in human sacrifice. The Dogon of West Africa defined their existence through art and the Balinese of Indonesia through drama and music. For the indigenous peoples of the American Plains, the key element of cultural life was the buffalo and, after European contact, the horse, warfare, and raiding. For contemporary society, the key is money. Money, as anthropologist Jack Weatherford notes, defines relationships, not only between buyers and sellers in the marketplace or between employers or laborers in the workplace but also between parent and child, among neighbors, between politicians and their constituents, and between friends. "Other than love and fear," writes economist Robert Guttmann (1994, p. xvii), "there is probably no more powerful motivating force in our lives than money."

But in other times and places, not everyone wanted money. Instead, people desired salvation, strength, adventure, or power. Even in other societies in which money is used, it is often viewed with suspicion and as a threat to the social order. Monetary relations, as opposed to relations of kinship or friendship, are viewed as impersonal and socially inconsequential. In coastal Malay fishing villages, men and women occupy different spheres of the economy. Men work on fishing boats for wages; women maintain the households, where everything is shared among members. Fishing crews are composed of people unrelated by kinship and tied together by commercial relations; households are composed of family members—sons, daughters, in-laws, or extended family members. Members of fishing crews are not related by kinship—largely because of a fear that if they were related, any conflict among crew members would spread among kin. Household work groups are composed of relatives who work together and share what they produce, and rarely is money exchanged. Because money is associated with the commercial sphere of fishing, its presence in the household could threaten the social bonds of kinship and is consequently dangerous. Thus, when men earn money, they immediately give it to their wives to absorb into the household, where everything is shared. The money is, in effect, cleansed of its association with the world of impersonal commercial relations; as anthropologist Janet E. Carsten notes, it is in effect "cooked" in the household and made acceptable.

Anthropological accounts are filled with instances such as this, where money is viewed as dangerous and threatening and has to be somehow cleansed of its association with the world of the impersonal market exchange. Even in advanced market economies such as ours, we make a distinction between relations characterized by monetary exchanges on the one hand and relations defined by kinship or friendship on the other. When we buy something at a store, our relationship to the person or persons we are buying from (or selling to) begins and ends with the market transaction, as opposed to, say, kin relations, which are permanent and enduring. There is a difference in your relationship to a friend who helps you move furniture as opposed to someone you hire to help. In our society, gifts have to be somehow cleansed of their association with the commercial world before they are presented by such means as wrapping them (as we will see in Question 6.4). Thus, all societies seem to make a distinction between spheres of exchange that involve long-standing intimate relations and spheres of exchange that are short-term, based on commercial relations, and defined by the use of money.

One reason that money is so important to us is that it is often the only thing we can use to get what we want or need. In Malay villages you could depend on kin or friends to provide you with what you needed, and even in our society, some things are available without money. But as we shall see, for our economy to function, things provided to us by family and friends are constantly diminishing as more and more of our needs are met only by the market.

We have a "market economy." Markets are very old; over the past 5,000 to 10,000 years, markets have existed for people to take goods and sell them to whoever needed them. Today, of course, the world is a market, and you can buy whatever you want or need without ever leaving your computer. However, as societies have become more complex and as economic activities have become more central to our lives, more and more of life's necessities as well as luxuries are available only through the market. Few of us grow our own food; we have to buy it. Few of us build our own shelter; we must purchase or rent it from whoever built or owns it. Few of us make our own clothes; again, to obtain them, we have to buy them with money. Thus, without money, we could barely survive. And, of course, we must work to obtain it. But what exactly is money, and where does it come from?

A Brief History of Money

Money, among other things, is a medium of exchange; that is, it is recognized by people as something to give or accept in exchange for other things. The exchange of goods, of course, does not necessarily require a medium of exchange. Often, people share items or give things as gifts. But societies throughout the world have made use of such objects as shells, furs, or other items of value as a medium of exchange. Precious metals were used as objects of exchange in Mesopotamia (roughly present-day Iraq) 5,000 years ago, and the use of coins dates back to the seventh century B.C. This was called **commodity money** because the substance had some value in itself and could be used for some practical purpose, such as manufacturing jewelry. China in the 12th century first used paper money, or "exchange" or "demand" notes, whose use spread to Europe some 200 to 300 years later. Thus, a trader in Venice might buy textiles from someone in Bruges and pay with a paper note backed by gold that the seller could retrieve from a third party. The issuing of paper money was a major step because it meant that the amount of money that could be created was theoretically unlimited; you just needed more paper. However, in practice, the printing of paper money was limited because people would not accept it unless it was backed by some precious metal—usually gold or silver—that people could retrieve with the paper.

However, there were some problems with commodity money; for example, the commodity being used (such as gold or silver) might be worth more in one area than another. And anyone could produce it; in the 19th century in the United States, there were some 30,000 different currencies in circulation. And banks or other institutions often lent out far more money than they had gold or silver on hand. That worked fine as long as everyone did not demand their gold or silver at once. But if they did, banks failed, and people lost faith in paper money.

The U.S. government addressed some of these problems by creating the Federal Reserve Bank in 1913 to control and stabilize the money supply and regulate the amount of gold banks were required to keep on hand to meet demand—generally equal to 10% of the deposits they held. That still allowed banks and other lending institutions to lend out and, in effect, create nine dollars of new money for every dollar deposited. But the Federal Reserve could still not address the limitations imposed on economic growth by tying money to a fixed commodity, such as gold. Solving that problem required two government decrees.

First, in 1931, the U.S. government announced that it would no longer allow citizens to convert their paper money into gold, although the value of money was still tied to the value of gold, and exchanges with foreign governments still occurred in gold. Then, in 1971, the U.S. government declared that its currency would no longer be backed by gold—or anything else for that matter. This marked the final shift from commodity money to **fiat money** or **credit money**—paper that was used as evidence of a claim to economic value but that, legally, was not redeemable for anything.

As might be expected, with dollars backed by nothing, the money supply could grow rapidly as banks and other financial institutions lent out more and more. We had entered the era of "debt" or "credit" money, when the only thing that limited the supply of money was the amount that governments and financial institutions could lend out. Thus, each time you charge something on a credit card, you have created debt money; you have injected money into the economy that you must now earn to repay—with interest. By 2003, credit card holders in the United States had created some $60 billion (an average of more than $8,000 a person), which, of course, they had to repay; and because only about half of credit card users pay the full amount owed, they had to repay it with interest.

When we think of money, we think of bills and coins. But that is only a small part (5 to 10%) of the money supply. The rest exists only as figures on paper (or in computers) in banks and in the records of other financial institutions. Credit money, for example, is simply that; it represents a promise by the borrower of money to repay it at some future date. Table 3.1 and Figure 3.1 show the kinds of money—or money stocks—in circulation in the United States, along with their growth since 1959.

As you can see, the money supply in 2009 was 35 times larger than it was in 1959. And this highlights a key consequence of debt money: Because money is created as debt and because debt requires repayment with interest, every dollar created through debt must generate itself and the additional interest on the debt, whether that is 5, 10, 20%, or more. Thus, if the lenders of money

 TABLE 3.1   INCREASE IN U.S. MONEY SUPPLY FROM 1959 TO 2009 IN BILLIONS

Years	Currency	M1	M2	M3	Non-M2 M3	% Change in M3
1959–1970	416.1	1959.1	5074.2	5256.1	202	-------
1971–1980	731.6	2910.3	10252.8	11905.2	1652.6	127%
1981–1990	1661.3	6102.2	24088.3	31002.9	6916.4	160%
1991–2000	3681.8	10550.1	37696.1	49151.9	11428.7	59%
2001–2009	6175	11896	58268.5	140701.3[1]	31993.3[2]	186%

M1 = Currency, traveler's checks, demand deposits, and other checkable deposits
M2 = M1, retail MMMFs, savings, and small time deposits
M3 = M1, M2, large time deposits, RPS, Eurodollars, and institutional money funds (http://www.federalreserve.gov/releases/h6/hist/h6histb.txt)

[1]The Federal Reserve stopped publishing M3 data in 2006. The data from 2006 to 2009 is estimated with information available at http://www.shadowstats.com/alternate_data.
[2]This includes estimated data from 2006 to 2009.

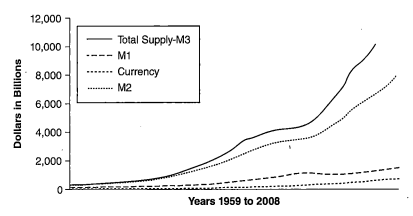

FIGURE 3.1 U.S. MONEY SUPPLY BY TYPE, 1959–2008

are to collect their interest, the money supply must grow. Put another way, once an economy allows people or institutions to make money with money—through loans at interest or through other financial instruments—perpetual economic growth becomes a necessity. If economic growth falls below a critical level (generally less than 3%) or, worse yet, declines, borrowers are unable to repay their debts, lenders cannot collect the principal or interest on their loans, banks and businesses fail, people lose their jobs, government revenue collections decline, and, ultimately, if the decline continues, the economy—and the society built upon it—collapses.

The Society of Perpetual Growth

While money is a source of individual well-being, we also have a measure of national well-being—something we call the **gross domestic product (GDP)**. The GDP is the total of goods and services bought and sold each year. For example, in 2007, the U.S. GDP was almost $14 trillion, and in Canada, it was more than $1.2 trillion. The world has been extremely successful at achieving economic growth, particularly in the past 200 years (see Figure 3.2).

Healthy economies grow at a rate of at least 3% a year, and therein lies a problem. If an economy declines for six months or more, it slides into a recession; anything more than that and an economy could be headed for catastrophe. Various countries over the past two decades, including Indonesia, Argentina, Russia, and Mexico, have experienced major economic crises that rivaled the experiences of the economic depression of the 1930s. But although it is necessary, perpetual economic growth is not an easy thing to achieve. China's economy, for example, has been growing at rates of 9–10% a year; to accomplish this growth, China in 2007 earned some $1.2 trillion from exports—an increase of 25% over the previous year. But China must continue to increase its exports and ship even more T-shirts, along with all the other commodities, in order to maintain an acceptable level of growth.

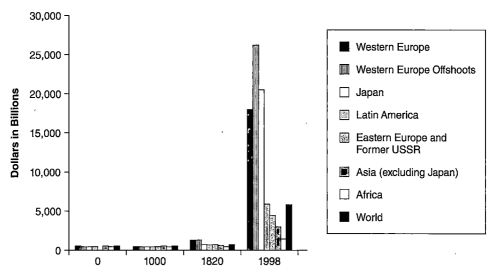

FIGURE 3.2 PER CAPITA GDP, 0–1998 A.D., BY REGIONS

Source: Data from Angus Maddison, *The World Economy: A Millennial Perspective* (Development Centre of the Organisation for Economic Co-Operation and Development, 2003).

To put perpetual growth into personal terms, imagine that in the year 2005, you were earning and spending $30,000 a year (or that some corporation earned $300 million). Because a growth rate of about 3% a year is necessary to maintain a healthy economy, by 2010, you (or our imaginary corporation) would have earned and spent $34,855 (more than $348 million), and by 2030, you must be earning and spending $63,507 ($635 million). If we factor in an inflation rate or additional growth of 3% on top of our necessary growth rate, the figures are even higher (see Table 3.2).

It would be an easy thing, of course, to just keep creating more and more money by giving more and more loans. The problem is that because money

TABLE 3.2	REQUIRED GROWTH IN INCOME AND SPENDING OVER A 25-YEAR PERIOD			
Year	Required Income Growth at 3% (with 0 inflation)		Required Income Growth at 6% (with 0 inflation) or Income Growth at 3% and Inflation at 3%	
	Individual	Corporate	Individual	Corporate
2005	$30,000	$300,000,000	$30,000	$300,000,000
2010	34,855	348,550,000	40,494	404,940,000
2015	40,495	404,950,000	54,661	546,661,000
2020	47,048	470,048,000	73,783	737,830,000
2030	63,507	635,070,000	134,434	1,344,340,000

itself is "worthless"—backed by nothing but the government's decree that it be accepted in payment for goods, services, and debt—to have worth, it must be converted into something of value: a house, a car, a pair of shoes, medical treatment, and so on. In other words, to keep the money supply growing, there has to be more and more stuff to buy. Furthermore, if the amount of money increases faster than the increase in stuff, people will pay more and more for whatever is available and you create inflation, where the value of money decreases. That is not necessarily a bad thing for most people, particularly those in debt; inflation means that the dollars with which you repay debts are worth less than when you borrowed them. On the other hand, people who are collecting debts—particularly banks and other financial institutions—do not like inflation because it makes the dollars they collect worth less than the dollars they lent out. Governments work very hard to minimize inflation.

This brief introduction to the origins and use of money and its growth should begin to give you a basic idea of the nature of the modern economy. But a problem remains. We mentioned that the economy must grow at a rate of at least 3% a year, that this requires a steady growth in the money supply, and that money itself is worthless until it can be turned into some commodity, such as T-shirts, shoes, or medical fees. Thus, not only must the money supply increase but so must the stuff that money can buy. The question, then, is where does all this perpetually growing stuff come from?

QUESTION 3.2   *Where Does the Wealth Needed to Sustain Growth Come From?*

Producing the goods and services that we acquire with money is a complex undertaking; it requires the mines, forests, factories, roads, financial institutions, legal institutions, educational centers, retail outlets, and much more that make up the productive economy. However, at another level, the process of producing stuff is a relatively simple one: We convert some nonmonetary resource—forests, lakes, music, family functions, collectively held land—directly or indirectly into money. That is, people find ways to make some good or service available on the market. In other words, we keep the economy going by a constant process of **capital conversion**.

Capital Conversion

There is a basic rule involved in maintaining economic growth: The more things people must pay for, the more the economy grows. For example, if you do your friend a favor by driving her to the store, you have advanced your friendship, but the service you provide does nothing for the economy (other than using gasoline and helping your friend buy something); on the other hand, if you charge her (and report the charge on your taxes), you have added to the nation's GDP. In a similar sense, the greater the number of goods and services that can be obtained only by purchasing them, the better it is for economic growth. This means that some things that we would not consider desirable—a divorce, an oil spill, an illness, or a natural disaster—are economically positive events because they result in more money being spent. Other things that we might think are desirable, such as sharing your car or your lawn mower, are negative because by allowing someone to use something without paying for it, you hinder economic growth.

Societies vary considerably in terms of what can be obtained from the market—that is, what can be bought and sold—and what is available outside the market. We can imagine two extremes: a "perfectly commoditized world" in which everything is available only on the market and you have to buy everything (air, space on the sidewalk, police protection, scenic views, etc.) and a world in which nothing is commoditized. In small-scale societies, particularly those without money, most needs were met by members supplying them to others. Food was hunted, gathered, or grown and shared within small or large family groups. Natural resources were owned collectively by the group, although some members may have been given preferential access. Medicinal plants were available to all. Even when money entered the economy of these societies, most goods and services remained outside the market.

But for an economy to grow, there has to be a constant transfer of things and activities into the monetary sphere. What do we obtain in life without money? Parental love, a companion's devotion, friendship, citizenship, voting rights, a sunset, and so on. This does not mean that there is not a constant attempt to commodify these things; for example, advertising agencies employ some of the most creative minds in the world to entice people to equate friendship with beer or love with diamonds. The travel industry would like you to believe that a sunset can only be enjoyed from the bow of a cruise ship or from some far-off beach. In Japan, lonely businessmen or elderly people can contact Rent-a-Family and have actors, including children, come to their hotel or home for a family meal—complete with family conversation; the company has a waiting list of 1,000.[1] The music industry has constantly appropriated and exploited grassroots culture and creativity by converting music forms from folk culture into forms that are sold to the public.

In the process of capital conversion lies the genius of the modern market economy. Through the operation of a myriad of rules, regulations, values, and laws, the modern economy encourages the conversion of items and activities that have no intrinsic monetary worth but are nevertheless valuable and even necessary in other ways into items and activities that can only be bought and sold in the marketplace (see Figure 3.3).

For example, whenever we convert some part of the natural environment—forests, mountains, animals, fish—into a commodity to be sold and bought, we have converted natural capital into money. Forests, regardless of their natural benefits, are monetarily worthless until they enter the market as wood products, tourist destinations, or the like.

---

[1]http://www.context.org/ICLIB/IC37/Bush2.htm; see also http://www.jetro.org/content/462/limit/1/limitstart/3.

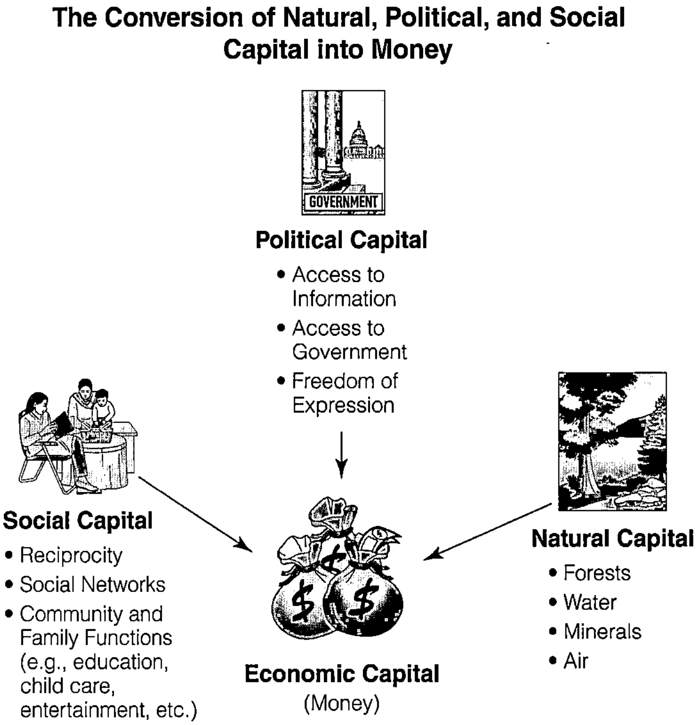

The Conversion of Natural, Political, and Social Capital into Money

Political Capital
- Access to Information
- Access to Government
- Freedom of Expression

Social Capital
- Reciprocity
- Social Networks
- Community and Family Functions (e.g., education, child care, entertainment, etc.)

Economic Capital
(Money)

Natural Capital
- Forests
- Water
- Minerals
- Air

FIGURE 3.3 THE CONVERSION OF NATURAL, POLITICAL, AND SOCIAL CAPITAL INTO MONEY

Water is something we think of as a necessity available to everyone, but today, more and more of our water supply is being commodified. Globally, only 10% of water usage goes to households; the other 90% is used by industry—65% of that for agriculture and meat production. The industrial usage is good for the GDP but not for the billion or more people who lack access to fresh drinking water. In the interests of economic growth, industry expects to double its consumption of freshwater in the next 25 years, leaving about two-thirds of the world's population with a severe water shortage.

We also convert our **political capital**—the freedom we have to regulate our own lives and the access we have to societal leaders and decision-makers—into money. For example, the need to maintain economic growth has resulted in the formation of powerful entities, such as multinational corporations with enormous economic and political power. CEOs can assign or withdraw resources at will, open and close plants, change product lines, or lay off workers with no recourse by persons or communities that are affected. In the interests of increasing GNP, the modern economy has transferred planning functions from governments accountable to their citizens to corporations accountable only to their shareholders.

Currently, over 40% of the richest institutional entities in the world are transnational corporations (see Table 3.3). One consequence of this

TABLE 3.3 THE TOP 100 GLOBAL FINANCIAL ENTITIES, 2006–2007

Rank	Country or Company	GDP/Revenue in Billions	Rank	Country or Company	GDP/Revenue in Billions
1	United States	12980	51	General Motors	192.6
2	China	10000	52	Chevron	189.5
3	Japan	4220	53	Nigeria	188.5
4	India	4042	54	DaimlerChrysler	186.1
5	Germany	2585	55	Toyota Motor	185.8
6	United Kingdom	1903	56	Peru	181.8
7	France	1871	57	Ford Motor	177.21
8	Italy	1727	58	Ireland	177.2
9	Russia	1723	59	Venezuela	176.4
10	Brazil	1616	60	Hungary	172.7
11	Korea, South	1180	61	Finland	171.7
12	Canada	1165	62	ConocoPhillips	166.7
13	Mexico	1134	63	Israel	166.3
14	Spain	1070	64	General Electric	157.2
15	Indonesia	935	65	Total	152.4
16	Taiwan	668.3	66	Morocco	147
17	Australia	666.3	67	Kazakhstan	138.7
18	Turkey	627.2	68	Singapore	138.6
19	Iran	610.4	69	ING Group	138.2
20	Argentina	599.1	70	Citigroup	131.0
21	Thailand	585.9	71	AXA	129.8
22	South Africa	576.4	72	United Arab Emirates	129.4
23	Poland	542.6	73	Allianz	121.4
24	Netherlands	512	74	Volkswagen	118.4
25	Philippines	443.1	75	Fortis	112.4
26	Pakistan	427.3	76	Crédit Agricole	110.8
27	Saudi Arabia	374	77	American Intl. Group	108.9
28	Colombia	366.7	78	New Zealand	106
29	Ukraine	355.8	79	Assicurazioni Generali	101.4
30	Exxon Mobil	339.9	80	Siemens	100.1
31	Bangladesh	330.8	81	Sinopec	98.8
32	Belgium	330.4	82	Slovakia	96.3
33	Egypt	328.1	83	Nippon Telegraph & Telephone	94.9
34	Wal-Mart Stores	315.7	84	Carrefour	94.5
35	Malaysia	308.8	85	HSBC Holdings	93.5
36	Royal Dutch Shell	306.7	86	ENI	92.6
37	Sweden	285.1	87	Aviva	92.6
38	Austria	279.5	88	Intl. Business Machines	91.1
39	BP	267.6	89	McKesson	88.0
40	Vietnam	258.6	90	Honda Motor	87.5
41	Algeria	253.4	91	State Grid	87
42	Hong Kong	253.1	92	Hewlett-Packard	86.7
43	Switzerland	252.9	93	BNP Paribas	85.7
44	Greece	251.7	94	PDVSA	85.6
45	Czech Republic	221.4	95	UBS	84.7
46	Norway	207.3	96	Bank of America Corp.	84
47	Portugal	203.1	97	Hitachi	83.6
48	Chile	203	98	China National Petroleum	83.6
49	Denmark	198.5	99	Pemex	83.4
50	Romania	197.3	100	Nissan Motor	83.3

Source: Data for the top 100 countries is available at Index Mundi at http://www.indexmundi.com/g/r.aspx?T=100&v=65 and the top 100 corporations at CNN Money at http://money.cnn.com/magazines/fortune/global500/2006/full_list.

development is that corporate interests, as opposed to human interests, dominate the policy agendas of nation-states and the international agencies that they create, support, and control.

Finally, economic growth and development also require the expenditure of social capital. **Social capital** refers to connections among individuals—social networks and the norms of reciprocity and trustworthiness that arise from them. Social capital resides in solidarities—people working together for the common good.

Social capital can improve our lives by making people aware of how our fates are linked while building social networks that help people fulfill individual goals. In U.S. communities that are rich in social capital, persons serve in local organizations, attend public meetings, vote, spend time working on community projects, visit friends frequently, entertain at home, and feel that "most people can be trusted" or agree with the statement that "most people are honest."

In his book *Bowling Alone*, Robert Putnam traces the history of social capital in America and concludes that, "By virtually every conceivable measure, social capital has eroded steadily and sometimes dramatically over the past two generations." Putnam attributes the decline of social capital to four factors. About half of the decline, he says, is a result of the slow, steady replacement of a long "civic generation" by a generation of their less involved children and grandchildren. He attributes another quarter to the advent of electronic entertainment—particularly television. The rest of the decline he attributes to time and money pressures on two-career families and the increase of suburban sprawl that creates communities with no centers.

It is significant, of course, that most of the factors Putnam identifies as contributing to the decline of social capital also contribute to economic growth. That is, we have converted social capital into economic capital by enacting rules and regulations that encourage suburban sprawl that, while reducing contact among people, creates new and larger homes, more expenditures on household items, and more road and bridge construction while creating a dependence on automobiles and all the expenses they involve. Two-income families exchange time that might be spent in family activities for increased monetary exchanges and income, while television watching, which further reduces family interaction, exposes people to thousands of hours of advertisements and media images that create new consumer needs and offer happiness through goods. It is noteworthy perhaps that in an earlier study, Putnam named television as the main culprit in the decline of American social capital.

To a great extent, the economic growth in core countries of the past 50 years has been produced by transferring social capital–rich functions, such as child care, food preparation, health care, entertainment, and maintenance of physical security, from households or communities—where they did not count in GDP figures—to the market—where they do count. The acceleration of the conversion of social capital into money over the past few centuries has completely transformed our social environments. When families gathered to collect food or slaughter game or livestock, multiple social interactions ensued. In the modern economy, those interactions are replaced by a simple exchange of money at the grocery checkout counter or interaction with an electronic checkout machine.

Converting nonmonetary capital into money, then, is essential for maintaining our economic system. But as economists have noted, the wealthier a country becomes, the harder it is to maintain growth. Consequently, economic policymakers must come up with more and more ways to enhance capital conversion. Next, then, let us examine how that has been done historically.

QUESTION 3.3   *What Kind of Economic System Is Necessary to Sustain Growth?*

Economic systems are about the distribution of goods and services—that is, the rules, mechanisms, institutions, and systems of relations through which people get what they need and want. This process can be as simple as the borrowing of a cup of sugar or a pair of shoes or as complex as the production, distribution, consumption, and disposal of such goods as automobiles, houses, or military weapons. Our modern economy is made up of a global market. As we mentioned, markets go back thousands of years. Communities would set up areas where merchants, farmers, and artisans could bring their goods or services for sale or barter. The farmers' markets that dot contemporary communities are examples of such places. But as new modes of transportation and manufacture developed, markets were no longer only specific places to trade but whole networks whereby silk manufactured in China could be sold in Paris or textiles manufactured in Benin sold in Constantinople. At some point, generally some 200 to 300 years ago, technological changes instigated what economist Karl Polanyi termed "the great transformation," or the Industrial Revolution.

"The Great Transformation"

One of the major questions regarding the maintenance of economic growth is the role of government. States have always played a major role in the economy. But some 18th-century economists argued that the state should play as small a role in the economy as possible. Ideally, people will supply only those goods and services for which there are demands, and generally, a balance will be established between what is demanded and what is supplied. In his classic work *The Wealth of Nations* (1776), Adam Smith saw the workings of the market as an "invisible hand," by which a benevolent God administered a universe in which human happiness was maximized—an ideal system whereby each person, seeking his or her own ends, would contribute to the betterment of society as a whole. Thus, by seeking money and wealth, each person would work toward supplying what others needed or demanded. For Smith, the market represented a utopian vision in which wealth was perpetually created for the benefit of all.

The problem was that an unregulated market, in which the generation of wealth is the only goal, resulted in abysmal working conditions, environmental degradation, and wild economic fluctuations that saw people suddenly plunged into poverty. In his book *The Great Transformation*, Polanyi addressed the tension between the need to allow the market—that is, the mechanisms for buying and selling—to operate freely without government interference and the need to somehow minimize the social and natural damages inflicted by the market. Allowed to operate unhindered, Polanyi suggested, the market would soon destroy the very foundations of society. It would disrupt social relations through the operation of the labor market; it would destroy the environment; it would reduce freedoms. On the other hand, regulating the market with laws regulating pollution, working conditions, and land use could destroy the market. It is the working out of this dilemma that Polanyi saw as one of the major driving forces of history since the early 19th century.

Governments have tried to maintain a balance, then, between regulation and noninterference in the workings of the market. At one extreme were the almost completely state-run economies of such socialist countries the Soviet Union, Cuba, and pre-1980 China. At the other extreme were capitalist economies, such as that of the United States, Australia, and most of Western Europe. But rarely were even the most capitalist economies free of significant state involvement, and the tension between the state and the market that Polanyi wrote of resulted in ebbs and flows of regulation.

For example, in late 19th-century America, market forces were allowed relatively free rein. It was the era of the so-called "robber barons"—such industrialists as John D. Rockefeller and Andrew Carnegie, who accumulated vast fortunes. Massive labor abuse resulted in labor wars, as states called out militias to break strikes. Almost anything could be sold; there was no government inspection of food or regulation of drugs, and there was no income tax. The backlash against market abuses led to increased state involvement in the economy in the form of labor laws, food laws, taxation, and state support of industries or sectors of the economy. State involvement in the economy grew after the world economic depression of the 1930s, when economic growth was negative.

British economist John Maynard Keynes advocated a policy of using government to regulate the economy through its spending, tax policies, interest rates, and so on. Government involvement in the economy, support of labor unions, and a progressive tax system in which marginal tax rates ranged as high as 90% resulted in rapid economic growth in the United States and Canada through the 1960s.

Then, in the 1970s, there was a period of slow economic growth and resulting pressure to change economic policies. Economists began to abandon Keynesian economic philosophy for one that argued for the withdrawal of the state from any involvement in regulating the economy, leaving as much as possible to the market. This economic philosophy—known as **neoliberalism**—is often synonymous with "globalization." Because the application of neoliberal principles will largely determine your career, where and how you get your jobs, and what goods and services you can acquire for what price—not to mention the natural, political, and social environment in which you live—it is useful to understand where it came from and what it is trying to accomplish.

The Emergence of Neoliberalism

Neoliberalism emerged with a group of economists, historians, and philosophers, including Ludwig von Mises, Milton Friedman, and Karl Popper, who gathered around political philosopher Friedrich von Hayek to create the Mont Pelerin Society (named after the Swiss spa at which they first met in 1947). Prompted by a concern over the spread of totalitarian societies and religious and racial intolerance, they argued that totalitarian philosophies not only endangered freedom but also threatened the belief in private property and the free market—without which, they argued, freedom cannot be preserved. They called themselves "liberals" because they adhered to ideals of freedom and "neo" because they adhered to neoclassical economic theory that was opposed to Keynesian economics and the idea of state involvement in the economy. Well-being, neoliberals argued, is best served by liberating individual entrepreneurs to operate in a framework of strong property rights, free markets, and free trade. The role of the state should be limited to safeguarding the integrity of money and maintaining military, police, and legal structures to secure property rights and protect markets. And when necessary, states should function to open markets in such areas as education, water, land, health care, and social security. Other than that, state intervention should be kept to a minimum because states can never have enough information to second-guess markets on matters such as prices and because state involvement allows special groups, such as unions, environmentalists, and trade groups, to distort the operation of the market. Neoliberals advocate privatizing any state-run activities, reducing the influence of solidarities, such as unions, and removing any and virtually all restrictions on business and finance.

Through the 1960s, few people were interested in neoliberalism; the economies of the major industrial nations, assisted by the state, were growing rapidly, and there was little interest in abandoning the Keynesian policies credited with growth. But in the 1970s, for various reasons, global economies began to stagnate, and in some countries, such as the United States, inflation became a major problem—so much so that in 1979, President Jimmy Carter went on television to appeal to Americans to stop driving up prices by spending so much!

One of the first applications of neoliberalism was in New York City in the 1970s. By the early 1970s, industry was leaving New York (and the United States), and people who could afford new housing were moving to the suburbs. This left the city with a diminished tax base and an impoverished and socially restive inner city—what became known as the "urban crisis." The initial solution was typical Keynesian economics: Expand public employment and public assistance. But when President Richard Nixon declared the urban crisis over in the early 1970s, he also reduced federal aid to the city. As the economic slowdown of the 1970s hit the city—combined with a reduced tax base and reduced federal aid—New York City faced bankruptcy. Financial institutions were unwilling to renegotiate the city's debts unless it met strict conditions, which included implementing wage and hiring freezes, cutting back spending on education, welfare, public health, and transport, and implementing user fees, such as tuition at the City University of New York (CUNY). They also required unions to put their pension funds in city bonds, which meant that if the city went bankrupt, workers would lose their pensions. The overall result was a diminished standard of living for New Yorkers—particularly the poor. But ultimately, the city became financially solvent.

New York City represented to neoliberals what could be done by imposing economic reform during a financial crisis or any other crisis. And it soon became the pattern with countries in trouble. The economic stagnation of the 1970s impacted heavily on Third World countries that, with the encouragement of banks, had borrowed heavily but could no longer repay their debts. As a condition for restructuring their loans, such multilateral institutions as the World Bank and the IMF imposed neoliberal economic policies on these countries. These policies included selling state-run enterprises to private buyers and reducing the value of their currency, making goods produced in the country cheaper for foreign buyers (thus encouraging exports) and making foreign (as well as domestic) goods more expensive for citizens (thus discouraging imports). These conditions also included reducing state funding for education, welfare, and health and imposing user fees for such things as attending school. David Harvey notes that few so-called developing countries escaped a debt crisis and the imposition of neoliberal economic policies. As a result, in repaying their debts and the interest on those debts, nations of the Third World have sent more than $4.6 trillion to creditors in wealthy countries, resulting, as financier George Stiglitz put it, in poor countries subsidizing the richest.

Market Externalization

Removing government involvement in the economy is central to neoliberal economic philosophy; without such involvement, business can be more profitable, create more jobs, and so on. One way that less government involvement can help economic growth is by allowing costs that are involved in the production, distribution, consumption, and disposal of goods and services to be externalized. For example, when you purchase a car, you pay for the manufacturer's cost of producing it, the retailer's expenses, and their monetary profit. But you pay no direct cost for the pollution that the car produces. When you buy a computer in the United States, you pay for the cost of producing and selling it; you do not pay anything directly for the cost of disposing of the toxic waste contained in the computer (in the European Union, the cost of disposing of computers is built into the sale price). All along the commodity chains—from the production of goods to their transport to their sale and disposal—there are costs that are not included in the price that people pay.

To illustrate the cost of externalities, let us examine the automobile in the United States. There are about 250,000 automobiles in the United States. Sixty-five percent of all households have at least two cars, and in 2008, Americans traveled some 2.98 trillion miles by car—double the miles traveled in 1960. Apart from marriage, the family, and the home, a car is arguably the most important thing Americans will ever have. Of every $8 the U.S. government spends on transportation, only $1 is spent for public transportation (buses, trains, etc.) and the remainder on car-related needs (roads, bridges, parking, etc.). We drive 4.6 trillion miles a year (compared to 180 billion passenger miles for rail and bus travel). As a consumer item, the automobile is essential to the U.S. economy. Car manufacturing accounts for about 4% of the GDP, and by one estimate, one in 10 jobs is car related. Individually, on average, we will spend at least six years of our lives, or about 18½ hours a week, in cars.

The car is also essential in expressing the American values of self-reliance, freedom, individualism, and progress. Cars appeal to teenagers because they represent a break from having to depend on others, mostly parents, for transportation. For others, they represent freedom and the ability to get on the "open road" and experience new things. They express our individuality; we bond with our cars and purchase those that best express our identity and self-image. Forty-six percent of people in one survey agreed with the statement that their car reflected their personality. And with automakers claiming to make constant improvements, cars are a significant symbol of progress. Of course, car manufacturers use these values to advertise their products and promote sales.

The cost of an automobile ranges from a few hundred dollars for a used clunker to thousands for an average purchase or even hundreds of thousands for super-luxury models. But, of course, there are all kinds of hidden costs; that is, what we pay for the sticker price is just a small portion of what we and others pay in total, as Catherine Lutz and Anne Lutz Fernandez (2010) illustrate in their book *Carjacked: The Culture of the Automobile and Its Effects on Our Lives*.

First, of course, there are the addition costs required for us to actually use the car. There is the gasoline, which amounts, on average, to about $7,000 a year. There are insurance costs plus—if you received a loan to buy the car—the interest payments. Then, there is maintenance and other assorted costs. All in all, the average family will spend approximately $1,000,000 for purchasing and using their automobiles.

Next, there are the financial costs of automobile accidents—some $433 billion a year, including medical costs, property damage, and legal and rehabilitation services. One quarter of the costs are uninsured and fall on individuals. Then, there are the infrastructure costs—the cost for police, fire, and other responders.

The automobile, as Lutz and Lutz Fernandez point out, also intensifies social inequalities and all the financial and social costs inequality create. The automobile is responsible for moving wealth upward by discriminating against those who do not have or cannot afford cars, putting an unequal load on the

Car inspection laws, intended to ensure automobile safety, also create economic opportunities for stores to rent tires to people unable to afford them so that their cars can pass inspection.

poor in buying and maintaining a car and benefitting financially those with investment in cars. The poorer you are, the bigger the chunk the auto takes out of your income. Transportation costs in America take from 15 to 28% of the income of all but the richest 20% of the population—a percentage that increases as incomes decline. The lack of a car is a major reason for unemployment among blacks. A Brookings Institute study showed that if blacks owned cars at the same rate as whites, it would half the employment disparity between the groups. The poorer you are, the higher your interest on car loans and the more expensive your insurance. One survey in California revealed that African Americans with clean driving records were paying nearly $1,000 more a year than drivers with similar records living in white zip codes. Indicative of the disparity between rich and poor in car costs, there is the appearance of rent-a-tire stores for people whose cars need to pass state inspections.

Cars not only exaggerate class differences, but they also make us sick. They are at least partially responsible for the additional 24 pounds Americans, on average, have added since 1960—a weight gain that also results in car engines having to use an additional 39 million gallons (out of 359 million) a day to move us around. And as people get larger, they buy bigger cars. Cars encourage us to drive short distances, resulting in a 42% decline in trips on foot over the past 20 years. People who shift from cars to public transit are five pounds lighter than when they drove.

Aside from the weight gain, another negative health effect is that the chemicals used inside cars in the plastics and rubbers are responsible for making us sick. To prevent damage from "offgassing," as they call it, health experts recommend that people park in the shade, use UV filters, and drive with the windows open. Cars and trucks produce five primary groups of pollutants: carbon monoxide; nitrogen oxides; toxins, including benzene and volatile organic compounds, or VOCs; ground-level ozone; and fine particulate matter. The health effects of exposure to these substances include upper respiratory tract and eye irritation and infection, increased likelihood of heart disease, low birth weight, lung and other cancers, and asthma (Lutz and Fernandez, 2010 p. 167).

People living within 150 to 500 yards of major roads or even within a mile are at higher risk for childhood cancers, brain cancer, and leukemia. Children living near roads carrying 20,000 vehicles a day are six times more likely to get leukemia.

Children in some areas of Los Angeles lose 1% of their lung function each year. And, of course, these conditions mostly affect the poor. In all, 35,000 deaths each year can be attributed to the contributions cars make to air pollution.

Finally, there is the carnage on the highway. While automobiles are safer than they used to be (largely because of the institution of some government standards), people drive more. Consequently, the death and injury rates continue to climb. In 2007, 41,059 people were killed in car crashes in the United States—an average of 112 a day. Car crashes are the leading cause of death for all Americans 1–34 years old. About 2.5 million people suffered injuries in car accidents in 2007, and since 1899, 2.4 million Americans have died—more than all U.S. wars combined. The use of cell phones while driving makes accidents four times as likely. In 2003, 955 people were killed by people driving while using their cell phones. Perhaps because of an association of driving and masculinity, in 2005, 2,575 male teenagers died at the wheel compared to 892 female.

As Lutz and Lutz Fernandez point out, when death by car is so common and our chances of crashing are one in five and of being permanently disabled is one in 83, it is a wonder that we believe that our cars are safe.

These, then, are some of the negative externalities of the automobile—that is, the price not included in the sticker price of the car. To all these costs, of course, we must add the military costs and deaths of maintaining our access to relatively cheap oil supply. As Ivan Illich pointed out in *Tools of Conviviality*, all of this to travel 20 miles an hour faster than on a bicycle.

In brief, then, rarely do consumers pay the real costs of production and consumption. These costs are passed on to future generations or to people in other countries in the form of low wages, polluted environments, health risks, and the like. None of this would be possible without nation-states to enact and enforce rules and regulations that allow its citizens to pass on the real cost of things in the form of environmental damage, health risks, and poverty to people in other countries and to marginalized people in their own countries or

Exercise 3.3 ➤

CALCULATING THE REAL COST OF THINGS

Each morning, most students begin their day by brushing their teeth, washing their face, and using the toilet facilities. Then, perhaps, they have a glass of orange juice and maybe a cup of coffee. But what are the hidden costs of these activities? That is, what sort of environmental, health, and economic costs are involved in these activities that we do not pay for directly?

Activity or Product	**Hidden Cost**
Brushing teeth	
Flushing the toilet	
Orange juice	
Coffee	

to future generations. Therefore, we need to examine the role of the nation-state in sustaining growth.

What Is the Role of the Nation-State in Sustaining Growth?

While neoliberal philosophy is the driving force behind what we call globalization, there is a basic contradiction in how it is applied. The central idea behind neoliberalism is to keep governments from interfering in the functioning of the market, but the nation-state still plays a vital role in how the economy functions. To begin to analyze this, let us return to the T-shirt that Pietra Rivoli purchased in Fort Lauderdale and examine the role of the state in its travels around the world.

T-Shirt Travels

For the sake of illustrating how nation-states assist economic growth, let us focus only on the cotton in Rivoli's T-shirt. Cotton is a major global commodity. Millions of 500-pound bales travel the world's shipping lanes to be converted into cotton goods. One 500-pound bale will produce enough cotton lint for 215 pairs of jeans or 1,217 men's T-shirts. Much of that cotton, including that in Rivoli's T-shirt, is grown in Texas.

However, cotton is a labor intensive product. Why, then, do T-shirt makers in China, where labor costs are lower, use Texas cotton and not, say, Chinese cotton? Part of the answer to that question is that Texas cotton is embedded in a web of policies enacted by the nation-state to ensure the profits of Texas cotton growers. For example, the government has long paid various kinds of subsidies to cotton farmers, amounting to billions of dollars a year. Without these government payments, Texas cotton farmers could not make a profit. In 2002, for example, it cost a U.S. farmer 86 cents to produce a pound of cotton, which then sold for 37 cents a pound. However, Texas cotton farmers were able to make a profit because the difference between the actual cost to produce the cotton and the price that farmers sold it for was paid by U.S. taxpayers. From 1995 to 2003, the county in which the ranch that produced the cotton for Rivoli's T-shirt is located received $86 million in subsidies. Of course, by allowing cotton producers to sell their cotton for less, the taxpayer subsidy also reduced the price that Rivoli paid for her T-shirt.

The government also helps cotton farmers by regulating the labor market—that is, the price that farmers pay for workers. The regulation of the labor market for cotton workers, of course, began with the slave trade. By permitting the import and ownership of human beings, the nation-state permitted southern cotton planters to keep their labor costs artificially low. In fact, given the high demand for labor in expanding factories in the United States in the 19th century, it is unlikely that anyone would have chosen to labor on southern farms, growing and picking cotton. When slavery ended, southern cotton planters introduced a system of tenant farming—made possible by laws that changed the status of the sharecropper to a laborer whose wages were paid in crops.

When labor was scarce during World War II, the U.S. Congress responded by authorizing the *bracero* program, which allowed Mexican labor to enter the United States for short periods to work in agriculture. Mexican farm labor, according to the growers, was much better than white labor, which was "lazy and draggy-like," or black labor, which, the growers claimed, exhibited "too much independence" (see Rivoli, 2005, p. 31). In fact, during periods of labor short-ages, immigration restrictions are lax, whereas when job shortages exist, anti-immigration sentiment tends to rise. The government also assists cotton farmers and all agribusiness by refusing to set a minimum wage for farm workers.

While all these government actions benefit cotton growers and consum-ers, it has a damaging effect on Third World countries. Farmers in those coun-tries, whose governments cannot afford to pay them what the U.S. government pays its farmers, cannot compete with U.S. growers. Furthermore, because U.S. farmers can charge less for their cotton and still profit, the subsidies de-press the world market price for cotton by 3 to 15%. The human impact of these policies is revealed by the rash of suicides among cotton farmers in the Andhra Pradesh region of India, who because of cuts in government subsidies for insecticides lost their entire crop.

The subsidies that the U.S. government paid to cotton farmers were ruled illegal by the WTO in 2006 and have now ceased. This decision was made in spite of the political support that the textile industry gets from U.S. politicians (and the money from the textile industry that goes to these same politicians). But why would the United States allow a nonelected, nonrepresentative body such as the WTO to override the policy of protecting Texas cotton growers, as the government had done for decades? To understand that, we need to know something about "free trade," its role in globalization, and how it affects us.

Free Trade

Free trade is another term commonly associated with globalization. To promote free trade means to remove barriers to the free flow of goods and capital between nations. Traditionally, these barriers consisted of tariffs (taxes) or quotas on goods from other countries that might compete with domestic industries; they might also include subsidies of the sort that the U.S. government paid to cotton produc-ers to give them an advantage in competing with foreign cotton growers. Today, the major watchdog of free trade is the WTO.

The WTO emerged, as did the World Bank and the IMF, from the Bret-ton Woods conference of 1944. It began as the Global Agreement on Tariffs and Trade (GATT) and became formalized as the WTO in 1994. The job of the WTO is to obtain agreements from countries to remove barriers to trade. These barriers may include taxes or tariffs on goods entering a country, subsidies or other payments that government provides to aid their own companies, and labor or environmental laws that the WTO rules are unfair restrictions to free trade.

Neoliberals argue that free trade stimulates economic growth and helps alleviate poverty and environmental degradation. Because economic prosperity provides people with more money, they argue, citizens can use that money to create a demand for a cleaner environment, take advantage of educational opportunities, purchase consumer items, and do all the other things that money allows. The problem is that not everyone gains from free trade. For example, neoliberals argue that the government should play no role in regulating the environmental damage that our lifestyle creates. Instead, they say, a clean environment should be viewed as another commodity that, if people wish, they can purchase. For that reason, when there is a choice between economic growth and a clean environment, growth should be the first priority. And this is basically how the WTO rules. For example, when researchers discovered that dolphin populations were being endangered by tuna fishing, the U.S. government reacted by issuing rules to protect dolphins and banned the importation of tuna from countries whose fishing fleets did not follow those rules. Mexico claimed that this law violated articles of the WTO and appealed to the WTO to have the United States rescind the rules or permit retaliatory tariffs to be applied to U.S. exports. The WTO ruled that the laws protecting dolphins were unnecessary barriers to trade.

But free trade and the jobs it takes from developed countries and moves to developing ones has advantages. For example, young women working in the Chinese factories visited by Rivoli were happy for the work; for all the terrible working conditions in the factories, the workers say that "[i]t sure beats work on the farm." And while millions of textile jobs in the United States have been lost to cheaper foreign labor, Rivoli says that those jobs would have been lost anyway to mechanization and technology.

Her point is that those who argue for tariffs on foreign cotton, yarn, and cloth create higher prices all along the line and reduce competitiveness. The cost of trying to protect U.S. textile manufacturers from foreign competition is estimated in the range of $7 to $11 billion a year, or more than $80,000 a year for each job preserved. Import tariffs are said to represent a tax on clothing of 48%. When the United States places restrictions on the quantity of textiles that can be imported, says Rivoli, this encourages foreign countries to maximize their incomes by producing more expensive products rather than lower priced items.

Avoiding Democratic Decision Making

For neoliberals, the only significant function of government is to advance trade and do whatever it takes to maintain economic growth. However, the problem they face is that in countries with democratically elected governments, citizens may demand more than that. They may want the government to pass environmental laws, enact higher minimum wage standards, provide more funds for education, enact laws to protect workers, or pass laws regulating the safety of consumer products—all things that neoliberals say are economically harmful.

Thus, in the United States, after the publication in 1962 of Rachel Carson's *Silent Spring*, voters demanded governmental action to ensure clean air and water, along with the preservation of other environmental resources. These demands for a cleaner environment led to the passage of the Clean Air Act of 1970 and the Federal Water Pollution Control Act of 1972. Both pieces of legislation, along with virtually every other attempt to pass environmental regulations, have been vigorously opposed by corporate interests. Governments all over the world, then, face a dilemma: How do they respond to public demands for the government to act to protect workers, children, consumers, and the environment while also responding to pressure from corporate interests not to pass legislation that might affect corporate profits and economic growth?

Generally speaking, governments have adopted three strategies to address this dilemma. The first is to pay lip service to social, political, and environmental concerns by emphasizing such values as democracy, freedom, social justice, and environmental sustainability while, in effect, doing little about them. The idea of environmentally sustainable growth is a good example. The idea of sustainable growth gained popularity as a result of a report issued in 1987 by a commission headed by Norwegian prime minister Gro Harlem Brundtland (World Commission on Environmental Development, 1987). The Brundtland report, *Our Common Future*, defined sustainable development as that which "meets the needs of the present without compromising the ability of future generations to meet their own needs." The problem is that whenever economic growth clashes with environmental concerns, economic growth almost always wins. Sustainability seems to mean the greatest amount of environmental damage the public will accept as the price for economic growth.

A second strategy that governments can adopt to avoid responding to public demands for, say, environmental action is to displace regulatory power onto unelected and largely remote global governance institutions, such as the WTO. In other words, by assigning the legal right to decide cases in which environmental protection conflicts with economic growth to dispute panels of the WTO, governments can absolve themselves of failing to respond to citizens' environmental demands. Allowing multilateral institutions such as the WTO to dictate environmental policy may explain the reluctance of some governments, such as that of the United States, to enter into multilateral agreements addressing the environment, such as the Kyoto Accord or the Basel Convention. What would occur if two multilateral bodies—one designed to protect the global economy and the other to protect the global environment—disagreed with each other? That may explain why efforts to form a Global Environmental Mechanism (GEM), as proposed by Daniel C. Esty and Maria H. Ivanova (2003), have been so difficult to implement. But the failure of governments to support the development of a GEM as vigorously as they have supported the WTO is indicative of global governmental priorities.

Finally, the third governmental strategy to avoid taking significant action on social or environmental problems that could conceivably endanger continued economic growth is to free corporations and the mass media to spin events and news to allay public fears and interests. For example, neoliberals in the United States have proposed privatizing Social Security, which would release billions of dollars now collected by the state for investment in the stock market and other financial instruments. Regardless of the pros and cons of the argument, the Social Security fund is fully solvent into the 2040s, and if the retirement of the large cohort of people born after World War II burdens the fund, a small rise in Social Security taxes would fix it. But for years, media reports have dwelled on the coming demise of the Social Security fund and the loss by millions of Americans of their Social Security pensions. Obviously, if the story of the coming demise of Social Security gains credibility, the chances of the public's approving privatization increases.

The Use of Force

The manufacturing of consent through the media or other public outlets is an example of "soft" power. However, when that fails, the state can always turn to "hard" power—the use of force. One definition of the nation-state is that it is the only entity that is granted the legitimate use of force. "Stateness," as Elman Service (1975, p. 15) put it, can be identified simply by locating "the power of force in addition to the power of authority." A killing by someone other than representatives of the state, as Morton Fried points out, will result in retribution by state police, militia, or military. Carol Nagengast defines the state as a form of social contract in which the public ostensibly has consented to assign to the state a monopoly on force to constrain and coerce people. Nation-states kill. R. J. Rummel estimates that nation-states in the 20th century killed close to 200 million of *their own* citizens: 61 million Russians killed from 1917 to 1987; 20 million Germans killed from 1933 to 1945; 35 million Chinese killed by the provisional Chinese communist government from 1923 to 1949 and 10 million killed by the Chinese nationalists; almost two million Turks killed from 1909 to 1918; and almost 1.5 million Mexicans killed from 1900 to 1920.

The application of force is essential to protect an economy's access to critical resources, to open countries to the sale of products, and to repress protests against policies that may be harmful to people. Free trade, for example, can be devastating to peasants and small farmers by forcing them to compete with large-scale agribusiness. For example, when the United States, Canada, and Mexico signed the North American Free Trade Agreement (NAFTA), thousands of small farmers and peasants in Mexico found that they could not grow and sell corn in their own country as cheaply as could U.S. corn growers. Forced to abandon their farms and migrate to Mexican cities or smuggle themselves into the United States to work, some joined a rebellion in the Mexican state of Chiapas to protest against the free trade agreement. The Zapatistas—as they called themselves in honor of a hero of the Mexican Revolution: Emiliano Zapata—began their revolt on January 1, 1994, the date that NAFTA went into effect, to protest its impact on peasants and small farmers.

The U.S. invasion of Iraq is an example of the attempted use of force to impose a neoliberal regime. After the invasion in 2003, the United States established the Coalition Provisional Authority (CAS) to govern Iraq prior to the holding of democratic elections. However, before elections could be held, the director of the CPA, L. Paul Bremer, imposed a set of orders that were intended to turn Iraq into a model demonstration of free trade and neoliberal economic theory. These orders included suspending all tariffs, customs duties, import taxes, and licensing fees on goods and services entering or leaving Iraq; giving security firms brought in to work in Iraq full immunity from Iraqi law; privatizing some 200 state-owned enterprises; permitting 100% foreign ownership of Iraqi businesses; allowing investors to take 100% of the profits they made in Iraq out of the country, with no requirement that the profits be reinvested; and prohibiting any requirement that foreign companies hire local workers, recognize unions, or reinvest any profits back into the country. In addition, CPA orders allowed foreign banks to open in Iraq and to take a 50% interest in Iraqi banks and, finally, lowered the corporate tax rate from 40% to a flat 15%.[2]

These orders constituted a corporate wish list of rules and regulations that virtually no democratic legislature could openly support, let alone implement. Furthermore, the CPA planned to build these rules into the Iraqi constitution so they would have to be acknowledged by any subsequent Iraqi government. This was particularly important because without guarantees that these economic policies would be retained by future Iraqi governments, no corporation or bank would risk investing money in the Iraq economy. The results of these orders included the firing of 500,000 state workers (most of them soldiers but including doctors, nurses, teacher, publishers, and printers) and the opening the borders to unrestricted imports (much to the dismay of local Iraqi business people), including construction materials, such as cement, that the Iraqis could have supplied at much lower costs. "Getting inefficient state enterprises into private hands," Bremer said, "is essential for Iraq's economic recovery." It is noteworthy that in the beginning of 2007, with the rising possibility of a U.S. defeat in Iraq, the Pentagon began a program to reopen state-run factories in order to provide jobs for the mass of Iraqi unemployed put out of work by the CPA.

The imposition of neoliberal policies on Iraq—a country in which the state had played a major role in the economy—was likely one of the main reasons for the Iraqi insurgency. With its emphasis on dismantling government programs to help the poor, eliminating public subsidies for such necessities as food, fuel, and medical service, cutting or eliminating funds for education, and then privatizing virtually everything, neoliberalism generates protest at various levels. By prompting manufacturers to move factories to countries where labor is cheaper (and thus putting thousands out of work), by limiting the power of the government to limit the environmental damage done by corporations (thereby polluting the environments of those with little political

---

[2]See all the orders at http://www.casi.org.uk/info/cpa.html.

power to prevent it), and by supporting tyrannical governments for the sake of economic "stability" (leaving millions in poverty), neoliberalism fuels dissent. To control and react to protest, the state has a growing arsenal of surveillance and deadly weapons to put down the protest. The growing militarization of the world is illustrated first by the enormous expenditures on weapons systems—even in countries that cannot yet afford to ensure that its citizens have enough food. Arms sales from developed to developing countries reached $28.8 billion in 2006, and overall, global military spending has passed the $1 trillion mark.

The importance of force is also evident in what some call the growing United States Empire. Chalmers Johnson suggests that the battery of military bases required to ensure U.S. access to energy and markets carries with it what he calls the "sorrows of empire," which will ultimately change the nature of the nation-state. These "sorrows" include a state of perpetual war that will lead to more violent attacks against U.S. citizens and an increase in reliance by smaller states on weapons of mass destruction; a loss of democracy and constitutional rights to an increasingly imperial presidency; a "shredded principle of truthful-ness," as propaganda and spin are used to glorify war, power, and the military itself; and, finally, economic decline and neglect of education, health, and indi-vidual well-being as more and more economic resources are spent to maintain a military empire. The current need of the United States to staff more than 750 bases around the world requires the "professionalism" of the armed forces, producing people who will fight because they are told to and because it is their job, regardless of the political goals of military operations. In World War II, we needed propaganda to convince the armed forces that they were fighting against evil; today, it is enough to be simply ordered into war.

QUESTION 3.5   *Why Do Economies Collapse?*

In spite of the best efforts of governments, economies do occasionally collapse. Thus, in the summer of 2007, the United States and the world experienced the beginning of the worst economic decline since the great depression of the 1930s. At least 30 million people—and possibly as much as 50 million—lost their jobs, more than 200 million people—mostly in developing economies—fell into poverty, and losses to the financial sector, to corporations, to homeowners, and to unincorporated businesses were more than $40 trillion, or two-thirds of the world's GDP (see Blankenburg & Palma, 2009). While economies began to again grow in 2010, hundreds of thousands of people remained jobless; in the United States, real unemployment estimates ranged from 16 to 18% of the workforce, while federal, state, and local governments struggled to deal with declining tax revenues.

We should first note that economic crises are not unusual. Since the year 1800, the most advanced economies in the world have experienced, on aver-age, over seven banking crises that lasted an average of over seven years each. In effect, the most advanced economies in the world have spent on average a quarter of their time in the midst of a banking crisis not dissimilar to the one that began in 2007 (see Reinhart & Rogoff, 2009).

One of the benefits of anthropology is being able to take a look at phenomena across history and culture; we can look at economic systems comparatively and historically and perhaps get a more nuanced view than that gained from someone whose view is skewed by specific cultural biases.

One common explanation for this latest global financial collapse is that it resulted from the collapse of a housing bubble in the United States. The story is that low interest rates in the United States, along with high cash inflows from overseas—particularly China—sent Americans on a house-buying spree that sent home prices soaring at an unprecedented rate. The bubble was further fueled by "subprime mortgages"—loans to people with few financial resources who soon defaulted on their loans. When people began to default and banks stopped lending, the housing market collapsed, resulting in the crash of home values and the wiping out of trillions of dollars of wealth. However, as we will see, it was a little more complex than that.

Much of the present debacle has also been blamed on Wall Street. Wall Street is about finance—or, more specifically, about making money with money. That is, Wall Street firms function by matching people or firms with money with people or firms who need it but for a price that takes the form of interest and/or dividends. For some, that is the essence of capitalism (see Polanyi, 1957). But historically, that is a relatively new thing. Recall that lending money at interest—the most basic form of making money with money—is defined in the Bible as well as the Qur'an as usury and is explicitly banned. It was not until the early Middle Ages that traders began to find a way around the ban, and it was in the Dutch Republic of the late 15th and early 16th century that a modern financial system emerged.

We need to examine why the crisis of 2007–2008 occurred, but it may first be useful to examine what may have been the first major economic collapse and then use that to better understand what happened recently. It occurred in 1636 and involved tulips.

Tulip Bulbs and Bubbles

The parallels between the Dutch economy and our own are revealing. The Dutch were inveterate investors seeking to make money with money. For example, in the period from 1610 to 1640, Dutch citizens invested at least 10 million guilders (when the annual average income was 200–400 guilders) in new capital intensive technologies, such as windmill pumping techniques to drain water, and increased farmland for crops to feed the growing urban populations (see de Vries and van der Woude, 1997, p. 29). They also invested money in the building of canals to connect cities and towns and in draining peat bogs—their major energy source.

Dutch citizens also made money financing the public debt. The Dutch state in 1600 had a debt of about 5 million guilders, which they financed by selling bonds to citizens that paid from 8 to 16% interest (de Vries and van der Woude, 1997, p. 114). By 1660, some 65,000 people (out of some 220,000 Dutch households) had invested money in state bonds, from which they were earning interest—that is, making money with money.

One of the most successful investments a person could make at the time was in the United or Dutch East Indian Company (Vereenigde Oost-Indische Compagnie, or VOC). The VOC was given monopoly rights to trade in Asia, along with the authority to build forts, raise armies, and negotiate treaties with Asian rulers. To finance the company, the board—made up of 17 lords and representing the first board of directors—issued stock in the company. The initial offering raised some 6.45 million guilders from shares bought by everyone from the wealthiest members of society to their servants. The VOC was the first multinational corporation and the first to sell stock. It was also incredibly profitable, paying an average of 18% return per year on investments for almost 200 years.

Of course, as today with the mortgage-backed securities blamed for the 2007–2008 crisis, not all investments proved as profitable. In 1636, during a decade when shares in the VOC were doubling in value, tulips—to most Dutch—looked like a good thing. Tulips enjoyed great popularity among the Dutch, who appreciated their aesthetic quality and the many-colored patterns of the flowers. Because some patterns were more desirable than others, the prices of tulip bulbs varied immensely.

Tulip bulbs can propagate through the formation of outgrowths on the mother bulb, and when the bulbs are invaded by a mosaic virus, it produces an effect called "breaking" that results in multicolored flower patterns that are highly desired. However, these patterns are only verified between June—when the bulbs can be removed from the ground—and September—when they must be replanted. Single bulbs were sometimes worth modest fortunes. A single Semper Augustus bulb sold for 5,500 guilders at a time—again, when the average yearly income was 200 to 400 guilders.

In the fall of 1637, Dutch citizens began to purchase tulip futures, specifying the kind of tulip they wished to purchase and entering into contracts with sellers. Most of the buyers had no intention of taking possession of the tulip bulbs, betting that the prices would rise and that they could then sell the rights to buy the tulips to people who wanted the bulbs. Often, the sellers did not have any bulbs but were betting that they could get them at a price less than they were offered from the

One type of tulip bulb, the Semper Augustus, sold for 5,500 guilders during the tulip craze, when the average yearly income was 200–400 guilders.

Tulip, c.1675 (gouache on vellum), Robert, Nicolas (1614–85)/Burghley House Collection, Lincolnshire, UK/The Bridgeman Art Library International

buyers. Thus, as de Vries and van der Woude (1997, p. 150) put it, "citizens crowded into taverns to buy and sell bulbs they could not deliver and did not want to receive." They were betting on the future price of bulbs.

Because there was no bank credit, payment was often promised in kind. In one case, for a pound of White Crown bulbs (a particularly common variety), one buyer offered FL 525 to be paid on delivery of the bulbs (presumably the following June) but four cows immediately. Other down payments consisted of "tracts of land, houses, furniture, silver and gold vessels, paintings, a suit and a coat, a coach and dapple-gray pair." Another buyer of a single viceroy bulb, valued at FL 2,500, paid "two *lasts* (a measure than varied by commodity and locality) of wheat, four of rye, eight pigs, a dozen sheep, two oxheads of wine, four tons of butter, a thousand pounds of cheese, a bed, some clothing and a silver beaker" (Kindelberger, 2000, p. 109).

Then, in February of 1638—for reasons that are unclear—prices being offered began to collapse, and investors who had depended on prices increasing faced economic ruin. Because they had only given the sellers a portion of the agreed upon price, they had to somehow come up with the rest, which they often did not have, depending instead on the expected rise in bulb prices. Furthermore, the sellers—using the contracts as collateral for loans—were faced with coming up with additional collateral, which they did not have. But because the future contracts were, at the time, unenforceable in court, there was no incentive to honor the contracts. Thus, investors lost large sums of money or the goods that they had used as down payment on their bulb purchases. Many amateur investors went bankrupt. However, in spite of this, the Dutch remained, in the 17th century, devoted investors, continuing to put their money in VOC stock or canal building, paintings, and clocks.

The Housing Bubble of 2007   What happened with tulips in 1636 is basically the same thing as what happened with houses in 2007. To better understand what happened, we need to begin with another market externality—the Exxon-Valdez disaster of March 24, 1989, when the oil tanker owned by Exxon Oil Company ran aground in Prince William Sound, Alaska, and spilled 10.8 million U.S. gallons into the sea. The central cast in our story was finance people who worked at the Wall Street firm of J. P. Morgan, one of the largest investment banks in the United States. As anthropologist and financial journalist Gillian Tett (2009) tells it, Exxon approached its bank, J. P. Morgan, for a $5 billion loan in order to cover possible penalties to the company because of the oil spill. The bank had no problem with the loan itself; Exxon was one of its best customers and one of the most profitable companies in the world. But it was concerned about the reserve requirement—a rule imposed by national and international regulatory agencies—that banks keep in reserve a portion of what is owed to protect them against default. The same reserve requirement applies to bank deposits; for example, if you deposit $1,000 in the bank, the bank may lend out about $900 of that to others, but it must keep $100 out of every $1,000 in order to meet depositors' demands for withdrawals. It must keep only 10% because no one expects everyone to want to withdraw their money (or fail to pay their loans) all at once. But banks have problems with reserve requirements because money that has to be held in reserve is money that is not working—that is not bringing in interest or fees. For banks to pay interest, they must invest deposits (or sell them) in order to make money to pay the interest. Thus, a problem that banks have is how can they put the money they hold in reserve to work? Banks sometimes deal with that problem by "offloading" a debt by selling it to another bank, but in this case, the people at J. P. Morgan were concerned that it would show disloyalty to its client, Exxon.

At J. P. Morgan, as Tett describes it, a group in the derivatives department headed by Peter Hancock thought they had a perfect solution to free up reserve money. They approached the European Bank for Reconstruction and Finance (EBRF), which had lots of money at their disposal, and asked whether, for a fee, they would insure the Exxon loan. That is, in the unlikely event that Exxon defaulted on its obligation, EBRF would make good on the loan. They called this a credit-default swap, or CDS. Once the EBRF agreed to do this, the derivatives team at J. P. Morgan went to bank regulators and asked the regulators to reduce the reserve requirement on the Exxon loan because, they argued, it was now insured, and even in the unlikely event that Exxon failed to pay, they would then collect from the EBRF. The regulators agreed. The result was that whereas originally J. P. Morgan would have had to keep about $700,000 in reserve, it now only had to keep about $180,000, thus freeing up more than $500,000 for the bank to lend or invest.

This may seem like a fairly esoteric banking deal, but it set the stage for the economic disaster to follow. The team at J. P. Morgan reasoned that they could use the same financial strategy for other loans that it held as it had on the Exxon loan. It could, in effect, industrialize the process, thus making it as easy for investors to buy credit derivatives as they could buy stocks and bonds. J. P. Morgan had about $10 billion of outstanding loans to some 307 major corporations. What if they took those loans and shifted them to a dummy corporation (thus removing them from the J. P. Morgan books), divided those assets in the form of the interest on the loans of the new corporation into smaller packages—or collateralized debt obligation (CDO)—and then sold them to investors (see Figure 3.4). They called these securities Broad Index Securities Trust Offerings, or BISTROS. Furthermore, what if they could find a large insurance company to guarantee those loans in the same way as the EBRF had guaranteed the Exxon loan? If they could do that, they reasoned, the bank regulators would let them greatly reduce the reserve requirements on the $10 billion of loans from the 307 corporations, thus freeing up millions of additional dollars for investment while also dispersing the risk that the loans would default (which they considered very unlikely) to other investors. They approached Joseph Caffano, the head of a small department at the giant insurance company AIG, and for a modest fee, Caffano committed AIG to insure

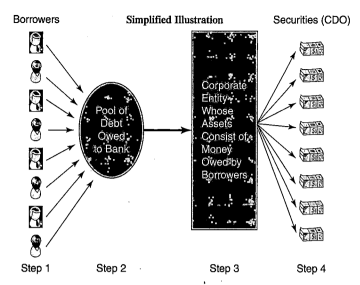

Borrowers   Simplified Illustration   Securities (CDO)

Step 1   Step 2   Step 3   Step 4

FIGURE 3.4 THE PROCESS OF CONVERTING DEBT
TO NEGOTIABLE SECURITIES

the securities issued on the corporate loans. And, finally, regulators agreed to lower the bank's reserve requirement.

The team at J. P. Morgan celebrated—not because they thought they had put one over on the regulators but because they had come up with a financial innovation that could free up billions—if not trillions—of dollars for investment and, consequently, help to speed economic growth. Furthermore, they had effectively dealt with the risk of loan default by insuring against it and at the same time distributing risk among a larger group, thus diluting the possible loss of any one person or financial entity. They had, they thought, contributed to a better financial world.

When other banks heard about the financial innovations of the derivatives team at J. P. Morgan, they enthusiastically followed suit, packaging loans or debt that they held into securities to sell to investors. These securities were also insured by AIG and others and seemed to have so little risk that investment rating services gave them double and triple A ratings—the same given to government issued securities, which are considered the safest form of investment.

Then, Bayerische Landesbank, a large German bank, approached the derivatives people at J. P. Morgan and asked them to package some $14 billion of U.S. home mortgages into securities to sell; however, that posed a problem. Unlike corporate loans, which had a long history that enabled banks to estimate the probability of default, there was no corresponding information for housing mortgages. Thus, it was difficult to assess how risky these securities would be. J. P. Morgan went ahead with the German bank but only after building in additional safeguards against default, and after doing one more BISTRO deal, they discontinued that line of investment.

However, other banks—largely to keep up with their competition—bundled trillions of dollars of home mortgages and other forms of debt (credit card loans, auto loans, commercial loans, etc.) into CDOs and then sold them to eager investors from pension funds, banks, insurance companies, charities, universities and colleges, and to anyone else who hoped to make an almost certain profit buying triple A or double A securities. One turning point may have come when large banks entered into agreements with home mortgage companies to buy any mortgage they sold to homebuyers in order to meet the demand from investors for more debt to package into securities. Mortgage companies could then make millions of dollars in fees for selling a mortgage to a homebuyer and immediately (often the same day) selling the mortgage to larger investment banks to package into CDOs. Consequently, the mortgage companies had little interest in whether a borrower had the means to repay the loan because they were quickly passing on the risk to the larger banks. These companies were so anxious to give mortgages that they offered them with no down payment—even in some cases offering mortgage buyers a free car or household of furniture. In some circles, these were called "liar loans" because there were no background checks on borrowers' income or resources; "neutron loans" because they killed the people but left the houses standing; or, finally, "ninja loans" or "no income and no assets." If the homebuyer expressed concern about repaying the mortgage, they were offered mortgages with low initial payments that later increased and told that if they had a problem paying the higher rate, they could, with home prices rapidly rising, sell the home at a profit or refinance the loan.

Of course, it did not work out; the housing bubble burst. The simplest way of looking at the collapse is that trillions of dollars were bet on the premise that the value of an asset—houses in this case—would continue to increase, when, in fact, the values fell—just as with tulips. As buyers defaulted on their loans, the value of the securities based on those loans either greatly declined or were impossible to sell because no one knew how much they were worth. Furthermore, derivatives based on commercial loans, credit card debt, and automobile loans were threatened by defaults. With banks losing money, holding assets of unknown worth, and not knowing the financial state of other institutions and borrowers and insurance companies unable to compensate investors for their losses, banks stopped lending, and the whole financial system threatened to freeze up. The insurance companies and banks that had guaranteed the securities were forced to pay out billions of dollars they did not have and were on the verge of collapse until the U.S. government came to the rescue with a trillion-dollar bailout. But the resulting banking crisis stopped the flow of money and credit, forcing the massive selling of assets (stocks, real estate, etc.) by people who needed to meet debt obligations, which further decreased asset value, affecting millions of business and throwing millions of people all over the world out of work.

Institutional Factors Contributing to the Collapse   As we try to understand the factors that contributed to the economic crises, we can identity certain ways that financial institutions work that contributed to the crash. For example, there were the perverse incentives whereby rating agencies were paid by the same companies whose securities they were judging. Moody's, one of the largest of the three major companies that rated the safety of securities, earned 40% of its income in 2005 from rating securitized debt. Others point to the complexities of the derivatives, such that it took a computer a day and a half to price a CDO. Still others point to the extent to which leverage or borrowing was used to purchase pricey CDOs in the expectation they would continue to rise in value. Finally, there was the need for investment houses to continue to successfully compete with others investment houses and earn what competitors were earning. That is, the people at J. P. Morgan and those at other banks had little choice but to jump on the derivative bandwagon; had they not done so, they would have failed to produce the profits other banks were realizing and would have lost some or all of their clients.

Consequently, there is much talk about changing the way that financial institutions work to ensure that it does not happen again. Suggestions include changing the incentive structure and making banker's and investment broker's bonuses somehow contingent on success. Another measure would be to more closely regulate derivatives and ensure that investors know more about the instruments they are buying. Other suggestions include increasing the reserve requirement. The problem with each or all of these institutional measures is that they run smack dab up against the prime directive—perpetual economic growth.

Quite simply, our economy requires that we spend or produce more this year than last and more next year than this in perpetuity. The minimum rate of growth required is roughly 3% after adjusting for inflation. If the economy grows at a lesser rate, it is considered sluggish or stagnant. It also means higher unemployment rates, more business failures, and low profits. In addition, there is one other factor that receives little attention that contributes to our understanding of economic growth and financial crises; that is, that the wealthier a country becomes, the more difficult it is to maintain economic growth. That is the reason emerging economies, such as China, India and Brazil, can grow from 6 to 10% a year, while wealthy economies struggle to attain the necessary 3 to 5%.

The problem, then, is that any attempt to rein in the financial practices of investment bankers may significantly affect the rate of economic growth. The financial sector, which 30 years ago comprised only about 5% of the GDP, now makes up 17% or more. With the decline of the U.S. industrial sector over the past 30 years, it is conceivable that had not investment banks generated the growth they did (as well as the bubbles that resulted), our economy might be in worse shape than had the folks on Wall Street not come up with their exotic financial instruments. Wall Street—as well as every other sector of the economy—was impelled to find new ways to make money to generate the necessary overall growth of the economy. That is why the derivatives team at J. P. Morgan was told that "[y]ou will have to make at least half your revenues each year from a product which did not exist before" (Tett, 2009, pp. 7–8).

This then gets to the central question—rarely if ever asked by economists: Why does the economy have to perpetually grow? The simple answer is that once a segment of an economy depends on making money with money, perpetual growth must ensue. That is, once money is lent or invested, the money must work, so to speak, to produce more money to account for the original amount lent or invested (the principal) plus the interest, dividend, or profit. The amount of growth required depends, obviously, on the interest, dividend, or profit required. If there is insufficient growth to generate the additional money, loans go unpaid and/or dividends or profits unrealized. Thus, going back to the present crisis, as long as house prices continued to grow, the system worked well, but once they ceased growing and, in fact, collapsed, the entire economic system was threatened.

The next question is how much growth is necessary given a specific level of debt? This is important because of the significant increase in debt obligations—nationally and globally—over the past few decades.

We can perhaps begin to understand the relationship between debt and growth with a household example. Let us assume I have a household that is earning $150,000 a year. I want to buy a new house that costs $600,000, so I get a loan from the bank for that amount, paying 7% interest over 10 years. The $600,000 represents money that did not exist before the bank issued it but will continue to exist in the form of an asset—the house. However, over the course of the loan (10 years), the total interest I will pay is $235,981. That represents completely new money that has to somehow be created over the course of the loan. Given my income of $150,000 and assuming that my other overall expenses remain constant, I must produce, on average, an additional $23,598 a year, or 15.7% a year of my total income in order to pay off the interest on the debt.

The numbers chosen to represent our hypothetical household were not randomly selected; the debt (the housing loan) roughly represents the total debt obligations of all sectors of the U.S. economy—some $57 trillion and growing—and the income represents roughly the total U.S. GDP of some $14 to $15 trillion.

Table 3.4 shows the current debt obligations of different segments of the U.S. economy as of January 2009.

TABLE 3.4   **U.S. TOTAL DEBT BY SECTOR—JANUARY 1, 2009[1]**

Debt Type	Debt Amount	Debt per Person
Federal government sector	$10.6 Trillion	$34,868
State and local government sector	$2.2 Trillion	$7,368
Household sector	$13.8 Trillion	$45,395
Business sector	$11.1 Trillion	$36,513
Financial sector	$17.2 Trillion	$56,579
Other	$1.9 Trillion	$6,250
Sum of all government and private sector debt	$56.9 Trillion	$186,717

[1] (Data from Grandfather Economic Report: http://mwhodges.home.att.net/nat-debt/debt-nat-a.htm)

Now, if we substitute the total debt of all entities in the United States (approximately 60 trillion), the present GDP (approximately $15 trillion), and assume that the average interest rate of all those debts is 7% (this includes credit card debt with rates at about 20%, bond rates, and treasury bill rates of perhaps 1 to 2% a year) and that the length of debt is approximately 10 years, then the total interest earned, expected investment return, and expected profit would total some $235,596 trillion, thus requiring a growth rate (not accounting for inflation or increases or decreases in asset valuation) of 15.7% a year, which is clearly unattainable and well above the average U.S. growth rate of 3 to 4% a year.

Thus, the current economic crisis has more to do with the internal logic of our economic system—particularly the need for perpetual growth and the constant return on capital—than it does anything else. Institutional factors, as such anthropologists as Gillian Tett (2009) and Karen Ho (2009) illustrate, certainly play a major role in contributing to the boom and bust nature of our economic system. But even those institutions must function in an environment that demands perpetual growth, and placing restrictions on how they operate may significantly hamper that goal.

CASE STUDY IN DOING ANTHROPOLOGY #3: ANTHROPOLOGY AND PUBLIC POLICY

Nation-states exist, in part, to regulate and promote the growth of national economies. Consequently, governments devise economic policies to achieve economic growth. However, market activities have effects that are often not considered in economic policy. We saw some of these **market externalities** in our examination of the real cost of an automobile, including environmental pollution, health problems, and so on. But policy planning rarely takes these externalities into consideration. One of the major contributions of anthropology in the area of public policy and planning is making people aware of the externalities of the market and trying to build into policy decisions recommendations to eliminate or at least minimize these negative externalities.

Anthropologists or persons with an anthropological background bring critical skills and perspectives to policy discussions. First, anthropology emphasizes the need to study the totality of societies and institutions, their economics, politics, agriculture, ecology, and so on. Second, a background in anthropology promotes an understanding of community aspirations and needs and inspires empathy—the ability to see things through the eyes of others.

Third, the insistence on examining public policy initiatives from various perspectives and from the viewpoint of others promotes an anticipation of undesirable consequences. Anthropologists are more likely to ask who is affected by policy interests and how the interests of those affected conflict or coincide.

Fourth, an anthropological perspective requires recognizing that policy making and implementation are not just political and social processes; they are also cultural. Policy decisions are always ideological; they contain assumptions—often implicit and unstated—about how society works, what people desire, and what are acceptable or unacceptable consequences of policy decisions. Even the categories of people that policies claim to address are cultural matters. Such categories as "the poor," "citizen," "professional," "national," "criminal," or "deviant" are culturally constructed categories. From an anthropological perspective, public policy regarding such issues as education, crime, economic development, human rights, or food production lead into issues that form the heart of anthropology: ideology and consciousness, norms and institutions, knowledge and power, meaning and interpretation, the global and the local, and so on.

Finally, anthropologists bring a needed critical perspective to policy making and are better able to mediate among policymakers with competing viewpoints regarding the most desirable ways of solving human problems. These competing views may range over the political spectrum—social democrat, liberal, conservative, neoconservative, Marxist, and so forth. On the one hand, a liberal might argue that preferential hiring and affirmative action will improve employment for minorities and that, as a result, crime rates will go down. On the other hand, a conservative might argue that harsher sentences will serve as deterrents to crime and thus increase public safety. In many ways, theories of action inherent in policy initiatives are like folk theories of medicine; people base their actions on and have great faith in them even though there is no ultimate proof or scientific research to support them. Furthermore, as anthropologists point out, policy may function to distance policymakers from the intended objects—"the poor," "deviants," "criminals"—of those policies. That is, policy may sometimes serve as a way to cloak highly subjective, ideological, and even irrational goals in the guise of rational and collective objectives.

Modern hog farms resemble factory complexes more than they do traditional family farms. The animals virtually never see daylight.

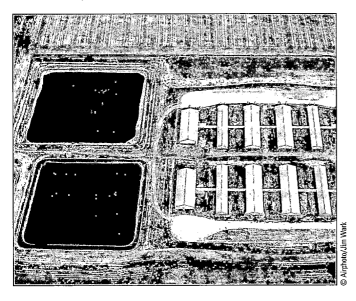

By taking a critical perspective on public policy and by carefully examining how different groups of people are affected by policy decisions, anthropologists often serve as public advocates, becoming spokespersons for people—often the relatively powerless—whose interests are being ignored by government, corporate, or nongovernmental policymakers. To examine how anthropology functions as a policy science and understand its distinct contributions to policy making, let us examine a case of agricultural policy as it relates to the growth of large-scale pig farms.

The Market Externalities of "Hog Hotels"

Over the past decade, there has been a significant growth in the United States of large-scale factory pig farms, or "hog hotels," as they are sometimes called. These farms have little to distinguish them from factories. Thousands of pigs are raised in multiple, long, low-lying metal buildings set on concrete foundations with rows of ventilation fans protruding from the sides and ends rather than in pasture and partial shelters. Elevated, bulk-feeding tanks complete the factory appearance of the facilities, where every stage of the production process can be monitored. Animal waste is deposited on cement floors, where it runs off into open waste pits called "lagoons." Large transport trucks pick up the pigs, which never see the light of day.

Hog hotels are the culmination of a growth of industrialized agriculture in which small-scale family farms are being replaced by corporate-owned facilities designed to minimize cost and maximize profit. But industrial agriculture, as we noted in Chapter 2 (Question 2.1), is one of the most energy-inefficient forms of food production in history. In addition, the growth of industrial agriculture generally ignores local concerns, has negative effects on the environment, and reduces employment. Furthermore, industrial agriculture concentrates such specialized operations as farming, food processing, and marketing into the hands of a relatively few corporations.

For more than half a century, anthropologists have been in the forefront of warning that national agricultural policy that promotes the industrialization of agriculture is a threat to family farms and communities and can have severe negative impacts on health and the environment. Anthropologist Walter Goldschmidt pioneered this work in the 1940s. Goldschmidt worked for the U.S. Bureau of Agricultural Economics (later closed under pressure from agribusiness), a branch of the U.S. Department of Agriculture that examined the impact of agricultural policy decisions. One of Goldschmidt's first studies compared two rural California communities—one consisting largely of small family farms and the other of absentee, corporate-owned farms. He found, in general, that the community with the greater number of independent farmers had higher production per land unit, higher family incomes, greater social cohesion, and more thriving churches, businesses, and service clubs. In the other community, dominated by energy-intensive corporate agriculture operating with federal irrigation subsidies, he found that labor was migratory and poor, town life marginal, and crime rates high.

Anthropologists Kendall Thu and Paul Durrenberger note that Goldschmidt's findings have been repeated again and again. Today, with the exception of organic farming, corporate-dominated, industrialized agriculture predominates. Thu and Durrenberger are among those who have taken an advocacy role, using their anthropological perspective to lobby for agricultural policies that are friendlier to small-scale family farms. Their major points are that large-scale pig farms are not economically superior to small-scale family farms and that they reduce jobs, create massive environmental problems, and

Anthropologist Laura B. DeLind's research exposed many of the externalities of hog production.

socially devastate communities that they enter. In other words, the externalities of large-scale pig production create environmental, social, and political problems. These problems are clearly revealed in a community study of the rural Michigan town of Parma by anthropologist Laura B. DeLind.

In 1983, the Michigan Department of Commerce sponsored a feasibility study to expand hog production by building ten 500-sow hog production units in Parma. The study projected that the new factory farms would increase hog production by 8% and realize a 24 to 27% profit—largely facilitated by tax breaks—for investors. However, although the feasibility study closely examined the economic benefits of the project, it paid no attention to its environmental, social, or health effects. In fact, town residents were not even consulted; they found out about the project only with the "pouring of the cement." But as soon as the building of the pig farm began, residents had lots of questions: What was being built? Why had the public not been consulted? How large a facility would it be? How would the pig waste be managed? What would it do to the creek, which passed only 200 feet from the 20-acre site? What would happen to the groundwater, the air, and property values? What environmental safeguards existed? These questions drew only assurances from government representatives and the company building the farm that there would be no problems.

By the time the residents had firsthand experience with their new neighbor and its three open-air anaerobic manure lagoons (42-million-gallon capacity), their worst fears were realized. Many reported a "horrific stench" that caused nausea, headaches, and respiratory ailments; burned eyes, noses, and throats; prevented sleep; and could be detected up to five miles away. Dead pigs were found piled up for days along the road, airborne particles were contaminating swimming pools, and fish disappeared from the creek. In response to complaints, residents were told that there was no detectable pollution or violation of state building or zoning codes; from the state's perspective, the operation was safe, legal, and unassailable.

However, when Parma residents were told that the facility was going to be expanded, they decided to fight it. They searched state regulations and laws and hired legal representation, finally forcing the hog facility to install new equipment and to regulate the pollution. They also succeeded in getting restrictions placed on any new hog farms. Then, in 1992, the company declared bankruptcy and, citing the cost of litigation and low hog prices, closed the facility, leaving behind 30 steel buildings and three lagoons standing empty on 20 denuded acres surrounded by chain-link fence and mercury vapor lamps. The company has since gone on to construct and operate new hog confinement facilities in Wyoming, China, and Korea.

On the surface, the story seems to be one in which a local community banded together to force an industry to be accountable to local citizens. But, says DeLind, that would be a flawed conclusion. Instead, she says, it is necessary to examine whether the project delivered on benefits to the local community promised by industry and government.

For example, the policymakers who produced the feasibility study promised that the hog company would purchase local corn as pig feed and decrease the local corn surplus. Instead, DeLind found, locally owned hog farmers purchased more local corn than did large-scale producers, who purchased their feed from nonlocal suppliers.

Project proponents and designers also promised to create local jobs. However, in the construction process, the company brought in its own construction crew; once in operation, the company employed some 22 to 27 people but only 10 or 12 were local people. Furthermore, the company filled all high-paid positions with persons from outside the community. Also, a local family-run antique apple orchard and historical museum, which employed four local people full time and a seasonal crew of some 28 locals and had been planning to expand, left the area because of the hog odors and severe environmental damage.

The community of Parma realized few if any of the economic benefits that were supposed to result from the large-scale pig farms. All the investors—some with ties to the governor's office—were from outside the area, and local property values collapsed because people were hesitant to purchase property because of the hog hotels. Even the broader claim that large-scale producers are more profitable than small-scale family farms has proved, on examination, to be questionable. What is actually happening is that large-scale producers are flooding the market with pork and driving down the price, so it costs small farmers more to produce the pork than the price they receive for it. However, large-scale agricultural corporations, which control pork production from production through packing, distribution, and marketing, can make up for the production loss in the packing, distribution, and marketing phases of their operations.

It is unlikely that these results would have come as a surprise had someone writing the proposal for the hog farms had some background in anthropology or other social science.

But there are more than environmental and economic consequences, as DeLind points out. There are also other externalized costs, including the human costs exemplified by one Parma resident with whom DeLind spoke, who said that "[i]t's hard to recall five years of hell." DeLind found that the confidence of Parma residents in the democratic political process had been compromised by their experiences with the pig farms. Government representatives assured Parma residents that there would be no odor—that they would never know the operation was there. When they then complained to state authorities, they were ignored. When they complained about the pollution to the creek, they were told that nothing could be done because there was no study of the creek before the hog farm was built. When they called and told authorities that there was pig manure floating in the creek, they were asked, "How do you know it's pig manure?" Rather than being attributed to drainage from the hog farm, a rise in the creek level was attributed to "roof runoff."

Prior to the hog hotel controversy, says DeLind, most Parma residents shared a sense that government was there to serve their needs and that if they expressed themselves they would get help. But the experience with the hog hotel demonstrated to them that authorities were reluctant to embrace their interests over those of power and profit. "Many high up political persons," said one Parma resident, "were invested in the operation. No one wanted to look too closely or to step on toes. It was a case of 'one hand washing the other.' For a long time we were laboring under the illusion that if we got to the right person, he would say: 'Wait a minute! You can't do this to the people of Parma.' That person does not exist."

When residents decided to fight the expansion of the pig farms, the community was wracked by the tension created in the community at meetings. Community meetings competed for time with family and children. Although the community ultimately forced the company to leave, the social fabric was destroyed as people fought back against company employees who harassed them, followed them home from meetings, and made middle-of-the-night phone calls. After a local night watchman was assaulted, the town residents formed a vigilante committee and, armed with guns and baseball bats, patrolled the community looking for intruders.

Corporate-owned and -run hog production facilities are realities of the current agricultural economy and are likely to become more common in spite of attempts by opponents to slow their growth and in spite of clear evidence that successful, modest-sized, family-operated hog farms contribute more to the economic and social well-being of rural communities than do their corporate counterparts. But anthropologists are among those who are striving for a greater input into agricultural policy. For example, in 1994, anthropologist Paul Durrenberger wrote an editorial for the *Des Moines Register*, Iowa's largest newspaper. The article was based on his and his associates' rapid appraisal fieldwork in North Carolina on the effects of large-scale pig farms and what they were doing to family farms and rural communities. Soon after the editorial appeared, he was besieged by industry leaders attempting to muzzle him, going so far as to meet with the president of the university at which Durrenberger taught. Durrenberger's associate, Thu, described the advocacy aspect of his work in a personal communication to anthropologist Alexander M. Irvin:

> My applied work involves a strategy combining research with advocacy through the media, public speaking, legislative testimony, expert witness work in the

courtroom, holding industries accountable for co-opting science, work with nonprofit organizations, and cooperation among community groups. . . .

Research and advocacy are necessary partners. Science never has, nor ever will, exist in a vacuum. If we do not advocate based on the rigor of our ethnographies, by default we have made a decision affecting the lives of those whose knowledge provided for our professional careers.

CONCLUSIONS

We began this chapter by asking, "What is globalization and what does it have to do with me?" We examined some global consumption patterns and then asked, "How do we define happiness and well-being?" We looked at what well-being means in some other societies and then examined our need for money, the emergence of money created by debt, and how this relates to the prime directive of our society, maintaining perpetual economic growth.

We then asked where the continuous creation of goods and services comes from and examined the process of capital conversion in which we transform such nonmonetary capital as the natural environment, political rights, and social capital into money.

Next, we asked what type of economic system is necessary to maintain perpetual growth. We sketched out the history of the modern economy—from the onset of the industrial revolution to the emergence of Keynesian economics to the emergence of neoliberalism, an economic philosophy that argues for the reduction of government involvement in the economy and that, generally speaking, promotes the acceleration of capital conversion.

But in spite of the directive that the state play little role in the economy, we explored how states in fact play a very important role in economic growth. The state does, when it can, enact legislation to protect its industries while trying to minimize the ability of others, particularly of poor countries, to protect theirs. We examined how nation-states help to manufacture consent regarding economic policies that favor growth and how, when necessary, the state uses force to gain access to resources, such as oil, and to impose policies on other countries favorable to itself.

Finally, we examined how a career in anthropology can be applied to some of the problems we discussed and examined the possibilities of a career in public policy, illustrated with a case study of anthropologists working to alleviate the damage created by industrial farming.

We concluded our questions by exploring the reasons why economies collapse. These crises are rooted in finance and the need of our economy to perpetually grow in order to generate the money required in the process of making money with money. When business activities cannot keep up, people cannot pay their debts, banks fail or stop lending, and the economy freezes. While this last crisis involved a crash of house prices, we noted that a rapid decline in asset prices is hardly unique, tracing them back to the tulip bubble of 1636–1637.

REFERENCES AND SUGGESTED READINGS

Introduction: My T-Shirt

The opening quote is from David Harvey's book *A Brief History of Neoliberalism,* p. 119 (Oxford University Press, 2005). Pietra Rivoli describes her exploration of the origin of her T-shirt in *The Travels of a T-Shirt in the Global Economy: An Economist Examines the Markets, Power, and Politics of World Trade* (Wiley, 2005). You can find a good summary of our consumption patterns in Bill McKibben's book *Deep Economy: The Wealth of Communities and the Durable Future* (Times Books, 2007) and the United Nations Development Report 1998: Overview (http://hdr.undp.org/en/reports/global/hdr1998). You can learn more about the biography of commodities in Igor Kopytoff's "The Cultural Biography of Things," in *The Social Life of Things: Commodities in Cultural Perspective,* edited by Arjun Appadurai (Cambridge University Press, 1986). You can find out more about how material progress affects happiness at http://www.technologyreview.com/Biotech/14091. You can check how countries rate on happiness from the World Values Survey. There is a simplified ranking at http://www.nationmaster.com/graph/lif_hap_net-lifestyle-happiness-net/AFR and ideas and information on measuring happiness in *Happiness: Lessons From a New Science* by Richard Layard (Penguin, 2005).

How Do We Define Happiness and Well-Being?

You can find lots of information on the history and meaning of money in Jack Weatherford's book *The History of Money: From Sandstone to Cyberspace* (Crown, 1997). Robert Guttmann's book *How Credit-Money Shapes the Economy: The United States in a Global System* (M. E. Sharpe, 1994) provides an excellent history of the emergence of credit money, and Jacob Needleman offers some philosophical insights into money in *Money and the Meaning of Life* (Doubleday, 1991). The discussion of money in a Malaysian village comes from Janet Carsten's article "Cooking Money: Gender and the Symbolic Transformation of Means of Exchange in a Malay Fishing Village," in *Money and the Morality of Exchange,* edited by J. Parry and M. Bloch (Cambridge University Press, 1989). The history of economic growth is contained in Angus Maddison's *The World Economy: A Millennial Perspective* (Development Centre of the Organisation for Economic Co-Operation and Development, 2003). You can find more information about the credit card habits of people in the United States at the Credit Research Center of Georgetown University (http://faculty.msb.edu/prog/CRC/).

Where Does the Wealth Needed to Sustain Growth Come From?

The idea of capital conversion is contained in an article by Pierre Bourdieu, "The Forms of Capital," in *Handbook of Theory and Research for the Sociology of Education,* edited by John G. Richardson (Greenwood Press, 1986). Information about global water usage comes from Maude Barlow's *Blue Gold: The Global Water Crisis and the Commodification of the World's Water Supply* (International Forum on Globalization, 2001), available online at http://www.thirdworldtraveler.com/Water/Blue_Gold.html. Robert Putnam's investigation of the decline of social capital in the United States is described in *Bowling Alone: The Collapse and Revival of American Community* (Simon & Schuster, 2000). A fuller examination of capital conversion can be found in *Global Problems and the Culture of Capitalism* (4th ed., Allyn & Bacon, 2008) by Richard H. Robbins.

What Kind of Economic System Is Necessary to Sustain Growth?

Adam Smith's 1776 classic *The Wealth of Nations*, edited by Edwin Cannan (Modern Library, 1994), is still worth reading to learn about the origins of the modern economy. Karl Polanyi's book *The Great Transformation* (Beacon Press, 1957), originally published in 1944, provides one of the best descriptions and analyses of the social effects of the industrial revolution and the dilemma posed by the choice of whether to regulate market excesses. One of the best descriptions of the history of neoliberalism is contained in David Harvey's book *A Brief History of Neoliberalism*, cited earlier. A financier's critical look at globalization is contained in Joseph Stiglitz's book *Globalization and Its Discontents* (Norton, 2002). The negative externalities of the automobile are described in Catherine Lutz and Anne Lutz Fernandez's book *Carjacked: The Culture of the Automobile and Its Effects on Our Lives* (Palgrave Macmillan, 2010). And the virtue of the bicycle is described in *Tools for Conviviality* by Ivan Illich (Marion Boyars, 2001).

What Is the Role of the Nation-State in Sustaining Growth?

Classic anthropological analyses of state formation and organization can be found in *Origins of the State* and *Civilization: The Process of Cultural Evolution* by Elman R. Service (Norton, 1975) and Morton H. Fried's book *The Evolution of Political Society: An Essay in Political Anthropology* (Random House, 1967). Carole Nagengast provides an excellent review of the literature on state violence in "Violence, Terror, and the Crisis of the State," in the *Annual Review of Anthropology*, vol. 23 (1994), pp. 109–36. R. J. Rummel provides a good history of state killing in *Death by Government* (Transaction Press, 1994). The major work on sustainability is contained in a report of the World Commission on Environment and Development: *Our Common Future* (Oxford University Press, 1987). Elaine Hartwick and Richard Peet provide a critique of sustainability in "Neoliberalism and Nature: The Case of the WTO," in a special issue of the *Annals of the American Academy of Political and Social Science*, vol. 590 (2003), pp. 188–211. The proposal for a Global Environmental Mechanism can be found in Daniel C. Esty and Maria H. Ivanova's article "Toward a Global Environmental Mechanism," in *Worlds Apart: Globalization and the Environment*, edited by James Gustave Speth (Island Press, 2003). A discussion of the role of the media in the Social Security debate is contained in *Social Security: The Phony Crisis* by Dean Baker and Mark Weisbrot (University of Chicago Press, 2001). Details about the imposition of neoliberal economic measures in Iraq can be found in Naomi Klein's article "Baghdad Year Zero: Pillaging Iraq in Pursuit of a Neocon Utopia," in *Harper's Magazine*, September 2004, available online at http://harpers.org/BaghdadYearZero.html, and the story about the reopening of closed factories in Iraq by the U.S. military in James Glanz's article "Iraqi Factories, Aging and Shut, Now Give Hope," *New York Times*, January 18, 2007, available online at http://www.nytimes.com/2007/01/18/world/middleeast/18factory.html. A discussion of the building of the American military empire is provided by Chalmers Johnson in *The Sorrows of Empire: Militarism, Secrecy, and the End of the Republic* (Henry Holt, 2004).

Why Do Economies Collapse?

For information on the financial crisis itself, see Stephanie Blankenburg and José Gabriel Palma's the global financial crisis in the *Cambridge Journal of Economics*

(2009: 33, 531–8) along with James Crotty's article, "Structural Causes of the Global Financial Crisis: A Critical Assessment of the 'New Financial Architecture'" (*Cambridge Journal of Economics*, 33, 563–80). Niall Ferguson provides an excellent history of finance in *The Ascent of Money* (New York: Penguin Press, 2008), as does Steve Fraser in *Every Man a Speculator* (Harper Perennial, 2005) and Charles P. Kindleberger in his 1978 classic *Manias, Panics and Crashes: A History of Financial Crisis* (4th ed.; Wiley). Carmen M. Reinhart and Kenneth S. Rogoff examine the history of financial crises in *This Time is Different: Eight Centuries of Financial Folly* (Princeton University Press, 2009). The major work on the Dutch economy is Jan de Vries and Ad van der Woude's book *The First Modern Economy: Success, Failure, and Perseverance of the Dutch Economy, 1500–1815* (Cambridge University Press, 1997). Finally, for excellent works in financial anthropology, see Gillian Tett's account of how the current economic crisis unfolded in *Fool's Gold: How the Bold Dream of a Small Tribe at J. P. Morgan Was Corrupted by Wall Street Greed and Unleashed a Catastrophe* (Free Press, 2009) and Karen Ho's *Liquidated: An Ethnography of Wall Street* (Duke University Press, 2009).

Case Study in Doing Anthropology #3: Anthropology and Public Policy
There is an excellent discussion of the role of public policy in anthropology in Alexander M. Ervin's book *Applied Anthropology: Tools and Perspectives for Contemporary Practice* (Allyn & Bacon, 2005). Chris Shore and Susan Wright's book *Anthropology of Policy: Critical Perspectives on Governance and Power* (Routledge, 1997) contains a more detailed critical analysis of anthropology and public policy. One of Walter Goldschmidt's major works on agriculture is *As You Sow: Three Studies in the Social Consequences of Agribusiness* (Allanheld & Osmun, 1978). Kendall Thu and E. Paul Durrenberger provide a description of the effects of large-scale pig farming in *Pigs, Profits, and Rural Communities* (State University of New York Press, 1998), a book that also includes Laura B. DeLind's study "Parma: A Story of Hog Hotels and Local Resistance" (pp. 22–38) as well as John Eikerd's analysis of the economics of large-scale and family-sized pig farms, "Sustainable Agriculture, Rural Economic Development, and Large-Scale Swine Production" (pp. 157–69).

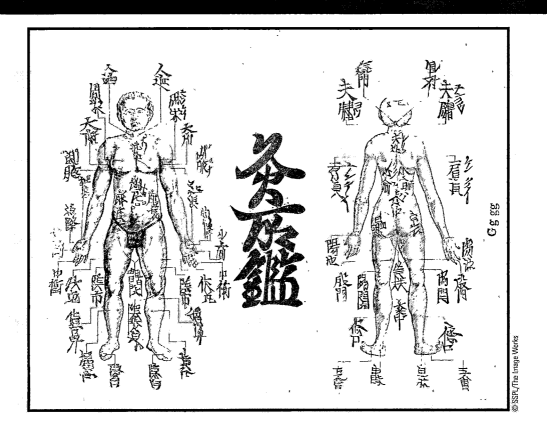

4

THE SOCIAL AND CULTURAL CONSTRUCTION OF REALITY

PROBLEM 4: WHY DO PEOPLE BELIEVE DIFFERENT THINGS, AND WHY ARE THEY SO CERTAIN THEIR VIEW OF THE WORLD IS CORRECT AND OTHER VIEWS ARE WRONG?

> *There is an obvious rightness about our own world view. It seems, in some way, to mirror reality so straightforwardly that it must be a consequence of direct apprehension rather than effort and imagination. Conversely, alternative beliefs possess an obvious wrongness. The more natural our own perspective becomes, the more puzzling become the strange propositions of ancestors, aliens and eccentrics. How did such mistaken ideas come to be held? However have they remained uncorrected for so long?*
>
> —**Barry Barnes**

INTRODUCTION

The Central Question

How is it that people can believe in a God whose existence cannot be proven? How can they believe in the existence of ancestor spirits, or witches, or devils or the power of magic to call forth spirits of the dead? But, of course, people do believe these things and even take these beliefs for granted. For example, most Americans believe in the existence of God, and according to most surveys, a vast majority of Americans believe in the existence of Satan and the possibility of demonic possession. Many Americans daily consult their horoscopes, believing that the position of the stars at their birth somehow affects their destiny. Some Americans believe in witchcraft; there are some 80,000 members of Wicca in the United States—people who are inspired by witches, wizards, druids, and kabbalists of largely European lore to practice what they consider to be magic and who claim that mind can alter matter—that the trained imagination can affect the material world.

How to deal with the problem of belief has long been a concern of anthropologists. When confronted with, say, a belief in witches, the temptation is to take for granted that the belief is mistaken. In that case, the task of the anthropologist is to explain how it is that people can believe in things that are wrong. Early anthropological efforts at understanding religion took this approach. Edward Tylor, considered by some to be the founder of modern anthropology, wrote in 1871 that religion and a belief in the supernatural developed through people's attempt to explain such basic phenomena as death and dreaming. What is the difference, Tylor imagined early human beings thinking, between a live person and a dead one or between a sleeping person and someone who is awake? They must have reasoned, Tylor said, that there was something— some kind of essence—that left the body in death or that traveled to distant places in sleep's dreams. From this reasoning, said Tylor, came a belief in the idea of a soul that animated the body but that fled the body in death and sleep. That is why, Tylor said, the word for "breath" and the word for "soul" are the same or similar in so many societies. And it was not unreasonable, said

Tylor, for these early philosophers to imagine that other animals and things were also animated by souls.

Once a belief in souls was arrived at, it was a small step to reason that there were places in which departed souls resided and a smaller step to believe that souls became gods. And it was logical, then, for human beings to appeal to these departed spirits for help in controlling life's uncertainties. For Tylor, then, beliefs in gods and spirits developed through the attempts of human beings to explain certain events—to understand why things happened as they did. The answers, he assumed, were wrong, but they were founded in the human need to explain and interpret experience.

French sociologist Émile Durkheim also asked, in his classic work *The Elementary Forms of the Religious Life* (1912), what suggests to the human mind the existence of God? Durkheim speculated, as did Tylor, that the secret must lie in the beliefs of early human beings. Thinking that the lives of early human beings could best be studied by looking at societies that were relatively underdeveloped, Durkheim read about the religious beliefs of the indigenous people of Australia—particularly their beliefs about **totemism**. The totem, said Durkheim, was some element of nature—an animal, an insect, a plant, or some celestial phenomenon—that served as a symbol for a group or clan. The totem was worshipped and was considered sacred and holy by the members of the group. It also served as a flag, or concrete representation of the group. If members of the group worshipped the totem and if the totem were a symbol of the group, was it unreasonable to suppose, said Durkheim, that it was the group—the clan itself—that was being worshipped?

But what would suggest to people the power of the totem—its sacredness? The answer, said Durkheim, lies in the constraints that people feel are imposed on them by the group and by society and in the special power that people feel when groups come together in celebration and **ritual**. And if in small-scale societies people worship the group through their symbolic representations, as clans worship themselves through their totems, is it not reasonable to suppose that in large-scale societies people worship society through their god or gods? That God is society?

There were many other attempts to explain what it was that suggested to human beings the idea of God. Sigmund Freud, for example, speculated that people projected onto an imagined God the power of the father—that in worshipping God, people were worshipping the father. Bronislaw Malinowski claimed that people turn to gods and spirits to influence life events that they feel helpless to control. All these early writers approached the question of God in particular and religion in general with the assumption that the beliefs were essentially in error. Nevertheless, they believed that religious beliefs served some purpose—increasing group cohesion or providing supernatural sanctions for the violation of group norms.

Recent anthropological attempts to understand belief have built on these early efforts, but the general thrust has been to try to understand how it is that people are persuaded that their view of the world is correct. Some researchers have even extended their studies to include so-called scientific beliefs, reasoning that the processes that result in people taking the existence of God for granted must apply as well to the taking for granted of a naturally ordered universe of atoms, molecules, genes, electrical and magnetic forces, social imperatives, and the like.

To answer the question of how it is that people can so easily believe that their view of the world is correct, we need to examine a number of concepts. Because language is one of the mediums we use to make our knowledge concrete and to communicate with others, it plays a major role in giving us a sense of the universe and ourselves. **Symbolic actions**—the rituals, myths, arts, literature, and music that we enjoy or participate in—all play a role, as we shall see, in organizing and making concrete a particular view of the world. Also, we need to explore how people learn to view the world as they do and how they defend their beliefs against skeptics. Certainly, the fact that others agree or disagree with us about the nature of the world will influence what we believe is true or not true and determine how we react to experiences that challenge a particular view of the world. What we believe must also be, in some way, a product of our social, economic, and political lives. Then, we need to ask why people sometimes radically change what they believe. Finally, we will examine how the frameworks for studying belief systems can be applied to such career areas as public relations and political counseling.

QUESTIONS

4.1   How does language affect the meanings people assign to experience?
4.2   How does symbolic action reinforce a particular view of the world?
4.3   How do people come to believe what they do, and how do they continue to hold to their beliefs even if they seem contradictory or ambiguous?
4.4   How can we account for the different meanings people assign to experiences?
4.5   How can people reorder their view of the world if it becomes unsatisfactory?

Case Study in Doing Anthropology #4: Political Counseling and the Power of Metaphor

QUESTION 4.1   *How Does Language Affect the Meanings People Assign to Experience?*

Language is one medium through which we make contact with the world that we take for granted. We tend to assume that it is only a transparent medium for the transmission of thought—a tool for communication. Anthropologist Edward Sapir challenged this view of language, suggesting that specific languages serve not only as a medium of communication but also to define and guide our perception of experience. That is, specific languages—French, English, Navajo, Chinese, Tupi, or any of the other thousands of languages that human beings speak—somehow order the experiences of those who speak them. Benjamin Lee Whorf later elaborated on Sapir's ideas and suggested that each language constitutes a frame of reference that orders a particular people's views of the world.

The relationship between language and thought can exist at various levels. The most obvious is at the level of vocabulary. For example, according to Sapir and Whorf, vocabulary reflects the social and physical environment of a people. For example, Whorf noticed that the Inuit have a variety of words for different kinds of snow, whereas we have only one, and the Aztecs of Mexico used the same word for "cold," "ice," and "snow." Sapir noted how the vocabulary of the Nootka of the northwest coast of North America precisely defined the variety of marine animals on which they subsisted, and the vocabulary of the Paiute, living in the desert regions of southern Utah and northern Arizona, where complex directions were needed for finding water, contained detailed descriptions of features of the landscape. Our own rich vocabulary for expressing units of time is linked to our concern for the temporal ordering of activities. Sapir suggests that the vocabulary of a language not only reveals what is important to the speakers of that language but also cues the speakers to be more sensitive to the named features of their environment.

Sapir and Whorf also explored the relationship between the grammar of a language and the modes of thought characteristic of its speakers. In English, Whorf points out, there are two dominant types of sentences: the subject-predicate type, such as "The book is green," and the actor-action type, such as "Sally runs." In both cases, the subject of the sentence—the book in the first case; Sally in the second—is spoken of as if it were an enduring object—something stable through time that acts or is acted on by something else. Whorf maintains that this indicates a pervasive tendency in English to view the world as being made up of objects, so experiences described in English lose the fluidity of passing experience. For example, we speak of time as if it were an object or a thing—as if we could isolate a piece of it ("I'll study for three hours") the same way we select food ("I'll take three hamburgers"). In English grammar, time occupies the same grammatical space as food. In this sense, our grammar reflects, reinforces, and perhaps determines our general view of the world as consisting of objects or substances, with everything perceived as an attribute of some object.

Another implication of our way of speaking of time has to do with our sense of controlling it. Because in English time may take the role of an object, we are able to quantify it and to speak of "saving" it or "wasting" it.

The ideas of Sapir and Whorf, generally referred to as the **Sapir-Whorf hypothesis**, are suggestive, and both were very careful to avoid claiming that there is a causal link between language and thought. Not all anthropologists are convinced there is an explicit link between the grammar of a language and the culture of the people who speak that language. But there is another sense in which language serves to give meaning to different events, and it has to do with the idea of **metaphor**.

"*Can I nuke something for you?*"

Americans use metaphors of war to explain and interpret many aspects of life, as in this cartoon.

Borrowing Meaning with Metaphors

One major characteristic of human language is its economy. That is, the same words we use to describe one area of experience can also be used to describe another area. If this were not so, we would need a distinct vocabulary for every distinct experience we wished to describe; instead of a working vocabulary of hundreds of words, we would need a working vocabulary of millions! Fortunately, we can escape that problem through the use of metaphor, taking linguistic expressions from one area of experience and applying them to another. Such expressions as "the shoulder of the road" or "the foot of the mountain" illustrate the metaphoric extension of parts of the human body to refer to features of the landscape. "Jane is a snake," "Sally is a fox," "Jeff is a dog," or "Charley is a pig" are expressions that represent metaphoric extensions from the animal world to the human world. Metaphors take language from one **domain of experience**, such as the domain of the body or the domain of animals, and apply it to another domain, such as landscape features or persons.

But when language is extended from one domain to another, meaning is also extended. In other words, metaphor involves not only speaking of one experience in terms of another but also understanding one experience in terms of another. For example, when we speak about argument, we might say "His point was right on target" or "Your claims are indefensible" or "She attacked my argument, and I had to defend my position." Or we might say "She shot down my argument" or "I think I won the argument." We speak about argument in terms of war, taking the language from the domain of war and applying it to the domain of conversation. But we have not only transferred words; we have also transferred meaning. We do not simply talk about argument in terms of war; we actually win and lose arguments.

What would happen if instead of metaphors of war, we borrowed metaphors from the domain of dance to comprehend argument? We might talk about the rhythm of the interaction or the grace of the performance. In fact, this would not be argument at all; instead of two protagonists in a win-or-lose situation, we would have two partners trying to coordinate their movements to arrive at a mutual accommodation.

Or think about the way our conception of illness is embedded in the language we use to describe it. We take language from the domain of war and use it to talk about health. We build our defenses against illness; we gt ill because

We are constantly trying to interpret animal behavior through our own social lens. Is this aggression, or might it be play or even a form of greeting?

our resistance was low. We fight a cold, destroy germs, wage war on cancer, and suffer heart attacks. The language that AIDS researchers use is full of metaphors drawn from war. Recent research reports that the AIDS virus weakens the "immune system attack force" or the "killer cells" that are meant to "destroy virus-stricken cells." As one researcher put it: "If you want to think of it with a war analogy, it's as though the soldiers are still on maneuvers, but they no longer have their weapons: When they encounter the enemy, they lose their weapons."

Not all societies borrow from the domain of conflict to give meaning to health. For example, the Navajo see illness as a displacement of the person from his or her proper place in the universe. Illness is thus a disruption of harmony.

The human body and war, of course, are not the only domains from which Americans borrow to assign meaning to other areas of experience. Americans also borrow from the domain of economic exchange. In English, time is spoken of not only as if it were a distinct thing but also as if it were a specific type of thing: Time is money; you're wasting my time; this gadget will save you hours; I don't have the time to give you; that flat tire cost me an hour; you need to budget your time; he's living on borrowed time; is that worth your while? Time in American culture is a valuable commodity—a scarce resource that we quantify, invest, and spend.

Sports represent another domain from which Americans borrow heavily for metaphors. For example, a male baseball enthusiast might describe a romantic encounter in this way: I met a girl, and I thought she'd play ball and that I'd not only get to first base but would score; but I struck out. A follower of astrology might describe the same event this way: I met a girl, and I thought we'd be Leo and Cancer, that we'd be in conjunction, and that she would be the sun to my moon, but our stars were crossed. The differences between the two descriptions of the same event involve more than a simple difference in language. Metaphors from different domains of experience assign different meanings to the same event. The baseball enthusiast, using a metaphor common to American youth, sees the experience as a contest to be won or lost

Exercise 4.1a ➤ | Carefully examine the photograph above. Describe what thing is happening in the photograph, and see if you can draw some conclusions about the nature of baboon society from your description.

and as a way of demonstrating proficiency. On the other hand, the follower of astrology sees the meeting as a fated, predetermined event; it involves not winning or losing but rather the discovery of pre-existent compatibility.

Love is a highly abstract concept, and the language of love is full of metaphors that try to put the concept into a domain of experience that helps us make sense of it. We try to make it concrete with metaphors of economic exchange: I make you feel good about yourself, and you in exchange make me feel good about myself. We use metaphors drawn from the world of work; we find people working out a relationship or working at it—and so on. Or we use metaphors and language drawn from electronics and communication; we get through to each other or talk about not being able to communicate anymore. Psychologists who write about love make frequent use of medical metaphors; they speak of a lack of love as a disease or of love as an addiction. In *Love: Emotion, Myth, and Metaphor* (1981), Robert C. Solomon provides an excellent discourse on such language of love.

Metaphors, then, are not simply verbal devices that we use to make our language colorful and economical. Rather, they are like theories, templates, lenses, or filters we can use to help us understand one domain of experience in terms of another. By using language from one domain of experience to describe another, we transfer whole domains of meaning: Arguments become wars, time becomes a commodity, and romantic encounters become contests. Moreover, the metaphors we use to describe experiences may predispose us to seek certain solutions to problems associated with those things and people. A Navajo cure seeks to return the patient to a state of harmony with the social and natural universe. Does our speaking of illness in terms of war and battle encourage us to take for granted that it is some kind of war? And if it does, how does that view determine the kinds of treatment for illness that we devise and seek? Does not the language we use to describe illness predispose us to cures that destroy the agent of disease rather than return the patient to health?

The fact that Americans borrow so heavily from the domains of war, sports, and economic exchange for metaphors suggests another way to understand how language operates to influence people's views of the world. Most societies seem to have one or more domains from which they borrow extensively for metaphor. These domains become **key metaphors** that give to each culture a style or cast that makes the culture distinctive. Thinking and speaking of many domains of experience in terms of a particular domain is a way of achieving a certain coherence in the meanings in any culture.

Kwakwaka'wakw Metaphors of Hunger[1]

Perhaps one of the most spectacular expressions of the elaboration of a key metaphor and the human imagination is found among the Kwakwaka'wakw

---

[1]The Kwakwaka'wakw have generally been referred to as *Kwakiutll* in most ethnographic studies—particularly the classic works of anthropologists Franz Boas. Kwakwaka'wakw is how they refer to themselves.

of British Columbia. Much of our knowledge of the traditional life of the Kwakwaka'wakw we owe to Franz Boas, one of the founders of American anthropology; his Kwakwaka'wakw assistant, George Hunt; and filmmaker and photographer Edward Curtis. Boas and Hunt's descriptions served as the basis for Ruth Benedict's description of the Kwakwaka'wakw in her classic work *Patterns of Culture* and, more recently, for Stanley Walens's analysis of Kwakwaka'wakw belief.

Walens suggests that the act of eating is a key metaphor for the Kwakwaka'wakw; that is, the Kwakwaka'wakw speak of many different things by using the vocabulary and language associated with hunger, eating, and food. A fundamental meaning the Kwakwaka'wakw find in their experience is that the universe is a place in which some beings are eaten by other beings and some beings must die so other beings may eat them and live. Eating gives life in at least two ways: It provides nutrition, but it also frees souls. The Kwakwaka'wakw believe that when a person dies, his or her soul leaves the body and enters the body of a salmon. But the soul cannot be freed until the physical body is destroyed; for this, reason the Kwakwaka'wakw place their dead on scaffolds where the body can be devoured by ravens and other birds. Once the soul enters the body of a salmon, it remains there, living in a salmon world that socially resembles the human world. However, when the salmon is caught and eaten by human beings, the soul is once again freed and enters the body of a newborn child. Thus, for the Kwakwaka'wakw, the act of eating becomes a metaphor through which much of their life is understood and described.

The importance of eating for the meanings the Kwakwaka'wakw ascribe to experience is manifested in the images of mouths that visually dominate Kwakwaka'wakw art, ritual, and **myth**. Their world, says Walens, is replete with the mouths of animals killing to satisfy their hunger, and their art is filled with gaping jaws of killer whales, fangs of wolves and bears, and tearing beaks of hawks, eagles, and ravens. Dancers wear masks of cannibal birds with nine-foot-long beaks that shatter human skulls to suck out the brains. Wild women with protruding lips who wait to rip apart and devour travelers and misbehaving children inhabit the woods. It is a world where suckling infants turn into monsters and devour their mothers.

The Kwakwaka'wakw use the eating metaphor to give meaning to a wide range of their experiences. Hunger is associated with greed, for, like unrestrained hunger, greed causes people to accumulate wealth far beyond what they need—often taking from others who are left without. Moreover, people who hoard

Metaphors of eating and being eaten abound in Kwakwaka'wakw life. In this religious ceremony, dancers portray cannibal birds with long beaks; a totem pole includes faces with gaping mouths.

Library of Congress, Edward S. Curtis Collection, LC-US262-49042

Exercise 4.1b ➤

There are some interesting parallels between the metaphors of eating and hunger among the Kwakwaka'wakw and the metaphors of sexual intercourse and sexual desire in America. Kwakwaka'wakw art, myth, and stories are filled with mouths and images of eating and hunger. What are some of the images that fill American expressive culture (advertising, for example)? Vomit is a life-giving substance for the Kwakwaka'wakw; what symbolizes life giving in America? Are there other ways Americans use sexual symbolism that are similar to the ways the Kwakwaka'wakw use hunger and food?

food are, in effect, hoarding souls, preventing the return of a soul from the spirit world. Consequently, the Kwakwaka'wakw place great emphasis on gift giving and generosity. Hunger is also equated with immorality. The Kwakwaka'wakw have few means of maintaining social control; there are no police or courts, and violence is often the only recourse available to people who believe they have been wronged. Because the Kwakwaka'wakw believe that human desires create conflict and destruction that can quickly get out of hand, people must work together to prevent and control conflict before it threatens to destroy the group. And hunger is metaphorically associated with children because they constantly demand to be fed and will, if allowed, devour all a family's food.

But to fully appreciate the impact of a metaphor, it is necessary to understand that by ordering and describing a view of the world according to a particular domain of experience, people are drawn to try to control their lives by controlling the domains of experience they use to represent aspects of their lives. The Kwakwaka'wakw believe that the real solutions to the problems of greed, conflict, and child rearing involve controlling hunger. Eating is highly ritualized and controlled; food must be carefully handled. Food must also be generously given to others to avoid accusations of greed. In fact, wealthy persons are said to vomit forth goods—vomit having for the Kwakwaka'wakw a distinctly different meaning than it has for Americans. For the Kwakwaka'wakw, vomit is a life-giving substance. Animals that regurgitate their food—wolves that vomit food for their young and owls that regurgitate the bones of small animals they have eaten—occupy a special place in the Kwakwaka'wakw world. And the socialization techniques of the Kwakwaka'wakw are geared toward teaching children to control their hunger. In sum, a single domain of experience—eating—has been elaborated by the Kwakwaka'wakw to give to their world a style and meaning that are unique to them.

The Metaphors of Contemporary Witchcraft and Magic

A metaphor is a theory—a system of interpretation that, once understood in the context of one domain of experience, can then be transferred to others. The metaphors may also be imbedded in myth and history as well as in everyday experience. A good example of that is modern witchcraft and magic.

Anthropologist Tanya M. Luhrmann details some of these practices in her book *Persuasions of the Witch's Craft: Ritual Magic in Contemporary England* (1989). Luhrmann joined various covens and groups in England whose membership consists of middle-class urbanites who situate their magic in "New Age" ideology—the "Age of Aquarius"—people who place an emphasis on natural foods, good health, and personal stability and whose magical practices consist largely of conjuring spirits, reading the tarot, and magical healing.

Modern magic is based on the assumption that mind and thought can affect matter without the intervention of the thinker's actions. It assumes that thought and matter are one. Magicians believe, says Luhrmann, that it is a distortion to treat objects as isolated and unique. One manual describes a world view that sees things as swirls of energy rather than things. The physical world, it says, is formed by energy as stalactites are created by dripping water. Human beings can cause a change in the physical world by altering these energy patterns, as we might change the flow of water forming the stalactites to change their form.

A key metaphor imbedded in modern witchcraft and magic is that of stratification—of "planes" and "levels." For the follower of white (good) witchcraft, or magic, or the tarot, the universe is divided into a complex collection of entities and beings, each of which exists on different planes, astral planes, or levels—of which the everyday plane of material life is but the lowest. After death, for example, the soul does not die but goes to exist on another plane, and some remain in contact with the material world. Other magical forces exist on other levels, but they too can be harnessed by human beings to influence events on the everyday plane of existence. Moreover, the properly trained human mind can, simply by imagining them, create forms on the astral plane that may in turn affect things in the material world.

Adherents of tarot cards use them to foretell the future and to interpret their own experiences in life.

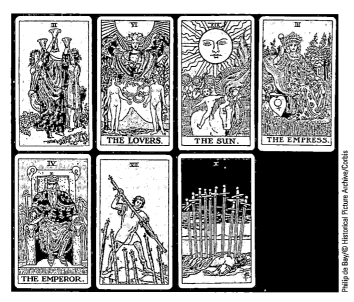

Becoming a magician, Luhrmann says, requires the acquisition of specialized and esoteric knowledge; consequently, magicians read books, arrange and attend rituals, go to meetings, and learn the tarot, astrology, mythology, and 17th-century Gaelic cures.

The tarot deck consists of 78 cards comprising an elaborate and complex system of metaphoric associations that link various domains of experience, ranging from an understanding of the planets and other celestial objects (sun, moon, etc.) to colors, material elements (e.g., mercury, iron, gold, etc.), emotions, personal qualities, and mythological beings. Each tarot card is said to have some meaning that is determined by its association with a specific planet, an element, an emotion or human quality, and so forth. Aleister Crowley, one of the founders of modern magic and witchcraft and a designer of the modern tarot deck, says that each card is, in a sense, a living being.

A magician uses the tarot cards to divine the future, but the cards also provide ways for people to interpret their own lives. The cards, says Luhrmann, provide people with a symbolic map with which to interpret and understand themselves as they transfer the meaning of the cards to their own lives and experiences. Thus, some may associate themselves with the Empress, calm and fecund, or they may say that someone has the temperament of a Hermes, mercurial and unpredictable. And in associating themselves with a particular card, people also associate themselves with a specific planet (e.g., Mars, dominant and aggressive), color (e.g., red, emotional and passionate), etc. In a sense, one may begin to define oneself in terms of the tarot and actually become the person that the cards delineate. The transfer of meaning creates meaning.

In examining the power of metaphor to define our realities, we must remember that there is no necessary connection between the domains from which people draw metaphors and the domains to which they apply them. There is no natural connection between commodities and time, war and health, eating and immortality, the tarot's Empress and someone's personality. These borrowings are the products of the human imagination. Many different metaphors can be applied to a specific experience, and one domain can never be the exact replica of the other. No man is really a tiger; no woman really a fox. How can there be "different levels" of reality? Metaphoric borrowings are intrinsically absurd. But we constantly seem to confuse one domain with another: We really do fight disease; we really win arguments. Thus, we need to explore by what magical means people are convinced that by controlling one domain of experience (e.g., eating), they can really control another (e.g., greed). Or that by imagining themselves in a different "level" of reality, they can actually contact the astral plane.

QUESTION 4.2   *How Does Symbolic Action Reinforce a Particular View of the World?*

Language represents one way that our experience of the world is socially filtered. By sharing a language, we also share a view of the world expressed in the vocabulary, grammar, and metaphors of the language. But language is not the only way that our social life mediates between our senses and the meanings that we assign to experience. We also participate in activities that express a particular view of the world. Especially important are such symbolic actions as ritual, myth, literature, art, games, and music. Symbolic actions carry bundles of meanings that represent public displays of a culture. They are dramatic renderings and social portrayals of the meanings shared by a specific body of people. More importantly, symbolic actions render particular views of the world in a way that makes them seem correct and proper.

This idea can be illustrated with the game of chess. Chess originated in India or China as a favorite pastime of the aristocracy. Its original meanings are unknown, but the game is often considered to be a representation of war. However, it is one in which each side has exactly the same number and kinds of pieces, and the two sides alternate their moves. If it is a symbolic representation of war, it is a highly stylized and carefully regulated war—unlike any that has ever been fought.

But chess is more than a game; it is a statement—a story about hierarchy and the social order. Pieces (pawns, rooks, knights, bishops, kings, and queens) are ranked in terms of importance and are given a freedom of movement corresponding to their ranking. Consequently, each game of chess is a story about social hierarchy that reinforces the validity of a social system based on rank order. Each time the game is played, the authenticity of this social system is proven true; the side with the highest-ranking pieces remaining is almost always the winner. And, significantly, the game validates the importance of the generals (the two players), who control the movement of their side's pieces on the board. It is the strategist, the thinker, who wins the war (game), not the soldiers. Even the king depends on the general. Because in every chess game each side starts out with the same number and kinds of pieces, it must be the strategist, the head of the hierarchy, who determines the outcome of the game and, by extension, the well-being of the society. Chess reinforces the axiom that rank is power, and power is achieved by outwitting an opponent; a pawn, in itself, can never defeat a queen any more than a peasant can threaten a king. There are winners and losers, but regardless of which side wins, the match in a crude way represents the superiority of the aristocracy over the peasants.

As a game, chess assures the players of the rightness of hierarchical forms of social organization. However, participating in a single game of chess is not likely to convince anyone that the world portrayed in the game works as the game says it works. Instead, the meanings that characterize a culture are repeated again and again in other symbolic actions—the most important of which may be ritual.

The Kwakwaka'wakw and the witchcraft and Western mystery groups provide good examples of how ritual portrays, reinforces, and provides evidence for a particular view of the world.

The Kwakwaka'wakw Cannibal Dance

The Kwakwaka'wakw view of the world, as we noted in Question 4.1, rests on metaphors of hunger and is graphically displayed in their language, myth, art, and ritual. One of the most important Kwakwaka'wakw rituals is the Cannibal

Dance. The following description of the dance is necessarily a simplified one, but it includes the basic outline of the ceremony.

The Cannibal Dance is a four-day spectacle that serves as the highlight of the Kwakwaka'wakw Winter Ceremonial, a period of celebration and ritual observance in which all worldly activities cease. It is a time set aside for the spiritual world of the Kwakwaka'wakw, filled with monstrous and powerful beings and animal spirits, to intersect with the real world. The dance varies in some detail from group to group, but in all, it is the focal point of a youth's initiation into the Cannibal Society, a group responsible for performing certain rituals. The initiate plays the role in the ceremony of the cannibal dancer, or *hamatsa*. Members of the Cannibal Society and others gather in a ceremonial house to call back the cannibal to the human world from his sojourn in the realm of Man Eater, one of the most important of the supernatural beings in the Kwakwaka'wakw pantheon of spirits.

At the beginning of the ceremony, the *hamatsa* (the initiate) is believed to be in the woods frantically searching for human flesh to devour. Some early ethnographic accounts of the dance report that he would actually eat human mummified remains. Meanwhile, members of the Cannibal Society gather around a fire in the ceremonial house to sing and recite prayers to entice the *hamatsa* into the house, periodically sending men out to see if he is approaching the village. Finally, the prayers and calls of the Cannibal Society attract the *hamatsa*, who arrives, dressed in branches of the hemlock tree, by pushing aside roof boards and jumping down among the celebrants. Jumping through the roof is supposed to symbolize descent from the spirit world above to the world of the living below. In a seeming frenzy, the *hamatsa* runs around the fire and then into an adjacent room, leaving behind only the sacred hemlock branches he had worn. During the four days of the ceremony, the celebrants try by various means to entice him back into the house and, in effect, tame and socialize him, convincing him to forsake his craving for human flesh and accept normal food. For example, in one part of the ceremony, the *hamatsa* flees the house and a member of the Cannibal Society is sent as the bait to attract him. The *hamatsa* rushes upon him, seizes his arm, and bites it. Each time he bites someone, he dashes into a secret room and vomits—an act that is repeated various times during the ceremony.

During pauses, members of the audience exchange gifts; wealthy persons are expected to give away more than others. Later, the *hamatsa* appears naked and is given clothes, but he flees again. At another point, a woman who serves as a co-initiate appears naked, carrying mummified remains; she dances backward, trying to entice the *hamatsa* to enter the house, but she fails. Finally, the group succeeds in subduing the *hamatsa* by bathing him in the smoke of cedar bark that has been soaked in menstrual blood. After the conclusion of the public part of the Cannibal Dance, the initiate and a few members of the Cannibal Society go to another house and eat a normal meal—the final symbol that the *hamatsa* has been tamed and that his craving for human flesh has been replaced with a desire for ordinary food.

Ritual can be viewed as a symbolic representation of reality that makes it seem as if the reality were absolutely true. In another sense, the ritual presents participants in the ritual with solutions to real problems in the same way as symbolic representations suggest real solutions. For the Kwakwaka'wakw, the *hamatsa* is the ultimate projection of the power of hunger, and his desire for human flesh is a manifestation of the forces that can destroy society. By symbolically taming the hunger of the *hamatsa*, the participants in the ritual are asserting their moral responsibility to control greed and conflict. The ritual is the acting out of the successful efforts of the group to overcome forces that threaten society. Here is how Walens puts it (italics added):

> The *hamatsa's* hunger is fearsome; but it is the same hunger felt by every human, and thus every human has the power to control it. Ultimately the *hamatsa* and the bestial ferocity he embodies can be conquered. Morally the force of controlled social action, the strength of ritual, can conquer even a Cannibal's hunger. In fact, ritual can totally alter the impetus of the Cannibal's hunger, changing it from a destructive act to an affirmation of self control, an act of creative power. *The winter ceremonials prove that no matter how terrible the power of hunger, no matter how many fearsome guises it assumes, no matter how many masks it wears, and no matter how many voices it speaks with, morality will be the ultimate victor.* So long as humans have the knowledge to use food correctly, they need never fear hunger nor its awful accompaniment, death. (1981, p. 162)

The Cannibal Dance also contains a powerful message about socialization. Children, like the *hamatsa*, come from the spirit world and enter the world naked. Like the *hamatsa*, children have a female assistant—their mother—who must feed and socialize them; they dance and kick in the womb, where they live off the flesh of their mothers. Children come into the world hungry, threatening to devour their parents' wealth. Thus, in the Kwakwaka'wakw view of things, all humans are cannibals who must be socialized and tamed. Through swaddling, ritual fasting, denial of food, and other actions, parents transform their children from cannibals into moral human beings. The Kwakwaka'wakw, through ritual enactment, have made their symbols real. Their world really is as the ritual depicts it, and their lives in part revolve around living the reality they have created.

This Haida sculpture, commonly called "Bear-Mother," depicts the story of a woman who marries a bear, and her agony suckling her half-human progeny. It also captures the idea of the unrestrained greed of the unsocialized child.

Smithsonian Institution National Museum of Natural History, Department of Anthropology, #E73117

The Ritual of Contemporary Witchcraft and Magic

> In a witches' coven in northeast London, members have gathered from as far
> away as Bath, Leicester, and Scotland to attend the meeting at the full moon. . . .
> The sitting room has been transformed. The furniture has been removed, and
> a twelve-foot circle drawn on the carpet. . . . Four candlesticks stake out the
> corners of the room, casting shadows from stag antlers on the wall. The antlers
> sit next to a sheaf of wheat, subtle sexual symbolism. In spring and summer
> there are flowers everywhere. The altar in the centre of the circle is a chest
> which seems ancient. On top an equally ancient box holds incense in different
> drawers. On it, flowers and herbs surround a carved wooden Pan; a Minoan
> goddess figure sits on the latter itself amid a litter of ritual knives and tools.
> (Luhrmann, 1989, p. 42)

This is the setting for one of the rituals that Tanya Luhrmann attended in the
course of her fieldwork on contemporary witchcraft and magic. These rituals,
she says, are particularly important because they comprise one of the ways that
people become convinced of the validity of their beliefs. Going on to describe
the ritual in this setting, Luhrmann writes:

> The high priestess begins by drawing the magic circle in the air above the
> chalk, which she does with piety, saying "let this be the boundary between
> the worlds of gods and that of men." . . . On this evening a coven member
> wanted us to "do" something for a friend's sick baby. Someone made a model
> of the baby and put it on the altar, at the Minoan goddess's feet. We held
> hands in a circle around the altar and then began to run, chanting a set phrase.
> When the circle was running at its peak the high priestess suddenly stopped.
> Everyone shut their eyes, raised their hands, and visualized the prearranged
> image: in this case it was Mary, the woman who wanted the spell, the "link"
> between us and the unknown child. . . . By springtime, Mary reported, the
> child had recovered, and she thanked us for the help. (1989, p. 42)

Rituals like this one, the Cannibal Dance of the Kwakwaka'wakw, or those
enacted in thousands of mosques, churches, and synagogues across America
are special occasions that not only involve the enactment of key metaphors
but also serve as special events set aside from everyday existence—events that
draw participants into an emotional involvement with the metaphors. Rituals really do produce special feelings; people are carried away with the symbolism, the music, and the social communion with others. It is easy in this
situation to come to believe that it is not the ritual itself that produces these
feelings but the forces or powers that the ritual is believed to summon or embrace. As Luhrmann puts it:

> Just because you have a profound experience during prayer, it does not mean
> that God exists. But people often find the distinction hard to handle: they
> tend to accept the magical or theological ideas because the involvement—
> the spirituality, the group meeting, the moving symbols, the sheer fun of the
> practice—becomes so central to their lives. (1989, p. 178)

In contemporary witchcraft and magic, great emphasis is placed on visualization and meditation as part of the ritual. The high priest or priestess may relate a story and ask the participants to imagine themselves in the story; it may be a walk through a moonlit wood or a voyage with Sir Francis Drake around the Horn of Africa. After the ritual, people report actually experiencing the salt spray on their face or the pitching of the sea, and they experience fellow participants as shipmates aboard Drake's ship, the *Golden Hind*. In other words, the ritual not only dramatically depicts a metaphor, but it also teaches the participants how to experience the world as if the forces, gods, and spirits were truly real. Consequently, it is not unusual, in any belief system, for people to claim when participating in ritual to have had a "mystical experience," to experience themselves as "one with the universe," or to be overwhelmed with love or light. Thus, ritual not only teaches us about the world depicted in our metaphors, but it also teaches us how to feel within the universe we create.

Dorothy Meets Luke Skywalker

Contemporary witchcraft and magic draw heavily from myth and literature for their language, symbols, and metaphors. Luhrmann reports that many of the magicians she came to know were first attracted to their beliefs when they read J. R. R. Tolkien's *Lord of the Rings*, Ursula LeGuin's *Earthsea Trilogy*, or Marion Zimmer Bradley's *Mists of Avalon*. The themes of many of these books and of contemporary witchcraft and magic in general are contained in Western popular culture. These books and movies contain **key scenarios**— stories or myths that, like ritual, portray certain values and beliefs. In the same sense that people act out and communicate their view of the world in ritual and come to learn how to feel in that world, they can be said to act out the scenarios contained in their myths.

Joseph Campbell spent most of his life studying the myths of people around the world. In one of his earlier books—*The Hero With a Thousand Faces*—Campbell concludes that myths from all over the world contain

Exercise 4.2 ➤

> From what you remember about both *The Wizard of Oz* and *Star Wars*, how does each represent the process of coming of age? Are there key differences in the stories that are significant? Consider the following questions: What does each of these heroes—Luke and Dorothy—seek? From whom do they obtain their power? What form does the power take, and why are the differences significant? What helpers join the heroes, and what is the hero's relationship to them? How do the heroes destroy evil, and what is the reaction to their heroic deeds? Finally, what lesson does each hero learn, and in what way have their adventures transformed them?

Lucasfilm/20th Century Fox/The Kobal Collection

MGM/The Kobal Collection

stories about a hero who embodies the most valued qualities of that society. The myths have a consistent scenario: A hero separated from home, family, or society embarks on a journey in search of something—knowledge, a magical object, a person, or even a vision. In the course of the journey, the hero encounters a mentor—someone who conveys some kind of power to the hero. When the hero encounters strange creatures or powerful forces that make it difficult to reach a goal, helpers appear to assist and protect the hero. Eventually, the hero faces death but, with the help of the mentor's power, escapes and ultimately reaches the goal.

If the scenario sounds familiar, it probably is; it has been the source for many stories, books, and films. For example, George Lucas wrote the script for his movie *Star Wars* by using Campbell's writings on mythology as a guide. The quest scenario is deeply rooted in American literature and myth. However, there are variations. Another popular American story that utilizes the quest scenario is Frank Baum's *The Wizard of Oz*, which differs from *Star Wars* in that instead of a male hero (Luke Skywalker), it has a female hero (Dorothy Gale). Consequently, the stories convey different meanings: One is a story of growing up male; the other a story of growing up female. Reading, watching, or listening to stories such as these—and identifying with the hero—helps people learn something about growing up. *Star Wars* and *The Wizard of Oz* are coming-of-age tales. Both emphasize the American value of finding oneself; both define the qualities that are required for success. Although one story describes how to be a male and the other how to be a female, both provide, to those who participate in them, scenarios for solving real problems.

QUESTION 4.3   *How Do People Come to Believe What They Do, and How Do They Continue to Hold to Their Beliefs Even If They Seem Contradictory or Ambiguous?*

In 1992, a New York newspaper sent one of its reporters, Dennis Covington, to cover a murder case in Scottsboro, Alabama. The case was unusual because a man was accused of trying to murder his wife by forcing her to stick her hand into a box full of poisonous snakes. Covington discovered that the accused husband and his wife were members of a religious group who believe that the Bible, specifically the Book of Mark, directs true Christian believers to handle poisonous snakes and to drink poisonous things:

> And these signs shall follow them that believe: In my name shall they cast out devils; they shall speak with new tongues.
>   They shall take up serpents; and they shall drink any deadly thing, it shall not hurt them; they shall lay hands on the sick, and they shall recover.
> (Mark 16:17–18)

What Covington did not know at first was that Holiness Churches exist throughout the United States. The church's origins go back to 1909, when a Tennessee farmer, George Hensley, claimed that this section of the Book of Mark appeared to him in a vision. He interpreted the vision as a message for him to build a church in which people would test their faith with poisonous snakes and poisonous drinks. During the course of the religious services, participants would be possessed by the Holy Spirit, who might speak to them through the possessed person. The practices of members of the Holiness Church are familiar to a couple of generations of introductory anthropology students through the now classic ethnographic film *The Holy Ghost People* (1968).

During a religious service at the Old Rock Holy Church in Alabama, participants handle poisonous snakes because they believe Scripture tells them to do so.

As he researched the story and came to know members of the local Holiness Church, Covington, who had been raised a Christian, began to attend church services. He was taken with the ritual, particularly the music that typically accompanies church services. He observed people handling poisonous snakes, drinking poisonous drinks, and speaking in tongues. What he did not expect was that he would become a believer and a practitioner himself. But that is exactly what did happen. Covington became a member of the church for a time, handled poisonous snakes, and even daydreamed about becoming a traveling preacher.

Abbas/Magnum Photos

Covington's conversion experience, although dramatic, is certainly not unfamiliar to anthropologists. The history of anthropological fieldwork is full of instances of the researcher being drawn into the beliefs of the people he or she is studying. Susan Harding reports that she began to use biblical parables to interpret her experiences while studying the beliefs and practices of the Christian Coalition of Jerry Falwell, and Tanya Luhrmann found herself using the concepts of contemporary witchcraft and magic to interpret her experiences while working among magicians and witches in London.

The Process of Interpretive Drift

The experiences of people such as Covington, Harding, and Luhrmann raise the question of how it is that people come to believe what they do. What causes them to put on new spectacles through which to see the world to convert to a new way of interpreting their experience? In understanding her experiences, Luhrmann (1989, p. 312) suggests that changing one's beliefs involves a process she calls **interpretive drift**: "the slow, often unacknowledged shift in someone's manner of interpreting events as they become involved with a particular activity." When someone begins to practice, even in play, some new belief, one becomes more skilled at seeing new patterns and new connections between things. Interpretive drift is similar to adopting a new theory or a new way of interpreting events.

Magicians, Luhrmann says, entered magic familiar with the vague notion that the mind can directly affect the material world. They may begin to read books on magic or they may attend parties where the host or hostess playfully pulls out a tarot deck or a Ouija board and begins to read fortunes or summon spirits. At this point, they may not be "believers," but they may find themselves playfully interpreting events in their lives according to the beliefs of magic, and they may begin to find the interpretations intellectually and emotionally satisfying. They may attend a ritual, find "energy surging through them," and attribute that feeling to the presence of some mystical force or power.

Luhrmann herself experienced this, and her description is illuminating. She relates how a few months after she first met magicians in London, she was reading a magical text riding on a train from Cambridge, and she thought she was beginning to understand the meaning of magical power:

> Indeed I imagined the force flowing through me and felt electrically vital, as if the magic current were pulsing through my body. In the midst of the phenomenological fantasy, a bicycle battery in the satchel next to me melted with a crisp, singed smell, and while no doubt coincidental it was disconcerting at the time. (1989, p. 318)

Later, while she was attending a ritual and again feeling a force, her watch stopped. Although it was, she admits, a cheap watch, watches are said to stop in ritual. She concludes:

> With the watch and the battery, I had ready-made, non-magical, culturally laudable explanations of both events: they were coincidental, and had I not

been involved in magic they would have been unsurprising. But I had been thinking about magic, trying to "think like" a magician, and these events were striking because they made the alternative way of looking at the world seem viable. (1989, p. 318)

Interpretive drift continues when there are systematic changes in the way the believer begins to interpret experiences and events. He or she begins to identify evidence of the new belief, and the beliefs soon come to make more sense—to seem more natural; the person begins to "believe" in his or her truth. Once participation in a belief system begins—once the assumptions begin to seem plausible and even compelling—the person may seek and find additional compelling evidence for the viability of the belief. Instead of thinking that his or her beliefs have "changed," the believer begins to believe that the new beliefs are simply "true."

Luhrmann reports that magicians and witches all have stories they tell that, for them, provide evidence for the veracity of their beliefs. For example, when she met Robert, he related how, 27 years earlier, he was vacationing in Brussels when he met Françoise. As they toured the city, Françoise confided to him that she was epileptic and that the new medicine that her doctor prescribed seemed to have no effect. After he returned to England, he wrote Françoise that he and his friends practiced spiritual healing and that if she would send a photograph and a lock of hair (as psychic links) and pray to the Virgin Mary, they would attempt a cure. After the first ritual, Françoise wrote that she had stopped having severe seizures and was having only minor ones. Robert and his friends repeated the ritual, and in her next letter, the woman reported feeling a tremendous inflow of energy—that she was feeling better and was seeking a job. Then, her letters ceased.

A few months later, Robert wrote Françoise asking if he could visit. She met Robert at the boat with her family, who expressed great pleasure in meeting the man who had "cured" their daughter. "When were you cured?" Robert asked, and Françoise told him it was after a car accident when she had been hurled through the windshield. They attributed this "healing" event to the power of the ritual.

There are, of course, various other interpretations for Françoise's cure. A doctor would say that the shock of the automobile accident resulted in the cure; a Catholic might say it was the prayers to the Virgin Mary; however, an occultist would attribute the cure to the magic rituals. Robert and Françoise found additional confirmation for their beliefs in the fact that the accident occurred at full moon on the pagan festival of Candlemas, exactly 13 weeks (a quarter of a year) after the first healing ritual was performed. For Robert, this event, even 27 years after it occurred, was a central memory—a central piece of evidence to him of the efficacy of magic and ritual. The magician dismisses the possibility of coincidence as an explanatory option; he or she learns that what might previously have been considered a coincidence is now considered a consequence of his or her magic.

Luhrmann reports that even the failure of ritual may be taken as evidence for its efficacy. For example, a person works a ritual for a new house; a few weeks later, a packet of advertising leaflets on home maintenance arrives in the mail. This may be reported with some self-mockery as the ritual working but not quite in the way intended. One coven performed a ritual for a woman who wanted to have a child. She stood in the magic circle along with another woman, who was to attempt to visualize the event, willing the spell to work. Members of the coven jokingly report that the woman for whom the spell was cast had no child, but the other woman in the circle had a child 10 months later.

The intellectual changes that accompany the adoption of a new belief are, says Luhrmann, illuminating, and the fact that they are illuminating makes the belief and its practice seem effective. That is, the new beliefs provide a sense of discovery and confirmation; they work to help believers make sense of themselves, events in their lives, and the world around them.

Luhrmann says that the key element in becoming a believer is practice— that is, the actual involvement with the practices of a specific belief. In other words, people do not first come to believe something and then practice the beliefs; rather, they first practice and then they come to believe. Covington did not first believe that the handling of poisonous snakes was evidence for the presence of the Holy Spirit and then begin going to church. He first attended the services, spoke with the people, and played with the ideas—and only then did he begin to find or seek evidence that converted him to the belief. His evidence was the power he felt and the visions he had while handling snakes—a power he attributed to the presence of the Holy Spirit. The power of practice might be expressed by saying that people do not go to church because they believe in God; rather, they believe in God because they go to church.

However, adopting new beliefs does not remove what others may see as contradictions, ambiguities, or just plain absurdities. And it does not remove alternative metaphors, theories, or beliefs for interpreting events. Consequently, people must have ways of protecting their beliefs—ways to defend them against skeptics. In other words, once a belief system is adopted—once it seems as though it is true—how can the believer continue to protect these beliefs even if they might seem foolish to others?

Explaining Why the Sun Moves Around Earth

For almost 2,000 years, Europeans believed that Earth was the center of the universe. They envisioned a two-sphere cosmos consisting of a vaulted heaven, on which were located the sun, planets, and stars that circled eastward across the heavens, and an earthly sphere that was at the center of the universe. This belief was reinforced by language; then, as now, people spoke of the sun rising and setting. This conception of the universe was incorporated into myth with the biblical story of Joshua stopping the sun in the heavens (Joshua 10:12–14). The idea of an Earth-centered universe fit well with a society in which humankind was afforded the central place in the universe.

In spite of the extent to which people took for granted an Earth-centered universe, there were problems with understanding the system. It was difficult to explain the behavior of planets that revolved around Earth because they sometimes seemed to reverse their course or increase or decrease in brightness. Moreover, some early scholars, such as Aristarchus—a Greek grammarian who

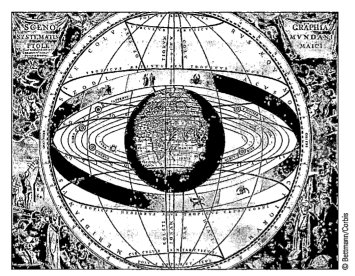

For centuries, Europeans believed in a cosmology that placed Earth at the center of the universe, with the sun, planets, and stars circling around it. The idea of a sun-centered cosmos was considered heretical.

proposed a sun-centered cosmology—were aware of alternative views. But people were generally able to explain away apparent contradictions.

The history of astronomy illustrates some of the ways by which people are able to sustain what they believe despite evidence to the contrary. For example, people can rationalize inconsistencies in what they believe; that is, they can find some way to explain away the inconsistency without changing their belief. For example, the behavior of the planets was a problem for medieval astronomers; sometimes, the planets could be observed reversing direction, a phenomenon now explained as a consequence of the differing speed of rotation of the planets around the sun. As Earth catches up to or is passed by a planet, the planet seems to reverse its motion. However, in the Ptolemaic system, the inconsistency was rationalized by proposing that planets moved in epicycles—figure-eight loops they supposedly made as they rotated around Earth. The epicycle concept also explained why a planet could vary in brightness because during its loops, its distance to Earth would vary.

British anthropologist E. E. Evans-Pritchard applied the term **secondary elaboration** to this type of rationalizing process. He illustrated secondary elaboration in his classic account of divination among the Azande of northern Zaire. A Zande who needs to make an important decision or discover the cause of an event consults a diviner. The diviner or oracle worker feeds a poison to chickens and addresses questions to the oracle that is thought to be manifest in the poison. The poison used by the Azande sometimes kills the chicken and sometimes does not, so the questions are put to the oracle in the form: if such is the case, kill (or do not kill) the chicken. The procedure is done twice to check its accuracy.

Sometimes, however, the oracle is wrong. It may reply positively to a question, but subsequent events prove the oracle false. It is, of course, easy for us to say we told you so, but the Azande can, if they wish, easily continue to believe in the power of the oracle by secondary elaboration. Instead of doubting the power of the oracle to predict, they can excuse the error by saying the oracle failed because the wrong poison was used, witchcraft interfered with the oracle, the poison was old, ghosts were angry, or the diviner was incompetent.

Beliefs can also be sustained by **selective perception**—seeing only what we want to see. For example, the Earth-centered universe was easily confirmed by the evidence of the senses. There was certainly nothing to indicate that Earth moved. In fact, the senses indicated just the opposite: If you dropped

Exercise 4.3 ➤

> One of the most persistent contradictions in Judeo-Christian thought has to do with the nature of God. The Judeo-Christian God, unlike creator figures in some other belief systems, is believed to be omnipotent: He controls everything. But, in addition, he is thought to be all good. The problem is, how can God be all powerful and all good when evil, suffering, and injustice exist in the world? If evil exists, he must allow it, in which case, he is not all good. Or if he is all good and if evil, suffering, and injustice exist, he must not be omnipotent. How might this contradiction be resolved while maintaining the idea of an all powerful yet all good deity?

an object, it fell straight down. If Earth moved, the object should fall to the right or left of the spot where it was dropped. You could see that the sun rises and sets. The Azande believe that witches are people who have inside them a substance responsible for making them witches. This substance can be discovered through autopsy and is believed to be inherited from one generation to another. Someone accused of witchcraft can thus be convicted or acquitted if an autopsy is done on kin who die. The corpse is cut open, and an expert in the procedure sifts through the intestines in search of the witchcraft substance. If it is found, as sometimes happens, it is held aloft for everyone to see.

A belief can also be sustained by **suppressing evidence**—not allowing evidence that contradicts a cherished belief. For example, in the Middle Ages, the Catholic Church denounced as heresy any attempt to suggest that Earth moved around the sun, and astronomers would simply ignore evidence that suggested that Earth was not at the center of the universe. For the Nuer, a herding people of the Sudan in northern Africa, the animal world is divided into things that are human and things that are not. Occasionally, however, a phenomenon threatens the distinction; if a monstrous birth (a severely deformed infant) occurs, it obscures the Nuer distinction between human and nonhuman. The Nuer solve the problem by saying the infant is a baby hippopotamus born to a human parent, and they place it in the river. They have suppressed evidence that threatens their view of the world.

Beliefs can also be sustained by an appeal to faith or mystery. The belief in an Earth-centered universe was sustained by an appeal to faith. If there were questions about it, people could be told that it was wrong to ask too many questions about the universe—that God sometimes worked in mysterious ways. The Catholic Church recognizes the concept of mystery in the anomalous features of such doctrines as the Trinity, the idea that God is one in essence but three in "person" (Father, Son, and Holy Ghost); the Eucharist, the idea that the bread and wine of ritual are the body and blood of Christ; and the Incarnation, the idea that the human and divine natures of Christ are united. The church embraces these ideas even though they are problematical in some way by declaring that each is a mystery—a doctrine whose truth cannot be demonstrated but must be taken on faith.

Beliefs can also be sustained by appeals to authority. The authority of Scripture supported the truth of an Earth-centered universe. And if all else fails, it is possible to use violence or deceit to protect a belief that is threatened. In the 17th century, when Galileo proposed to support the idea that Earth revolves around the sun, he was imprisoned and tortured by church officials until he finally recanted. He spent the rest of his life under house arrest.

People who practice contemporary witchcraft and magic often find themselves defending their beliefs and practices to skeptics and sometimes even to themselves. Some may claim that the magic and ritual really do work and that their beliefs and practices are as valid as any scientific belief or practice. They may produce testimony from people who actually witnessed spirits or who were cured of some illness immediately following a ritual. Others may try to rationalize their beliefs by saying that magic may seem unprovable or unreasonable, but, they say, a great deal of life seems unreasonable. Others may justify and defend their beliefs by an appeal to history: magic, the tarot, and astrology are ancient practices whose antiquity gives them authority and validity. They may recite the exploits of great magicians of the past: John Dee, Nostradamus, Eliphas Levi, and so on.

Some people may rationalize or legitimate their beliefs by focusing on their spirituality, freedom, or aesthetic beauty. Some may take a relativist perspective that says it is impossible even to question the "objective" status of magic and witchcraft, claiming that all understanding is subjective; others may assert that their beliefs are objectively false but valid as myth. These represent, Luhrmann points out, different standards of truth—standards that are collectively defined. For some, these standards are acceptable; for others, they are not. But the main point is that if people choose to adopt and defend a given set of beliefs, they are able to do so. However, that still leaves the question of why, when there are various way of looking at the world—various metaphoric constructions of reality, so to speak—do people select one metaphor over another?

QUESTION 4.4   *How Can We Account for the Different Meanings People Assign to Experiences?*

A central problem in anthropology, as we noted at the beginning of this chapter, is explaining how, when human beings generally have the same perceptual abilities, they have such different ways of interpreting experience. Why is it when some people look out upon the world, they assume it is filled with danger, while others see the world as benign? Why do some view others as friendly and welcoming, while other see them as dangerous or threatening? The explanation generally is that there must be a fit between what people believe about the world and the type of society that they live in. That is, the views we hold about the world—values, attitudes, beliefs,

Jonathan Player/The New York Times/Redux Pictures

Anthropologists Mary Douglas developed the grid/group framework to explain how the constraints that guide our social behavior also determine how we view the world.

and tastes—must generally support the patterns of social relations characteristic of our groups or society. It would be as difficult to believe that everyone is equal and should enjoy the same privileges while living in a hierarchical society as it would be believing that some people are innately more gifted than others in a society in which all were equal.

Perhaps the most ambitious attempt to explain why we choose certain metaphors over others—why certain views of the world just "seem right"—is the framework developed by anthropologist Mary Douglas and her associates. Called *grid/group theory* or *cultural theory*, it proposes that there are five—and only five—cultural types or social environments that are possible, with each characterized by different patterns of social relations and each with a characteristic world view. That is, each cultural type generates attitudes, beliefs, tastes, and values that support and justify that type of social organization—that each type is associated with a perceptual screen that makes particular visions of reality seem more or less plausible and provides for its members a particular cultural bias.

The five cultural types are defined on the basis of variations in two different types of social constraints that act on each person and guide their behavior. These constraints are labeled "group" and "grid." Group is the extent to which an individual is incorporated into bounded limits. Group constraints or pressures influence whether persons are free to move from group to group or they are constrained by group boundaries. Group will determine whether a person can gain support and sustenance from a single group or if he or she must seek support from many groups. Think about the experience of making the team or not making it.

Grid refers to the degree to which an individual's life is limited by externally imposed prescriptions. Do the rules of the group or society limit a person's interactions with others? Are people more or less free to define their relations to others or are roles, statuses, and rankings clearly demarcated by the society? Think about being able to date or marry whomever you want or being restricted to date or marry only people from certain social categories.

We can then categorize groups or societies relative to whether they are a high or low group, and a high or low grid. For example, at the high end of the grid dimension, people cannot freely interact with each other; rigid social classifications keep them apart and tightly regulate their interactions. People, as such, do not have the freedom to transact their interactions with each other. Males do not engage in female spheres, sons do not define their relationships with their fathers. Grid is visible in segregated times and places, and there are visible signs of rank, such as clothing, insignias, or linguistic forms. Societies at the low end of the grid dimension, on the other hand, have few ascribed statuses. Persons are able to transact their statuses with others more freely and more often.

High group is characterized by well-defined social boundaries, whereas low group is characterized by loose boundaries. Contrast the elaborate steps a person must follow to convert to Catholicism or Judaism and the ease in which he or she can declare themselves Methodists or Unitarians.

Combining grid and group allows us to identify five types of social environments, whose social organization and outlook on the world can be identified with the labels "fatalist," "hierarchist," "egalitarian," "individualist," and "hermit" (see Figure 4.1).

Let's begin with the hermit, the person living alone, generally geographically isolated and supplying for him- or herself all basic needs. The hermit feels neither the constraints of group nor of grid. He or she has no obligations or responsibilities to a group and does not need to negotiate his or her place in society with anyone. Few people, of course, live as hermits, but they do occupy a special place in our mythology. The hermit is in an unusual position; because he or she feels neither the power of grid nor the constraints of group, he or she must, in some way, encompass all (or none) of the world views characteristic of the other four types, ranging in mythology from the wise man on the mountaintop to the Kwakwaka'wakw cannibal who must be forced to accept the constraints of grid and group.

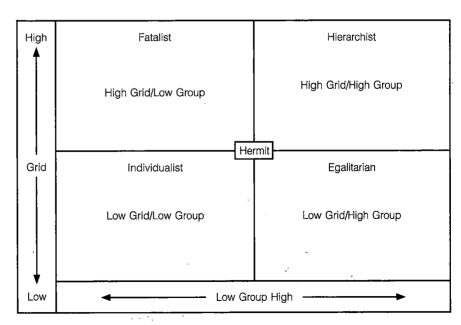

FIGURE 4.1 THE FIVE CULTURAL TYPES

The hierarchist feels strong group pressure and strong grid restrictions; the hierarchist's place in the group is strongly ascribed as the group is divided into separate, ranked and graded compartments, with resources (wealth, privilege, etc.) distributed unequally among members. Because a high degree of control is necessary to maintain these internal classifications and divisions and to police the restrictions on behavior, this type of social environment is associated with complex societies. A typical example would be the military, in which there are strong group boundaries ("us" and "them") and in which the person's place and his or her obligations and responsibilities to others are rigidly proscribed and divided into ranked identities—privates, lieutenants, majors, generals, and so on—with each identity carefully marked by dress and behavior. Sports teams, corporations, and formal religious institutions (e.g., the Catholic Church) tend to be high group and high grid. Hierarchies place great emphasis on loyalty to the group. Their motto might be "all for one and one for all," and they would consider the bureaucrat a hero, and, politically, would trend conservative.

The egalitarian is low grid but high group. There are strong boundaries around the group—that is a significant difference made between "us" and "them." The strong boundary between "us" and "them" is often maintained by portraying "them" as dangerous or corrupt, with the group serving as the main protector of members from outside threats. However, within the group, people are relatively free to negotiate their relations with others in a setting in which all are viewed as equal. Communal societies are representative of this kind of cultural type, as are grassroots or activist organizations or almost any ad hoc group (e.g., college club). There is weak leadership (because all are supposed to be equal), and there is a distrust of formal authority, although charismatic leaders are often sought. The motto of egalitarians is "A world in ourselves and in each other," their hero might be the holy man, and their politics would trend liberal/progressive.

Individualist groups are low on the grid and group dimensions. Because there are few rules defining a person's place in society, the social environment is strongly competitive. Relations between persons will be ambiguous and subject to negotiation. It will be a "free market" social environment—one where persons advance by making (and breaking) alliances, taking advantage of every opportunity, even (and especially) if it is at the expense of others. In this social environment, says Douglas, others are experienced as anonymous and merciless. In this setting each person will view corruption, self-seeking, and aggression as the characteristic features of human social life. The Wall Street trader or the typical college student might exemplify this cultural type. Of course, a college student may shift his or her social position by joining a Greek organization (egalitarian—all "brothers" and "sisters") or he or she may join a sports team (hierarchical) in which he or she would not only enter into a strongly bounded group but also have a specific role coordinated by a formal authority: the coach. The motto of the individualist is "Every man/woman for him/herself," the hero is the pioneer, and the political leaning would be libertarian.

Finally, there is the fatalist. Persons in this social environment have little control over personal transactions, as their place in society is relatively fixed, with little room for personal autonomy. There is little hope for rewards other than those that come from fulfilling one's allotted station in life. Because there is no group boundary, the person is excluded from whatever groups exist and the power that constrains the person is remote and impersonal. The dominant attitude in this social environment is one of passivity. The elderly in the United States may fall into this cultural type—limited by their age but with decreasing group support. The peasant farmer or, in many societies, the poor, fall into this cultural type. Their motto might be "What am I doing here," they would likely have no heroes, and, politically, they are likely to be nonvoters (see Figure 4.2).

A particular group or society may vary to the extent they represent the four types of social environment and range along different spots of the grid/group axis. However, a society or group can function only so long, as members hold a way of looking at the world that, at least to some degree, reinforces the desired pattern of social relationships characteristic of the society or group. A ranked society or group must, at least to some degree, promote a view that some individuals are *naturally* more talented or gifted than others and will seek evidence in nature and elsewhere that this is true, as an egalitarian society must promote the view that all are "born equal."

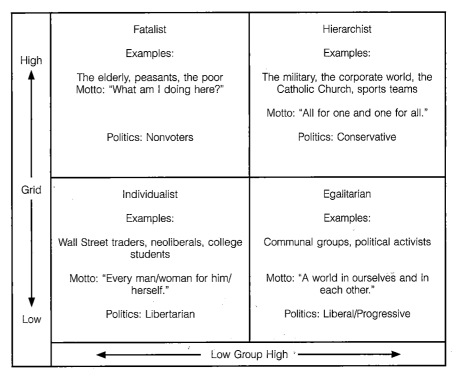

Grid	Low Group ←	→ High
High	Fatalist Examples: The elderly, peasants, the poor Motto: "What am I doing here?" Politics: Nonvoters	Hierarchist Examples: The military, the corporate world, the Catholic Church, sports teams Motto: "All for one and one for all." Politics: Conservative
Low	Individualist Examples: Wall Street traders, neoliberals, college students Motto: "Every man/woman for him/herself." Politics: Libertarian	Egalitarian Examples: Communal groups, political activists Motto: "A world in ourselves and in each other." Politics: Liberal/Progressive

FIGURE 4.2 Some Characteristics of the Four Major Cultural Types

What Kinds of World Views Are Associated with Each Cultural Type?

In outlining the different social environments and asserting that each will promote in their members characteristic beliefs, values, tastes and attitudes, grid/group theory assumes that each offers only a partial view of reality but that nevertheless each can find in reality evidence that their characteristic beliefs are, in fact, the correct ones. In other words, reality is flexible and subject to interpretation. Looked at another way, social constraints operate to guide perception in a specific direction—toward certain views of reality and away from others. However, at least up to a point, persons can find in experience validation for their specific viewpoint. If experience consistently contradicts what a specific orientation predicts and the contradictions could not be "explained away," the orientation could not be maintained.

To illustrate the "fit" between cultural types and views of the world, let us examine the view of human nature characteristic of each. To the fatalist, human nature is unpredictable: Some people may be benevolent, but more are hostile; if people were predictable, it would undermine the key idea in fatalism that everything is beyond our control. The "tarot metaphor," examined previously, with the idea of predetermined personal characteristics, would likely be attractive to the fatalist.

For the individualist, human beings must be assumed to be greedy and self-seeking. If they were otherwise, it would undermine the rationale for competition and taking every advantage that one could over others. After all, if you do not do it to them, they will do it to you. The metaphor of courtship as a game to be won or lost would "seem right" to the individualist as might the Darwinian metaphor of "survival of the fittest."

For hierarchists, human beings are born sinful but can be redeemed by good institutions. Otherwise, how could they justify strong leadership and formal rules of interaction? The view of children as "cannibals" who must be tamed through the restrictive rules and regulations of the group, characteristic of the highly ranked Kwakwaka'wakw society, provides a good example of the hierarchist's view of human nature. For egalitarians, if human beings were naturally greedy—as in the individualist cultural type—or sinful—as seen by the hierarchist—it would deny their key precept that individuals can be motivated by pursuing the good of the collective. Thus for the egalitarian, human nature must be inherently good but corrupted by "the system" or by evil institutions. We would expect metaphors of dance to appeal to egalitarians (see Figure 4.3).

Of course, the range of human behavior is capable of supporting any of these interpretations, and even if it does not, a person can nevertheless rationalize contrary experiences in such a way as to support a specific viewpoint. Thus, the individualist can insist that what others might see as altruistic behavior is simply a ruse to gain some advantage.

Because each social environment would generate a specific way of viewing human nature, it would also influence what persons in each environment

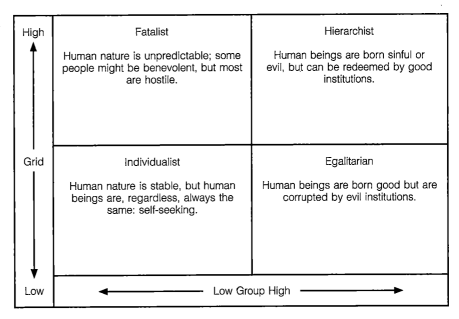

FIGURE 4.3 Assumptions About Human Nature

believed about social relations. For example, the fatalist would view a love relationship as unpredictable and beyond their control; he or she would expect little in the relationship and be happy for any reward or pleasure. Individualists would be likely to view love and relationships through cost-benefit analyses (costs and benefits to themselves). If he or she were not getting what they expected from the relationship, he or she would end it. Hierarchists would view love as a dependable division of labor (in all matters of love and relationships). Each party in this relationship would have their characteristic role or duty with a clear division of authority. Egalitarians would depend more on an "It is us against the world" (or at least "It is us against the other(s)") attitude and view each party in the relationship as equal.

One of the powerful implications of grid/group theory is that it helps explain why, in policy debates over such issues as poverty reduction, taxes, and even climate change, people argue so vehemently, are certain they are correct, and have such a hard time seeing others' points of view. For example, take climate change and how one's policy position is affected by social environment and its characteristic view of nature itself. Hierarchists tend to view nature as perverse but tolerant. If we were to imagine nature as a ball on a surface (see Figure 4.4 and Thompson et al., 1990, p. 27), it would be such that you can push nature—e.g., extract resources, experiment freely, dump waste, etc.—but only if we follow rules and the advice of experts; otherwise, how could we justify the rule of authority? Individualists would view nature as benign; you can push as hard as you want, but nature will always bounce back. In this view, nature's resources are virtually unlimited; otherwise, gaining as much as

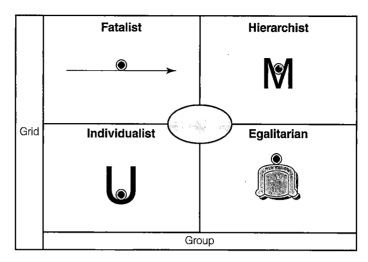

FIGURE 4.4 The Social Construction of Nature

possible is untenable. On the other hand, to the egalitarian, nature is ephemeral; if we push too hard, it will go over the edge. From this perspective, resources are limited; otherwise, why should everyone share equally? Finally, for the fatalist, nature is capricious; we never know what it has in store for us.

Because one's attitudes, values, and beliefs must support the pattern of social relations characteristic of the group or society to which they belong, members of each of the cultural types will have a characteristic view or story on climate change. The hierarchist's story is that we can solve the problem through international protocols, such as Kyoto, along with national commitments to limit greenhouse gas emissions. This solution supports the hierarchists' commitment to authority and to formal rules of interaction and to the idea that nature, like individuals in society, can be threatening but can be managed through careful organization and planning. If problems arise, according to the hierarchists, experts will develop new technologies to solve our problems.

The egalitarian story is that nature is ephemeral—that it may last only a brief time (as egalitarian groups tend to be short lived)—and consequently, the problem with climate change is rapidly declining resources and overconsumption. The fault lies in corrupt institutions that must be overhauled, along with the promotion of a simple lifestyle. For the egalitarian, grassroots action is the solution to climate change.

For the individualist, nature is benign and resilient. A view of nature as endangered could not fit with the individualist's view that one must take every opportunity to accumulate wealth and get ahead. To address climate change, the individualist would rely on laissez-faire markets to spur competition and innovation. For the individualist, the benefits of climate change (e.g., the transformation of dry climates into fertile ones) may even balance out the costs (e.g., flooding of coastal areas, severe weather patterns, etc.).

Exercise 4.4 ➤

> **SOCIAL ENVIRONMENT AND MUSICAL TASTES**
> Because grid/group theory suggests that even our tastes are influenced
> by our predominant social environment, we should be biased toward
> different movies, foods, or music. For example, try to find songs whose
> lyrics would best correspond to specific social environments of cultural
> types. Would specific musical genres (e.g., folk, country and western,
> rap, etc.) be more attractive than others to individualists, hierarchists,
> egalitarians, or fatalists?

The fatalist's story is based on the view that nature is unpredictable. Natural forces are beyond human understanding, much less human influence.

Thus, each cultural type or social environment as defined by grid and group constraints will develop its own arguments and legitimizations and, hence, its style of knowledge and characteristic beliefs, attitudes, values, and tastes.

Mary Douglas's framework is provocative, and some of the attempts to apply it to areas as diverse as the social settings of research scientists, the perceptions of time and space in egalitarian sects, styles of financial accounting (see Douglas, 1982), and responses to disasters (Dowty et al., 2010) are certainly suggestive. Her framework implies that our commitment to a metaphor, world view, paradigm, or theory is a function of our patterns of social interaction and that what makes a metaphor "feel" better is its fit with our social experience rather than any fit with some fixed, external reality.

However, the framework is not without some difficulties. For example, how do we delineate the specific groups or societies to which individuals belong? Can we characterize whole countries, as some have done, by using this framework? Can the United States be characterized as "individualistic" or the United Kingdom, with its history of a strong class structure, as hierarchical? Can we classify Italy, as some have done, as "fatalistic"? While there may be some truth to these labels, there are certainly groups within each of these countries that can be labeled differently. In fact, all four groups must exist; otherwise, each one would not have the others to define themselves against. And what happens as individuals move from one type of social environment to another? Do their views, attitudes, and beliefs change? Some research suggests that they do (see Bloor and Bloor, 1982).

QUESTION 4.5   *How Can People Reorder Their View of the World
If It Becomes Unsatisfactory?*

The meanings that people assign to their experiences do not change easily. We very much take for granted that the view of the world created by the interaction of our own experiences of the world with the mediums of language, symbolic actions, humor, and collective judgments is the right view. But beliefs do change. Often, changes in the meanings that people assign to their experiences are triggered by social upheavals, in which the old way of looking at the world, for whatever reason, is no longer satisfactory. If sufficient numbers of people share this unease, they may together try to change their view of the world and the organization of society. Anthropologist Anthony F. C. Wallace suggests the term **revitalization movements** for these attempts to construct a more satisfying culture.

Generally, a period of social or economic upheaval or oppression leads to the development of a new or revised belief system that promises to return the society to a real or mythical previous state or offers a new vision of the world that promises to relieve the oppression or frustration. During such social upheavals, the usual explanations for events are unsatisfactory, traditional solutions to problems no longer work, and rituals may be abandoned. Doubt engendered by social upheaval is replaced with a new certainty born of religious fervor or conversion. Two examples of revitalization movements are the Ghost Dance among Native Americans and the Shakers, a religious group that came to America from England and settled in upstate New York.

Wovoka and the Ghost Dance

As settlers moved west in the 19th century, they came into contact with hundreds of Native American groups. As more and more people migrated west, conflict over land resulted in wars between these groups and U.S. military forces. The Indian wars covered a period from about 1850 to 1880. During this time, the U.S. government negotiated and signed treaties with Native American groups guaranteeing Indian rights over specified areas of land as well as financial compensation, food, and other provisions.

But as more white settlers moved onto Native American territories, the U.S. government insisted on renegotiating these treaties. For example, the Sioux had been given rights to the Black Hills of South Dakota; however, after gold was discovered there, the government unilaterally insisted on renegotiating the treaties and reduced Sioux land by more than half in 1889. (However, in this case, courts later ruled that the government's act was illegal and that the Sioux had never ceded their rights.) In addition, the buffalo were virtually exterminated—sometimes in a conscious effort by the U.S. military to destroy the economic basis of native society.

As a result of the Indian wars, treaty negotiations, government deceit, and the influx of new settlers, native groups were restricted to reservations, made dependent on government rations, and denied such traditional pursuits as hunting and horse raiding. Government deliveries of food and provisions were often late or did not arrive at all, and diseases brought to the New World by European settlers, to which the indigenous population had little resistance, decimated the population. Children were taken to boarding schools

National Anthropological Archives, Smithsonian Institution, Neg. No. 1659-A-1

Wovoka, the major prophet of the Ghost Dance, is shown here in a photograph taken by anthropologist James Mooney in 1891.

away from the reservations and prohibited from speaking their native languages. Government agents—often at the insistence of Christian missionaries—banned traditional ceremonies and rituals. In brief, the social fabric of indigenous society was virtually destroyed. Those traditional things that help filter experience—language, ritual, and the ability of groups to collectively sustain particular views of the world—virtually vanished.

Revitalization movements usually receive their impetus from a prophet who claims to have received a vision or dream about a new way of viewing the world or a set of moral injunctions governing people's lives. The major prophet for the Ghost Dance was a Paiute named Wovoka. In 1889, Wovoka had a vision in which he was taken up to heaven, where he saw God and all the people who had died performing their traditional games and activities. God told him he must go back and tell people to live in peace with whites and with each other. He was also given instructions for a ritual dance. He was told that if this dance were performed for five days and nights, people would be reunited with their friends and relatives in the other world.

Converts to Wovoka's message spread the word from Nevada to Native American groups throughout the United States and Canada. Wovoka's message was sometimes reinterpreted as it spread from native group to native group. In some versions, the world would be destroyed and only the Native Americans brought back to life; in others, Euro-Americans and Native Americans would live together in harmony. In some versions, the buffalo would return. In some cases, a specific date (such as July 4 or the time of major traditional ceremonies) was set for the millennium. In some versions, Wovoka was even said to be the son of God. Whatever the interpretation, the Ghost Dance, as it became called, was adopted by numerous groups who were seeking a revival of a way of life disrupted by Euro-American expansion.

Among the groups that enthusiastically adopted the Ghost Dance were the Sioux. Emissaries sent in 1889 to visit Wovoka returned with descriptions of his vision and power. One account of the delegates' report is contained in James Mooney's work on the Ghost Dance. An anthropologist working for the Bureau of American Ethnology, Mooney traveled around the country interviewing key figures, including Wovoka, and collecting firsthand accounts of the dance from Euro-Americans and Native Americans. Here is his description of the report of the Sioux delegates:

> They were gone all winter, and their return in the spring of 1890 aroused an intense excitement among the Sioux, who had been anxiously awaiting their report. All the delegates agreed that there was a man near the base of the Sierras who said that he was the son of God, who had once been killed by

the whites, and who bore on his body the scars of the crucifixion. He had now returned to punish the whites for their wickedness, especially for their injustice toward the Indians. With the coming of the next spring (1891) he would wipe the whites from the face of the earth, and would then resurrect all the dead Indians, bring back the buffalo and other game, and restore the supremacy of the aboriginal race. (1965, p. 64)

Based on these messages, the Sioux began to dance in October 1890. However, for the Sioux, the Ghost Dance turned into a tragic reminder of Euro-American oppression. Frightened that the dance might turn into open rebellion, the Indian agent on one of the Sioux reservations called in the military. Some of the Sioux fled the reservation, chased by the Seventh Cavalry, General George Custer's group that had been decimated by a combined Native American army at Little Bighorn in 1876. After a promise of a safe return to the reservation, the fleeing Sioux surrendered their arms at a place called Wounded Knee and were surrounded by the Seventh Cavalry equipped with Gatling guns. As soldiers rummaged through the Sioux shelters searching for guns, someone fired a shot and the army opened fire, killing hundreds of men, women, and children.

The Ghost Dance virtually ceased among the Sioux after the massacre at Wounded Knee, but it continued among other groups, each of which hoped for the return of their traditional culture. Today, it represents one attempt of a people to build a new culture—a new system of meaning—after the destruction of a previous one.

Mother Ann Lee and the Shakers

The next example of a revitalization movement comes from one of the most dramatic periods of religious change in American history: the first half of the 19th century. During that period, hundreds of religious movements warning of the coming end of the world led to the establishment of religious communities. This was a period of great social change as Americans began the transition from a rural agricultural to an urban industrial society. It was marked by considerable population movement, the spread of poverty, and the breakdown of the family as the prime maintainer of societal norms. Revitalization movements represented an attempt to reformulate society in ways that remain relevant today. Virtually all of them reacted to poverty by eliminating private property and requiring communal ownership of all things; reacted to inequality by recognizing the equality of men and women; and reacted to what they perceived as the breakdown of the larger society by requiring a separation of their communities from the larger society. Although almost all the movements eventually failed, the goals of many remain viable.

The Shakers, or the United Society of Believers in Christ's Second Appearing, as they called themselves, were one of the most interesting and most successful. The Shakers are known largely for their vows of celibacy and rejection of sexual intimacy. But that was only a portion of their ideology.

The founder of the Shakers was Ann Lee. We know little of her life other than information obtained from early 19th-century accounts written by her followers. These sources tell us that she was born in Manchester, England, in 1736. At eight years of age, she was working 12 to 14 hours a day in the textile mills of Manchester, one of the worst urban slums in England. When she was 22, she attended a series of religious revival meetings held by a group led by Jane and James Wardley. The Wardleys had been Quakers but broke away to form the Wardley Society, developing an expressive kind of worship characterized by emotional chanting, shouting, and shaking, from which they got their name: the "Shaking Quakers."

Lee is reported to have exhibited an antipathy to sex early in her life and had been reluctant to marry. But when she was 25, pressured by her family, she married a blacksmith, Abraham Standerin; in a rare decision for its time, she continued to call herself by her maiden name. Her first three children died in infancy and the fourth was stillborn. The chronicle of her life states that she was paralyzed by grief and guilt and became convinced that sex and marriage were the root of all evil and the cause of her misery. She gained support (over the objections of her husband) from the Wardleys and declared her celibacy.

The Wardleys preached that the second coming of Christ was near and that because God was male and female that the manifestation of Christ's second coming would be a female. The movement embraced the public confession of sin, and Lee poured out all her transgressions and then joined the Wardleys to preach. She, her father, brother, and husband—all of whom had joined her—were arrested for causing a public nuisance. While in jail, she had a vision of Adam and Eve "committing the forbidden sexual act" and began publicly preaching against it. During one of her arrests, she claimed to have had a vision in which Jesus appeared to her and revealed that she was his chosen successor—that she was to be the Word of God—the second coming of Christ as a woman.

The Wardleys accepted her vision, and stories began to circulate about the miraculous healing power of Mother Ann Lee, as she came to be called. One woman claimed that she had a cancer of the mouth, and when Lee touched it, it disappeared. Others related how Lee was beaten for her beliefs but showed no injury. She later had another vision that told her to take her religion to America. In 1774, along with her husband, brother, niece, and four others, she journeyed to America to establish a church. Escaping New York City just ahead of the British in 1776, they journeyed to upstate New York and established a settlement just outside Albany.

The turning point for the Shakers in America came in 1780. There was a religious revival of Baptists in the nearby community of New Lebanon, and Calvin Harlow and Joseph Meacham, Baptist ministers, heard about the Shakers and traveled to see Mother Ann Lee. They were so impressed with her and what she had to say that Meacham became her first important convert in America.

Mother Ann Lee died in 1784, perhaps as a result of a journey she and members of her group undertook in 1781 to bring her message to others in

New England. The journey was marked by persecution and beatings. But the movement continued to spread, and at its height in the 1840s, there were more than 6,000 members spread over 25 communities—from Maine to Florida and into the Ohio Valley.

The social message of the Shakers was relatively simple. Sexual relations were banned, men and women shared authority, there were separate living arrangements for men and women, members were required to publicly confess their sins, and property was held in common. There was also a prohibition on eating pork, and most Shakers ate no meat at all, even avoiding milk, butter, and eggs. The Shakers professed pacifism and sought to maintain a separate government apart from the rest of society. Each community was organized into groups called *families* and had a ministry consisting of males and females—usually two of each. Their religious principles included the idea that God is a dual being—male and female—that Mother Ann Lee was the second coming of Christ as spirit, and that the millennium had commenced with the establishment of their church.

Much of what we know of the Shakers in the 19th century comes from a book by Charles Nordhoff: *The Communistic Societies of the United States: From Personal Observations.* Nordhoff was a widely respected journalist who traveled among Shaker settlements in 1874, recording his observations and interviewing members of the settlements. During his visit to Mount Lebanon, he interviewed Frederick Evans, probably the most prominent Shaker of his time, who had met with President Abraham Lincoln to plead that Shakers be exempted from military service, a request that Lincoln granted. Evans described for Nordhoff the advantages of Shakerism, asserting that celibacy is healthful and that it prolongs life: "The joys of the celibate life are far greater than I can make you know. They are indescribable."

Nordhoff reports that the Shakers comprised a cross-section of professions—teachers, lawyers, farmers, students, and merchants—and a cross-section of religious denominations—Jews, Baptists, Methodists, and Presbyterians but no Catholics. Because celibacy was a requirement, the Shakers could not reproduce themselves and had to recruit new members. In the early years, they obviously did this with considerable success. They built their communities to be representations of heaven on Earth and gave them heavenly names: City of Peace, City of Love, City of Union, Holy Mount, and so on. They became master builders whose physical structures were the envy of all and whose authentic furniture still brings astronomical prices today. Their organization of space,

Shaker men and women shared authority but lived separately. In their religious meetings, both genders participated but did not interact with each other.

their posture, the way they cut their food—all exemplified simplicity and symmetry. The only time that restrictions on posture and movement were suspended was during religious meetings. The same people who ordinarily walked straight, tiptoed, and never raised their voices sang, shouted, and whirled in dizzy circles.

It is difficult to speculate what led the people who joined the Shakers to accept their beliefs. Women were attracted to the movement because of its promise of equality, and all may have been attracted to the strong group support offered in Shaker communities. In many ways, the physical layout, rituals, and rules of the Shaker communities seemed to be a denial of anything urban—anything suggesting economic or social exploitation. The communities thrived from 1800 to 1850 but began to decline after the Civil War as fewer and fewer people were attracted to the message. A small community of believers in Sabbathday Lake, Maine, remains to carry on the Shaker tradition.

CASE STUDY IN DOING ANTHROPOLOGY #4: POLITICAL CONSULTING AND THE POWER OF METAPHOR

In 2004, linguist and University of California at Berkeley professor George Lakoff unexpectedly became one of the most celebrated political consultants in the United States. Lakoff characterizes his political views as progressive, and after Republican victories in the national election of 2004, Lakoff wrote a book—*Don't Think of an Elephant: Know Your Values and Frame the Debate*— to serve as a handbook for Democratic activists. In the book, he outlined some of the reasons that he believed the Democratic Party lost the 2004 election. The

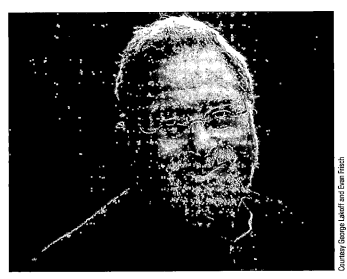

Linguist George Lakoff is applying his expertise to advising political candidates on the best way to express their political message.

Courtesy George Lakoff and Evan Frisch

book became so popular among Democrats that they were handing it out by the boxload, and Lakoff was asked to speak to hundreds of politically progressive groups around the country. The story of how a Berkeley professor of linguistics and "cognitive science" became a political consultant is one that illustrates how to make a career out of what you can learn in anthropology.

Don't Think of an Elephant is about "framing." **Frames**, according to Lakoff, are mental structures that shape the way we see the world; as a consequence, they also shape our goals, plans, and actions as well as determine our values—what we believe are good or bad outcomes of our beliefs and behaviors. For example, if Harry does not spend much money, we can set that in the frame "Harry is thrifty" or the frame "Harry is cheap." Thus, the choice of frame influences how we view Harry.

Frames, of course, are metaphors—that is, linguistic devices whose use (or misuse) carries enormous influence in our views of the world. Consequently, as Lakoff emphasizes, metaphors are powerful political tools. If someone can determine the metaphors people use to think about issues, that someone in effect gets to frame the debate about the issue.

Take the issue of taxes. Republicans, who are generally opposed to most forms of taxation, began to use the term *tax relief* in advocating tax reduction. The term is, for those opposing taxes, an effective metaphor for their ideas; it frames taxes as an affliction from which we need "relief"—much as we need relief from a headache. Furthermore, those who bring relief are heroes, removing this affliction from us. However, taxes need not be viewed as something we need relief from; why not, suggests Lakoff, view taxes as an investment—a down payment on our children's future. Instead of taking about "tax cuts," call them "service cuts" or "benefit cuts." People who may not like seeing some of their income go to taxes may feel different about not receiving the services (police, firefighting, education, road maintenance, etc.) or benefits (Social Security, education loans, scientific research) supported by our tax investments.

Moral Politics: The Nation as a Family

George Lakoff was one of the pioneers illustrating how metaphors form the foundation of how we conceptualize the world, as discussed earlier in this chapter. He first began delving into politics and metaphors in the early 1990s. He was puzzled by the distinction between liberals and conservatives in U.S. politics. How and why could people hold such different views on issues such as taxes, abortion, crime, and so on, when everyone was faced with pretty much the same so-called "facts." Furthermore, he could not figure out what the positions held by liberals and conservatives on one issue had to do with their positions on other issues. What does your position on abortion have to do with your views on taxes, gun control, environmental issues, or foreign policy? He remembered a paper that one of his students had written on how people think of the nation as a family; we speak of "founding fathers," the "Daughters of the American Revolution," "Uncle Sam," "Big Brother," and "sending our sons and daughters off to war." Thus:

- The nation is a family.
- The government is a parent.
- The citizens are children.

The idea that we think of the nation as a family is not unusual. We generally try to conceptualize abstract ideas, such as a nation, in terms of things that are more concrete, such as communities or families. It was then that Lakoff realized that while Americans do seem to think and talk about the nation as a family—deeply embedded in conservative and liberal politics are different metaphors for the family. Conservative politics, says Lakoff, are based on what he called a strict father notion of the family, whereas liberal politics is filtered though the metaphor of the nurturant parent family. These family metaphors, says Lakoff, define morality—that is, our concepts of right and wrong—good and bad. And the positions that conservatives and liberals take on various issues are moral positions. You could sum up the differences between liberals and conservatives, says Lakoff, by asking "If your baby is crying at night, do you pick it up?"

The strict father metaphor, which is at the heart of conservative politics and morality, conceives of a traditional nuclear family in which the father has the prime responsibility for protecting the family and the authority to set strict rules for children's behavior. The mother has the responsibility to take care of the house, raise the children, and uphold the father's authority. Children must honor and obey their parents. Honoring authority, in this model, builds character, self-discipline, and self-reliance—all key personal attributes in the strict father view of the world. Love and nurturance are present in this family model but cannot trump parental authority. The goal of the strict father family is to produce children who, when mature, are self-reliant, self-disciplined, and able to survive on their own.

The nurturant parent family—the metaphor that forms the foundation for liberal political beliefs, according to Lakoff—emphasizes love, empathy, and nurturance, with the goal of producing children who are responsible, self-disciplined, and self-reliant and who respect and care for others. Children are obedient not because they fear punishment but because they love and respect their parents. In this family model, good communication is critical because parents must be able to explain their decisions and how they serve the function of protection and nurturance. In this way of thinking, children should be happy and fulfilled in their lives and be able to empathize with others. According to Lakoff (1996, pp. 33–34), "When children are respected, nurtured and communicated with from birth, they gradually enter into a lifetime relationship of mutual respect, communication, and caring with their parents."

At the root of each family model is a set of assumptions about the world. In the strict father metaphor, the world is seen as a place in which evil lurks and which is inherently dangerous. It is also a difficult place because it is competitive; in this world, people are "winners" or "losers." There is absolute "right" and "wrong." Children are born "bad," in the sense that they will do whatever they want to do; the father is there to ensure that they do "right." In this kind of world, the family needs as a moral authority to enforce obedience—through physical punishment if necessary—a father who can:

- Protect the family in a dangerous world.
- Support the family in the difficult world.
- Teach his children right from wrong.

On the other hand, the metaphor of the nurturant parent family assumes that the world—despite its dangers and difficulties—is basically good, that it can be made better, and that it is one's responsibility to work toward that goal. Children are born good, and parents, sharing responsibility and working together, can help them become nurturing and caring adults—just as, in the world, cooperation and shared responsibility can make the world a better place. Thus, the goals of the nurturing family are to:

- Work together to make the world and each other better.
- Promote empathy and caring in children and others.
- Teach children how to be nurturing, responsible adults.

Each of these models of the family contains a strong moral component. From the strict father perspective, a good person is someone who is disciplined enough to be obedient, to know right from wrong, to be self-reliant, and to pursue one's own self-interest; a bad person is someone who does not learn discipline, does not know right from wrong, and cannot take care of oneself. For the nurturant family perspective, a good person is happy and therefore is able to help and support others; a bad person is not responsive to the needs of others, is unable to empathize with them, and is self-centered and uncooperative.[2]

In the conservative worldview, model citizens are those who:

1. Have conservative values and act to support them
2. Are self-disciplined and self-reliant
3. Uphold the morality of reward and punishment
4. Work to protect moral citizens
5. Act in support of the moral order

By the same token, conservative demons fall into five categories:

1. Those who are against conservative values (strict father morality), such as feminists, gays, and other "deviants"
2. Those who lack self-discipline (e.g., unwed mothers, the unemployed, drug users)
3. Protectors of the "public good" (e.g., environmentalists, consumer advocates, affirmative action supporters) who want government to interfere with the pursuit of self-interest
4. Those who oppose the way the criminal justice and military systems work or advocate gun control—seen as taking guns away from those who would protect their families
5. Advocates for equal rights for women, gays, nonwhites, and ethnic Americans because they work to upset the moral order

On the other hand, in the liberal worldview, model citizens are people who:

1. Are empathetic
2. Help the disadvantaged
3. Protect those who need protection

---

[2] We can see Lakoff's ideas as a reflection of the grid/group analysis we examined earlier in this chapter. However, where grid/group theory proposes that there must be four social environments, Lakoff is proposing only two.

4. Promote and exemplify fulfillment in life
5. Take care of themselves in order to do all of the above

Liberal demons include:

1. The mean-spirited, selfish, and unfair who have no empathy
2. Those who would exploit the disadvantaged (e.g., union-busting corporations)
3. Those whose activities harm people or the environment
4. Those who oppose public support of education
5. Those who oppose health care for the general public

When you map these metaphors for the family onto such policy issues as social welfare, abortion, environmental protection, and many others, you get very different perspectives. For liberals, the role of government is to nurture and help people; for conservatives, government must teach self-discipline and self-reliance so people can help one another.

Lakoff offers a couple of important qualifications to this view of U.S. politics. First, everyone is familiar with both of the family metaphors and more than likely uses each in specific situations. Thus, for example, a worker who is a strict father at home may be a nurturant union organizer at work; a woman who is a nurturant mother at home may be an authoritarian supervisor at work. Second, people do not always see the world through the frame that is most in their self-interest. For example, even though a tax cut may harm the vast majority of people, they will support it if they believe that "good people" ought to be able to keep all the money they earn. Thus, people tend to vote according to the family model they most identify with, not according to whether they are hurt or harmed.

Armed with this knowledge, what might it tell us about why people take the political positions they do? To illustrate, let us examine the policy debates over same-sex marriage.

Policy Views: Same-Sex Marriage

Marriage is another one of those abstract ideas that we give meaning to through metaphor. We can conceptualize marriage as a *journey* through life together, a *partnership*, a *union* or *bond*, a *haven* or *home*, or a relationship in which we can enjoy *legitimate sex*. Thus, the issue of redefining marriage generates a lively argument. The question is, why are conservatives so opposed to same-sex marriage, and why are liberals generally supportive? And if we know the answer to that question, how can we apply that knowledge to gain acceptance for the progressive position?

To begin with, language is again critical. Conservatives prefer to use the term *gay marriage* because it connotes gay sex, which may make even some liberals uncomfortable. On the other hand, *same-sex* marriage lacks that connotation and may therefore be more acceptable.

For conservatives, the idea of same-sex marriage does not fit the strict father family model. In that model, marriage must be heterosexual; the father must be manly, strong, and decisive—a model for sons and someone for daughters to look up to. But there is nothing in the nurturing parent model to rule out same-sex marriage. Liberals are baffled by conservatives' objections to same-sex marriage. No heterosexual marriage is being threatened. What liberals fail to understand is that same-sex marriage threatens conservative political values.

In arguing against same-sex marriage, says Lakoff, conservatives use two powerful ideas: definition and sanctity. To convince people of the acceptability of same-sex marriage, activists have to show that conservatives have the definition of marriage wrong. Marriage is not defined by the gender of the partners but by the realization of love through a lifelong public commitment. Love is sacred in America, as is commitment, and the sanctity of marriage comes from love and commitment.

Marriage, says Lakoff, comes with a variety of prototypes. The ideal marriage is happy, lasting, and prosperous; it includes children, a nice home, and friendships with other married couples. The typical marriage also has its ups and downs and its difficulties with children and in-laws. And marriages often end in divorce. However, none of these characteristics—definition, rituals, sanctity, or hopes and dreams—demand that the marriage be heterosexual. The idea that marriage is heterosexual, says Lakoff, is a widespread cultural stereotype.

Activists for same-sex marriage, says Lakoff, must not ask people to approve of "gay marriage"; instead, they need to ask people whether they think it is the government's function to tell people whom they can or cannot marry. Same-sex marriage is about equal rights under the law; it permits people who are in love to make a lifetime public commitment to each other. In other words, the issue must be framed so people are not being asked to approve gay marriage but are being asked to approve of a person's right to choose whom they will marry.

Lakoff's point is that policy debates—whether they be about taxes, same-sex marriage, student loans, abortion, or foreign policy—are not only a matter of rational discussion. In the language that is used to frame the debates are embedded concepts of morality that are grounded in family-based concepts of right and wrong. The debates are about the right forms of morality (e.g., people must not depend on others versus we should help people in need), and these conceptions of morality stem from a particular model of the family.

Translating Theory into Action

The most compelling part of Lakoff's hypothesis is the notion that in order to reach voters, all the individual issues of a political debate must be tied together by some larger frame that feels familiar. Lakoff suggests that voters respond to grand metaphors—whether it is the metaphor of a strict father or something else entirely—as opposed to specific arguments and that specific arguments only resonate if they reinforce some grander metaphor.

Conservatives have gotten their philosophy out in 10 words: strong defense, free markets, lower taxes, smaller government, and family values. Lakoff proposes a progressive 10-word philosophy: *stronger America* (not just defense but our economy, health care system, education, environment, and so forth); *broad prosperity* (markets should be structured to bring widely distributed prosperity, not concentration of wealth at the top); *better future* (need to invest for the future); *effective government* (not less government but better government); and *mutual responsibility* (a moral system built not around a strict father but around mutual caring and responsibility).

Looking at the issue of framing, one might ask whether it is manipulative— tricking people into looking at the world one way rather than another. Lakoff makes it clear that you cannot depend on language alone; the ideas expressed have to be acceptable. Framing taxes as investments may certainly help convince people that contributing to the collective good is desirable, but unless there is a clear message on the specific goods to be developed, the idea of investment itself is not likely to convince people that they need to contribute more.

CONCLUSIONS

We began by asking how it is that people can believe in things that cannot be proven—for example, why people are convinced of the existence of God, of unseen spirits, or of the powers of witchcraft. The answer to this question requires examining the role of language, ritual, myth, and humor, along with other features of social life that persuade people of the correctness of their beliefs or that convince them to change what they believe.

How does language affect the meanings we assign to our experience? The ideas of Edward Sapir and Benjamin Lee Whorf demonstrate that the vocabulary of a language may direct perception to certain features of the environment and the grammar of a language may encourage certain ways of looking at the world. The selection of metaphors also has an impact on the meanings we assign to experience. By taking language from one domain of experience and applying it to another, we carry the meaning of one domain to the other.

We explored the ways in which symbolic action reinforces a particular view of the world. For example, ritual symbolically depicts a certain view of reality in such a way that it convinces us of the truth of that reality. Examples include the Cannibal Dance of the Kwakwaka'wakw, which portrays the values of Kwakwaka'wakw society and provides members with a way to control their lives, and the rituals of contemporary English magic and witchcraft, which convince participants that mental forces can influence the material world.

We then examined the process through which people might come to believe what they do—a process that Tanya Luhrmann called "interpretive drift." People come to their beliefs by practicing them or participating in rituals that encourage them to seek and find evidence for their veracity and then to defend their beliefs against the objections of skeptics. At some point, people cease to think that they have changed their beliefs and come to believe that the new beliefs are simply true.

Next, we examined how our social environment might guide how we interpret experience. The grid/group framework of Mary Douglas identified five cultural types or social environments, with each cultural type generating characteristic attitudes, beliefs, tastes, and values that support and justify that type of social organization; each type has its own perceptual screen that makes particular visions of reality seem more or less plausible and provides for its members a particular cultural bias.

We saw how, under certain conditions, people might be led to radically change what they believe. The experience of social upheaval may lead, as it did among the Plains Indians, to a new system of belief that promises to reorder society and, in the case of the Ghost Dance, promises to resurrect the past. In the case of the Shakers, the social change that marked the transition from an agricultural economic base to industrialization inspired an attempt to formulate a religious community that might bring the millennium and reshape the social order.

Finally, we examined the way in which knowledge of how people construct their worlds can be relevant for careers in such areas as public relations and political consulting.

REFERENCES AND SUGGESTED READINGS

Introduction: The Central Question

The epigraph comes from Barry Barnes's book *Scientific Knowledge and Sociological Theory* (Routledge & Kegan Paul, 1974). The major work of Edward Tylor is found in his book *Primitive Culture* (Murray, 1871), and Émile Durkheim's theories are outlined in his brilliant work *The Elementary Forms of the Religious Life* (Collier, 1961), originally published in 1912. An excellent review of early anthropological theories of religion can be found in E. E. Evans-Pritchard's very readable work *Theories of Primitive Religion* (Clarendon Press, 1965). An excellent review of how anthropologists have addressed the human way of knowing can be found in Malcolm R. Crick's "Anthropology of Knowledge" in the *Annual Review of Anthropology*, vol. 11 (1982), pp. 287–313.

How Does Language Affect the Meanings People Assign to Experience?

Edward Sapir's works span the period from 1910 to 1939; many of them appear in a volume edited by David G. Mandelbaum: *Selected Writings of Edward Sapir in Language, Culture, and Personality* (University of California Press, 1949). Benjamin Lee Whorf's works are collected in a book edited by John B. Carroll: *Language, Thought, and Reality: Selected Writings of Benjamin Lee Whorf* (Technology Press, 1956). A good summary of the work of Sapir and Whorf can be found in *Language, Thought and Experience* by Paul Henle (University of Michigan Press, 1958). The treatment of metaphor is from George Lakoff and Mark Johnson's *Metaphors We Live By* (University of Chicago Press, 1980). Robert C. Solomon discusses the metaphors of love in *Love: Emotion, Myth, and Metaphor* (Anchor Press/Doubleday, 1981). The notion of key symbols or metaphors comes from the work of Sherry Ortner, particularly her article "On Key Symbols" in the *American Anthropologist*, vol. 75 (1974), pp. 1338–46. Some of Franz Boas's work on the Kwakwaka'wakw is contained in *Kwakiutl Ethnography*, edited by Helen Codere

(University of Chicago Press, 1966). The description of Kwakwaka'wakw metaphors comes from Stanley Walens's *Feasting With Cannibals: An Essay on Kwakiutl Cosmology* (Princeton University Press, 1981). The discussion of contemporary witchcraft and magic is based on the work of Tanya M. Luhrmann's *Persuasions of the Witch's Craft: Ritual Magic in Contemporary England* (Harvard University Press, 1989). A discussion of the tarot occurs in *The Book of Thoth* by Aleister Crowley (U.S. Games Systems, 1995). A review of the role of language in socialization is provided by Bambi B. Schieffelin and Elinor Ochs in "Language Socialization" in the *Annual Review of Anthropology*, vol. 15 (1986), pp. 163–91.

How Does Symbolic Action Reinforce a Particular View of the World?

Information on the Kwakwaka'wakw Cannibal Dance, along with other aspects of Kwakwaka'wakw ritual and mythology, is given in Franz Boas's *Kwakiutl Ethnography*, cited earlier, and Franz Boas and George Hunt's *Kwakiutl Texts (Memoir of the American Museum of Natural History)*, vol. 5 (1905). A classic work is Ruth Benedict's *Patterns of Culture* (Houghton Mifflin, 1934). Interpretations of the Cannibal Dance are found also in Stanley Walens's *Feasting With Cannibals: An Essay on Kwakiutl Cosmology*, cited earlier. A social analysis of *The Wizard of Oz* can be found in David Payne's "The Wizard of Oz: Therapeutic Rhetoric in a Contemporary Media Ritual" in the *Quarterly Journal of Speech*, vol. 75 (1989), pp. 25–39. Joseph Campbell's *The Hero With a Thousand Faces* (Princeton University Press, 1949) is one of the classic works on mythology. The anthropological literature on ritual and symbolic action is extensive. Roy Wagner's "Ritual as Communication: Order, Meaning, and Secrecy in Melanesian Initiation Rites" in the *Annual Review of Anthropology*, vol. 13 (1984), pp. 143–55, provides an excellent review of works on ritual, as does John D. Kelly and Martha Kaplan's "History, Structure, and Ritual" in the *Annual Review of Anthropology*, vol. 19 (1990), pp. 119–50. The discussion of contemporary witchcraft and magic is based on Tanya M. Luhrmann's *Persuasions of the Witch's Craft: Ritual Magic in Contemporary England*, cited earlier.

How Do People Come to Believe What They Do, and How Do They Continue to Hold to Their Beliefs Even If They Seem Contradictory or Ambiguous?

Dennis Covington's experiences with the Holiness Church are described in his book *Salvation on Sand Mountain: Snake Handling and Redemption in Southern Appalachia* (Addison-Wesley, 1995). The history of snake handling and of the Holiness Church can be found in Weston La Barre's *They Shall Take Up Serpents: Psychology of the Southern Snake Handling Cult* (University of Minnesota Press, 1962) and Thomas Burton's *Serpent-Handling Believers* (University of Tennessee Press, 1993). The discussion of contemporary witchcraft and magic is based on Tanya M. Luhrmann's *Persuasions of the Witch's Craft: Ritual Magic in Contemporary England*, cited earlier. The analysis of medieval astronomy comes from Thomas Kuhn's *The Copernican Revolution: Planetary Astronomy in the Development of Western Thought* (Harvard University Press, 1957). The description of Azande witchcraft and divination appears in E. E. Evans-Pritchard's classic *Witchcraft, Oracles and Magic Among the Azande* (Oxford University Press, 1937). The example of the Nuer monstrous birth comes from Mary Douglas's *Purity and Danger* (Praeger, 1966).

How Can We Account for the Different Meanings People Assign to Experiences?

The major sources for grid/group or cultural theory are Mary Douglas's works *Natural Symbols: Explorations in Cosmology* (Barrie and Rockliff, 1970), "Cultural Bias" in the Royal Anthropological Institute's Occasional Paper No. 35 (1978), and *How*

Institutions Think (Syracuse University Press, 1986). One of the more ambitious attempts to apply gird and group is *Risk and Culture: An Essay on the Selection of Technical and Environmental* Dangers by Mary Douglas and Aaron Wildavsky (University of California Press, 1982). An excellent summary and application of the framework are provided in *Cultural Theory* by Michael Thompson, Richard Ellis and Aaron Wildavsky (Westview Press, 1990). *Essays in the Sociology of Perception*, edited by Mary Douglas (Routledge and Kegan Paul, 1982), contains studies on how to apply grid/group theory to areas ranging from communal sects, industrial scientists, and accounting procedures. More recently, Rachel Dowty, Peter May, William Wallace, and Colin Beech in "Organizational Culture and the Katrina Response in Louisiana" applied the framework to explain why different government agencies or groups responded to the Katrina disaster (in *Dynamics of Disaster: Lessons on Risk, Response, and Recovery*; Rachel Dowty and Barbara Allen, eds.; Earthscan, 2011).

How Can People Reorder Their View of the World
If It Becomes Unsatisfactory?

Anthony F. C. Wallace provides a discussion of revitalization movements as well as the ritual process in *Religion: An Anthropological View* (Random House, 1966). The material on the Ghost Dance comes from James Mooney's *The Ghost Dance Religion and the Sioux Outbreak of 1890* (University of Chicago Press, 1965) and from Alice Kehoe's *The Ghost Dance: Ethnohistory and Revitalization* (Holt, Rinehart and Winston, 1989). The earliest work on the Shakers is contained in *Testimonies of the Life, Character, Revelations and Doctrines of Our Ever Blessed Mother Ann Lee*, published in 1816 by J. Tallcott and J. Deming, and much of what is known about Ann Lee is described by Nardi Reeder Campion in *Mother Ann Lee: Morning Star of the Shakers* (University Press of New England, 1990). Charles Nordhoff's *The Communistic Societies of the United States* was first published by Harper and Brothers in 1875 and was reissued by Dover Publications in 1966. An excellent summary of Shaker life and the relationship of their beliefs to their architecture and living arrangements can be found in *Seven American Utopias: The Architecture of Communitarian Socialism, 1790–1975* by Dolores Hayden (MIT Press, 1981). A recent comprehensive description of the history and life of the Shakers is contained in Stephen J. Stein's *The Shaker Experience in America: A History of the United Societies of Believers* (Yale University Press, 1992). For a general review of other religious movements, see James W. Fernandez's article on religious change in Africa: "African Religious Movements" in the *Annual Review of Anthropology*, vol. 7 (1978), pp. 195–234.

Case Study in Doing Anthropology #4: Political Counseling
and the Power of Metaphor

George Lakoff's work on politics can be found in *Moral Politics: What Conservatives Know That Liberals Don't* (University of Chicago Press, 1996) and *Don't Think of an Elephant: Know Your Values and Frame the Debate* (Chelsea Green, 2004). Stuart Ewen's book *PR: A Social History of Spin* (Basic Books, 1996) is one of the best at explaining the history and impact of public relations on our lives and at explaining how images are used to control and manipulate our definition of reality.

Mother and children (wood). Yoruba Culture/British Museum, London, UK/The Bridgeman Art Library International

CHAPTER

5

PATTERNS OF FAMILY RELATIONS

PROBLEM 5: WHAT DO WE NEED TO KNOW BEFORE WE CAN UNDERSTAND THE DYNAMICS OF FAMILY LIFE IN OTHER SOCIETIES?

179

> If ever thou purpose to be a good wife, and to live comfortably, set down this with
> thyself: mine husband is my superior, my better; he hath authority and rule over
> me; nature hath given it to him . . . God hath given it to him.
>
> —W. Whately, *The Bride Bush*, London, 1617
>
> A Woman Without a Man Is Like a Fish Without a Bicycle.
>
> —Automobile bumper sticker, ca. 1975

INTRODUCTION

Soap Operas and Family Relations

Could a foreign visitor to the United States learn anything about American family life from watching our soap operas? Consider this plot from a popular soap of a few years ago: Holden is having an affair with Lilly while his wife Angel is undergoing psychiatric treatment because she had been sexually molested by her father, who was shot and killed by Kalib, Holden's brother. In the meantime, Darryl is having an affair with Francine while he and his wife, Carol, are arranging to have a child through a surrogate mother. Francine's sister Sabrina has run off with Antonio, an apparent drug dealer who has shot Bob, the sisters' father.

A visitor certainly might conclude from the popularity of this soap opera that Americans like to watch stories of illicit love, incest, infidelity, greed, and marital and family conflict. And although the behaviors of these soap opera characters may not really represent the daily lives of American husbands and wives, fathers and mothers, or sons and daughters, they must represent enough of reality to allow viewers to identify with the characters and their situations. In some ways, the plots and the relationships between the characters must seem plausible and reveal something about the dynamics of American lives. Our assumption in this chapter is that a person who understands and appreciates soap operas in America would have a good understanding of the dynamics of American life. But what relevance does that have for understanding family life in other societies?

Americans are not alone in their fascination with soap opera plots. Most societies have fictional dramas and real-life tales about family life that reveal people's concerns. Brazilians, for example, like Americans, are fanatical soap opera watchers, but the characters, situations, and plots are different from those on American television, and these differences reveal variations in family structure and dynamics. The focus in Brazilian soap operas tends to be on the **family of orientation**—father, mother, self, and siblings—rather than on the **family of procreation**—husband, wife, and their children. The theme of class mobility dominates Brazilian soaps, as do plots about women from poor, rural families marrying wealthy men from the city. Love is depicted as dangerous and often unrequited, as when a woman is hopelessly in love with a man destined to marry someone else. In Brazilian soaps, characters almost always interact with family and friends; in American soaps, they interact much more frequently with strangers. In addition, the setting for Brazilian soaps is usually the home—the sphere of private life. In American soaps, the setting is often the workplace or some other location in the sphere of public life.

Soap operas reveal the reasons for domestic strife. They depict individuals with choices to make—choices that impact others. They reveal character motivation and development. In whatever form they take—traditional dramas, real-life tales, or soap operas—stories are an interesting way to learn about family life in different societies. If you decided to learn enough about family life in another society to enable you to write a plausible soap opera for members of that society, you would probably understand a good deal about the dynamics of their family life.

What, then, would we need to know in order to write a good soap opera about families in other societies? First, we explore the composition of a typical family and how the family is formed and maintained. We examine how the themes of sexuality, love, and wealth (all prominent in American soap operas and familiar themes in the stories of other societies) are dealt with and what kinds of situations or conflicts can disrupt family life. Finally, we explore how the understanding of patterns of family relations can be relevant for careers.

QUESTIONS

5.1   What is the composition of the typical family group?
5.2   How are families formed and ideal family types maintained?
5.3   What are the roles of sexuality, love, and wealth?
5.4   What threatens to disrupt the family unit?

Case Study in Doing Anthropology #5: Combating HIV/AIDS

To make this task more manageable, we focus on family life in three societies: the Ju/wasi, the Trobriand Islanders of the South Pacific, and the traditional Chinese farm family. These societies have been selected for three reasons. First, they represent very different levels of social, cultural, and technological complexity. The Ju/wasi were gatherers and hunters living in small, mobile groups; the Trobriand Islanders were horticulturists living in villages of up to 400 people. The traditional Chinese represented a large agricultural society. Second, family structure and roles vary significantly among the three, but together, they depict family types and relations that are representative of many if not most societies around the world. Finally, the three societies have been well studied in the anthropological literature. We discuss these societies in what anthropologists refer to as the ethnographic present; that is, although the actual descriptions may refer to situations that existed in the past, we describe them as if they still exist. In reality, the Ju/wasi, the Trobriand Islanders, and the rural Chinese are, to varying degrees, very different today than they were when the anthropologists whose work we mention studied them.

QUESTION 5.1   *What Is the Composition of the Typical Family Group?*

To understand family composition in different societies, we need certain concepts and tools. One place to begin is by examining how most unmarried Americans would respond if asked about the composition of their families. They would probably list their mother, father, brothers, and sisters. If asked who else, they would likely add grandparents, aunts, uncles, and cousins. If they were married, they would add their husbands or wives and children. Figure 5.1 shows how this family structure would be diagrammed by using genealogical notations.

Certain features of the typical (although not universal) American family stand out. Americans consider themselves equally tied by kinship to both their mother and father and to their maternal and paternal kin. In other words, Americans reckon kinship **bilaterally**—through both parents. As we shall see, this is not true of all societies. Second, Americans make no linguistic distinction between their mothers' siblings and their fathers' siblings; both are referred to as aunts or uncles. Nor do they distinguish linguistically between the children of aunts and of uncles; all are referred to as cousins. For most Americans, the most important family grouping is the **nuclear family**—the group consisting of a father, a mother, and their biological or adopted children.

Families in other societies may be composed very differently. For example, although Americans give equal recognition to people's ties to their mothers or their fathers, other societies place greater emphasis on ties to one parent or the other. In some cases, only people related through either the mother or the father are considered family. Societies that emphasize persons' ties to their mother are said to have **matrilineal kinship** systems; those that emphasize persons' ties to their father are said to have **patrilineal kinship** systems. However, in few societies is an individual's relationship to one side of the family or the other totally ignored; rather, in most societies, relationships with mothers' families and fathers' families are viewed differently. For example, Americans traditionally inherit their surnames from their fathers, thus embracing the patrilineal principle, but in case of divorce, the American legal system usually gives priority to the matrilineal principle by awarding custody of children to their mother.

The three examples of societies used in this chapter—the Ju/wasi, Trobriand Islanders, and traditional Chinese—each define the composition of the family and relations between members differently.

1. The traditional American household generally begins with a husband and wife pair moving from the households of their parents.

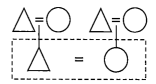

2. The arrangement is formalized with the birth of children, which produces a new nuclear family.

3. At some point the household might be composed of three generations, as married children join the household with their children.

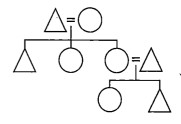

4. At a later stage, the household might consist of the original couple or a single person.

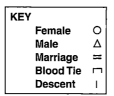

KEY		
Female	O
Male	Δ
Marriage	=
Blood Tie	⌐
Descent	I

FIGURE 5.1 COMPOSITION AND DEVELOPMENT OF THE AMERICAN NUCLEAR FAMILY

The Family Composition of the Ju/wasi

For most of the year, the Ju/wasi live in groups numbering from 10 to 40 people, related bilaterally (through both parents), who hunt and gather in a territory associated with a particular waterhole. Camp groups are often organized around a brother-and-sister pair who claim ownership of the waterhole. They bring their spouses and children into the group; in turn, the spouses might bring in their brothers, sisters, and even their mothers and fathers.

A typical camp might look like the one described by Elizabeth Thomas in her classic work *The Harmless People* (see Figure 5.2). Membership in a camp

1. Most Ju/wasi camps are organized around brother–sister pairs who claim ownership of a waterhole.

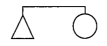

2. Brother and sister are joined at the camp by their spouses and relatives of their spouses. The nuclear family is the main economic unit.

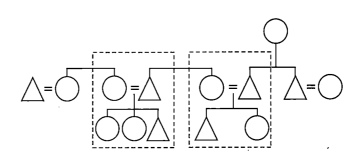

3. Bridegrooms join the camp of brides' parents for brideservice.

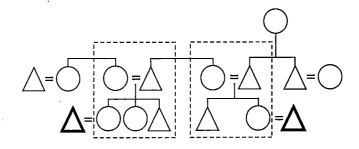

4. Camp composition changes as a result of changing social relations.

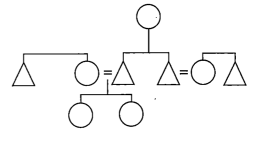

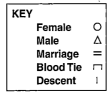

KEY

Female	O
Male	Δ
Marriage	=
Blood Tie	⊓
Descent	Ι

FIGURE 5.2 COMPOSITION AND DEVELOPMENT OF THE JU/WASI CAMP

is fluid. People move freely from camp to camp based on hunting alliances or because conflict develops in the group. However, within the camp, the basic family group is the nuclear family of husband, wife, and children. Children spend most of their time with their mothers. The Ju/wasi acknowledge the fact that pregnancy results from sexual intercourse (not the case in all societies). They also believe that conception takes place at the end of the woman's menses, when the man's semen joins with the last of the menstrual blood.

One feature of Ju/wasi society that figures prominently in the dynamics of family life is the custom of **brideservice** at marriage. When a couple marries, the groom is expected to come and live in the bride's parents' camp and work for her parents for as long as 10 years. Tales of family life among the Ju/wasi are often built around the effects of this arrangement on family dynamics.

The Family Composition of the Trobriand Islanders

The people of the Trobriand Islands live in some 80 villages, whose populations range from 40 to 400. Each village is surrounded by cultivated fields of yams, taro, and other crops, waterholes, fruit trees, and palm groves. Each village is further divided into hamlets, and each hamlet ideally consists of a **matrilineage**, or *dala*, as the Trobrianders call it—a group of men related to each other through the female line, along with their wives and unmarried children (see Figure 5.3).

The matrilineages are ranked relative to one another, and each village has a chief who is the eldest male of the highest-ranking matrilineage. Because each person is a member of the lineage of his or her mother, neither a man's wife nor his children can be members of his own *dala*.

The Trobrianders' mythology and beliefs about procreation dramatically depict the matrilineal element in their lives. Their mythology contains stories of how, a long time ago, pairs of brothers and sisters emerged from the ground to begin each *dala*. *Dala* members trace their descent back to their mythological ancestors, and they base their claims to specific plots of land on the fact that it was from thence that their ancestors emerged. There is obviously an incestuous theme in Trobriand myth because the originators of each lineage were brothers and sisters. However, Trobriand theories of procreation ostensibly deny a role to men in conception. They reinforce the matrilineal principle as well as the tie between brothers and sisters.

The Trobrianders say that when a person dies, the person's soul or spirit becomes young and goes to live on an island called Tuma. There, the soul ages, but it regenerates itself by bathing in the sea. As the skin is sloughed off, a spirit child, or *baloma*, is created, which returns to the world of the living and enters the womb of a woman of the same matrilineage as itself. In effect, a Trobriand matrilineage exists in perpetuity because souls and spirits travel back and forth between the land of the living and the island of the dead.

The *baloma* may enter the woman through her head or it may be carried by water into her womb. In some areas of the Trobriand Islands, if a woman wishes to become pregnant, her brother brings a pail of water to her dwelling. In fact, a woman cannot conceive without the "permission" of her brother. Consequently, the act of conception among the Trobrianders is a matter of three agencies—a woman, the spirit or *baloma* of a deceased ancestor, and the woman's brother. Although sexual intercourse is said to play no role in

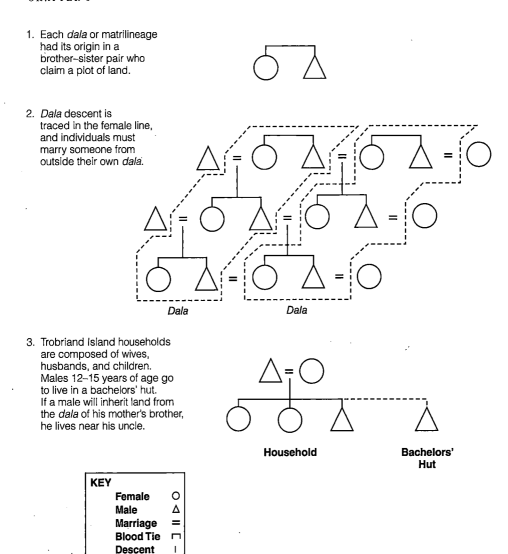

1. Each *dala* or matrilineage had its origin in a brother–sister pair who claim a plot of land.

2. *Dala* descent is traced in the female line, and individuals must marry someone from outside their own *dala*.

Dala   Dala

3. Trobriand Island households are composed of wives, husbands, and children. Males 12–15 years of age go to live in a bachelors' hut. If a male will inherit land from the *dala* of his mother's brother, he lives near his uncle.

Household   Bachelors' Hut

KEY
Female   O
Male   △
Marriage =
Blood Tie ⊓
Descent |

FIGURE 5.3 COMPOSITION OF THE TROBRIAND ISLAND *DALA* AND HOUSEHOLD

conception, it does play a role in the development and growth of the fetus. Trobrianders believe that the man's semen provides food and nourishment for the fetus and that is why children physically resemble their fathers. Sexual intercourse is also said to open the womb for the child to emerge.

Although Trobriand procreation beliefs may, at first glance, seem strange, in the context of their ideas about descent, they make perfect sense. When a person is believed to be descended exclusively from the mother, possible relations and ties to the father are excluded not only socially but also physically. In fact, we find corresponding beliefs about conception in strongly patrilineal societies. Earlier, we examined how Carol Delaney (1991, p. 27), in her book on Turkish village society—*The Seed and the Soil*—explains how villagers have what she calls a "monogenetic" theory of procreation. "It is the males," as she puts it, "who give life; women merely give birth." Turkish villagers use an agricultural metaphor to describe procreation: men provide the seed; women are the soil. It is the seed that contains life; the soil simply nurtures it. The man is believed to plant the seed, and the woman is said to be the field in which the seed is planted. This metaphor emphasizes the male role and diminishes the female role in the patrilineal family system of the Turkish village.

The Trobrianders can rationalize and "prove" their beliefs about procreation very easily. Bronislaw Malinowski, who spent four years studying the people of the Trobriand Islands, tells of their response when he suggested to them that sexual intercourse plays a role in procreation:

> I sometimes made myself definitely and aggressively an advocate of the truer physiological doctrine of procreation. In such arguments the natives would quote, not only positive instances of women who have children without having intercourse; but would also refer to the many cases in which an unmarried woman has plenty of intercourse and no children. This argument would be repeated over and over again, with specially telling concrete examples of childless persons renowned for profligacy, or of women who lived with one white trader after another without having any baby. (1929, pp. 185–6)

To what extent the Trobrianders really deny a role to men in procreation is a matter of some debate. Annette Weiner, who worked with them in the early 1970s—some 50 years after the pioneering work of Malinowski—reported that they no longer denied the direct role of men in conception. However, she also reported a case in which a grandmother claimed that she had used magic to make her granddaughter pregnant when the woman conceived while her husband was away.

Regardless of the extent to which the Trobrianders recognize the role of coitus, their ideas about descent and procreation reflect important features of the composition of their families. First, the key family relationship for them is not, as it is among the Ju/wasi, between husband and wife; it is between brother and sister. Second, the father of the family is an outsider to his children—a member

Exercise 5.1 ➤

The procreation beliefs of the Trobriand Islanders prompted debate among anthropologists about whether the Trobrianders really did believe that men played little or no role in reproduction or whether, to emphasize the matrilineal principle, they pretended not to acknowledge the male's role. In either case, we would expect to find in societies that emphasize the patrilineal principle that a woman's role in reproduction is de-emphasized. What kind of belief about reproduction can you think of that would deny the importance of the female? How does this compare with the biological roles of men and women in American society?

of another family group. Ideally, his interest is in his sister's children because it is they who are members of his matrilineage. Third, because the matrilineal **extended family** group—the *dala*—is more important than the nuclear family, the Trobrianders merge certain people under the same kin term—the same way Americans refer to different kinds of kin as aunt, uncle, or cousin. In the Trobrianders' case, a person refers to all women of his or her matrilineage of the same generation by the same term; for example, a man refers to his mother as well as his mother's sisters by the term *ina*. A woman refers to her brother and to all other men of her matrilineage and generation as *luta*. Thus, a man has many "sisters," and a woman has many "brothers."

Another consequence of matrilineal kinship is that a man inherits property not from his father but from his mother's brothers, and it is ideally in his maternal uncle's village that a young man goes to live. The fact that these ideal conditions are not always met creates some of the drama in Trobriand family life.

The Family Composition of the Chinese

Family life in traditional rural China centers on the patrilineal extended family household of a married couple, their married sons and daughters-in-law, and their grandchildren and unmarried daughters (see Figure 5.4). To understand the traditional Chinese family, you have to understand the idea of temporal depth, for in China, the **patrilineage** exists as much in time as it does in space. When Americans speak of family, they generally limit it to the living; in traditional China, the family includes a long line of patrilineal ancestors. Anthropologist Francis L. K. Hsu notes that the identity of each male is defined by his relations to the dead as much as it is by his relations to the living. His social worth and destiny are but reflections of the actions of his ancestors. He thus exists, as Hsu says, "under the shadow of his ancestors." Likewise, the spirits of the dead depend on the contributions of the living. These contributions are ceremonially made at altars—prominently positioned in each home—from which people send gifts to their ancestors by burning paper money, paper clothes, or other paper articles.

Given the interdependence between living and dead men of the patrilineage, it is apparent why it is essential to a Chinese male to have male descendants to look after his well-being and provide for him in the afterworld. Male children and grandchildren are living proof to a man that his line will continue. For this reason, unlike the Ju/wasi or Trobriand Islanders, the Chinese express a marked preference for male children. Males are needed to maintain the patrilineal descent group because if the only children born are daughters, their children will belong to the patrilineage of their husbands and the father's family line will die out. A son, as the Chinese put it, is a major happiness; a daughter is but a small happiness. Here is how one woman summed up the Chinese attitude toward daughters to Margery Wolf, who did research in the Taiwanese village of Peihotien: "Why should I want so many daughters? It is useless to raise your own daughters. I'd just have to give them away when they

1. The traditional Chinese family exists in time as well as in space. Descent is traced patrilneally for generations.

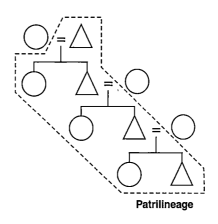

Patrilineage

2. An ideal family would be similar to that of the Lim household in Taiwan.

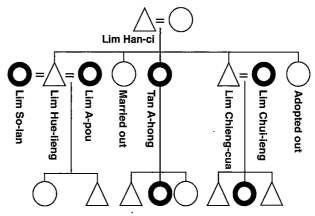

3. Most Chinese extended households eventually break up into separate nuclear family units, with wives of sons joining their husbands' households.

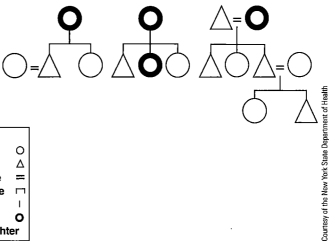

Courtesy of the New York State Department of Health

KEY	
Female	O
Male	△
Marriage	=
Blood Tie	⊓
Descent	I
Adopted Daughter	●

FIGURE 5.4 COMPOSITION AND DEVELOPMENT OF THE TRADITIONAL CHINESE FAMILY

Source: Margery Wolf, *The House of Lim: A Study of a Chinese Family*, 1st Edition, © 1960. Reprinted by permission of Pearson Education, Inc., Upper Saddle River, NJ.

were grown, so when someone asked for them as infants I gave them away. Think of all the rice I saved" (1968, p. 40).

A more lethal implication of the relative importance of sons and daughters in China is the differential rates of infanticide and abortion of males and females. In the area in which Hsiao-Tung Fei did research, there was a ratio of 100 girls to 135 boys in the age group 0–5. The population data suggest that a larger proportion of females had been killed.

In addition to a long line of male ancestors, an ideal Chinese household should include several generations of fathers and sons sharing a common hearth or cooking stove and an ancestral altar—the symbols of the household. In the architecture of Peihotien, houses are constructed in such a way that they can easily be extended to accommodate additional sons and grandsons who bring their wives to live in the family home. In reality, it is very difficult to maintain this ideal; most households in villages such as Peihotien are small, consisting of a married couple and several dependent patrilineal relatives.

QUESTION 5.2   *How Are Families Formed and Ideal Family Types Maintained?*

Regardless of the size of family units or descent systems, in virtually all societies, families require the socially recognized union of a male and female. Generally, this takes the form of marriage—a publicly recognized joining of two people or two families. But although marriage makes or sustains families, the manner in which such an arrangement comes about varies significantly in different societies. In American society, for example, children begin learning about courtship and marriage at an early age; five- and six-year-olds are teased about their "boyfriends" or "girlfriends," and playing house together is a popular preschool pastime. Americans begin serious courting in their early teens and usually go through a series of relationships before choosing a partner for their first marriage—most often when they are between the ages of 18 and 30. Although the choice of a marriage partner is supposedly based on feelings of love and sexual attraction, other factors also influence it. Like people in virtually all societies, Americans are prohibited by the **incest taboo** from marrying certain categories of kin, such as brothers or sisters, children or parents, or, in some cases, cousins. Ideally, a spouse should also be chosen from an appropriate income, ethnic, gender, and racial group. The conflict that may arise when an inappropriate marriage partner is chosen is often depicted in soap opera plots.

The marriage ceremony in American society is traditionally arranged and financed by the bride's family, and after the honeymoon, the couple ideally establishes an independent residence. Based on love expressed in regular sexual intercourse, their relationship is later transformed by the arrival of one or more children—a wife transformed into a mother and a husband transformed into a father. That is the ideal for most Americans, and it is the disruption of that ideal that is the stuff of soap opera plots.

In the Ju/wasi culture, most marriages are arranged by the couple's parents, and the bride-to-be frequently objects to the chosen spouse or to the prospect of marriage itself.

The cycles of events that create or sustain the family among the Ju/wasi, Trobriand Islanders, and traditional Chinese illustrate the diversity of such arrangements. The soap opera themes of these groups would be quite different.

The Family Cycle of the Ju/wasi

Ju/wasi men and women, like Americans, begin to learn about courtship, sex, and marriage early in life. Because there is little privacy in a Ju/wasi camp and children sleep with their parents, they are soon playing at marriage and imitating the bodily movements of parents making love. Most young men and women have had sexual experiences by the time they are 15. A Ju/wasi man usually marries for the first time between the ages of 18 and 25, when he is able to hunt and work for his wife's parents. Marriage is important for a man for a number of reasons. It marks him as an adult worthy of taking part in Ju/wasi public life, he gains a sex partner, and he gains a mate to provide his food. Although men are obligated to share and formally distribute the meat they obtain in the hunt with everyone in the camp, women are not obligated to share what they gather outside their nuclear family group, and women gather from 60 to 80% of the food in a camp.

Women often marry as early as 12 to 14 years of age—generally before their first menstruation, which occurs at about 17. Girls have fewer reasons to marry than men. Single or married men are always available as sex partners, and because the product of male labor, meat, is widely shared, a woman need not have a husband to ensure her share of the hunt. However, a girl's parents have good reasons for getting her married as soon as possible. The earlier she is married, the longer she and her husband will remain with her parents until she is of age and the longer her husband will work for her parents. Moreover, the bride's family gains an alliance with another family and is less likely to get involved in open conflict between men over their daughter.

A couple's parents almost always arrange their marriage. Typically, the mother or father of the male approaches the family of the girl with a proposal for marriage. If the girl's parents approve of the match, the families exchange gifts to indicate their agreement. An appropriate husband for a daughter is a man who is not too much older, is not yet married, is a good hunter, and is willing to accept responsibility. The prospective groom should also be cooperative, generous, and unaggressive.

The Ju/wasi not only avoid choosing a spouse who is a close kinsperson, but they are also restricted in the choice of a marriage partner by their naming system. There are only about 30 to 40 names that can be chosen for newborns, and people with the same first name consider themselves connected, regardless of their actual kinship relation. For example, if two people are named Toma, then everyone related by kinship to one Toma will be considered related in the same way to the other Toma. Consequently, if a man's name is Toma, all the brothers and sisters of everyone else named Toma would be considered his brothers and sisters, all the sons and daughters of other Tomas would be considered his sons and daughters, and so on. Therefore, a marriage partner should occupy neither an actual prohibited kinship category nor one created by the naming system. For example, a woman could not marry a man with the same name as her father or a man whose father had the same name as her father because she and the man would refer to themselves as brother and sister. When Richard Lee was working with the kinship system of the Ju/wasi, he found that interpretations of the naming system varied, and disagreements about the kin connection between people would always be resolved by the interpretation of the older person in the relationship.

Once a suitable match is made, one more obstacle to the marriage remains. Perhaps because they have little to gain or much to lose, young women often object strenuously to the marriage or to their parents' choice of a husband. Kicking and screaming are ways women demonstrate their objections. If they protest long and hard enough, the marriage will be called off; if the protest is not sufficient to call off the arrangements, a marriage ceremony takes place. Members of both families build a hut for the couple that is set apart from the bride's family village. Friends bring the couple to the hut, and the girl, head covered, is placed in the hut. Coals from the fires of both families are brought to start the fire in the couple's hut. Friends stay, joking, singing, and dancing, while bride and groom stay apart. Often, especially if the girl is young, a relative stays with them in the hut until she begins to adjust to her new status. These "honeymoons" are often the source of continuing conflict.

Working among the Ju/wasi, Marjorie Shostak forged a close relationship with a Ju/wasi woman, Nisa, who described her wedding night. Nisa said that she cried so much and objected so strongly to spending the night with her new husband, Bo, that her parents asked a female relative, Nukha, to sleep between Nisa and Bo. She soon discovered that Nukha was having sex with Bo, and after a few nights, she told her parents. They took her and moved to another waterhole, leaving Nukha and Bo behind.

Typically, half of all first marriages fail among the Ju/wasi, and they may enter several marriages over the course of their lives. Nisa's second marriage, to Tashay, followed the same lines as her first; on her wedding night, she cried and cried and finally ran away into the bush. Relatives tried to explain the benefits of marriage and to convince her to accept Tashay. When she finally agreed, Tashay took Nisa to his parents' home to live, and Nisa's parents followed. But not until Nisa and Tashay had been living together for a long time did they have sex. Nisa remembers the aftermath of their first lovemaking as being painful, and it was a long time before she allowed it again and began to enjoy it.

The Family Cycle of the Trobriand Islanders

Courtship and sexual play begin early in the Trobriand Islands. Children play erotic games at the ages of seven and eight and begin seeking sex partners at ages 11 to 13. Trobriand adolescents are permitted to display their affection for each other openly. Girls scratch, beat, thrash, or even wound their lovers; boys accept this treatment as a sign of love and display their wounds as proof of manliness and success in courtship. They sing about love—successful and unrequited—and take great pains with their physical appearance. Here is what Malinowski says about adolescent courtship:

> An adolescent gets definitely attached to a given person, wishes to possess her, works purposefully toward his goal, plans to reach fulfillment of his desires by magical and other means, and finally rejoices in achievement. I have seen young people of this age grow positively miserable through ill-success in love. (1929, p. 63)

Because sexual activity before marriage is common and expected among the Trobrianders, the couple has often already been living together, and the marriage simply formalizes an existing relationship. Although the couple may take the initiative in arranging a marriage, parents approve or disapprove of the choice of a spouse and sometimes arrange matches. There are certain categories of people a Trobriander may not marry. All Trobrianders belong to one of four **clans**—groups whose members consider themselves to be descended from a common ancestor. They must observe **exogamy**—that is, marry out of their own clan and into another. In addition, the incest taboo applies to all close relatives, particularly brothers and sisters, who include all members of a matrilineage of the same generation. Trobriand myths tell of disastrous consequences of brother-sister incest that resulted in both parties' committing suicide. Sexual relations between a father and daughter are prohibited, although Trobrianders tell stories about it and joke about the idea of a father being overwhelmed by the beauty of his daughter. From the Trobriand viewpoint, fathers are not related by kinship to their daughters. The best marriage for a man is to a woman from his father's clan, for then his children, who will trace their descent from their mother, will be members of his father's clan. Consequently, the close relationship a man has with members of his father's clan will continue into the next generation.

Among the Trobriand Islanders, lineage is traced through the mother, and individuals must marry outside their own clan. Here, a Trobriand chief on Kiriwina Island is shown with family members at the home of one of his two wives.

Peter Essick/Aurora Photos

There is no formal marriage ceremony; the girl simply stays overnight in her boyfriend's house. The next morning, the bride's mother brings the couple cooked yams to indicate the bride's family's approval of the marriage. If girl's parents do not approve, they demand that their daughter return home with them. Significantly, the Trobrianders consider sharing food to be more intimate than having sex. Later, the wife's mother and maternal uncle bring raw yams for the couple while the groom's father and maternal uncle begin collecting **bridewealth**—such valuables as stone ax blades, shells, and money—to give to the wife's kin and her father. The requirement of bridewealth makes young men depend on members of their matrilineage. This differs from the brideservice required of a Ju/wasi man because brideservice does not obligate a man to members of his family (see Question 5.1).

During the first year of marriage, the couple lives in the hut that served as the groom's adolescent retreat, and during that year, the groom's mother brings meals for them to share. At the end of the year, the groom's mother builds a stone hearth for the couple, and at that point, the wife becomes responsible for the cooking.

The end of the first year of marriage marks a dramatic change in the husband-wife relationship. They no longer eat together, and the sexuality that bound them together as adolescents must be publicly submerged. After the first year of marriage, it is shameful for anyone to refer to the couple's sex life together. People may tease each other with such sexual taunts as "fuck your mother" or "fuck your father," but the epithet "fuck your wife" could get a person killed. In public, a husband and wife never hold hands or display affection. Their lives become segmented into a private domain—in which affection and emotion can be displayed—and a public domain—in which the meaning of their relationship is dictated by their obligation to help ensure the continuity and honor of their respective matrilineages.

The matrilineal principle in the life of a Trobriander husband and wife requires each to have a continued involvement with others outside the nuclear family. In addition to his ties to and concerns for his wife and children, the husband is also involved in the family life of his matrilineage—his sisters and their children. The wife is continually involved with her and her children's matrilineage—particularly her brothers. This involvement is economic and centers around wealth—particularly yams, banana leaf bundles, and skirts—all of which women ultimately control.

One reason men marry is to obtain yams. Yams are more than food in the Trobriand Islands; they are valuable symbols or objects of wealth and are used as gifts to create and sustain relationships among people. They are particularly important in marriage transactions and in the continued tie of a woman to her matrilineage. Trobriand family yam gardens belong to the wife, but they are tended first by her father and later by a "brother." Each year at harvest time, the yams grown in her garden by her father or brother are ceremoniously taken to her. The amount and quality of the yams grown by a woman's brother are usually proportional to the bridewealth given to the wife's family by the groom's family when the couple was married. Early in the marriage, these yams are stored in the rafters of the couple's hut, and the husband uses them as valuables to be redistributed to his kin who contributed the bridewealth. Later—often 10 to 15 years later—if the kin of a man's wife recognize him as important, they construct a yam house for him to store the yams they bring each year. The amount and quality of the yams stored and displayed by a man are indications of the regard in which his wife's kin hold him and of his status in the community. The yam house is, according to Weiner, like a public bank account.

As a man seeks a wife to obtain the yams grown for him by his wife's brother, brothers seek husbands for their sisters—not only for the children nurtured by the husbands for their wives' matrilineage but for the brother-in-law's help in obtaining banana leaf bundles. Sisters are obligated, with the help of their husbands, to prepare bundles of banana leaves to be used to finance the funerals of members of their matrilineage. The woman makes some, but her husband may have to purchase additional bundles. Members of the deceased's matrilineage give them away at funerals to people who were important in the life of the deceased. The more important the person was to the deceased, the greater the number of banana leaf bundles he or she receives. In this way, members of a matrilineage uphold their honor and status; to fail to fulfill these obligations would bring dishonor to the matrilineage.

The development of Trobriand family life, then, must be understood in the context of the movement of such goods as yams and banana leaf bundles between husband and wife and members of the wife's matrilineage. It is the successful completion of the cycle of exchanges of yams and banana leaf bundles that ensures the stability of a marriage and a matrilineage.

The Trobriand nuclear family promotes stable bonds between husband and wife, although divorce is frequent and easy to obtain. The wife usually takes the initiative. Most divorces occur in the first year of marriage; they are rare after the couple has been together for a few years.

Although fathers are not technically members of their children's family, they are very important in the lives of the children. Once children are weaned, they sleep with their fathers, and fathers are later responsible for enhancing their beauty with presents of shells, necklaces, and tiny tortoise-shell earrings. These objects are evidence of a father's presence in the life of his child; in fact, Weiner says, the term for a child with unpierced ears is translated as "fatherless." So important is the tie that develops between a man and his son that when the son marries, the father may try to convince him to remain in his village rather than moving to the village of his maternal kin, as expected.

The Family Cycle of the Chinese

The key relationship in the Ju/wasi family is between husband and wife; among the Trobriand Islanders, it is between brother and sister. In China, the family centers on the relationship between father and son. Marriage in traditional China is less a matter of a man getting a wife than of bringing a childbearer into the household. As Hsu (1967, p. 57) describes it, "A marriage is made in the name of the parents taking a daughter-in-law, not in the name of the son taking a wife."

Because marriage has far less to do with relations between husband and wife than with those between the husband's family and a daughter-in-law, marriages in traditional China are almost always arranged—often far in advance—and there is little if any courtship. When a boy is six or seven years old, his parents might hire a matchmaker to find a girl who will eventually be an appropriate bride for their son. Because they believe that the time of a person's birth influences his or her personality and fate, the parents might also enlist the services of a diviner to make the appropriate match. The matchmaker takes a red paper with the time and date of a girl's birth to a prospective groom's family. The boy's mother brings this paper (or papers, if there is a choice of brides) to a fortune-teller, who predicts the compatibility of the boy and girl. If the fortune-teller deems a girl appropriate, the matchmaker tries to convince the girl's parents to accept the match. If she is successful, the bridewealth—the marriage gifts of the husband's family to the wife's parents—is then negotiated.

Another way parents can obtain a wife for their son in traditional China is to adopt an infant girl, who will be reared in the household and will later marry the son. Although this kind of arrangement is not as prestigious as bridewealth marriage, it has two advantages. Because the prospective bride is raised in the household of her future mother-in-law, she is more likely to be obedient, and it is not necessary to pay a brideprice for an adopted daughter-in-law. The major disadvantage is that the prospective bride and groom are raised virtually as brother and sister and often find it difficult to make the transition to husband and wife.

The adoption of a boy to serve as a husband for a daughter is a third way to arrange a marriage in traditional China. Adoption occurs only when a family has no sons. The adopted boy then assumes the family name so his sons continue the line of his adopted father. Such marriages are not as respected as others, and a man who is adopted into his wife's family bears the stigma of having abandoned his parents and ancestors. For poor or orphaned boys, however, the prospect of heading a thriving household might outweigh such a stigma.

Compared to the Ju/wasi or Trobriand marriage ceremony, the Chinese wedding is very formal and, for the groom's family, very expensive. A diviner determines the date and hour of the wedding and even the exact time the bride will arrive in her sedan chair. The day before the wedding, the girl's **dowry** is sent to the groom's home in a procession accompanied by a band, drummers, and ushers. The dowry consists of such goods as leather chests, tables, stools, cosmetics, housewares, or clothing and cloth but never land or a house. On the day of the wedding, the groom is carried in a sedan chair to the house of the bride; when he arrives, she shows token resistance, and she and her mother weep. Then, she is carried to the groom's house in a red sedan chair decorated to suggest the early birth of sons. Offerings are made at the ancestors' altar to ensure the success of the marriage. Then, the couple is taken to pay respects to the boy's parents—the formal introduction of the

In a traditional Chinese wedding, the bride's mother places a rose in the bride's hair and then transfers it to the groom. Then, the couple proceeds to the household of the groom's parents, where they will make their home.

bride to the groom's household. Feasting and dancing accompany the wedding—sometimes lasting for three or four days.

After the wedding, there is little time or place for romantic relations between husband and wife. Hsu reports that after the marriage, husband and wife sleep in the same bed for only seven days, and there is no public expression of affection between them. Once the wife enters into her husband's family, she finds herself among strangers—virtually cut off from her parents and siblings. She must treat her mother-in-law with respect and acquiesce to the demands of sisters-in-law or other members of her husband's family. She occupies the lowest place at the table. She can occasionally go back to her mother and sob at her change of status, but as the Chinese proverb puts it, spilled water cannot be gathered up. She does not acquire full status in her husband's family until she produces a male child. Until then, the husband must show indifference to his wife, addressing her through a third party; after the birth of a son, he can refer to her as the mother of his child. It is as if a man's wife is related to him only through his children. For the groom, marriage is simply a continued expression of his duty to his father and his ancestors. In no way is his new relationship with a wife to interfere with that duty; rather, the marriage is an expression of his filial devotion and obligation to produce male heirs.

Whereas divorce is a fairly common among the Trobrianders and among the Ju/wasi, it is virtually unheard of in traditional China. A husband can take mistresses with impunity, but in theory, he can murder an adulterous wife. Wives have no rights of divorce. A wife may flee her husband's household, commit suicide, or become a prostitute, but a woman who wishes to leave her husband and in-laws has few other alternatives.

QUESTION 5.3   *What Are the Roles of Sexuality, Love, and Wealth?*

The themes of sex, love, and wealth are pervasive in American life as well as in American soaps and sitcoms. Young men and women use their sexuality and appearance to influence one another and to gain potential partners and spouses. Later, as husbands and wives, they attempt to manage their wealth (if they have any) to fulfill social obligations and to maintain or rise in status. Often, they seek to cement their status as individuals and as a family by having children. As mothers and fathers, they face the task of guiding their children and trying to ensure their success and happiness.

The manipulation and negotiation of sexuality, love, and wealth dominate many of the plots of American soap operas. However, the ideas about romantic love expressed in these plots often are not shared in other societies. Examining these ideas among the Ju/wasi, Trobriand Islanders, and Chinese—and imagining how they might be expressed in soap·operas—can help us understand our own beliefs about these things.

Sex, Love, and Wealth Among the Ju/wasi

Wealth plays virtually no part in the lives of the Ju/wasi, but for women especially, sex, love, and beauty are very important. A Ju/wasi woman's sexuality is her major means of negotiating the conditions of her relationships with others. Sexuality is important first for her own well-being. Nisa told Shostak that if a girl grows up not learning to enjoy sex, her mind does not develop normally; if a grown woman does not have sex, her thoughts are ruined and she is always angry. Moreover, a woman's sexuality maximizes her independence. Sex attracts lovers, and a love relationship—being voluntary—recognizes the equality of the participants. By taking lovers, a Ju/wasi woman proclaims her control over her social life because she can offer her sexuality to men as a means of vitalizing them. Nisa talked candidly about sex, male impotence, and the contributions women make to men. She said:

> A woman can bring a man life, even if he is almost dead. She can give him sex and make him alive again. If she were to refuse, he would die! If there were no women around, their semen would kill men. Did you know that? Women make it possible for them to live. Women have something so good that if a man takes it and moves about inside it, he climaxes and is sustained. (Shostak, 1983, p. 288)

There is one trade-off for Ju/wasi women who use their sexuality. Men see them as sources of male conflict and consequently as potentially dangerous.

Unlike sexuality, motherhood is not easily bartered by Ju/wasi women. In other societies, including our own, parents are apt to stress how much they have sacrificed or suffered for their children, thus using motherhood or fatherhood as a way of creating obligations and ties. It makes little sense for a Ju/wasi woman (or man, for that matter) to make such a claim. Children owe their parents little; there is no need for bridewealth or dowries for marriage, and food and kin to care for them are plentiful. The dynamics of Ju/wasi families are built on the need of individuals to avoid permanent ties and obligations and to maintain their independence.

Sex, Love, and Wealth Among the Trobriand Islanders

Whereas the maintenance of sexuality is important throughout life among the Ju/wasi, among the Trobriand Islanders, it is important for women only prior to their marriage. Armed with the magic and bodily adornments contributed by her father but without the wealth—yams, banana leaf bundles, and other valuables— she will later acquire, an unmarried woman uses her sexuality to negotiate her relationships with others. Once married, she ceases to emphasize her beauty and sexual attraction and instead emphasizes her fertility and motherhood. Once measured by her father's concern for her and her own sexuality and beauty, a woman's worth is determined after marriage by her ability to collect yams for her husband, produce children, and provide banana leaf bundles for her matrilineage.

Men's sexuality is viewed very differently. Because the Trobrianders claim that men play no role in reproduction, their sexuality is never very important. Their physical attractiveness, however, is important, for this is what attracts lovers and later a wife to collect the yams by which a man measures his status. Beauty is especially important for chiefs. They must maintain an aura of sexual attractiveness in order to attract more wives, whose fathers and brothers will supply the wealth they need to maintain their position of influence.

Wealth also forms different kinds of links for Trobrianders. Because the Ju/wasi have little wealth to contend for and what there is (e.g., meat) is widely shared, the links men create with their wives' families are based not on wealth but on their labor. However, among the Trobrianders a man who wants to marry must use the wealth of members of his matrilineage as bridewealth payments to his wife's family. He is required to return this wealth to members of his family by redistributing the yams he later receives from his wife's brothers. Moreover, the yams he receives from his brothers-in-law are in some ways payment for the children his wife produces, who are members of the wife's and brother-in-law's matrilineage.

Sex, Love, and Wealth Among the Chinese

The themes of sexuality, love, and wealth are played out very differently in the traditional Chinese rural family. Whereas both Ju/wasi and Trobriand adolescents have considerable freedom to use their sexuality to attract and influence others, quite the opposite is true in China. If a girl comes from a family that is influential and wealthy enough to make an attractive match for her, she will have little to do with boys. Virginity is valued and necessary for a Chinese bride; for a Ju/wasi or Trobriander woman, it is almost no consideration. In China, if a girl has been mixed up in an affair, her only chance of marriage is to someone in a distant village.

Romantic love and sexuality are also irrelevant in the relations between traditional Chinese husbands and wives. A wife's function is to produce children. A man who can afford it takes concubines. A man who cannot afford it but does so anyway is criticized not for his infidelity to his wife but for squandering the wealth of his ancestors and descendants.

In fact, sexuality figures very little in the life of a Chinese woman either before or after her marriage. Her sexuality is simply not negotiable; instead, it is as a mother that most Chinese women establish significant relations. Her value exists in her potential to become the mother of a boy. Becoming a mother cements her relations with her husband, her father-in-law, and her mother-in-law, and it is her motherhood that secures her later life. Although a son is obligated to care for his aged mother, the obligation is not so great as it is to care for a father. To compensate, a woman must establish bonds of emotion and affection with her sons. She may do this with the assistance of her husband. After a boy is six or seven, fathers become aloof and withdrawn in order to assert and reinforce their authority and control over a son. A mother can use her husband's aloofness from his son to strengthen the son's ties to her. Even if she enjoys good relations with her husband, she will try to reserve the son's affections for herself while preserving the son's respect for his father.

The only exception to the motherhood over sexuality rule is the woman who is unable to obtain a husband or who loses one. Such a woman may become a concubine or prostitute. Margery Wolf tells the story of Tan A-Hong in the Taiwanese village of Peihotien, who was adopted by Lim Han-ci to be the wife of a son who later died. When this happens, adopted daughters are often sold to dealers who buy attractive women to train as prostitutes, to wealthy families as slaves, or to prostitutes, who initiate them in their livelihood for support in their old age. Lim Han-ci arranged to have Tan A-Hong adopted into another family, but for whatever reason, the adoption did not work out. Tan A-Hong moved to southern Taiwan and became a prostitute. She ultimately moved back to Peihotien, bringing with her an adopted daughter, whom she reared in her way of life to care for her.

The attitude toward prostitutes in traditional China is not the same as it is in the United States. The Chinese do not condemn women who choose prostitution. According to Margery Wolf, prostitutes are said to be "more interesting" than other women, but people rarely make judgments about them because too many village girls "go out to work" to support family members.

Exercise 5.3 ➤

The American family is obviously different from the Ju/wasi, Trobriand Islander, or traditional Chinese family. The Ju/wasi are hunters and gatherers, the Trobriand Islanders are horticulturists and fishers, and the Chinese are peasant farmers, whereas our families are embedded in an urban industrial society. But there are features of family life in all three that are similar to life in the American family. Your problem is simply to list those features of family life among the Ju/wasi, Trobriand Islanders, and Chinese that resemble American families. Put another way, what features of American family life would be familiar to a Ju/wasi, a Trobriand Islander, or someone from rural China?

QUESTION 5.4   *What Threatens to Disrupt the Family Unit?*

Threats to family formation and maintenance are, as might be expected, major sources of soap opera drama. If soap operas are in any way accurate reflections of American life, infidelity, sickness, authority struggles, and economic hardship are the principal threats. Moreover, as our soap operas constantly remind us, any threat to an established marriage endangers the continued existence of the family unit. Ideally, the American marriage is sustained by love; if either partner says "I don't love you anymore," it is generally grounds for divorce. Diminished sexual attraction or sexual activity or acts of sexual infidelity are other grounds. Economic problems also threaten the stability of the American family; if a couple does not have the resources to sustain or to fulfill their obligations, strains inevitably develop.

There are also threats to the stability and maintenance of traditional Chinese, Trobriand, and Ju/wasi families, but they differ from those that threaten the American family.

Threats to the Ju/wasi Family

The major threat to family stability among the Ju/wasi is conflict between husband and wife over infidelity or the efforts of a husband to secure a second wife. Like many societies around the world, the Ju/wasi allow **polygamy**. Men are allowed to have more than one wife (**polygyny**), and apparently, women are permitted to have more than one husband (**polyandry**), although this is rare. In fact, polygamy is the exception rather than the rule. A survey conducted by Lee in 1968 of 131 married Ju/wasi men found that 93% were living monogamously, 5% were living in polygynous unions, and 2% were living in polyandrous relationships.

One reason why polygamy is rare, even though having more than one wife is a sign of prestige, is the family difficulties it creates. According to Shostak, a popular saying is "[T]here is never any peace in a household with two women in it." Stories of the complications resulting from polygamous unions are an endless source of humor for those who are single or monogamous. Here is how Nisa described polygyny in her society to Shostak:

> When a man married one woman, then marries another and sets her down besides the first so there are three of them together at night, the husband changes from one wife to another. First he has sex with the older wife, then with the younger. But when he goes to the younger wife, the older one is jealous and grabs and bites him. The two women start to fight and bite each other. The older woman goes to the fire and throws burning wood at them yelling "What told you that when I, your first wife, am lying here that you should go and sleep with another woman? Don't I have a vagina? So why do you just leave it and go without having sex with me? Instead you go and have sex with that young girl!" Sometimes they fight like that all night, until dawn breaks. A co-wife is truly a terrible thing. (Shostak, 1983, p. 172)

Although polygamy is rare, marital infidelity is not. At one waterhole with 50 married couples, Lee recorded 16 couples in which one or another of the partners was having an affair. The Ju/wasi recognize certain benefits in taking lovers. For a woman, extramarital affairs add variety as well as economic insurance. Here is Nisa again:

> When you are a woman, you just don't sit still and do nothing—you have lovers. You don't just sit with the man of your hut, with just one man. One man can give you very little. One man gives you only one kind of food to eat. But when you have lovers, one brings you something and another brings you something else. One comes at night with meat, another with money, another with beads. Your husband also does things and gives them to you. (Shostak, 1983, p. 271)

Men say that the emotion and passion of extramarital affairs are wonderful: "Hearts are on fire and passions great," as the Ju/wasi say. When Shostak asked a young married man about his lover, he said they fantasized about running away. She asked what it would be like, and he smiled and replied, "The first few months would be wonderful!" However, extramarital affairs are likely to be threatening to a husband, and they are the most common cause of conflict and violence among the Ju/wasi. Wives are important to Ju/wasi men because as long as they have wives they are dependent on no one. Male adulthood requires acquiring and demonstrating a willingness to fight for a secure marital status.

Nisa's marital history provides an example of Ju/wasi family conflict. After the death of her second husband, Tashay, Nisa married Besa. Nisa says that even though they began fighting soon after the marriage, she became pregnant. Besa then abandoned her at a settlement where they had been working, and she miscarried. Shortly after, she met some people from Besa's village and told them to tell Besa that their marriage was over. She began a relationship with Twi, an older man, who asked her to live with him, and together, they went to live in the camp of Nisa's brother. Besa returned, saying he had come to take her back with him. Nisa refused to go. Besa and Twi fought, and Besa, the younger man, pushed Twi down. Later, Nisa and Twi separated because Nisa's brother Dau liked Besa and sent Twi away.

Nisa still refused to return to Besa and resumed an affair with a past lover that lasted for a time—until he died. Then, she began to see another man named Bo, but Besa returned to renew his claim over her. Violence again erupted—this time between Besa and Bo; they pushed each other and called each other insulting names, such as "Big Testicles" or "Long Penis." In an almost final confrontation with Besa, Nisa publicly stripped off her apron and cried, "There! There's my vagina! Look Besa, look at me! This is what you want!" Besa, consoled by a man who accompanied him, left. Soon after, Nisa and Bo married. Besa also remarried, but later, he began again to approach Nisa about renewing their relationship.

The story of Nisa's relationship with Besa reveals how much a Ju/wasi man may have invested in a marriage and how he is obligated to resort to violence against his wife's lover, even if she has rejected him.

Threats to the Trobriand Island Family

Among the Trobriand Islanders, it is not threats to the husband-wife relationship that are critical but threats to the matrilineage. Because the matrilineage is the major social unit, the honor of that family group relative to other groups is a central concern to all members. Lineages among the Trobriand Islanders are ranked according to the closeness of their genealogical connection to the founders of the lineage. Each lineage must be able to maintain its position vis-à-vis others through the ceremonial presentation of valuables, particularly yams and banana leaf bundles. So important are yams in the relative ranking of matrilineages that groups try to demonstrate their wealth by giving more yams to others than they receive. However, because giving may be taken as a claim of superiority, it can be dangerous; as the Trobrianders put it, "When you give too much, people worry."

Although it may seem implausible, yams could become the focus of a Trobriand soap opera plot. For example, a man's political power, measured in yams, is a direct result of the support he receives from his wife's kin—it is her yams, grown for her by her father and brother, that create status for her husband. However, the annual yam gifts received by a husband can also be a source of conflict. If the amount or size of yams harvested does not live up to a husband's expectations, he may be insulted. On the other hand, if a woman's brother is unhappy over the bridewealth he received from the husband's family or the support given by the husband to his sister in collecting banana leaf bundles, he may purposely communicate his unhappiness by not working hard in his sister's yam gardens. Other plots could be devised about unrequited love, attempts of fathers to convince their sons to remain in their father's villages, and even about incest. But a theme that would be sure to attract a Trobriand audience would be about sorcery.

The Trobrianders claim to know of spells and magic that are capable of killing. Generally, only chiefs have this power but others can seek out a chief and, for a price, convince him to use his power against their enemies. Someone who is believed to have this power is feared and respected; Trobrianders tell of instances in which they were challenged and retaliated with sorcery. Vanoi, an important Trobriand chief, told Weiner about being challenged by a Christian convert who openly mocked Vanoi's knowledge of sorcery. Vanoi offered the man a cigarette, saying that he should smoke it if he doubted the chief's knowledge of sorcery. The man did; he became ill later that night and died a week later.

A person who uses sorcery against another is dominating that person, and because each person's fate is tied to that of the matrilineage, a threat to one is considered a threat to all. That is why any death among the Trobrianders is a serious matter. Because all deaths are attributed to sorcery, every death is a sign that someone from another lineage is challenging the power of a matrilineage. Each funeral marks an attempt by the members of a matrilineage to reassert its power; at the same time, the mourners assert their innocence of sorcery. The matrilineal kin of the deceased do this by distributing banana leaf bundles and other valuables to those who have come to publicly mourn the passing of the deceased and to assist with the funeral arrangements by decorating and carrying the corpse. In recognition of their contribution to the life of the deceased, they receive gifts. The deceased's matrilineage empties its treasury to announce its strength in the face of the threat to its integrity that is signaled by a death.

Maintaining one's identity and that of the matrilineage is a never-ending process among the Trobrianders because death threatens the network by removing someone from it. Here is how Weiner sums up the meaning of death for them:

> Because of the expanding possibilities in a person's life, each Trobriander represents her or his matrilineal identity—originally conceived through a woman and an ancestral baloma spirit—as well as the accumulation of all the other relationships that parenthood and marriage made possible. Therefore, a death demands attention to this full totality, as the members of a matrilineage seek both to repay all "others" for their past care and to hold on to them now that this death has occurred. (1988, p. 161)

Threats to the Chinese Family

The biggest threat to the traditional rural Chinese family is, of course, the absence of a son. The lack of a male heir endangers not only the continuance of a household but the entire patrilineage through time. A man without sons—a spirit without descendants—has no one to offer incense for him and no altar on which his spirit can find refuge and honor. However, the existence of a son is no guarantee of smooth family relations. Fathers have enormous authority and power over sons, and sons are obligated to worship, respect, obey, and care for their fathers. But fathers often become overbearing or use force to assert their authority. Wolf says that Lim Han-ci in the village of Peihotien (see Question 5.3) was unusual in the frequency with which he administered physical punishment to his sons; he once beat them with a hoe handle and left bruises that lasted for weeks. However, regardless of how harshly a person may be treated (and most Chinese boys are, if anything, spoiled), breaking away from one's father is considered a violent act. Wolf reports the case of the conflict between Lim Han-ci and his eldest son, Lim Hue-lieng, which illustrates the dilemma of a father-son split and the difficulties that can arise in adopted marriages. When Lim Hue-lieng was a child, Lim Han-ci adopted Lim A-pou, then nine months old, to be reared as the eventual wife of his son. Growing up in the Lim household, Lim A-pou was a model daughter-in-law. She accepted reprimands and punishment without becoming sullen, she did not complain, and she was a hard worker. However, her relationship with her prospective husband was not a happy one. When Lim Hue-lieng was 19, he committed what in traditional China is an act of moral violence; he left home and severed his relations with his father. If a son dies before his father and so is unable to care for the father in his old age, the father ritually beats the son's coffin to punish him. Lim Hue-lieng was able to leave home only because he had become a leader in the *lo mue*—a secret society that is involved in crime and extortion but that also protects the downtrodden and contributes heavily to religious festivals.

Years after leaving home, much to the excitement of the villagers, Lim Hue-lieng returned to Peihotien, reconciled with his father, and went through a simple ceremony that transformed him and his foster sibling, Lim A-pou, into husband and wife. Although it must have been obvious to her that Lim Hue-lieng would be less than an ideal husband, Lim A-pou did not protest, for what alternatives did she have? She could not return to the family she left as an infant, and to remain in the Lim household after refusing to marry Lim Hue-lieng would be impossible. Moreover, there were advantages to marrying the eldest son; it would give her status and influence in the household. Thus, when Lim Hue-lieng took a succession of mistresses after the marriage and even took one to live in the family house, Lim A-pou complained very little. Because she had a son by Lim Hue-lieng, her status as the mother of the son of the eldest son in the family was secure.

Dramatic splits between fathers and sons are rare in traditional China. More frequent is conflict between brothers over the division and sharing of the family wealth at the death of a male head of the household. In most other rural, peasant societies around the world, the male head of the household designates his heirs before his death. He may in some fashion divide his property among his offspring—**partible inheritance**—or he may leave all his property to one or another descendent—**impartible inheritance**. In China, the ideal is for brothers to continue to live together and share the inheritance—usually under the direction of the eldest son—thus avoiding the division of property. In fact, however, brothers rarely continue to share, and ultimately, conflict between them leads to a division of household property.

Wolf documents the ultimate disintegration of the Lim household after the death of Lim Han-ci and the resulting arguments over property by the sons and their wives. When Wolf went to live in the Lim household, Lim Han-ci and his oldest son, Lim Hue-lieng, had already died. The two remaining family units consisted of the family of the second-oldest son, Lim Chieng-cua, and the family of Lim Hue-lieng's widow, Lim A-Pou. While Lim Han-ci was alive, his power and influence and his control over the family's wealth was enough to maintain the extended family. Once he died, conflict between Lim A-pou and her son on the one hand and Lim Chieng-cua on the other led to the division of family property. The wealth that had held the extended family together served, finally, to drive it apart. After dividing the property, brothers or their families often continue to live in the same house, but they partition it into separate family units with separate stoves, as did the son and grandson of Lim Han-ci. The once extended household becomes, in effect, a family compound.

Exercise 5.4 ➤

An international television production company has hired your company, Creativity Enterprises, to write a pilot episode of a soap opera to be marketed in rural China. The plot of the soap you will create will revolve around the Wang family. The Wangs are a relatively well-off farming family that lives in rural China. The characters in the soap opera are to include the following family members:

Wang Zhou, the 55-year-old male head of the family
Wang Lim, the wife of Wang Zhou
Wang Xiao, the eldest son of Wang Zhou
Wang Lao, the wife of Wang Xiao
Wang Jiang, the second son of Wang Zhou
Wang Jane, the wife of Wang Jiang
Wang Sally, the 20-year-old unmarried daughter of Wang Zhou
Wang Nai-Nai, the mother of Wang Zhou
Xiao and Lao have four children—two boys and two girls
Jiang and Jane have two children—both girls

You may, if you wish, add other characters to the story. The story line should be simple but clear, and you are free to embellish the characters in any way you want, but keep in mind that the soap must appeal to a rural Chinese audience.

CASE STUDY IN DOING ANTHROPOLOGY #5: COMBATING HIV/AIDS

As we have seen, knowledge of family relations helps us understand a whole range of things—from parent-child relations to marriage and courtship patterns to ideas about love, sexuality, and wealth. Understanding these relations can have practical applications in many different careers having to do with family relations—such as spousal abuse, divorce, or parent-child conflicts—or any occupation that requires knowledge about intimate human relations. Anthropologists, for example, apply this knowledge to the study, prevention, and cure of sexually transmitted diseases—particularly in programs of HIV/AIDS prevention and cure. Very often, family values and attitudes play a role in effective HIV/AIDS prevention programs, particularly in non-Western cultures and societies.

The major problem in AIDS prevention (and the prevention of sexually transmitted diseases in general) is how to persuade people who are sexually active to protect themselves and their sex partners. Condom use is one of the simplest and most common measures. But even when people are aware of the risk of contracting a sexually transmitted disease, they fail to take this easy precaution. The questions are, "What do medical practitioners and those working in AIDS prevention need to know to design effective prevention programs, and what can anthropologists do to help?" and "How can knowledge of family relations help design HIV/AIDS prevention programs?"

AIDS Prevention in Mexico

In his book *The Night Is Young: Sexuality in Mexico in the Time of AIDS*, Hector Carrillo describes his research in Guadalajara, Mexico, on cultural barriers to implementing HIV/AIDS prevention programs. One study conducted in Mexico in the late 1990s—when some 200,000 people of a population of 91 million lived with HIV or AIDS—surveyed some 10,000 people, including young people between the ages of 18 and 24, gay men, female sex workers, intravenous drug users, and migrants. People were asked about the number of sex partners they had had in the past year and whether they had used a condom in their last sexual encounter. Researchers found that young people had an average of 1.8 sex partners a year but used a condom with their last partner only 50% of the time. Intravenous drug users had an average of 14.8 partners a year but went without condom use more than 60% of the time; gay men averaged 8.6 partners a year and were unprotected more than 20% of the time. Even female sex workers failed to use condoms more than 15% of the time.

Carrillo began his research assuming that to understand the dynamics of AIDS prevention, health workers need to understand people's attitudes toward sexuality, love, and trust, and to do that, they need to know a little about the traditional Mexican family and how people learn about and form attitudes toward sexuality and its various forms.

Traditional HIV/AIDS prevention programs consist of workshops, clinics, media campaigns, and brochures and assume that if people know about HIV/AIDS and if they openly discuss its dangers and the means to prevent infection, they will take precautions against it. These assumptions were based on theories of behavior derived from psychology, education, and communications in which people are considered to be rational actors who, when informed about a danger, will modify their behavior to reduce the risk. Thus, brochures for university students emphasize the dangers of AIDS and the need for open communication between sex partners and suggest that women insist that their partner wear a condom. The problem in Mexico, as Carrillo demonstrates, is that

In spite of the information about preventing HIV/AIDS that is available from schools, doctors, public health clinics, and elsewhere, cultural factors often prevent people from applying what they learn to their own situations.

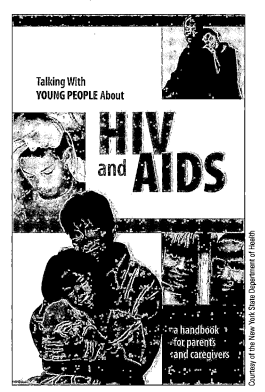

Talking With
YOUNG PEOPLE About

HIV and AIDS

a handbook
for parents
and caregivers

Courtesy of the New York State Department of Health

Hector Carrillo's research in Mexico sought
to discover cultural factors that inhibited
condom use.

significant cultural factors undermine people's ability to act "rationally," even when knowledgeable about the risk.

Sexual Silence

The advice from AIDS prevention specialists that sex partners openly communicate their concerns about infection conflicts with what Carrillo describes as the "code of silence" about sexual matters in the Mexican family. Children and parents in Mexican homes rarely talk about sex. Of Carrillo's 37 informants, 29 had never had a conversation about sex with their parents. People did learn the biology of sex in schools, but the approach was clinical, with no discussion of such sex-related topics as love, trust, and power relations. Instead, people learned about sex from friends and the popular media—often having to navigate through misinformation and myth. Most informants learned about sex on their own, with some input from friends. The code of silence especially hindered gay men and women from discussing their sexual orientation with parents. Even when children revealed their sexual orientation to parents, there were attempts to hide the fact from others. Many gay men assumed their parents knew about their homosexuality but preferred to maintain silence; they assumed the silence represented a tacit acceptance by family members of their sexual orientation, and they feared they would withdraw that acceptance if anyone openly broached the subject. However, in families, people did learn about what was "normal" and to participate in the reproduction of sexual silence by keeping transgressive sexual behavior under wraps to preserve the appearance of normalcy.

Because people are reluctant to talk openly about sex, a common way of talking about it is through sexual jokes or exchanges (*albures*); in these exchanges, sexual topics are embedded in metaphors [e.g., "Did you get up yet?" (Did you get an erection?) or "Should I put this in your car?" (Can I fuck you?)]. Persons soon learn that sexual joking is a socially acceptable way to communicate about sex, especially with friends, and they soon develop the skills to participate in these exchanges. Carrillo suggests that AIDS educators who support open communication about sex are likely to dismiss the code of silence and *albures* as remnants of a cultural past that needs to be changed. However, individuals who participate in the silence or become adept at sexual joking obtain benefits in the form of tacit acceptance of their sexual behavior and orientation as well as enjoyment generated by the exchanges. Nevertheless, sexual silence and sexual joking represent a discrepancy between public health messages that emphasize direct communication for HIV prevention and safe-sex negotiation on the one hand and social reality on the other.

Power Relations

Another barrier to effective HIV/AIDS prevention is the traditional relationship in which women are supposed to be submissive to men within and outside the family. Mexican families are patriarchal, and *machismo*—an exaggerated masculinity—requires the subordination of women but grants sexual freedom to men outside the monogamous marital relationship.

Sexual relations in North American society often imply a dominant and submissive relationship. The language we use to talk about sex reflects that inequality. As we noted in the previous chapter, men often use metaphors from sporting contests to talk about sex, and the language of sexual intercourse is used to express victimhood ("screwed") or domination.

In Mexico, the unequal relationship between husband and wife and men and women extends as well to male sex partners in which the active, penetrating male still maintains his *machismo*, whereas the passive, receptive male during anal penetration (*joto*) is seen as a *maricon* ("queer"). Furthermore, gay men occupy a lower status than men who are bisexual. If the fact that a man is drawn only to men is made public, he is stigmatized. Bisexual men on the other hand can rationalize their choice of a male partner by claiming to have been drunk or "very horny."

However, as Carrillo notes, gay men who hide their sexual orientation from family, friends, and employers are perpetuating their second-class citizenship and end up living the kind of double life that would be unacceptable in more open societies. Nevertheless, they are comfortable in being able to find acceptance in social networks and meeting places and to find a niche for themselves as *homosexuales*, gays, or lesbians in a world that is otherwise hostile to their lifestyle.

The difference in power between sex partners has been assumed to be a major cause of HIV risk—particularly for women when the more powerful partner does not want protection. Women also suffer disproportionately because while men are expected to have had many sex partners, "good" women are supposed to be sexually inexperienced. When a woman requests a condom, she implies that she is sexually experienced and is assumed to be "loose." Consequently, many women are reluctant to request that a partner use a condom for fear of being stigmatized as promiscuous.

Men who assume the submissive role in gay sex tend also to be reluctant to insist that their partners use a condom, in much the same way that women are reluctant to insist on condom use by their male partners. One of Carrillo's gay informants described an instance in which he decided to have sex with a bisexual man whom he knew and to whom he was attracted. The man called him to meet at a bar and from there went off, parked, and had unprotected sex, with Carrillo's informant being penetrated. In describing the encounter, the man said that he did not request a condom because he saw the encounter as an opportunity that he did not want to lose; furthermore, he reasoned, because the man was bisexual and had a girlfriend, he posed less of a risk.

And the fact that the man had a girlfriend put the informant in an even more submissive position, assuming a role that some women in Mexico must adopt when they are afraid of losing a male partner.

Another male informant was attracted to a male construction worker who one day stopped to talk to him. The informant offered him a soda, the man went with him to his apartment, and they made out. The informant was HIV positive but was afraid to tell his partner for fear of a negative and even a violent reaction. The man anally penetrated him. He felt guilty but also said that the partner had some responsibility for his own protection.

Trust and Fidelity

Another reason that people are reluctant to use a condom or request that their partner do so is because they fear that the request may carry implications of mistrust or infidelity. Requesting a condom, says Carrillo, could be construed as meaning "I don't trust you" or "I have been unfaithful." The danger of this kind of misunderstanding is increased if partners have not used a condom on previous occasions or if sexual partners have known each other for some time. As a result, a partner might consent to unprotected sex rather than face issues of suspicion, mistrust, infidelity, and dishonesty. As one of Carrillo's informants put it, "People can go to ten safe-sex workshops and say, '[S]urely this will help a lot; I won't have sex anymore without protection,' but then it is difficult to propose to the sexual partner to have sex with protection. It is difficult to do in real life."

Sex and Love

Beliefs and attitudes about sex, love, and passion also pose barriers to condom use. Successful sexual encounters require abandonment or surrender (*entrega*), said Carrillo's informants. In the sexual encounter, lovers must suppress "rational" thinking because rationality could destroy the sexual moment. As one informant put it, sexual passion involves "the surrender of your internal whole, of you yourself as a whole." Another said, "It's necessary to allow yourself to be taken by the moment, by the caresses, not think that you are in a relationship, not pressure yourself [to think], because then it all dies." The informant added, "My partner used to do something that totally turned me off. We would start touching and she would say, 'Did you wash your hands?' She killed me with that."

Carrillo's informants are expressing a view common to Western thought and literature that sex is dominated by a logic that is different from that of everyday life. In this sense, the sexual experience requires what Carrillo calls an "altered state." It is permissible, informants said, to "think" before and after sex—but not during. There is also the implication of a distinction between passionate sex and safe or rational sex. As one informant put it, in today's world with HIV/AIDS and other sexually transmitted diseases, you must practice "rational sex." "You must," he said, "first be aware of what you are doing. . . . It is best to use the methods that we have at hand such as condoms, lubricant, to prevent sex from destroying our lives." The informant was not necessarily advocating safe sex because, he added, "Let me clarify that I am talking about sex without eroticism and without love. In it there is no surrender. It is only the flesh for the flesh and pleasure for pleasure." Although safe sex was advisable for health reasons, he nevertheless preferred the "irrationality" of passion and surrender. The implication is that the introduction of preventive measures would cause the whole sexual interaction to collapse.

Why Is the Message of Traditional AIDS Prevention Programs Sometimes Ignored?

Clearly, even when people were knowledgeable about HIV risk, the programs designed by HIV/AIDS prevention educators did not guarantee that people would protect themselves. The existence of cultural barriers to using or requesting condom use—the code of silence, inequality in sexual relationships, implications of mistrust and infidelity, and the meaning of the sex act—did not prevent people from using condoms on occasion. But judgments about whether to use or request a condom were based on an intuitive decision regarding how much risk was involved—not only in using or not using a condom but in destroying the sexual moment by talking about it.

    Carrillo suggests that there are two conflicting views of the sexual moment. One involves an emphasis on sexual desire, sexual passion, and love. This viewpoint emphasizes the value of emotions, the dynamics of the sexual relationship, and the value of seeking validation, satisfaction, and communion with sexual partners. The second view, articulated in HIV prevention literature, is highly medicalized and places priority on rationality, informed decision making, self-control, and sexual health. As Carrillo puts it, "In Mexico, while the former view of sex highlights spontaneity, mutual surrender, and abandonment, the latter has stressed self-control and the need to contain sexual passion."

    The question is how to reconcile these competing views of sex so as to develop a more effective means of preventing infection. That is, how can one introduce the awareness of disease risk and preventive measures without inhibiting the spontaneity of sex?

Exercise 5.5 ➤

> **DEVELOPING A PROGRAM FOR PREVENTION OF STDS**
> For this exercise, you need to play the role of an HIV/AIDS prevention specialist and help design a program for your culture to promote condom use. You need to answer the following questions:
>
> 1. What are some of the cultural barriers that might inhibit condom use? Are any of them similar to those in Mexico?
> 2. What are some measures that you would suggest to help people who are sexually active overcome these barriers?

Designing AIDS-Prevention Programs

Not everyone was satisfied with traditional Mexican sexual values and attitudes. Women wanted to change their subordinate status in regard to men, gays wanted a more open attitude toward sexual variation, and the young in general wanted a change in the attitude that relegated talk about sex to a few friends or to joking relationships. But people did not know how to effect such changes and often perpetuated the values and behaviors that reproduced the very attitudes and values that they wanted to change. Thus, women would use their subservience to negotiate their relations to men, and gays—who wanted a more accepting attitude—adopted double lives to hide their sexual preferences from family, friends, and fellow workers.

This is not to imply that Mexicans were uninterested in sexual topics, particularly gay sex. The issue was explored in many television shows imported from the United States as well as in Mexican soap operas. For example, on one soap opera, *La Vida en el Espejo*, Mauricio—one of the show's central characters and the eldest son of an upper-middle-class family in Mexico City—was a gay male who began to realize his homosexuality, told his family, fell in love with another masculine man, and eventually brought his lover into the family. The audience was able to observe the growth in family and personal relations and see romantic affection between the men. This show was broadcast in prime time, six nights a week, for around four months, with little negative reaction.

However, says Carrillo, it is still necessary to develop prevention measures to promote greater self-reflection. People need to be made more aware of the factors that might prevent them from practicing safe sex and thus be better able to recognize warning signs and how their own and others' beliefs about sex, intimacy, and trust put them at risk to contract a deadly disease. He concludes that for an effective HIV/AIDS prevention program, people must be able to keep the risk of infection in the back of their minds, be able to act when there is a red flag, and thus be able to take the initiative to use or request protection and refuse to engage in behaviors that put them at risk for infection. Such a program requires health educators to show flexibility in considering locally preferred forms of sexual interaction, to recognize sexual partners' immediate relational and health-related needs, and to work with the relational complexities of sexual and romantic interactions.

Richard Parker and his associates at the Brazilian Interdisciplinary Association on AIDS (ABIA) designed and implemented an AIDS prevention program of the sort that Carrillo recommends. They targeted their program toward male sex workers in Brazil and sought to heighten the workers awareness of the cultural barriers

Anthropologist Richard Parker has focused on the social and cultural construction of gender and the social and cultural aspects of HIV/AIDS.

© Vagner de Almeida/Courtesy Richard Parker

to HIV/AIDS prevention that Carrillo described for Mexico and, at the same time, help them find alternative sources of income other than sex work.

The young men involved in the program had significantly higher rates of unprotected anal sex than older men. For example, in one study, 41.5% of those under the age of 24 reported receptive anal sex without a condom, and only 53.4% reported condom use for insertive anal sex.

The goal of the ABIA program is to introduce young male sex workers to anthropological fieldwork methods to enable them to conduct research on the issues and factors that affect their lives and explore how these issues may play out in the lives of other young men. The process aims to facilitate self-reflection and, ultimately, to develop effective sexual health promotion tools. In the initial training session, program directors train young men in ethnographic fieldwork—interviewing, recording information, oral history, and so on. In the second stage, program participants conduct ethnographic research with other youths. They address such questions as: What does it mean to be a man in Brazilian society? What are the stereotypes of men who have sex with other men? How do we perceive our bodies? How do men talk to each other— if they talk—about pleasure and desire? If they do not talk about such issues, are there other ways in which they communicate nonverbally about them? In the third phase of the program, the young men use the results of their research to develop flyers, pamphlets, storybooks, and outreach workshops, such as short plays that are presented in community centers and schools. Theater plays are developed, such as one staged in Rio de Janeiro called *Cabaret Prevenca*. The play ran for three months in a large theater and consisted of 16 scenarios that focused on specific issues that emerged from the men's ethnographies. The play was later turned into a documentary film that was distributed nationwide.

The assumption of most anthropologists working in the area of HIV/AIDS prevention is that the ability to critically understand and evaluate your own behavior and beliefs from an anthropological perspective will provide you with the power to make better behavior choices.

CONCLUSIONS

In this chapter, we have examined the structure and dynamics of family life among three peoples—the Ju/wasi, the Trobriand Islanders, and the traditional, rural Chinese—by asking four questions. The first question had to do with the composition of the typical family group. Each society has different rules regarding whom a person regards as a family member. In some societies, such as that of the Trobrianders, family membership and descent are reckoned through females (matrilineal descent), whereas in other societies, such as that of the traditional Chinese, descent is reckoned through males (patrilineal descent). In still other societies, such as that of the Ju/wasi, family membership is reckoned through both parents (bilateral descent). In China, the family is extended in time to include many generations of living and dead ancestors. For the Ju/wasi, the major social unit is the nuclear family; for the Trobrianders, it is the matrilineal extended family; and for the Chinese, it is the patrilineal extended family.

The next question concerned how the family is formed and the ideal family type maintained in these societies. Among the Ju/wasi, the parents of boys and girls arrange marriages—often when their children are very young—but if the girl protests strongly, the marriage does not take place. Among the Trobrianders, young men and women court freely and often choose their own marriage partners, but their choice must be approved by their parents. In traditional China, parents almost always arrange a marriage—often with the assistance of a matchmaker. Sometimes, female infants or young girls are adopted into families to later marry a son. The economic responsibilities for making a marriage also vary. Among the Ju/wasi, a man is obligated to perform brideservice for the wife's family; among the Trobrianders as well as in traditional China, a man's family is obligated to pay bridewealth to a wife's family. Key relationships also vary in the different family types. For the Ju/wasi, the key relationship is between husband and wife; for the Trobrianders, it is between brother and sister; for the Chinese, it is between father and son.

Another question had to do with the roles played by sexuality, love, and wealth in family life. Love and sexuality figure prominently in the life of the Ju/wasi. Women especially emphasize the power of their sexuality and men's dependence on it. Wealth has almost no role among the Ju/wasi. Among the Trobrianders, men and women begin sexual activities early in their lives, and they place great emphasis on being sexually·attractive and on romantic love. However, once they are married, couples de-emphasize the sexual aspects of their lives—at least publicly. Instead, they work to repay the bridewealth payment made to the wife's family and grow yams for the husband to present each year to his sister's husband. Wealth is important to maintain the social rank of the matrilineage. In traditional China, sexuality and love play little part in family life. The main obligation of a woman is to produce a son; it is her fertility, not her sexuality, that men value. Wealth is needed by a man's family to pay bridewealth to the wife's family at the time of marriage. Wealth is also required to sustain the patrilineal extended family of a man, his sons, and his sons' sons.

The forces that threaten the family unit were the topic of the fourth question. Marital infidelity is the greatest threat to the Ju/wasi family, and divorce is frequent, especially early in a marriage. For the Trobrianders, the more serious threats are to the matrilineal extended family. Because an act of sorcery is believed to cause the death of a family member, it is a serious threat to the family unit, as is the consequent depletion of economic resources. Divorce is almost nonexistent in traditional China. The failure to produce a male heir threatens the continuity of the family, as does the death of the head of the patrilineal extended family. Disputes among brothers over the distribution of family wealth often result in the breakup of the extended family.

Finally, we examined how knowledge of intimate relations in a society can be applied to the development of programs to promote sexual health and how health professionals must consider the cultural factors that increase a person's risk of contracting a sexually transmitted disease. Then, we examined an example of a program developed by using anthropological theory and method.

References and Suggested Readings

Introduction: Soap Operas and Family Relations
The epigraphs come from Lawrence Stone's *The Family, Sex and Marriage in England, 1500–1800*, pages 55–56 (Harper & Row, 1977) and from an automobile bumper sticker first observed in the mid-1970s. Susan S. Bean provides an analysis of American soap operas in "Soap Operas: Sagas of American Kinship," in *The American Dimension: Cultural Myths and Social Realities*, edited by William Arens and Susan P. Montague (Alfred, 1976). Conrad Phillip Kottak provides the study of Brazilian soap opera in *Prime Time Society: An Anthropological Analysis of Television and Culture* (Wadsworth, 1990).

What Is the Composition of the Typical Family Group?
The descriptions of the Ju/wasi are drawn largely from Richard Lee's book *The Dobe !Kung* (Holt, Rinehart and Winston, 1984) and Marjorie Shostak's *Nisa: The Life and Words of a Ju/wasi Woman* (Vintage Books, 1983), with additional information drawn from Elizabeth Thomas's *The Harmless People* (Knopf, 1959). The description of the Trobriand Islander family is taken from Annette B. Weiner's *The Trobrianders of Papua New Guinea* (Holt, Rinehart, and Winston, 1988) and from Bronislaw Malinowski's *The Sexual Life of Savages in North-Western Melanesia* (Halcyon House, 1929). The material on China comes largely from Margery Wolf's *The House of Lim* (Prentice Hall, 1968); Francis L. K. Hsu's *Under the Ancestors' Shadow* (Anchor Books, 1967); and Hsiao-Tung Fei's *Peasant Life in China: A Field Study of Country Life in the Yangtze Valley* (Routledge & Kegan Paul, 1939). Additional information on traditional Chinese families can be found in *Village Life in China* by Arthur H. Smith (Little, Brown, 1970). Carol Delaney gives the description of the procreation beliefs by Turkish villagers in *The Seed and the Soil: Gender and Cosmology in a Turkish Village Society* (University of California Press, 1991).

How Are Families Formed and Ideal Family Types Maintained?
The observations about the significance of brideservice and bridewealth come largely from Jane E. Collier and Michelle Rosaldo's "Politics and Gender in Simple Societies," in *Sexual Meanings: The Cultural Construction of Gender and Sexuality* (pp. 275–329), edited by Sherry B. Ortner and Harriet Whitehead (Cambridge University Press, 1981). A good introduction to kinship and social organizations is Burton Pasternak's *Introduction to Kinship and Social Organization* (Prentice Hall, 1976).

What Are the Roles of Sexuality, Love, and Wealth?
The extent to which women in different societies are valued or emphasize their sexuality or their role in procreation is discussed by Collier and Rosaldo in their article cited previously and by Michelle Rosaldo and Jane Monnig Atkinson in "Man the Hunter and Woman: Metaphors for the Sexes in Ilongot Magical Spells," in *The Interpretation of Symbolism*, edited by Roy Willis (Wiley, 1975). A good

general review of works on the cultural construction of sexuality can be found in an article by D. L. Davis and R. G. Whitten's "The Cross-Cultural Study of Human Sexuality," in *Annual Review of Anthropology*, vol. 16 (1987), pp. 69–98.

What Threatens to Disrupt the Family Unit?

Sylvia Junko Yanagisako provides a good analysis and review of factors that influence family structure in "Family and Household: The Analysis of Domestic Groups," in *Annual Review of Anthropology*, vol. 8 (1979), pp. 161–205. An interesting collection of articles by anthropologists on divorce, largely in America, can be found in *Divorce and After*, edited by Paul Bohannan (Doubleday, 1970).

Case Study in Doing Anthropology #5: Combating HIV/AIDS

The information on sexuality in Mexico comes from Hector Carrillo's book *The Night Is Young: Sexuality in Mexico in the Time of AIDS* (University of Chicago Press, 2002). The statistics on condom use in Mexico are from an article by C. A. Hernandez-Giron and others, "Factors Associated With Condom Use in the Male Population of Mexico City," which appeared in the *International Journal of STD & AIDS*, vol. 10, no. 2 (February 1999), pp. 112–7; the account of the HIV/AIDS prevention program for male sex workers in Brazil is described in the article by Miguel Munoz-Laboy and others, "Promoting Sexual Health Through Action Research Among Young Make Sex Workers in Rio de Janeiro, Brazil," which appeared in *Practicing Anthropology*, vol. 26, no. 2 (2004), pp. 30–34.

THE CULTURAL CONSTRUCTION OF IDENTITY

PROBLEM 6: HOW DO PEOPLE DETERMINE WHO THEY ARE, AND HOW DO THEY COMMUNICATE WHO THEY THINK THEY ARE TO OTHERS?

> *When an individual enters the presence of others, they commonly seek to acquire information about him or to bring into play information about him already possessed. They will be interested in his general socioeconomic status, his conception of self, his attitude toward them, his competence, his trustworthiness, etc. Although some of this information seems to be sought almost as an end in itself, there are usually quite practical reasons for acquiring it. Information about the individual helps to define the situation, enabling others to know in advance what he will expect of them and what they may expect of him. Informed in these ways, the others will know how best to act in order to call forth a desired response from him.*
>
> —Erving Goffman

INTRODUCTION

The Importance of Self

Of all the products of our culture, the one we most take for granted is our self. We are not born knowing who we are or what our place is in the social landscape; we learn to be American or Japanese, male or female, husband or wife, or Amy, Richard, Michael, Rachel, or Rebecca. As we become who we are, we learn how we stand in relation to others. We learn how we relate to others as son, daughter, student, friend, or lover. In this sense, society is a collection of **social identities** distributed over a landscape. Individuals strive to arrive at some identity/destination from which they can relate to other social identities while they seek confirmation from others that they occupy the position in the social landscape that they claim to occupy.

To appreciate the importance of the self, try to imagine a society in which every person is physically indistinguishable from every other person. How would people in such a society know how to behave toward each other? Whenever we interact with another person, the interaction must be based on some idea of who the other is: Friend? Stranger? Family member? Teacher? At the same time, the other person must have some idea of who we are—a conception of the relationship that exists between us. The necessity of knowing the social identity of others is apparent when strangers meet and, directly or indirectly, seek to elicit information about one another. Each tries to place the other in some identity at some spot in the social landscape.

Imagine next a society in which every person is completely unique. In this case, every interaction would be different, and there would be no way to learn from one situation how to behave in another similar situation. Each person would need to have an infinite variety of behaviors with which to interact with an infinite number of types of people. We avoid this situation by categorizing people—placing them in groups—so not everyone in our social universe is unique. We group them into categories based on such criteria as gender (female or male); ethnicity (Irish, Italian, Chinese); personal characteristics (short, tall, husky, thin); and so on.

Try to imagine, also a social landscape in which no person acknowledges any other person or communicates in any way who he or she thinks the other person is. This, too, would represent an impossible situation. People would have no way of acquiring from others confirmation that they occupy the social identities they think they occupy. In reality, others—who by their behavior toward us confirm that we occupy the spot in the landscape we claim to occupy—in large part construct our social identities. Put another way, nobody is anybody except in relation to somebody.

Finally, try to imagine a social landscape in which everyone communicates to everyone else that they occupy the wrong spot on the landscape. Every person actively disagrees with every other person about his or her identity. This situation would be chaotic, if not impossible.

To examine how people in a society determine their identities and communicate who they think they are to others, we explore the ways different societies define the person, the ways individuals are differentiated from others, the manner in which individuals find out who they are, how they convey to others who they are, and the consequences of disagreements over identity. Finally, we consider how we can apply what we learn about identity to solve problems regarding body image.

QUESTIONS

6.1   How does the concept of personhood vary from society to society?
6.2   How do societies distinguish individuals from one another?
6.3   How do individuals learn who they are?
6.4   How do individuals communicate their identities to one another?
6.5   How do individuals defend their identities when they are threatened?

Case Study in Doing Anthropology #6: Fat Talk

QUESTION 6.1   *How Does the Concept of Personhood Vary from Society to Society?*

Personal names in all societies are intimate markers of the person, differentiating individuals from others. Names can also reveal how people conceive of themselves and their relations to others. For Americans, names are perhaps the most enduring aspect of the self. Assigned at birth, our names remain with us throughout our lives. Some people may choose to modify them—to shorten Kathleen to Kate or Philip to Phil. In whatever form a name takes, it represents the self. How much of the self is revealed by a name varies by culture and situation. College students meeting for the first time exchange personal names, rarely bothering with family names. Theirs is a self that is independent of any group or past. When American businesspeople meet, they exchange first names, last names, and business titles. Businesspeople are linked to their organizations. When Moroccans from different towns meet, the names they offer to others include not only the name of their family but also the name of the town from which they come. The Moroccan self is embedded in family and place of origin. Among the Gitksan of British Columbia, the names people use depend on their social position; when they enter adulthood, get married, or assume a higher rank in Gitksan society, they change their names. The Gitksan self is inseparable from one's position in society.

The differences in naming practices among different societies reveal the different ways societies conceptualize what a person is and how that person relates to the group. Most Americans believe that individuals are stable, autonomous entities who exist more or less independently of whatever situation or status they occupy. As Americans move from status to status or place to place—from student to husband or wife or from employee to father or mother—they believe themselves nevertheless to be the same person. Otherwise, each time we changed situations or statuses, we would in effect become different people and would have to change our names. In this regard, Americans are highly **individualistic**.

This does not seem to be the case in other societies, where individuals are not seen as entities distinct from their social position or group. In societies such as the Gitksan, the relationship between the person and the group or the person and his or her social position is **holistic**; the person cannot be conceived as existing separately from society or apart from his or her status or role. The holistic view of the self is expressed in Gandhi's metaphor of individuals as drops in the ocean; the drops cannot survive without the ocean, and the ocean loses its identity without the drops.

The Egocentric and Sociocentric Self

These differences between individualistic and holistic conceptions of the self led Richard A. Shweder and Edmund J. Bourne to distinguish two distinct ways in which the person is conceived in different societies: the **egocentric** and the **sociocentric** views of self. In the egocentric view, typified in many ways by the Western view adopted in American society, each person is defined as a replica of all humanity—the locus of motivations and drives and capable of acting independently from others. For Westerners, the individual is the center of awareness—a distinct whole set against other wholes. Social relations are regarded as contracts between autonomous, free-acting beings. Individuals are free to negotiate their places in society, and the dominant idea is that everyone is responsible for what and whom he or she is. Moreover, individuals possess such intrinsic qualities as generosity, integrity, or beauty. In the egocentric view of the person, a high value is placed on individualism and self-reliance.

The cowboy image projected by John Wayne personified the idealized American self—individualistic and self-reliant.

Robert Bellah and his coauthors have examined American ideas of the individual in *Habits of the Heart*. The American self, they say, seeks to work out its own life plot by individually pursuing happiness and satisfying its wants. Unlike individuals in some other societies, Americans seek to cut themselves off from the past, especially from their parents. Each wishes to become his or her own person—to find his or her self. Young men and women need to demonstrate that they can stand on their own two feet and be self-supporting. This belief in a self-reliant, independent self underlies the American belief in success as the outcome of free and fair competition among individuals in an open market. Most successful Americans, say Bellah and his associates, claim that they achieved success through their own hard work and seldom acknowledge the contributions made by their families, their schooling, or their positions as members of the upwardly mobile middle class. The only way they can say they deserve what they have achieved is if they have succeeded through their own efforts. It is as if Americans believe that they have given birth to themselves.

In contrast to the egocentric view of the person, say Shweder and Bourne, the sociocentric view of the self depends on context. The self exists as an entity only within the concrete situation or role occupied by the person—in much the same way that Gitksans' names are linked to their position in society and not to some autonomous, separate self. From a sociocentric view, there is no intrinsic self that can possess such enduring qualities as generosity, integrity, or beauty. Such qualities can apply only to concrete social situations. Instead of saying that a man is generous, a sociocentric perspective would be "He gives money to his friends." Instead of saying that a woman is principled, the perspective would be "She does not give away secrets."

Personhood in Japan and America

Some anthropologists attribute a sociocentric view of the self to the Japanese. Christie Kiefer explains that the Japanese are more apt to include within the boundaries of the self the social groups of which the person is a member, as opposed to the American self-concept, which does not extend beyond the physical body. Japanese children are not trained to be self-reliant, as American children are. They are taught that interdependence between the person and the family or group is more important than independence.

Robert Smith notes that the Japanese view of the self is expressed in their language. For example, the Japanese language lacks anything resembling our personal pronouns. In American society, children quickly learn to use the two personal referents *I* and *you*; Japanese boys, though, must learn six, and girls must learn five. The personal referent used in Japan depends on the relationship of the speaker to the listener. It expresses how the self is defined relative to a specific social interaction.

In addition, says Smith, the Japanese language lacks vocabulary that is status-neutral. Rather, it is characterized by what the Japanese call *keigo*, or "polite speech." *Keigo* has the effect of establishing at the outset of a conversation the relative social standing and degree of intimacy of speaker and listener. Japanese speakers use different forms of address depending on their social position relative to the person to whom they are speaking. Because the Japanese language is based on status, people must be careful of the linguistic forms they use in conversation. When conversing with someone in a superior social position, the speaker must linguistically acknowledge his or her inferiority. Japanese advertisers have a problem with *keigo* because actors should not give imperative commands (e.g., "drink Coke") for fear of offending people. They solve the problem by using low-status people who are nonthreatening (such as clowns, coquettish women, or children) to issue the commands.

The sociocentric Japanese also differ from the egocentric Americans in their approach to social interaction. Americans believe it is desirable to assert themselves; some even undergo assertiveness training. Americans believe that it is desirable for people to stand out—to take charge. The Japanese believe that social interaction should be characterized by restraint or reserve—traits they identify as *enryo*. Americans may aggressively present themselves to others; the Japanese are more reticent. With *enryo*, giving opinions is avoided; this attitude is best summed up in the Japanese proverb "The nail that sticks up shall be hammered down."

Nevertheless, the Japanese do conceive of themselves as separate entities. They are as attached to their personal names as Americans are—if not more so. Moreover, the Japanese believe in self-development. But for the Japanese, the autonomy of the individual is established not in social situations where they actively distinguish themselves from others, as Americans do, but

Exercise 6.1 ➤

People begin to learn from childhood the ways in which their self relates to others and their groups. That is, from the behavior of others toward them, they come to see themselves as distinct entities or as beings intimately linked to others. Schools in America are significant environments for learning about self. Try to list the ways in which American school settings—and how children act in them—convey to children their degree of individuality and responsibility for their actions. Are there ways in which individualism is submerged? Might school settings differ in the extent to which the egocentric, as opposed to the sociocentric, self is developed?

away from society, where self-reflection and introspection are legitimate. It is through introspection that the Japanese find their true heart (*kokoro*) and are put in touch with their true nature—their *hara* ("belly") and *jibub* ("self").

In the remainder of this chapter, we will look at the self less from our own egocentric perspective and more from the sociocentric perspective—as something contingent and relative to the situation. Our focus will be on that part of the self that is defined by social relations and social processes and that is subject to change and redefinition.

QUESTION 6.2   *How Do Societies Distinguish Individuals from One Another?*

Differences and similarities among persons are the materials from which we construct social landscapes that allow us to distinguish individuals from one another or assign them to one group or another. From these similarities and differences, we construct our social identities. However, all societies do not use the same similarities and differences to construct a social code nor do they use these similarities and differences in the same way. Some characteristics of persons—of the **identity toolbox**, so to speak—are almost universally used to differentiate and to group them. For example, family membership, gender, and age are used in every society as categories of a social code. Other characteristics, such as ethnic group membership, skin color, and wealth, figure prominently only in some societies. Consider the variety of personal characteristics that students and teachers in a suburban New York high school use to construct a social landscape. They include (not necessarily in this order): participation or nonparticipation in sports, performance in sports (as measured by the number of points an individual has contributed to a team), participation in extracurricular activities, dress, scholastic achievement, will to achieve, disruptive or nondisruptive behavior, willingness to cooperate with teachers and administration, gender, ethnicity (Italian, "nothing" [American], Irish, African American, Hispanic), family wealth, health, age, grade, and so on.

Perhaps the most important set of characteristics used to define the self is related to kinship and family membership. In traditional societies, kinship is the central organizing principle—the main determinant of a person's social identity. Anthropologists working with traditional societies are often "adopted" by a family. This act, although also a signal of acceptance, serves the practical purpose of assigning an outsider a social identity through which others can approach him or her. To have no kinship label or designation in such societies is to have no meaningful place in the social landscape.

The language spoken is another important identity marker that is sometimes viewed as essential for the maintenance of a group identity. The way a language is spoken is often important; think about how Americans use dialect to identify people as being New Englanders, New Yorkers, Texans, and the like. Language is often strongly tied to a national identity, and many countries have established institutions to oversee the "purity" of the national language. The Académie

Française is charged with keeping the French language free of foreign borrow-ings, such as "le hot dog" or "le hamburger." In some countries, conflict be-tween groups focuses on issues of language. For example, in Quebec, efforts of one group to preserve French as the official language of the province—and thus protect what it sees as essential to group identity—have led to a movement for independence from the English-speaking remainder of Canada.

The importance of group identity can also be observed in Northern Ireland, where the fundamental marker people use to locate others is religious affiliation. An important skill the Irish people acquire is "telling": determining whether another person is Catholic or Protestant. Adults in Northern Ireland claim that they can tell people's religious affiliation by such cues as their area of residence, the school they go to, their given names and surnames, speech, clothing, and even facial appearance. Some have suggested that group identity as either Protestant or Catholic is the most important defining feature of social identity. This is reflected in the joke about a man who is stopped on a Belfast street and asked his religion. "Jewish," he replies. "Yes," says the questioner, "but are you a Catholic Jew or a Protestant Jew?"

Northern Ireland also illustrates the importance of having either a **positive identity** or a **negative identity**. Members of each group attempt to build a positive identity, to attribute to themselves characteristics they believe are desirable, and to construct a negative identity for others by attributing un-desirable characteristics to them. In Northern Ireland, people often do this by comparing themselves with the other religious group: Catholics to Protestants and Protestants to Catholics. Catholics build a positive identity by emphasiz-ing their Celtic heritage and their "decency," whereas Protestants emphasize their past military triumphs and their loyalty to Great Britain. Protestants be-lieve themselves to be "neater" and "cleaner" than Catholics; Catholics think of themselves as the only true Irish.

Constructing Male and Female

Although some personal attributes of individuals are used to construct identi-ties in almost all societies, they are not always used in the same way. Gender is a good example of an identity feature that Americans take for granted, assum-ing it is a biological construct. But gender is a cultural creation; that is, differ-ent standards apply to being male and being female.

Gender assignment begins at birth with the announcement that "It's a girl" or "It's a boy," conveniently ignoring some 4% of births in which the infant has various combinations of male and female characteristics (e.g., an infant with one testis and one ovary, an infant with one testis and aspects of the female genita-lia, or an infant with ovaries and some aspect of male genitalia). Once the an-nouncement of gender is made (or after a surgical procedure in which the infant is "corrected" to fit into either the male or female category), the infant is given a gender-appropriate name, dressed in properly designed or colored clothing, and spoken to in gender-appropriate language. Parents use more diminutives (kitty, doggie) when speaking to girls than to boys; they use more inner-state words (happy, sad) with girls than with boys; and they use more direct prohibitives (no! no! no!) to boys than to girls.

Parents and other caregivers then teach male children that it is manly to endure pain and to be strong and tough. Male children are discouraged from expressing discomfort and encouraged when they can withstand it. On the other hand, female children are comforted when they hurt themselves. Traditionally, American male children are encouraged to be aggressive and competitive; they learn to compete in games and play with toys that require aggressive behavior. Females are taught to be caring and helpful; they are given toys, such as dolls, that encourage "feminine" behavior.

Schools in the United States reinforce gender roles in areas such as sports participation. Douglas Foley, in his description of student life in a Texas high school, notes the special role that coaches play in socializing males into their gender roles. Unlike regular teachers, says Foley, they are less likely to be considered sissies. They occupy a special place in the culture of schools and of small communities. They are more likely to have outside interests, more likely to be known and respected in the community, and more likely to become school administrators and leaders.

Cheerleaders reinforce gender roles, says Foley, by performing at pep rallies and games. Cheerleaders, he reports, were objects of envy and gossip and were considered by men to be objects to possess, dominate, and gain status through. They were objects of longing who prompted among men public bravado and private longing and frustration. Girls who could not be cheerleaders joined the pep squad, which would lead cheers and decorate the town and school.

These gender roles were further reinforced through the ritual of the powder-puff football game in which the men dressed as girl cheerleaders and burlesqued female behavior while girls dressed in football attire and played a game of football. As Foley (1990, p. 51) put it:

> Males used this moment of symbolic inversion to parody females in a burlesque and ridiculous manner. Males took great liberties with the female role through this humorous form of expression. The power of these young males to appropriate and play with female symbols of sexuality was a statement about males' social and physical dominance. Conversely, the females took few liberties with their expression of the male role. They tried to play a very serious game of football. The females tried earnestly to prove they were equal. Their lack of playfulness was a poignant testimony to their subordinate status in this small town.

The number of gender categories recognized in societies also differs. For example, many Native American societies traditionally recognized a third gender— that of *berdache* among the Cheyenne and Lakota and the *nadle* among the Navajo. The *berdache* or *nadle* is a biological male who does not fill a standard male role. Such individuals are not seen as men nor are they defined as women. They occupy a third role—one that is culturally defined, accepted, and—in some cases—revered. Male children in the Navajo, Lakota, Cheyenne, and other groups could thus choose from two gender categories rather than learning that gender roles are defined by physiology. Among the Lakota, male children learned that if they desired, they could adopt the dress and work roles of women and have sex with men, although the *berdache* role did not necessarily involve sexual behavior. However, the *berdache* or *nadle* did not play only women's roles; some were noted for their hunting skills and exploits in war. In American society, in contrast, persons who do not assume the gender roles associated with their anatomy are defined as deviant, abnormal, or nonconformist.

Anthropologist Harriet Whitehead suggests that Americans have difficulty recognizing a third gender in part because they make ethnocentric assumptions about what characteristics are most important in defining gender roles. Americans define gender largely by sexual preference—whether a person prefers to have sex with a male or a female. They pay less attention to preferences in dress, behavior, and occupation. Native North Americans traditionally placed a different emphasis on these characteristics. Groups that included the socially legitimate identity of *berdache* or *nadle* defined gender primarily by choice of occupation; the gender of a sexual partner was least important.

Language, Gender, and Race

Societies provide a social landscape along with the symbols or codes through which a person's place in the landscape is conveyed to others. For individuals, these symbols or codes serve as toolboxes from which to fashion an identity. Societies may vary in the extent to which people are allowed to negotiate their place in the landscape, but all allow people some leeway.

As we mentioned, language is one of the tools that people have to signal how they want to be placed in society. For example, voice pitch does tend to differ because men's vocal tracts are longer, thus giving men a deeper voice. But children, whose voice tracts are not yet different in size, will unconsciously lower or raise their pitch to conform to gender expectations, which is the reason that you usually tell the gender of children from their voice. As Penelope Eckert and Sally McConnell-Ginet point out in their book *Language and Gender*, people use language to present themselves as a certain kind of person—to project an attitude or a style along with gender. Virtually all parts of language can be used in this way. The phonology—that is, the sounds—of a language can convey gender. For example, if the /s/ sound is made by pressing the tip of the tongue against the teeth, it is still recognized as /s/, but the result is a slight lisp associated in the United States with femininity in women and gayness in men.

Grammar can signal gender. Thus, in French, there are male and female forms of nouns; in English, the third person singular *he* or *she* forces us to differentiate gender. In Japanese, there are sentence-final particles that add to or soften the force of an utterance, with so-called women's language characterized as milder. Thus, "I'm going" can be said as a mild assertion (*iku wa*), as a neutral assertion (*iku*), or as an emphatic assertion (*iku ze/iku zo*), with the last being characterized as more masculine.

What is said may also convey gender. Profanity is reserved largely for males and is prohibited for women and children. There are still laws on the books in the United States prohibiting the use of "foul" language in the presence of women and children, and as late as 1999, a man was indicted and convicted in Michigan on such a charge.

Whether or not to speak can convey gender. Children, for example are encouraged to speak or to remain silent. Among the Araucanian of Chile, men are encouraged to talk because it is a sign of masculine intelligence and leadership, whereas the ideal woman is submissive and silent in her husband's presence.

Conversational styles may also convey gender. Linguist Robin Lakoff was one of the first to draw attention to the way that a woman's identity in society influences how she speaks. Women, says Lakoff, are constrained to minimize their expression of opinion with such various linguistic devices as tag questions ("This election mess is terrible, *isn't it?*"), rising intonations on declaratives ("When will dinner be ready? *Six o'clock?*"), the use of hedges ("That's *kinda* sad" or "It's *probably* dinnertime"), boosters or amplifications ("I'm *so* glad you're here"), and indirection (e.g., saying "I've got a dentist's appointment then," thus conveying an inability or reluctance to meet at that time and asking the other person to propose another time).

The general thrust of Lakoff's argument has to do with the relative powerlessness of women, stemming from their relatively weak social position. Speaking "as a woman," suggests Lakoff, requires avoiding firm commitment or expressing strong opinions and, in general, being constrained to use a "powerless" language.

Others point out that such tags also signal a willingness to listen to alternative perspectives and may strengthen a speaker's position by enlisting support for their ideas and positions. Others suggest that the tags are not so much a matter of gender but a matter of power because men with little power also speak the same way. But Lakoff's work focused attention on how language is central to building identities and conveying ideas of self.

Some very simple linguistic devices can be used to change identity. For example, someone may choose to use or not to use profanity. This choice is a way of positioning oneself in the social landscape. Imagine, suggests Eckert and McConnell, an adolescent girl who begins to use profanity. She may be trying to demonstrate autonomy from her teachers or other adults or distinguish herself from her "preppy" peers. She may be trying to demonstrate her connection to her mother who swears or her friends who swear. She may be trying to project the air of a grownup or of a rebellious, assertive, or angry person. Perhaps she is trying to separate herself from friends and moving toward some tough people. The point is that she has drawn from her identity toolbox some linguistic symbols that serve to position her in a different part of the social landscape. She may, of course, also use other tools. She may choose different modes of dress and change the places where she hangs out. Regardless, she is active in projecting the way that she wants others to see her—something we all do virtually all the time.

Language can also be used to construct "others"—groups from which people want to separate themselves. In his classic article "Racism in the English Language," Robert B. Moore discusses how judgments about race are coded into the way we speak. References to the color black are scattered throughout the English language—generally with negative meanings: having a black outlook, to blackball or blacklist someone, or to be a black sheep. The word *tribal* is often applied to discussions of African politics but not European affairs. Thus, rivalries between Ibo and Hausa and Yoruba in Nigeria or Hutu and Tutsi in Rwanda are referred to in the press as "tribal conflicts," but conflicts between Serbs and Croats in the Balkans, between Protestants and Catholics in Northern Ireland, or between Basques and Southern Spaniards in Spain are not described that way.

Ward Churchill discusses the consequences of naming sports teams the "Braves," "Chiefs," "Redskins," "Seminoles," and "Savages"—names that he suggests are deeply demeaning to Native Americans. Because apologists claim that this is just "fun," with no harm intended, Churchill suggests we spread the fun around and use nicknames from other groups to name sports teams, such as the Kansas City "Kikes," the Hanover "Honkies," the Dayton "Dagos," the Wisconsin "Wetbacks," and so on. Churchill draws attention to the way we use language—often unknowingly—that stigmatizes the identities of others.

QUESTION 6.3   *How Do Individuals Learn Who They Are?*

We are not born with an identity; it is something we learn. Moreover, identities are not static phenomena. In all societies, people are constantly changing their identities as they move through the life cycle. Consequently, there must be ways in which identity changes are announced.

In a classic work published in 1908, Arnold van Gennep introduced the concept of **rites of passage**. These rituals mark a person's passage from one identity to another, as going into different rooms might mark a person's progress through a house. Van Gennep identifies three phases in rites of passage: First, the ritual separates the person from an existing identity; next, the person enters a transition phase; finally, the changes are incorporated into a new identity. These phases of rites of passage are not equally elaborated in specific ceremonies. The separation phase, for example, is a major part of funeral ceremonies designed to help the living let go of the deceased; transition is a major part of initiation ceremonies marking the passage of a person from, say, childhood to adulthood; and incorporation is emphasized in marriage ceremonies, which, in most societies, mark the transfer of a person from one social group to another.

Anthropologists have even begun to study how American corporations use ceremony and ritual to help employees define their identities within the work organization. Some corporations use ceremonies not only to change a person's identity but to remind others in the organization of unacceptable behavior. The W. T. Grant Corporation reportedly humiliated poorly performing store managers by throwing custard pies in their faces, cutting their ties in half, and inducing them to push peanuts across the floor with their noses. W. T. Grant was later dissolved through bankruptcy.

A more successful example of the use of ritual to define identity in business is the Mary Kay Cosmetics ceremonies to enhance employees' identification with the company. Each year, awards were presented to sales personnel—all of whom were women—in a setting that has been compared to the Miss America pageant. Dressed in evening clothes, honorees were seated on the stage of a large auditorium in front of a cheering audience. The ceremony celebrated the personal saga of founder Mary Kay—how, through personal determination and optimism, she was able to adjust to her separation from her husband, support her children as a salesperson, and ultimately found her own company. A bee-shaped pin with the legend "Everyone can find their wings and fly" symbolizes the ideology of the corporation.

The Transition to Adulthood

Prominent in most societies around the world are ceremonies that mark the transition of a male from boyhood to manhood—most involving some kind of test of courage. Anthropologist David Gilmore claims that one reason so many societies incorporate tests of masculinity and tortuous initiation rituals for males is that the male identity is more problematical than the female identity. For every individual, there is in the beginning of life a subliminal identification with the mother, and men must make greater efforts to differentiate themselves from their identification with their mothers. Consequently, societies incorporate rituals that symbolically separate the boy from his mother while also incorporating him into manhood.

One example cited by Gilmore is the Maasai, a cattle-herding people of East Africa. For a Maasai male to attain the identity of "worthy man," he must own cattle, be generous to others, and be autonomous and independent—capable of defending his homestead and his honor. He must also demonstrate bravery on cattle raids against neighboring groups. The road to being a man (what the Maasai call a *moran*) begins with a boy's father looking for a sign that the boy is ready to assume the responsibilities of manhood. Tepilit Ole Saitoti tells in his autobiography how he begged his father to let him be initiated. One day, Tepilit confronted a huge lioness that threatened the family's cattle and killed it. Shortly after, his father gathered the family and said: "We are going to initiate Tepilit into manhood. He has proven before all of us that he can now save children and cattle."

The central feature of the Maasai initiation is circumcision. Circumcision is intensely painful because the cutting, which may last up to four minutes, is done with no anesthetic. Placed on view before male relatives and prospective in-laws, the boy must remain absolutely still and silent. Tepilit describes how, shortly before his circumcision, he was told: "You must not budge; don't move a muscle or even blink. You can face only one direction until the operation is completed. The slightest movement on your part will mean you are a coward, incompetent, and unworthy to be a Maasai man."

By participating in male-bonding rituals such as this food fight in a college fraternity, young American males establish new identities as members of a group.

Americans also have their rites of passage into adulthood—some of the most spectacular being those associated with high school and college fraternities. As with the Maasai, sexual identity, including separation from the female identity, is often a major theme in these ceremonies. To illustrate, we describe a study whose initial focus was an instance of fraternity gang rape. The study began in 1983 when anthropologist Peggy Reeves Sanday learned from one of her students of a gang rape at a college fraternity. Sanday's subsequent research produced a vivid portrait of how college fraternity behavior depicts the male identity in American society.

Gang rape—or "pulling train," as it is called in fraternities—begins with the coercion of a vulnerable young woman who is seeking acceptance or may be high on alcohol or drugs and who may or may not agree to have sex with a certain man. When she passes out or is too weak or intoxicated to protest, a "train" of men have sex with her. Although the incident that triggered Sanday's study occurred in a fraternity on a large, prestigious college campus, gang rape is not unique to college fraternities. It is also associated with sports teams, street gangs, and other groups of men for whom the act often serves, according to Sanday, as a male bonding ritual. Pulling train occurs with some frequency. During one six-year period in the mid-1980s, there were 75 documented cases on college campuses, and in the investigation of the event that led to Sanday's study, witnesses reported that it occurred on that campus once or twice a month. It is likely that many cases go unreported. One reason is that perpetrators and victims often do not recognize it as rape. Most men, suggests Sanday, believe that if a woman has consented with one man, does not vigorously resist, and is not violently overpowered, the sex act does not constitute rape. Rather, they say, the woman is "asking for it." These men are unaware that any sex act in which the woman is not able to give consent constitutes a legal definition of rape. Victims may not recognize it as rape either and may take the responsibility, saying "I went too far" or "I let things get out of hand." Other victims are reluctant to report it because of the publicity or negative treatment they receive from authorities. When fraternities are involved, colleges often cloak these events in secrecy to protect the offenders, the victims, and themselves.

As Sanday and her associates interviewed fraternity members, women who were associated with them, and victims of rape, they sought to explain what it was about male identity, as represented by college fraternities, that encourages these actions. Three things seemed to stand out in her account. First, there is a heavy emphasis in fraternities on male bonding and male-bonding behavior to the extent that a college man's self-esteem and social identity depend on first gaining entry to a fraternity and then being accepted by the brothers. Fraternities confer status; on most college campuses where they exist, they are recognized as places "where the action is." They also provide reassurance, security, and ready-made identities. Membership in a fraternity transforms outsiders into insiders.

Second, sex constitutes a major status and identity marker. Masculinity is defined and demonstrated by sexual conquest. For example, in the fraternity in which the gang rape occurred, a major activity was "hitting" or "riffing" on women or "working a yes out." This involves persuading a woman to have sex by talking, dancing, or drinking with her. Men who are expert riffers gain status; those who are unsuccessful are in danger of being labeled "nerds," "wimps," or, worse, "fags." Sex in this case is a public thing. Men in the fraternities that Sanday interviewed bragged publicly about their sexual conquests and arranged for brothers to witness them. Some fraternities posted weekly newsletters listing brothers' sexual conquests.

A third element in the identity of fraternity men concerns their attitudes toward women. Many of the fraternity members interviewed by Sanday implied that women were sex objects to be abused or debased. A woman's identity among fraternity men was determined largely by her sexual interactions with them. Women who are sexually unresponsive are "frigid" or "icicles"; women who allow advances only up to a point and refuse intimacy are "cockteasers"; and women who have sex with many men are "sluts" or "cunts." Such labels indicate that the role of girlfriend is virtually the only role with no negative connotations that a woman can play. In one fraternity, brothers marked women who attended their parties with "power dots": black, red, yellow, white, or blue stickers they attached to a girl's clothing at parties to indicate how easy the girl was to pick up.

For fraternity men, the debasement of women is interwoven with the themes of male bonding and sexual conquest. Part of the reason men bond in college, says Sanday, is to achieve domination and power they think is owed to males. One fraternity man explained how verbally harassing a girl increases male bonding: "I mean, people come back the day after a party and say, 'You should have seen me abuse this girl.' They're real proud of it in front of everyone."

Sanday uses the term **phallocentrism**—"the deployment of the penis as a concrete symbol of masculine social power and dominance"—to describe the use of sex and the debasement of women to demonstrate masculinity.

Exercise 6.3 ➤

In her book on gang rape, Sanday also discusses the role of pornography in the definition of male and female identities in America. She suggests that pornography in America depicts women as subservient to men and that it reinforces sexist attitudes and encourages behavior toward women characteristic of men in fraternities. Do you agree or disagree and why?

Phallocentrism as well as the themes of male bonding, sexual prowess, and the debasement of women are all manifested in the act of pulling train. It is a form of bonding, it publicly legitimizes a male's heterosexuality, and it makes women an object of scorn and abuse.

Sanday is quick to emphasize that not all college men subscribe to the ideology of phallocentrism and not all fraternity men measure their masculinity by sexual conquest and the victimization of women. In the case that initiated Sanday's study, all the girls who knew them described the six men charged with gang rape as "among the nicest guys in the fraternity." Individually, probably none of them would have committed the act they were charged with. However, in the context of the fraternity, gang rape is the credible outcome of a process of identity formation that is manifested in fraternity life in general and in the fraternity initiation ritual in particular.

The fraternity initiation ritual on most college campuses is the culmination of a period of pledging in which initiates are required to perform various demeaning acts. Particulars may vary from fraternity to fraternity and campus to campus, but in general, the ritual stigmatizes the initiates as infants, children, or girls and then proceeds to cleanse them of this negative identity before incorporating them into the fraternity as full-fledged brothers.

In one fraternity initiation described to Sanday, the initiates were blindfolded and stripped down to their jockstraps. Then, they were told to drop their jockstraps and were ridiculed: "Look at the pin-dicks, pussies, fags. They're all a bunch of girls, it's amazing they don't have tits." As the brothers screamed at them, their testicles were rubbed with Ben-Gay. After about 10 minutes, a brother spoke, saying: "Sorry we had to do that, but we had to cleanse you of your nerd sin." Then, the pledges were put to tests of trust. In one case, a pledge was thrown to the ground; one brother placed a sword at his crotch and another brother placed a sword at his chest. The pledge was then asked if he trusted the brothers not to kill him. As the pledge nodded yes, the brother brought the sword down on his chest; because it was made of wood, it shattered. In another fraternity, initiates were taken blindfolded to a bathroom and told to eat some feces out of a toilet bowl and trust they would not become sick. As they picked it out and ate it, they realized they were eating bananas.

The final stage of most fraternity initiations generally includes a secret ritual in which the pledges come before the brothers, who are dressed in robes and hoods or other ritual paraphernalia. In one ritual reported to Sanday, a brother addressed the initiates with the following words:

> You have shown trust in the fraternity and trust in the brothers. We know we can trust you now. A bond has been formed between us. No one has experienced the hell you have except us and the brothers before us. Bonded by strength, loyalty, and trust we are one. Cleansed of weakness and filth, we are men. As men we stand tall. As men we stand for the fraternity, and [name of fraternity] stands for us. (Sanday 1990, p. 163)

In these ceremonies, the abusers of the initiates then gain credence by accepting those they have just heaped with abuse. One initiate described to Sanday how he felt at this point:

> I felt exhilarated. I kept saying, "Oh wow!" and hugging my big brother and shaking hands with everybody. I was incredibly happy. I was made to feel worthless by the fraternity as an individual, and now that it was all over, I was made to feel wonderful by the fraternity as a brother. My worth was celebrated by the same process that had previously denied it, because of the change that it had effected within me. I now saw myself as a brother, and what may feel terrible to an individual confronted by brothers feels tremendous to an individual who is a brother. (Sanday 1990, p. 149)

Sanday concludes that fraternity initiation rituals serve to solidify a fraternity man's identity by separating him from his previous identity as a member of a family and perhaps separating him from his mother. The ritual incorporates the man into a group whose activities reinforce a male identity, defined largely by degradation of the negative identity of female and acted out in sexual conquest and abuse of females. Pulling train is an expression of male sexuality and a display of the power of the brotherhood to control and dominate women. In other words, gang rape is but one instance of the abuse and domination that begin in the initiation and are continued later in relations with women and new pledges. Sanday says that once initiates have suffered abuse as a means of establishing their bond to the fraternity, they are obliged to abuse new generations of pledges and party women as a way to honor the original contract and renew the power of the brotherhood.

QUESTION 6.4 *How Do Individuals Communicate Their Identities to One Another?*

There is an episode in Jonathan Swift's *Gulliver's Travels* in which Gulliver learns of an experiment conducted by professors at the Academy of Lagado. They believe that because words are only names for things, they can abolish words by having people carry with them everything they need to engage in discourse with others. Gulliver describes such a "conversation": Two people meet, open their packs of things, "talk" by using them for an hour, pack up their things, and go off.

In many ways, our interactions with others are similar to the interaction of the inhabitants of Laputa. We also communicate with things by using them to make statements of our identity—who we think we are or who we want to be. The clothes we wear, the way we speak, the things we possess, and the people we associate with are all used to display an identity that we think we have or that we desire. For example, if sex or gender is used as a criterion to distinguish individuals, there must be ways of displaying sexual differences so others can read them. For example, men in some groups in New Guinea wear

Trobriand Islanders define and maintain their social identities by participating in the *kula* ring—a ritualized pattern of gift giving involving the exchange of necklaces and armbands.

penis gourds, and in 17th-century Europe, men wore codpieces to emphasize their male anatomy. In areas of Africa, people from different villages have different hairstyles; in America, teenagers encode their schools, gangs, or teams by the jackets they wear. People signal their connectedness to others by holding hands, by wearing rings, or by feasting and drinking together.

One of the most influential works in the history of anthropology is a book written by Marcel Mauss, modestly entitled *The Gift*. Mauss identifies what he calls the **principle of reciprocity**: the giving and receiving of gifts. His major point is that gifts, which in theory are voluntary, disinterested, and spontaneous, are in fact obligatory. The giving of the gift creates a tie with the person who receives it and who, on some future occasion, is obliged to reciprocate. To Mauss, what is important is not what is given but the relationship that is maintained or established by the gift. The types of things given and received signal the identities of the participants in the exchange and the kind of relationship that exists between them. If the gifts are roughly of equal value, the relationship is one of equality. But if the gifts are unequal in value, the person who gives the more valuable gift is generally of higher status than the receiver.

A well-known example of gift giving in the anthropological literature is the *kula* ring of the Trobriand Islanders—the circulation of gifts among trading partners on different islands. The seagoing Trobrianders leave their homes on islands off the eastern coast of New Guinea and travel from island to island, visiting and trading. Noteworthy in their travels is their pattern of gift giving. Each man has trading partners on the islands he visits, and these partnerships are signaled with gifts of red-shell necklaces or white-shell armbands. As a man travels and trades objects, he also gives and receives necklaces and receives armbands. A man who receives either an armband or a necklace does not keep it but passes it along to another trading partner. There is a set pattern to the exchange: Necklaces travel from island to island in a clockwise direction, whereas armbands move counterclockwise. The time between exchanges and the distances between the islands are so great that it may take two to 10 years before the necklaces and armbands make a complete circle.

The *kula* ring serves as a concrete representation of the ties between individuals. Any change in the pattern of gift giving reflects a change in the nature of the social ties. In addition, special gifts that are individually owned are also circulated, and the owner's status and renown grow as the goods he owns circulate along predetermined paths. A successful *kula* operator participates in many such exchanges and can profit from them by keeping items for as long as he can before

Exercise 6.4 ➤

> Suppose you were to travel to Gulliver's island of Laputa. If you could communicate to people only with objects that you carried with you and if you could take only five things with you to "tell" people about yourself, what would they be?

passing them along. Of course, if he keeps them too long, others will be reluctant to exchange, so a good deal of social skill is required to *kula* successfully.

Another famous example of gift giving is the potlatch ceremony of people on the northwest coast of North America. Among the Gitksan, the potlatch is a feast at a funeral; someone who dies vacates a spot in the social landscape or, more specifically, leaves empty a name. The Gitksan are organized into patrilineal clans or houses. Each house has associated with it a fixed number of personal names, and each name has associated with it specific spiritual powers, honors, and objects of wealth. As a Gitksan moves through the life cycle, he is given different names associated with his higher standing in the group. The name he holds when he dies is vacated until it is claimed by or given to someone else. If the name vacated belongs to a chief or someone else of high rank, numerous people may try to claim the name and the honors and privileges associated with it. In the competition that follows, the person who contributes the most wealth to the potlatch or funeral feast is the one who gets the name. The higher ranking the name, the greater the wealth that is given away. Around 30 years ago, the cost of a name was anywhere from $100 to $500, and some chiefs have held eight to 10 names at one time. However, the more names held by a Gitksan, the greater is the burden of upholding the power and honor of each name by being generous, loyal, and upstanding. A person who disgraces his name by doing something wrong (such as having an automobile accident or being put in jail) must give a feast to "clean the name."

However, the potlatch feast does more than allow a Gitksan to obtain a new name and identity. It also serves to symbolically reorder and validate the names—hence, the social positions—of everyone at the feast through the distribution of gifts. Members of the house of the deceased generally serve as hosts to members from the deceased's father's house. The guests are feasted for the services they perform at the funeral (they prepare the corpse and dig the grave) and as repayment for the gifts they formerly gave the deceased to help him acquire his name. Hosts seat guests according to rank. Guests who think they have been given a "wrong" seat—one that assigns them to a lower rank than they think they deserve—complain to the leader of the host group, who gives them a gift of money to "wipe away" the disgrace or insult. When the guests are seated, the hosts announce the gifts they are giving to the guests, along with the name of the person from the host group who contributed the gift. Higher-ranking guests receive more gifts at a potlatch than lower-ranking guests. Thus, the seating arrangements and the value of the gifts given to guests at the feast serve to announce or publicly notarize the social position or identity of each guest.

Exchanges that convey recognition of identities need not be limited to material goods. The exchanges also may consist of emotion and sentiment. Hawaiians, for example, define a desired identity in part by expressions of gregariousness and hospitality. The emotional qualities of a person's relationships are one criterion by which others judge, interact with, and respond to that person. For example, if you accept an offer of hospitality in Hawaii, it is a signal that you recognize the generous nature of the offer and you wish to maintain the social link. If you reject the offer of hospitality, it is seen as a hurtful sign that you do not recognize the generous nature of the person making the offer and do not wish to maintain the relationship. Hawaiians attempt to keep social pathways open with altruistic exchanges of love (*aloha*), sincerity, feeling (with heart, *na`au*), and warmth (*pumehana*).

Gifts and Commodities

An important characteristic of traditional *kula* and potlatch goods is that they had a history; a Trobriander who received a necklace or armband could likely recite the history of the object—sometimes from its creation through all the persons who had, at one time or another, possessed it. These goods had the quality of heirlooms in our own society: the family wedding ring that has been worn by brides for three generations; the watch that was owned by a great-grandfather; the quilt that was made by a great-aunt. The history of these kinds of objects, especially when they are given as gifts, forms a vital part of their identity and, consequently, of the identity of the person who gives them. They say something special about the relationship between the giver and the receiver of the gift. The same is true to a lesser extent of gifts that are produced by the giver; they carry a special meaning apart from the object itself. A lamp made and given as a gift is often far more meaningful than a lamp purchased at a department store. However, we often must choose the gifts that we give from among thousands of mass-produced, largely impersonal goods available in department and chain stores. Herein lies a dilemma.

In his book *Gifts and Commodities: Exchange and Western Capitalism Since 1700*, James Carrier argues that since the 16th and 17th centuries, the production and distribution of goods have become impersonal—that the spread of industrial and commercial capitalism has meant the spread of alienated objects and relations. In previous times, commodities were personalized in various ways. The relationship between the producer and/or the seller of goods was a personal one between relatives or friends; the buyer knew who made and sold the object purchased. Even when stores replaced home trade and markets, the buyer knew the storeowner, who further personalized the goods by buying them in bulk and individually packaging and displaying them. The buyer-seller relationship was further personalized by the extension of credit from seller to buyer and by the customer loyalty expressed by the buyer to the seller. Today, the buyer knows neither the producer nor the seller; if the item is bought on credit, it is through a credit card issued by some distant bank based on the filing of an impersonal application—the transaction accomplished completely by mail. Eyes never meet.

Carrier labels goods that carry no special meaning **commodities**—to distinguish them from what he calls **possessions**. Gifts, says Carrier, must be possessions before they carry meaning in an exchange. Commodities involve a transfer of value and a countertransfer: A sells something to B, and the transaction is finished. But in a gift exchange, a more or less permanent link is established between giver and receiver. Gifts are inalienable—they are bound to people after the presentation; commodities are independent of their sellers (or producers). It is easy to return, destroy, or give away a commodity; it is a dilemma to do any of those with a gift. Ralph Waldo Emerson vividly expressed the difference between gifts and commodities when he wrote:

> The only gift is a portion of thyself. Thou must bleed for me. Therefore the poet brings his poem; the shepherd, his lamb; the farmer, corn; the miner, a gem; the sailor, coral and shells; the painter, his picture; the girl, a handkerchief or her own sewing. This is right and pleasing . . . . when a man's biography is conveyed in a gift. (Carrier, 1993, p. 56)

Or, as Emerson said again: "It is a cold, lifeless business when you go to the shops to buy me something that does not represent your life and talent" (Carrier, 1993, p. 56).

As mentioned previously, for Americans, the contrast between commodities and gifts poses a special problem. Most of the items that we give as gifts are store bought, often mass produced commodities. Their history is brief and undistinguished: an item of clothing assembled in some factory in Mexico or Indonesia by a young woman earning perhaps a dollar an hour; a sports item assembled in some factory in South America, shipped to a warehouse in Chicago, and sold in a mass-produced catalog; a radio, VCR, or CD player assembled in Korea, distributed by a Japanese company, and sold in an American chain store. These are commodities rather than gifts. Their meaning is contained in their worth or utility—in their materiality. The meaning of a gift is different; the perfect gift is priceless—its materiality immaterial.

For Carrier, the problem is how, in a world filled with impersonal, alienated commodities—goods without history, so to speak—can we turn these things into personal items with meaning and history—into possessions that carry something of the buyer's identity? In gift giving, how do we turn commodities into items that say something about the relationship between the giver and the receiver? How do we make commodities meaningful?

We convert commodities into possessions and gifts, says Carrier, by a process of appropriation. For example, when a person takes an impersonal space—a dorm room or a rented apartment—and decorates and modifies the space, he or she has appropriated it and given it meaning. When we buy food at the supermarket, we appropriate it by preparing or cooking it. When a person buys an automobile, one that is virtually identical to thousands of others of the same make, model, year, and color, and comes to think of it as unique—as an expression of his or her identity—that person has appropriated an object and made it a possession. Shopping itself, says Carrier, is a way of appropriating commodities; the "wise shopper" chooses what is "right" for him or her or what is "right" for the recipient of a gift.

Manufacturers and sellers try to aid the process of converting a commodity into a possession by stamping their products with a distinct identity. A good example is Harris tweed, which most buyers associate with some Harris Islander weaving on a loom in his shed, creating the item as his ancestors have done for centuries, and even giving each item its own serial number. In fact, the yarn is spun in textile mills and then woven on looms given to the weaver with the frames warped so no special skill is necessary to weave the cloth. Other than being narrower, the only difference between the looms the Harris Islanders use and those used in factories is that the Harris Island weaver supplies the power with a foot treadle rather than a machine.

Endorsements from sports or movie celebrities help consumers transform a commodity into a possession, and displaying goods in catalogs in a way that helps the buyer appropriate commodities has become a fine art. For example, Carrier notes how the Smith & Hawken catalog for gardeners forges a personal link between object and producer by detailing the historical origins of the tools and linking them to historical figures—almost always English and most from the 18th or 19th century. The text communicates this message by using such words as "origins," "can be traced back to," "was invented by," and so on. Lands' End catalogs display pictures of employees, thereby linking commodities to the people who work at Lands' End, even though these employees are not always the actual producers of the goods.

Comfortably Yours, a medical supply distributor, sells items to the old and infirm by telling readers about the people who use them. For example, the text describes how the company owners bought a particular item for a particular person and how pleased the recipient was. The company has managed to wrap its commodities directly in the cultural framework of the gift.

Gift Giving and Christmas in America

The dilemma of converting commodities into gifts is particularly acute during the Christmas holiday season, when most gift giving takes place in America. Christmas as we know it did not really emerge until the height of the Industrial Revolution. Its precursors included the traditional end-of-the-year festivities that took place in England, where gifts consisted of food or feasts given by superiors to their dependents. In the 1770s, in New York City, people began celebrating December 6, the day of St. Nicholas, instead of the New Year on Jauary 1st. This was actually something of an anti-Christmas celebration; St. Nicholas was Dutch, and the colonists were celebrating things Dutch to protest British rule over what had been New Amsterdam before British colonization. It was not until 1809 that the holiday began to spread and St. Nicholas turned into Santa Claus, giving gifts of candy to children. The appearance in 1823 of Clement Moore's *A Visit From St. Nicholas* (or *'Twas the Night Before Christmas*, as it later came to be known) marked the movement of the holiday to the end of the year. At this point, children began to get toys rather than food. But even then, Christmas was celebrated largely on New Year's Day and in the industrial northeast.

The next major step in the evolution of Christmas was the appearance in the United States of Charles Dickens's *A Christmas Carol* in 1843; it was an immediate sensation, especially with its victory of Bob Cratchit, Tiny Tim, and their world of the home over Scrooge and the cold, impersonal world of work. By 1865, Christmas was declared a national holiday (28 states had already declared it a holiday), and in 1862, the Thomas Nast image of Santa Claus began appearing in *Harper's Weekly*, completing his construction as a fat, jolly old man dressed in fur-trimmed robes (inspired, Nast later admitted, by the fur-trimmed clothing of the wealthy Astor family). By the 1880s, writers were already beginning to complain about the commercialization of Christmas.

Most social scientists who have written about Christmas agree that it is largely a celebration of the family, serving especially to distinguish the world of the family from the outside world of work. Christmas serves to affirm the identity of Americans as members of specific family groups, and the circle of kin with whom gifts are exchanged defines the boundaries of the family. In one study conducted in a midwestern city, some 90% of all gifts exchanged at Christmas were exchanged with family members. Moreover, many of the items not exchanged within the family hardly qualify as gifts at all. Thus, the office party where people draw lots to discover the person for whom they will buy a gift, the party in which everyone gets a gift but there is no exchange, and the presentation to the letter carrier or the garbage collector hardly qualify as gift giving. In these situations, there is little concern for reciprocity. Christmas heightens a person's sense of family identity, expressing how warm the family is and how cold the world outside may be.

Thus, it is within the family that the Christmas gift is most important and where the gift must contain something of the biography of the giver and the history of the relationship—where the gift must be a possession rather than a commodity. The question is how to resolve the problem of using commodities as family gifts—how to transform commodities to make them suitable as statements of the special role that family and family relations play in defining our identity. Apparently, this problem is not a new one. The dilemma of giving gifts that were manufactured and sold in stores apparently existed as

In American society, the yearly ritual of Christmas shopping provides a means of converting impersonal commodities into personalized gifts that show one's love for family members and close friends.

© Monika Graff/The Image Works

early as the mid-19th century, and department stores tried to convince buyers to purchase their gifts in stores by advertising them as "special Christmas stock." Even today, with Christmas decorations, music, and special attractions, such as the ever-present Santa Claus, retailers attempt to inject the spirit of Christmas into their stock of goods.

But there are other ways that consumers try to appropriate commodities and turn them into Christmas gifts. First, we may simply say that the nature of the gift itself is immaterial—that "It's the thought that counts." A second way is to purchase things that are not very useful, giving frivolous or luxurious gifts or items that are Christmas-specific, such as Christmas tree decorations or clothing with Christmas decorations on it. Third—and very important—there is the wrapping rule: Christmas gifts must be wrapped. The wrapping itself converts the commodity into a gift. Difficult-to-wrap presents (such as a piano, a horse, or a bicycle) must be decorated with a bow. The only kinds of things that need not be wrapped are items made by the giver, such as breads or jams. These items need only a bow and a card.

Finally, says Carrier, there is the shopping itself—that is, the time and worry we spend getting the "right" gift for the "right" person. Why, he asks, do we go through all this? It is onerous, it is stressful, and it is expensive. But one-third of all retail sales are made in November and December, half of which are accounted for by Christmas shopping. People complain about the materialism of Christmas and Christmas shopping, but people shop intensely for Christmas.

In the face of this bother and complaint, why do Americans, even devout Christians, spend so much effort on Christmas shopping? Why not give homemade gifts? Indeed, why give presents at all? Why not give a Christmas card instead? It is true that the giving of purchased gifts reflects a number of motives, ranging from displays of affluence to a desire to shower a loved one with lovely things. However, these more commonly recognized motives do "not explain the intensity of Christmas shopping and people's ambivalence towards it" (Carrier, 1993, p. 62).

Carrier suggests that the answer to this riddle lies in the fact that shopping itself is a method of appropriation—of converting a commodity into a gift—as we exercise choice from among the mass of commodities presented to us. As Carrier puts it:

> Christmas shopping is an annual ritual through which we convert commodities into gifts. Performing this ritual indicates that we can celebrate and recreate personal relations with the anonymous objects available to us, just as it strengthens and reassures us as we undertake the more mundane appropriations of everyday life during the rest of the year. (1993, p. 63)

It also demonstrates to people, says Carrier, that they can create a world of family—a world of love—out of the impersonal commodities that flood the world "out there." Christmas is a time when Americans make a world of money into a world of family—a time of contrast between the impersonal world of commodities and the personal world of possessions and gifts.

QUESTION 6.5   *How Do Individuals Defend Their Identities When They Are Threatened?*

In defining themselves and others, people sometimes disagree on their relative positions on the social map; they disagree on their respective identities. Anthony F. C. Wallace and Raymond Fogelson refer to these situations as **identity struggles**—interactions in which there is a discrepancy between the identity a person claims to possess and the identity attributed to him or her by others. Consider the medicine fight among the Beaver Indians of British Columbia. The Beaver believe that a man's identity relative to others is determined by the amount of supernatural power or "medicine" he possesses. This power determines a man's success in hunting and protects him and his family from illness and misfortune. Any personal misfortune a man experiences, such as illness or failure to kill game, is interpreted by others as a loss of supernatural power and, hence, a loss of prestige. However, the man experiencing the misfortune does not interpret it in the same way; for him, the misfortune is not caused by a loss of his supernatural power but by someone using supernatural power against him. In other words, his view of his identity is different from what he believes is attributed to him by others. The person experiencing the misfortune will then dream the identity of the attacker and publicly accuse him. The accused may deny the charge, responding that his accuser is experiencing misfortune because he has committed some wrongful act. Thus begins the medicine fight—a series of accusations and counteraccusations that sometimes leads to violence.

Making Moka in Papua New Guinea

The Beaver claim or defend their social identities through spiritual means. More common is the manipulation of material goods. The Melpa, who live around the area of Mt. Hagen in the Central Highlands of Papua New Guinea, provide an example. The people of Mt. Hagen live by growing crops such as sweet potatoes and raising pigs. Pigs serve not only as a source of protein but also as signs of wealth that are required for gift exchange.

The most important identity in the Highlands social landscape is that of Big Man. Because they are leaders and among the wealthiest in terms of pig ownership, Big Men are the most independent from others. A man who is poor and depends on others for food and sustenance is called by a term that translates into English as *rubbish man*.

Becoming a Big Man requires courage in warfare. War, in the form of highly ritualized battles with spears and arrows or raiding and murder, has long been a part of Papua New Guinea Highland society. Big Men play a pivotal role in planning war as well as establishing peace—either with their oratorical skills or with their wealth. The greatest skill required of a Big Man, however, is making *moka*. As described by anthropologist Andrew Strathern, *moka* is a form of ceremonial gift exchange in which a man makes an initial gift to a trading partner and then receives in return more than he gave. Ceremonial gift exchanges serve two purposes: They establish and maintain links between individuals and groups, and they establish a rank system that enables men to earn status and prestige and become Big Men. Big Men from the same clan can make *moka* with each other, but it is most common for a man to have partners outside his clan and among ex-enemies or groups tied to his through marriage. Items that are given in exchanges include pigs, shells, bird plumage, salt, decorating oil, and stone axe blades. Pigs and shells once were the most important items, but today, Australian money, bicycles, cattle, and even trucks are used.

The major idea in making *moka*—and, consequently, establishing the status of Big Man—is for a man to give his trading partner more than he received at the last exchange. Thus, if A gives 100 pigs to B and then B returns a countergift of 150 pigs that A cannot repay, then B is the Big Man because he gave the last gift. A diagram of a series of *moka* exchanges between two trading rivals might look something like this:

First exchange: A gives x amount of goods to B.
Result: B owes x amount of goods to A.
Second exchange: B give two times x goods to A.
Result: A owes x amount of goods to B.
Third exchange: A gives two times x goods to B.
Result: B owes x amount of goods to A.

Because a man has returned the debt he owes his partner and added an increment equal to the debt after each exchange, the result of the interaction is that one person always owes the other. The two participants never reach the point where things are even; the pattern of gift exchange assures that one party is always indebted to the other. The basic rule is to give more than you receive. It is strictly the incremental change in the debt that allows a man to say he made *moka*.

The negotiation of identity between *moka* partners is never an isolated affair because a man is rarely able to make *moka* solely on the basis of what he possesses at a given time. For example, if a man wants or is being pressured to make *moka* with a rival to whom he must give six pigs or 10 shell bracelets and he does not have that many pigs or bracelets at that time, he must either call in outstanding *moka* obligations others owe him or must get what he needs from friends or kin. Thus, any given exchange may involve a host of people and groups. A map of the circulation of *moka* goods around Melpa society would provide a pretty good idea of how different people and groups are related to others and would indicate the social identity of each person in the exchange network. These exchanges serve for the Melpa as public statements of social identities—the relations between people and groups—at any given time. It is as if everyone in an American town publicly announced the present state of their social relations with every other person and group in town.

At a fairly typical *moka* exchange, many Big Men from different groups may make *moka* at once. The ceremony takes place at a ceremonial ground associated with a particular clan or lineage—usually built by the Big Man of that group. Preparations for the *moka* exchange begin months before the actual presentation, and Big Men of donor groups negotiate the timing of the exchange. Those who are ready can push the *moka* through, but those who are not ready and who do not have enough to give to their trading rivals in the other group risk defaulting to their partners. Those who do not possess enough wealth to give may try to delay the timing of a *moka* ceremony but may be taunted as procrastinators or as "rubbish men."

Before making *moka*, each man reviews his partnerships and ties to others—perhaps dropping some and adding others. Men scheduled to receive gifts at the *moka* exchange make initiatory gifts of shells, pigs, and legs of pork to their *moka* partners. Discussions about the ceremony are held at the ceremonial ground of the main group, and the men scheduled to give gifts set up stakes to indicate how many pigs they will give away to their partners. They also clear the ceremonial ground, make speeches, and review the history of the relations between the two groups. At each meeting, the Big Men try to contract for more gifts, egging on their clanmates to give more pigs to their trading partners and increasing the competitive spirit. They insist that they must surpass in wealth the gifts they received from their partners the last time they received *moka*. The climax of these discussions is the showing of the gifts at the ceremonial grounds. Once this is done, the final transfer takes place with dancing and oratory.

When the presentation is made, the Big Men among the donors step forward and make speeches. On the final day, men and women of the recipient group converge on the ceremonial grounds while the donors decorate themselves with pearl shell pendants, fine bark aprons and belts, pig grease or tree oil, and charcoal and red ochre. At the ceremony, the donors run up and down the row, crying "hoo-aah, hoo-aah" and performing a war dance. Their speeches are boasts, claiming that by the amount they have given, they have "won." Here is an excerpt of such a speech:

> My sister's sons, my cross-cousins. I am your true cross-cousin, living close to you. My sisters' sons, my cross-cousins, you say you see big pigs, big shells, well, now I have given you large pigs on the two olka stakes, given you a bicycle too, given you all the food you like to eat. Further, I have given you two steers, and so I win. I have given you all the things which are your food; I give you two steers also and so I win. (Strathern, 1971, p. 241)

Recipients who do not receive what they expect at the ceremony (and they never know exactly what they will get until the ceremony takes place) complain loudly and bitterly. Thus, the ceremony is an anxious occasion in which the honor and, consequently, the social identities of both donor and recipient are on the line. Sometimes, actual fighting breaks out. If a man does not meet his commitments to his partner and does not give gifts commensurate with what he received at the last ceremony, his partner can do little but shout insults or physically attack him.

At the end of the ceremony, an orator counts the gifts while the recipient offers stylized thank-yous. The recipients of *moka* then gather their shells and pigs and knock over the pig stakes, except for one that is left standing as proof that the donors have made *moka* at their ceremonial ground.

CASE STUDY IN DOING ANTHROPOLOGY #6: FAT TALK

One of our most important identity features is our body shape. Although desired body shapes vary cross-culturally and across historical periods, in the West today, a thin person is judged to be superior to a heavier person. When researchers asked children ages six to nine to examine three body silhouettes and to describe the kind of person represented by each body type, the children described the thinner figure as friendly, kind, happy, and polite, whereas they described the heavier figure as lazy, lying, and cheating. When 10- and 11-year-olds were shown drawings of other children, they consistently ranked heavier figures lowest—even below drawings of children with missing limbs or a child in a wheelchair.

Weight is also a handicap in the educational system, where teachers perceive heavy children as having more behavioral problems than others and as being less well liked by their classmates. Later in life, people who are overweight face hostile work environments and job discrimination because workers judged unattractive by their peers, particularly women, are consistently described in more negative terms.

Consequently, many people are engaged in a constant effort to achieve or approach the ideal body type—one that is defined mainly by the media, where models and media personalities are consistently thin and well below average weight. According to one study, as many as 60% of white middle-class girls in the United States report that they are dieting.

In addition to determining how people are judged by others, body weight is also a health issue. The U.S. Centers for Disease Control and Prevention (CDC) reports that 64% of U.S. adults are overweight or obese as measured by a body mass index of 25 or more.* Furthermore, in spite of the number of people who report that they are dieting, people are getting heavier. The CDC reports that in 1991, only four states in the United States had obesity rates of 15 to 19%, with none above 20%. By 2009, 14 states had obesity rates of 20 to 24%, 23 had rates from 25 to 29%, and nine states had obesity rates over 30%.

---

*The body mass index (BMI) is a number that shows body weight adjusted for height. BMI can be calculated with simple math by using inches and pounds or meters and kilograms. For adults age 20 years or older, BMI falls into one of these categories: underweight, normal, overweight, or obese. Thus, for example, a 5 foot 6 inch adult is considered overweight at 155 pounds or above and is considered obese at 190 pounds (see http://www.cdc.gov/nccdphp/dnpa/bmi/index.htm).

The reasons that people are getting fatter are complex but probably have something to do with the need for the food industry itself to grow and, consequently, to get people to eat more. It may also be a consequence of an increase in consumption of processed foods, which are more profitable for food companies.

In order for the food industry to grow, it tries to get people to eat more.

© Bob Daemmrich/The Image Works

Weight gain may also be a function of declining exercise levels and the increased hours that people must work at relatively sedentary jobs to keep up economically. Regardless of the reasons, the gap between the body shape we desire and the one we have has social, psychological, and health consequences.

The relationship between self-image and body shape is particularly relevant for female adolescents, as anthropologist Mimi Nichter discovered in a three-year study among high school girls in Arizona. Adolescent girls are particularly vulnerable to body image issues because during adolescence, girls gain up to 25 pounds of body fat and hence are likely to be more critical of their own bodies. Young girls, says Nichter, are imbedded in a morality play in which thinness is good, fatness is bad, and dieting is the way to get in shape. Nichter's survey revealed that a majority of the girls in her study were thinking about their bodies either "all of the time" (24%) or "a lot of the time" (31%), and 90% of the white girls in the study were dissatisfied with their weight.

Nichter's research is relevant not only for what it can tell us about body image and identity but also because her research illustrates how anthropological perspectives can be applied to address problems related to body image and identity. Identifying a problem is one thing, as Nichter shows; trying to do something about it is another.

Anthropologist Mimi Nichter.

© Yankee Image/Peter Miller. Courtesy Mimi Nichter

Body Image and Identity

The adolescent girls in Nichter's study formed their idea of the "perfect" body largely from television, films, magazines, and, of course, Barbie. The ideal woman was tall (5 feet 7 inches) and had long hair (preferably blonde), long legs, flat stomach, clear complexion, and "good" clothes. But weight was the key factor because being "thin" was believed to be the ticket to happiness and popularity. As with many adult women that Nichter knew, the girls seemed to see the world in terms of fat and thin.

Although the girls rarely talked about weight with classmates whom they judged to be "fat," they nevertheless made moral judgments about them, believing that if overweight people really wanted to lose weight, they could. Not losing weight implied that a girl was unconcerned with her personal appearance or was lazy. The lack of respect for overweight girls, says Nichter, was a theme that repeatedly emerged in discussions with the students. One girl explained:

> I have a friend that's overweight and I feel that she should—I mean, I don't have anything against her 'cause she's overweight—but I guess it makes me mad that she doesn't do anything about it. She could do something about it and she doesn't. It's like her responsibility . . . like last night I went over there and right when I walked in she had a bag of Doritos—she was just, I mean, it's just like she's constantly eating. She's addicted to food. She just can't stop. (2000, p. 42)

Fat Talk

The adolescents interviewed by Nichter expressed their concern with body image with what Nichter labeled "fat talk." Fat talk characteristically began with a statement such as "I'm so fat," to which others would respond "No, you're not." Fat talk took the form of almost ritualized exchanges centering on the topic of body weight. As one 14-year-old girl put it:

> All the girls are always saying, I'm so fat. Then I'm like "No, you're not." Then they're like, "Yes, I am." Some girls I know that say that . . . they're really skinny and they just wannabe . . . they just want people to say that they're skinny so that they'll feel better about themselves. I go, "no, you're not," but they keep on saying, "I'm so fat," so that can hear me saying that they're not fat. (2000, p. 45)

Fat talk, says Nichter, serves various purposes. A girl's statement "I'm so fat" is a call for support from others and an affirmation that she is not fat. In some cases, it may allow girls to draw attention to negative identity characteristics before others do. When it is uttered in the locker room, it may be a defense reaction to revealing her body; in the cafeteria line before making a calorie-rich choice, it may be recognition that she knows she should not be eating that much or a public statement of responsibility and concern for her body image. Fat talk is also a way that girls express solidarity with each other, show that they have common concerns, and build consensus among the group.

Even girls who are not overweight feel obligated to engage in fat talk to avoid separating themselves from the group or appearing too satisfied with their appearance. There is even a danger in being thin because any statement by other girls to the effect "You're so skinny" is tantamount to an accusation. As one tall, thin teenager put it when asked if she ever said "I'm so fat":

> Well, I don't know. It's just like I feel I'm stupid if all my friends are like, "Oh, I'm fat," and I don't say it, I feel like I'm bragging about myself, so I automatically

say it anyway. . . . So I don't know. . . . Sometimes I do feel fat, but other times I don't really feel that I'm fat but I still say it. I mean, it's not like I'm looking for a compliment, it's just I don't want to feel like I'm bragging about myself by not saying it. (2000, pp. 53–54)

The concern about body image seems so great that even girls whose weight is normal or below normal seem to fear being fat. Nichter asked a thin girl if she ever felt fat. The girl responded by relating a dream in which she was looking in a mirror and appeared really fat, but when she looked down at herself, she looked skinny. It was as if, suggests Nichter, inside her was lurking a fat girl waiting to be seen and leaving her with feelings of shame.

Much of fat talk consists of plans for dieting. Nichter notes, however, that there is more talk about dieting than actual denial of food and little evidence of the pathological eating behaviors often reported in the popular media. As one of the girls said: "I'm always on a diet, but then I'll end up like, you know, eating something when I'm really hungry. You know, something really gross and then I'll feel really guilty about it. Then I'll still be in that diet. I'm always trying to be on a diet" (2000, p. 68).

Fat talk, says Nichter, represents the tendency of women in Western society to subject themselves—particularly their body image—to constant self-inspection and self-assessment. Even if they are not doing something about their body appearance, they are at least talking about it and conveying to others that they are responsible people who care about their appearance. Fat talk represents a woman's affirmation, reinforcement, and ritual acknowledgment of the fact that her body image is her main identity feature.

However, as pervasive as concerns over weight were among white girls, Nichter discovered that African American girls had different views about weight. Most reports on African American girls indicate that they are much more satisfied with their body weight and less likely to diet than white girls. Furthermore, most African Americans do not define being overweight as being unhealthy. Researchers in one study of 500 African American women found that 40% of those who were overweight as measured by the body mass index thought that their figures were attractive. They also agreed, almost unanimously, that their weight had not created difficulties in their personal relations. In her study of 50 African American adolescents, Nichter reports that 70% were satisfied with their bodies.

Exercise 6.6 ➤

MEN AND BODY IMAGE
Men rarely talk about dieting—or at least not as much as women do. However, concerns about body image are certainly not restricted to women. How, then, do men address the gap between their body image and the cultural ideal represented in advertisements and the media? Do men talk about this issue, and if so, how is it articulated?

For African American girls, the ideal woman seemed to be defined not by body type but more by personality. They said that beauty was not solely a matter of body shape. They said it was important to be beautiful on the inside as well as the outside. One girl explained, "African American girls have inner beauty in themselves that they carry with them—their sense of pride." It is more important to be "looking good," making the most of what you have and presenting a positive public image. Regardless of her body shape, said the African American girls, if a woman dresses right and grooms herself, projects a positive self-image, and has the personality to carry off her individual style, she is "looking good."

The Problem

The negative self-image and obsession with body weight revealed in fat talk—particularly by white adolescents—is complicated by a number of factors. The first is the difficulty for adolescents (or anyone, for that matter) to remain thin in a society that abounds in junk food. In the high school in which Nichter conducted her research, pizza and French fries were the most popular foods, and a balanced diet consisted of a candy bar and a diet coke. The girls socialized over food, and vending machines selling soda and candy bars provided the main source of snacks. School sports teams and clubs earned money for their activities by selling candy, and those with candy bars were obligated to share them with their friends. In her survey, Nichter asked the girls what they typically had for lunch; of those who ate the school lunch, 20% had French fries or chips, 20% had nothing (just something to drink), 8% had ice cream or candy, and only 6% had a salad. In addition, more financially strapped schools are forming partnerships with fast-food chains and allowing fast-food advertising in the schools or on TV commercials shown in the school.

The popularity of soda makes maintaining body weight particularly difficult. Conservative estimates are that children and teens drink more than 64 gallons of soda each year—much of it caffeinated. This is triple the amount consumed by teens in 1978. The average 13- to 18-year-old soda drinker drinks more than two cans a day, and 10% drink five or more cans a day. For some young people, soda comprises 20 to 40% of their daily caloric intake.

In addition to being urged to eat more fast food and to drink more soda, female adolescents are also exposed at home to concerns about their weight and negative judgments about their body image. As one 14-year-old girl put it, "I was brought up to think being thin. . . . Like I'd say, 'Mom, have a piece of pie,' and she'd be like 'No, I'm on a diet.' So I mean I've known diets since I was in kindergarten" (Nichter, 2000, p. 122).

Although many girls reported to Nichter that their families are supportive, more indicated that their body weight created problems at home. One-third of the girls reported being teased by siblings or parents about their weight and of being sensitive to and pained by the teasing. In many cases, there was little or no parental appreciation of the bodily changes that the girls were experiencing during adolescence.

Girls with overweight parents or relatives spoke about having the "curse" and trying to escape the fate of fat family members by exercising and dieting. And by listening to their mothers' or grandmothers' fat talk, girls learned that there was no end to fat work. They learn that body shape concerns persist throughout their lives—further compounding their obsession with body weight. Nichter (2000, p. 120) concludes:

> As troubled as I had felt while listening to girls' self-deprecating comments about their own bodies, their stories of their family environment left me equally, or perhaps even more, disturbed. Both at school and at home, girls seemed to be surrounded by excessive concerns over physical appearance and talk of feeling fat. Was there no respite from dissatisfaction with one's body? Was the message of self-acceptance truly absent from girls' households, or was it spoken and they failed to hear it. . . . It is telling, not to mention depressing, how few white and Latino mothers in our study tried to foster positive self-image on the part of their daughters.

In sum, the way that body image is presented in Western culture creates a dilemma for high school adolescent girls. They are forced to adapt to a standard that creates a negative self-image and an obsession about weight. Nichter realized that some action needed to be taken when she asked a 16-year-old girl what she wanted to do over the summer. Expecting the girl to tell her that she wanted to travel or visit friends or family, Nichter was a little taken aback when the girl responded that she wanted to lose 15 pounds. If she lost 15 pounds, she said, "I'd be more self-confident. I'd be able to walk past the soccer team and not feel all embarrassed. I could just walk up to those guys and say, 'Hi, how are you doin'?' I'd feel so much better about myself if I were thinner" (Nichter, 2000, p. 181).

Addressing the Problem

As an anthropologist, Nichter could take a critical look at her culture's obsession with women's body image and examine the negative effects it had on adolescent girls. Nichter concluded that schools and families were not providing girls with effective instructions on the developmental process, on eating well and exercising, and on critical thinking regarding media images and advertising. Classes on nutrition and exercise were ineffective, suggests Nichter, because they generally did not recognize that "health work," including diet regulation, was closely related to "beauty work." In addition, the school provided easy access to fatty food and soda in lunchrooms and vending machines. The question is, what to do about it? What kind of intervention could be mounted in the school to help adolescent girls address the anxiety over their appearance and, at the same time, promote a healthy lifestyle?

To begin, Nichter and her associates asked the girls what kind of program they would like. The girls responded that they wanted the opportunity to get more information on eating better and exercising. The girls also recommended including students from all grades in the program. On the basis of these recommendations, Nichter implemented the program at a high school and two community sites with 22 girls from ninth to 12th grades.

The goals of the program, says Nichter, were to build on what the girls already knew about the virtues of avoiding junk foods and the value of eating more fruits and vegetables and to help them address their high consumption of caffeinated sodas and harmful dieting practices. The program would also attempt to expand the girls' notions of beauty beyond "Barbie beauty" and to help them develop the skills to work on themselves more holistically.

However, the first step would be to raise awareness of the unrealistic body images being promoted in the media. The girls needed to understand and appreciate the diversity of healthy body shapes in the real world. Consequently, on the first day of the program, Nichter presented a slide show of images from magazine advertisements of white, Latino, and African American girls. The group first discussed how the media attempted to limit the differences among the models and attempted to make them conform to some ideal body type and appearance. Accompanying the slide show was a script drawing on lines from teens who reacted to the ads ("I'd kill for her body," "She's so perfect," "When I go to the mall and I see all those beautiful girls, I just wonder why I was born"). The girls discussed among themselves how notions of beauty adversely affect relationships between girls, creating jealousy and conflict. The girls then discussed the presentation and got a cross-cultural view of notions of ideal beauty. The discussion made it obvious to all participants that media images were marketing discontent, and even girls who were white, blonde, and thin were driven to be dissatisfied with their appearance.

Another goal of the program was to get girls of different backgrounds and ages together to talk about body image in the collective sense rather than talking about bodies individually. They particularly wanted white and Latino girls to hear from African American girls about their sense of beauty, style, and movement. The girls learned that what was desirable in white culture was not necessarily what was valued among African Americans. Consequently, they were able to expand on notions of style and looking good common among African American girls. One of the students in the class had a background in fashion design, and she draped girls in different colors while others gave feedback about how specific colors complemented or detracted from their appearance.

Some of the classes were devoted to nutrition sessions, with dietary assessment and cooking demonstrations. They analyzed the foods they had eaten and discussed how and why they made the food choices they did. They addressed such questions as "Why can some people eat and eat and eat and never gain weight and other people just look at food and get fat?" "Is there a way we can turn fat into muscle?" "What does the word *metabolism* really mean?" and "What should I do if I really pigged out?"

They had sessions on the necessity of physical exercise. They discovered that some girls were reluctant to participate in physical activities because they were afraid that if they breathed hard or sweated, it would reveal that they were out of shape. An African dance specialist was brought into the class to discuss body movement and self-esteem, how to move with grace and confidence, and how movement and grace come more from inside than from how we look on the outside. They had some weight training and developed inexpensive alternatives for exercise equipment.

They also needed to involve the families. Very few of the families had told the girls that weight gain was a normal part of puberty, and parents were unable to explain it to their daughters. Parents also tended to avoid talking about the topic because they were reluctant to discuss sensitive topics that might lead to arguments. Parents needed to be made aware that excessive talk about dieting normalized girls' dissatisfaction with their bodies. Parents needed to provide more direction on diet. Family meals, the researchers discovered, were the exception rather than the rule. Only 26% of the girls reported eating with their families every night, 19% reported eating with their families four to six times a week, and 26% reported that they ate dinner with their families once a week or less. The frequency of eating family meals declined as the grade level went up. Most nights, one-third of the girls were deciding themselves what they would eat. The most common foods were sandwiches, macaroni and cheese, and spaghetti; salads were consumed less than 5% of the time. Most girls reported that their parents were just too tired after working all day to prepare family meals. As a consequence, parents are less able to monitor their children's diet.

It is probably too early to know how effective Nichter's program was in helping the girls alleviate anxiety over their body shapes or in helping them develop healthier diets and exercise regimes. But, clearly, an anthropological perspective can illuminate issues that are not addressed in most health education classes and can identify issues that families need to address as part of their children's normal maturation process.

CONCLUSIONS

The concept of the self, or personhood, varies from society to society. In the *egocentric* view, the person is viewed as an autonomous, discrete individual; in the *sociocentric* view, the self is viewed as contingent on a situation or social setting. The sociocentric view is often taken by social scientists who are interested in the social processes by which social identities are formed and maintained.

Societies distinguish individuals from one another by using such criteria as age, gender, kinship, ethnicity, and language. Differences and similarities in characteristics among individuals are used to construct social landscapes on which each person's place or identity is indicated. The characteristics that determine identity, such as gender, are treated differently in various societies.

One way that individuals learn who they are is through rites of passage or initiation ceremonies, such as those practiced in college fraternities.

Initiation rituals prepare individuals to accept new ways of looking at themselves and others.

People must also be able to communicate their identities to one another. One way to do this is through the process of gift exchange and the principle of reciprocity. The *kula* ring—the circulation of gifts among trading partners by the Trobriand Islanders—is an example. Americans and other people in modern industrial societies have a special problem with gift giving, needing to somehow convert an impersonal, store-bought commodity into a personal and meaningful gift. We examined how this is a special problem at Christmas, and we explored some of the ways in which Americans solve it.

Individuals must be able to defend their identities if they are threatened. An example of how this is done is making *moka* by the Big Men among the Melpa, who thus claim and defend their places in the social landscape.

Finally, we examined how an anthropological perspective on identity and body image could be used to develop programs to help adolescent girls address body image concerns and promote a healthy lifestyle.

REFERENCES AND SUGGESTED READINGS

Introduction: The Importance of Self
The epigraph is taken from the opening passage of Erving Goffman's classic work *The Presentation of Self in Everyday Life* (Doubleday, 1959). The Gandhi reference is from Ramashray Roy's *Self and Society: A Study in Gandhian Thought* (Sage, 1985).

How Does the Concept of Personhood Vary From Society to Society?
An excellent treatment of the relationship between names and identity can be found in Richard D. Alford's book *Naming and Identity: A Cross-Cultural Study of Personal Naming Practices* (HRAF Press, 1988). The discussion of naming among the Gitksan is from John W. Adams's *The Gitksan Potlatch: Population Flux, Resource Ownership and Reciprocity* (Holt, Rinehart and Winston of Canada, 1973). The discussion of the differences between the sociocentric and egocentric self comes from Richard A. Shweder and Edmund J. Bourne's "Does the Concept of the Person Vary Cross-Culturally?" in *Cultural Conceptions of Mental Health and Therapy*, edited by A. J. Marsella and G. M. White (D. Reidel, 1984). The discussion of American individualism comes from Robert Bellah and others' *Habits of the Heart* (University of California Press, 1984). The nature of the self in Japan is discussed in Robert J. Smith's *Japanese Society: Tradition, Self and the Social Order* (Cambridge University Press, 1983) and in Christie W. Kiefer's "Psychological Anthropology" in the *Annual Review of Anthropology*, vol. 6 (1977), pp. 103–19.

How Do Societies Distinguish Individuals From One Another?
The information on identity in Northern Ireland comes from Ed Cairns's "Intergroup Conflict in Northern Ireland" in *Social Identity and Intergroup Relations*, edited by Henri Tajfel (Cambridge University Press, 1982). Judith Lorber describes the process of gender construction in *Paradoxes of Gender* (Yale University Press, 1995), and Anne Fausto-Sterling provides a rationale for recognizing at least five sexes in "The Five Sexes: Why Male and Female Are Not Enough" in *The Sciences*,

vol. 33 (March/April 1993), pp. 20–4. An excellent account of the *berdache* role can be found in Walter L. Williams's *The Spirit and the Flesh: Sexual Diversity in American Indian Culture* (Beacon Press, 1986) and Harriet Whitehead's "The Bow and the Burden Strap: A New Look at Institutionalized Homosexuality in Native North America" in *Sexual Meanings: The Cultural Construction of Gender and Sexuality*, edited by Sherry B. Ortner and Harriet Whitehead (Cambridge University Press, 1981). Susan U. Philips discusses the ways language is used to convey gender identity in "Sex Differences and Language" in the *Annual Review of Anthropology*, vol. 9 (1980), pp. 523–44, as do Penelope Eckert and Sally McConnell-Ginet in their book *Language and Gender* (Cambridge University Press, 2003). Robin Lakoff's ideas about gender and conversational style are detailed in her book *Language and Woman's Place* (Harper and Row, 1975). Douglas Foley describes gender relations in a Texas high school in *Learning Capitalist Culture: Deep in the Heart of Tejas* (University of Pennsylvania Press, 1990). For a review of anthropological studies of human sexuality, see "The Cross-Cultural Study of Human Sexuality" by D. L. Davis and R. G. Whitten in the *Annual Review of Anthropology*, vol. 16 (1987), pp. 69–98. Robert B. Moore's work on racism in the English language comes from his book *Racism in the English Language* (Council on Interracial Books for Children, 1976), and Ward Churchill's discussion of team nicknames appears in his book *Indians Are Us?* (Common Courage Press, 1994).

How Do Individuals Learn Who They Are?

The classic work on rites of passage is Arnold van Gennep's *The Rites of Passage*, translated by Monica B. Vizedom and Gabrielle L. Chaffe, which was originally published in 1906 (University of Chicago Press, 1960). A description of how American businesses use rites of passage is in Harrison M. Trice and Janice M. Beyer's "Studying Organizational Cultures Through Rites and Ceremonies" in the *Academy of Management Review*, vol. 9 (1984), pp. 653–69. David D. Gilmore's work is represented in *Manhood in the Making: Cultural Concepts of Masculinity* (Yale University Press, 1990). The account of the initiation of a Maasai man is from *The Worlds of a Maasai Warrior* by Tepilit Ole Saitoti (Random House, 1986), an excerpt of which is reprinted in *Anthropology 90/91*, edited by Elvio Angeloni (Dushkin, 1990). Peggy Reeves Sanday's account of gang rape is in *Fraternity Gang Rape: Sex, Brotherhood, and Privilege on Campus* (New York University Press, 1990). Another account of American college life is Michael Moffatt's study *Coming of Age in New Jersey: College and American Culture* (Rutgers University Press, 1989). An interesting account of sorority initiation rites is contained in Gary Schwartz and Don Merten's "Social Identity and Expressive Symbols" in *American Anthropologist*, vol. 70 (1968), pp. 1117–31.

How Do Individuals Communicate Their Identities to One Another?

The use of *Gulliver's Travels* to illustrate the importance of goods in identity work is taken from Annette Weiner's *The Trobrianders of Papua New Guinea* (Holt, Rinehart and Winston, 1988). The classic work on the importance of the gift is Marcel Mauss's *The Gift: Forms and Functions of Exchange in Archaic Societies*, translated by Ian Cunnison and published originally in 1925 (W. W. Norton, 1967). The material on the Gitksan is from John W. Adams's *The Gitksan Potlatch*, cited earlier. The original description of the *kula* ring formed the foundation of Bronislaw Malinowski's classic *Argonauts of the Western Pacific*, originally published in 1922 (E. P. Dutton, 1961). A reinterpretation of the *kula* ring can be found in Annette Weiner's *The Trobrianders of Papua New Guinea*, cited earlier. The discussion on gifts and commodities is based on James G. Carrier's book *Gifts and Commodities: Exchange and Western Capitalism Since 1700* (Routledge, 1995) and his article "The Rituals of Christmas Giving" in *Unwrapping Christmas*, edited by Daniel Miller (Clarendon Press, 1993).

How Do Individuals Defend Their Identities When They Are Threatened?

Anthony F. C. Wallace and Raymond D. Fogelson's "The Identity Struggle" can be found in *Intensive Family Therapy*, edited by I. Boszormenyi-Nagy and J. L. Framo (Harper and Row, 1965). The description of the Beaver medicine fight is from Robin Ridington's "The Medicine Fight: An Instrument of Political Process Among the Beaver Indians" in *American Anthropologist*, vol. 70 (1968), pp. 1152–60. The material on making *moka* comes from Andrew Strathern's *The Rope of Moka: Big Men and Ceremonial Exchange in Mount Hagen, New Guinea* (Cambridge University Press, 1971).

Case Study in Doing Anthropology #6: Fat Talk

Mimi Nichter's research on body image among female adolescents is described in *Fat Talk: What Girls and Their Parents Say About Dieting* (Harvard University Press, 2000).

7

THE CULTURAL CONSTRUCTION OF SOCIAL HIERARCHY

PROBLEM 7: WHY ARE MODERN SOCIETIES CHARACTERIZED BY SOCIAL, POLITICAL, AND ECONOMIC INEQUALITIES?

> Every social hierarchy claims to be founded on the nature of things. It thus accords itself eternity; it escapes change and the attacks of innovators. Aristotle justified slavery by the ethnic superiority of the Greeks over the barbarians; and today the man who is annoyed by feminist claims alleges that woman is naturally inferior.
>
> —Robert Hertz, 1909

INTRODUCTION

The Rationale for Social Inequality

The maldistribution of wealth, status, and privilege is a significant problem throughout the modern world. To Americans, it is visible in the starving faces that stare out from our television screens in documentaries and on the evening news—interspersed with advertisements for such luxuries as automobiles, cosmetics, and household conveniences. Some people can purchase the finest amenities, whereas others lack the basic necessities of life, such as food, shelter, and health care. There are few, if any, modern nations in which one portion of the population does not in some way enjoy privileges that other portions do not share.

Small wonder, then, that the worth of the 358 richest people in 1996 was "equal to the combined income of the poorest 45 percent of the world's population—2.3 billion people." Worse still, "the world's 200 richest people more than doubled their net worth in the four years to 1998, to more than $1 trillion. The assets of the top three billionaires [were by then] more than the combined GNP of all least developed countries and their 600 million people" (Harvey, 2005, p. 35). And this inequality has continued to increase.

A common figure used to measure inequality is family wealth distribution. For example, in the United States, wealth distribution as of 2007 shows that the bottom 80% of the population held 15% of the country's wealth, whereas the highest 1% held almost 35% of the wealth (see Table 7.1). Examining income distribution historically, we find that in the United States, income inequality grew from 1983 to 2007, with the bottom 80% of the population having a smaller share of the national wealth (decreasing from 18.7% to 15%) and the highest 25% having a greater share (increasing from 47.5% to 50.5%). More telling perhaps is the fact that over the course of his or her lifetime, a child in the United States has a better than 50% chance of being on food stamps—90% if he or she is black.

Another way to measure income distribution is by using something called the **Gini coefficient**. The Gini coefficient—a measure of variability developed by Italian statistician and demographer Corrado Gini—can be used to

TABLE 7.1 DISTRIBUTION OF NET WORTH AND FINANCIAL WEALTH IN THE UNITED STATES, 1983–2007

	Total Net Worth		
	Top 1 Percent	Next 19 Percent	Bottom 80 Percent
1983	33.8%	47.5%	18.7%
1989	37.4%	46.2%	16.5%
1992	37.2%	46.6%	16.2%
1995	38.5%	45.4%	16.1%
1998	38.1%	.45.3%	16.6%
2001	33.4%	51.0%	15.6%
2004	34.3%	50.3%	15.3%
2007	34.6%	50.5%	15.0%

Data from http://sociology.ucsc.edu/whorulesamerica/power/wealth.html

measure any uneven distribution. It produces a number between zero and one, where zero corresponds to perfect income equality and one means that a single person receives all the income and everyone else has zero income.

The measure is based on something called the *Lorenz curve*. Imagine a graph in which the vertical, or y, axis represents the number of households in a country and the horizontal, or x, axis represents the total income they receive. If every household had the same income, then the plotted line would rise evenly (see Figure 7.1a); that is, 20% of the households would have 20% of the income, 40% of the households would have 40% of the income, and so on. This is the line of perfect equality. On the other hand, if one person had 100% of the income, the graph would look like Figure 7.1b, which represents the line of perfect inequality. It most cases, the line would look something like the curve in Figure 7.1c. The Gini coefficient represents the area between the line of perfect equality and the Lorenz curve drawn based on the actual distribution of income.

Table 7.2 shows the Gini coefficient for selected countries in selected years. With a Gini index of 24.4, Hungary has the most equal distribution of household income, and with a Gini index of 70.7, Namibia has the most unequal distribution of income. Various factors influence the Gini coefficient, such as the level of industrialization of different countries, the nature of their economic systems, and the extent to which tax systems seek to redistribute income. Regardless, the coefficient does a reasonably good job of providing a portrait of income distribution for different countries and the degree of inequality this distribution reveals.

Another way of visualizing the global distribution of wealth is to look at a map of the United States that names each state after the country whose GDP it matches (Figure 7.2).

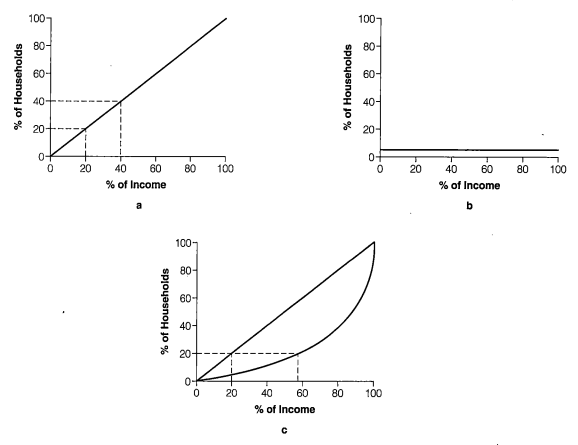

FIGURE 7.1 THE LORENZ CURVE AND THE GINI COEFFICIENT

Some people believe that the hierarchical ordering of people and groups is unavoidable. In their view, scarce resources, occupational specialization, and the power of an elite group to control the behavior of others necessarily result in some form of social stratification. Others maintain that stratification is not only avoidable but is counter to human nature. According to anthropologist Thomas Belmonte:

> Since the emergence of stratification, man's history (his changing ways of relating to nature and other men) has stood opposed to his humanity. The emergence of power-wielding elites laid the basis for a new kind of anti-collective society whose vastly accelerated growth was founded, not on the reconciliation of antagonisms between men, but on their origination and amplification in slavery, caste, and class. (1989, p. 137)

Those who support Belmonte's view note that in such societies as those of the Ju/wasi and Inuit, there are no "poor," "rich," "inferior," or "superior" people. This is not to say that these societies are totally egalitarian; even in small-scale societies, valued statuses are not available to some members.

TABLE GINI COEFFICIENT FOR SELECTED COUNTRIES

Country	Gini Index 1992–2007
Denmark	24.7
Japan	24.9
Sweden	25.0
Czech Republic	25.8
Norway	25.8
Croatia	29.0
Hungary	30.0
Pakistan	31.2
Romania	31.5
Australia	32.2
Canada	32.6
Belgium	33.0
Spain	34.7
United Kingdom	36.0
New Zealand	36.2
India	36.8
Russian Federation	37.5
Senegal	39.2
Indonesia	39.4
United States	40.8
China	41.5
Central African Republic	43.6
Uruguay	46.2
Costa Rica	47.2
Mexico	48.1
Guatemala	53.7
Brazil	55.0
South Africa	57.8
Botswana	61.0
Namibia	74.3

Source: United Nations World Development Report, 2009, http://hdrstats.undp.org/en/indicators/161.html/161.html, https://www.cia.gov/library/publications/the-world-factbook/index.html.

FIGURE 7.2 U.S. STATES NAMED AFTER THE COUNTRIES THAT MATCH THEIR GDP

Source: All data from 2007. Reprinted by permission of David Ghirardelli.

Rather, the question is why modern societies are characterized by such extremes of poverty and wealth.

In this chapter, we examine how societies construct social hierarchies and why some groups erect social edifices that encompass social dominance and submission, high and low status, and oppressors and oppressed and how inequality persists. We examine why most people in stratified societies—those at the top and those at the bottom—consider social ranks to be "in the nature of things." We ask how people at the bottom levels of the hierarchy—those in poverty, for example—adapt to their conditions, and we explore whether a nonstratified community can exist within a large-scale society. Finally, we examine the contributions of anthropology to addressing problems that arise from social, political, and economic inequality.

QUESTIONS

7.1   How do societies rank people in social hierarchies?

7.2   Why do social and economic inequalities persist?

QUESTION 7.1   *How Do Societies Rank People in Social Hierarchies?*

Social hierarchies in different societies vary along several dimensions: the criteria used to differentiate people into one level of society or another, the number of levels that exist, the kinds of privileges and rights that attach to people at different levels, and the strength of the social boundaries that separate the different levels. For example, in American society, people are stratified by income and personal possessions into **social classes** (e.g., lower class, middle class, and upper class). They are classified by cultural or family background into ethnic groups (e.g., Italian, Jewish, Hispanic, or white Anglo-Saxon Protestant) or by physical appearance or skin color into racial categories (e.g., black or white). They are also classified by gender and age as well as by standards such as education. People in the United States may move from class to class, and they may choose to emphasize or de-emphasize their ethnic group membership, but generally, their racial category and gender are fixed.

In India, the population is stratified into hundreds of different castes. In a caste system, individuals are assigned at birth to the ranked social and occupational groups of their parents. A person's place in the social order is fixed; there is no mobility from one caste to another. Castes are separated from one another by strict rules that forbid intermarriage and other forms of inter-action, such as eating together, speaking to each other, or working together.

In any stratified society, people's access to jobs, wealth, and privilege is determined largely by their position in the hierarchy. For example, castes in India were based on traditional roles. The Brahmins—priests whose lives were devoted to worship and teaching—occupied the top of the caste hierarchy. Directly under them were the Kshattriya castes, whose members comprised the soldiers, politicians, and administrators. Next were the Vaisya castes—composed of farmers and merchants. At the bottom of the hierarchy were the Sudra castes, which were devoted to the service of other castes. The Sudra castes included "untouchable" or "unclean" persons whose occupations were believed to be polluting to others. Untouchables included washermen, tanners, shoemakers, and sweepers—people whose occupations required them to come into contact with animal or human wastes. The Indian government has outlawed discrimination against untouchables based on caste membership, but it persists nevertheless.

Exercise 7.1 ➤

Below is a list of personal attributes. Your task is to rank them by number from most to least important to you in judging a person's social or personal worth—no ties allowed. If you wish to add an attribute not included in the list, feel free to do so.

_____Personal appearance
_____Monetary income
_____Gender
_____Age
_____Religion
_____Ethnic or community origin
_____Family background
_____Intelligence (as indicated by school performance)
_____Athletic ability
_____Personal possessions (clothes, car, etc.)
_____Personality (describe:_____)

Youth and Class

In 1999, the frozen bodies of Yaguine Koita and Fode Tounkara, 14-year-old boys from Conakry, Guinea, were found in the landing gear of a plane at Brussels International Airport. On one of the bodies, authorities found a note addressed to the political leadership of Europe. The letter began:

> Gentlemen, members and leaders of Europe, we appeal to your solidarity and kindness to help Africa. Please help us, we are suffering enormously in Africa, we have problems, and some weaknesses with regard to children's rights. . . . We have war, disease, lack of food, etc. . . . In Guinea we have many schools but a big absence of education and training. Therefore, if you see that we are sacrificing ourselves, and expose our lives it is because we are suffering a lot in Africa, and we need your support to fight poverty and end war in Africa. Nevertheless, we want to study and we ask you to help us study so that we can live like you but in Africa. Finally, we beg you to accept our apologies for taking the liberty to address you this letter because you are eminent personalities, which we ought to respect. (quoted in de Boeck and Honwana, 2005, p. 7)

There is a lot to be learned from that incident: the global gap between rich and poor, the desire of the global poor to emulate the global rich, the rationale for migration from poor to rich countries, and so on. But it also points at the emergence of youth as a major social category. They are, in the words of Alcinda Honwana and Filip de Boeck, "makers and breakers." They are makers in the sense of the cultural contributions they make and the innovations they introduce. They are breakers in the form of alcohol use, unprotected sex, violence, and crime.

Jean Comaroff and John L. Comaroff note that there are startling similarities among youth all over the world. On the one hand, they are excluded from local economies—particularly the shrinking blue-collar sectors—and cut off from state assistance as neoliberal policies reduce government expenditures on the unemployed. Cut off from wage-earning citizenship, they take to the streets as the only space available to them. They are overwhelmingly male, and their exclusion marks what the Comaroffs call a "crisis of masculinity" evidenced in U.S. gangsta rap, African gang rape, soccer violence, and school shootings, such as that at Columbine High School and Virginia Tech.

On the other hand, youth has gained unprecedented autonomy. Its disenfranchisement has led to the creation of a kind of "counternation," with its own spaces, its own forms of recreation, and its own forms of illicit enterprise—from drug trafficking and computer hacking in the urban United States to the "bush" economies of West and Central Africa, where the young trade diamonds, dollars, guns, and gasoline and supply illicit services. The young, say the Comaroffs, "have felt their power, born partly of the sheer weight of numbers, partly of a growing inclination and capacity to turn to the use of force, partly of a willingness to hold polite society to ransom" (2001, p. 18).

There is among the genteel mainstream, they say, this nightmare image of youth as a larger-than-life figure wearing expensive sports shoes, listening to gangsta rap, and having a cell phone tied to the global underground economy. Is this not, they ask, a "sinister caricature of the corporate mogul"—the "dark side of consumer capitalism"? It is this image that led U.S. Representative William McCollum of Florida to exclaim that contemporary youth "are the most dangerous criminals on the face of the earth." The image of dangerous youth is also evident in the growing movement in the United States to incarcerate youth offenders as young as 10 years old. Of course, such descriptions and actions are generally applied to juveniles from poor or "high crime" neighborhoods. Thus, in the United States, three-quarters of youth in jail are black or Hispanic; a black teenager is six times more likely than a white kid to be sent to jail for a first-time violent offence, and a black teenager is 48 times more likely to be jailed for a drug offence than a white kid.

To some extent, the congressman is correct; by criminalizing behaviors associated with marginalized groups—by criminalizing certain drugs (such as cocaine and marijuana) while legalizing others (alcohol)—the society creates a marginalized criminal class that legal authorities are then justified in watching closely. Is it so surprising, then, that juveniles see themselves, as the Comaroffs put it, as "mutant citizens of a new world order"?

Status and the Petty Cruelties of High School

The dilemma of youth as a marginalized social category is also evident in the obsession with social structures that youth create. These are particularly evident in the American high school. In one high school studied by Murray Milner Jr., there were six primary groups on campus, arranged in a

Finding their own space to gather is one way that kids cope with constraints on their behavior.

status hierarchy: the "Preps" (image-conscious types), the "Jocks" (highly athletic—usually involved in at least two sports), the "Rockers" (alternative, grunge, skateboard types), the "Nerds" (academic, studious), the Punks/Weirdos (seen by other groups as nonconformists—apathetic to the school social hierarchy), and the "Gs" (gangsters and wannabe gangsters). Everyone agreed that two groups in particular distinguished themselves from the rest—the Preps and the Jocks.

Various symbols were used to differentiate the groups, including clothing, music preferences, activities, and even the physical locations in which they gathered. Status was in play in the constant judgments about clothing, body image, associates, and general appearance high school students make about each other. Status, according to Milner, was such an obsessive concern of students that who they sat with at lunch was a greater concern than school grades.

Milner asks why high school students are so obsessed with status and concludes that making judgments about each other is the only power students really have. They have little economic or political power; they must attend school all day and have very little say in what goes on there; they are pressured into learning such esoteric subjects as European history, algebra, and chemistry that have little immediate relevance to them. The one power they do have is creating their own status system—generally using criteria very different from those promoted by teachers and parents and constantly evaluating each other based on these criteria.

But since status, says Milner, is relatively finite, the only means that students have to increase or maintain their social standing is by lowering the status of others. That is, you move up by putting others down—by "dumping" on them. The way this is done is through "petty cruelties" that take the form of gossip about such things as body weight, friends or associates, clothing, and speech. Web-based social networking sites are becoming a means of public ridicule popular among teenagers. And, of course, petty cruelties can extend to bullying and outright violence.

The concern for status is also evident in the degree of sexism in schools. Sexism is prevalent in many formal school rituals, such as the prom—with its glorification of romance that empowers men—and in beauty contests and the elevation of male sporting events—with their generally female cheerleaders. You also see it in the acceptance of misogyny in rap lyrics. Interestingly, while racism in schools seems to have declined significantly, sexism is as strong as ever. The question is why?

Paul Willis's study of working class youth in Great Britain offers an interesting explanation—one that may apply also to marginalized people of color in the United States.

Willis's book *Learning to Labor: How Working Class Kids Get Working Class Jobs* is about how a class society reproduces itself from generation to generation. Why do working-class kids always tend to end up in working-class jobs? It is not, says Willis, solely because of the ideology of the school and its middle-class biases. The kids themselves, by their behavior, essentially do the job of funneling themselves into the working class. They do this by refusing to follow the agenda of the school, rebelling against its discipline, and rejecting what they see as "mental" labor, as opposed to "manual" labor. Their own behavior dooms them to failure in the one institution that might lead to better jobs.

Manual labor is glorified as manly; mental labor, on the other hand, is seen as feminine, and to be feminine, for working-class youth, is to be an "ear'oles," a "pouf," or a "wanker"—all sexually laden insults. Thus, to be masculine, working-class youth must reject the educational agenda of the school. In rejecting school work as effeminate, the "lads," as they called themselves, must also reject anything associated with women and demonstrate their control and domination over them physically and sexually.

QUESTION 7.2   *Why Do Social and Economic Inequalities Persist?*

There is a basic contradiction in Western values: We extol equality, but massive inequalities persist and, in fact, grow nationally and internationally. We boast of the ability of people to get ahead and send armies to "spread freedom" but constantly devalue the worth of labor. People in the United States boast of achieving a color-blind society—even choosing a person of color as a national leader—but racism and its historical consequences persist.

Equality, of course, is an elusive term. Differences of various kinds are present in any social grouping—let alone any society. Even highly egalitarian gathering and hunting societies assign differential values to members based on gender, age, and skills. But there is a difference between that and relegating some members of society to social positions where some enjoy lives of extraordinary luxury while others struggle to obtain the basic necessities, such as food, shelter, clothing, and medical care. The problem is that many believe that modern societies have removed the barriers that prevent people from acquiring wealth and well-being—that if people live in poverty, it is because of their own personal choice or because they somehow lack the will and initiative to "get ahead." As evidence, they point to individuals who, born in poverty, have become millionaires or to people of color who have attained wealth, status, and worldwide fame. However, lacking in these perceptions is consideration of the structural features of our economy and society that result in maintaining huge gaps in wealth and well-being. Three of these are debt, the devaluing of labor, and the new racism.

Debt and the Redistribution of Wealth

In many ways, debt is the foundation of our present economic system. Money is created by debt and would not exist without it; that is, banks and other private financial institutions (not the government, as many believe) create most of our money by lending it. Whenever a person uses his or her credit card or obtains a car loan or mortgage, most of this money is literally created "out of thin air." Banks operate on what is called the *fractional reserve system*; that is, for every dollar they receive in deposits, they are permitted to lend approximately nine dollars on the assumption that not everyone will demand their deposits back at the same time. The system has the benefit of ejecting money into the economy to promote the buying and selling of goods. The problem is that loans come with the expectation of a return greater than the amount lent; that is, the debtor must pay back the principal on the loan plus interest. The same, of course, is true of money "lent" to corporations or to any business, government, or private enterprise for which the lender or investor expects a return on capital. However, the problem with debt is that it is, in effect, a regressive tax; that is, it funnels money from the less rich among us to the more rich. How does it do that?

We can divide people into two economic categories: net debtors who pay out more in interest than they receive in interest (and/or dividends) and net creditors who receive more than they pay out. Virtually everyone pays interest; they pay interest on credit cards, mortgages, car loans, and so forth. Furthermore, whenever someone pays rent or buys food, clothing, or virtually any commodity, part of the price he or she pays consists of interest that the person collecting the rent or payment or selling the commodity or service must pay banks or investors as the price of money they borrowed in order to do business. On the other hand, most people have money in a savings account, insurance policy, or invested in stocks or bonds—from which they receive interest or dividends. However, some people take in far more in interest and dividends than they pay out, and these represent only a small percentage of the population. Figure 7.3 shows one distribution of debtors and creditors based on a German study in the mid-1980s (see Kennedy and Kennedy, 1997).

The figure illustrates that the vast majority of the population pays out more in interest than it receives in interest and/or dividends. The result is that debt creates a net flow of money from those of lower income to those of higher income or from net debtors to net creditors. Put another way, those people or institutions (e.g., banks, insurance companies, pension funds, etc.) that can rent money to those that need it—whether they are individuals or other institutions—multiply their wealth from interest or dividends received

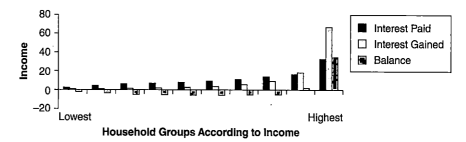

FIGURE 7.3 COMPARISON OF INTEREST PAID AND GAINED BASED ON INCOME GROUP

Source: Adapted from Kennedy and Kennedy, 1995.

from borrowers. Debt is, in effect, a regressive tax that redistributes money upward to the more wealthy and, consequently, maintains and increases economic inequality.

Looking at debt another way, we must recognize that debt (or money) is a commodity whose sale creates profits for those who lend it—in the same way that television sets, iPods, automobiles, cosmetics, or any good or service is a commodity that people sell for profit. That is why banks and other financial institutions seek borrowers—why, when students arrive on campus every fall, there are people encouraging them to obtain credit cards; money that is not returning more money is, in effect, as useless as any unsold product or service. Furthermore, when a vast majority of the population requires indebtedness to maintain their lifestyles, money—and the privileges that go with it—moves upward. One can generally choose whether to buy a television set or even an automobile, but in our economy, debt is as essential as food or shelter.

Devaluing Labor

Another reason inequality persists is the devaluing of labor. There has always been tension between those who own the means of production and those who are hired to work those means. It was around this tension that Karl Marx and Frederick Engels built their critique of capitalism. According to Marx, classes arise when a group—a ruling class, landlords, bosses, and so on—gains control of the **means of production**. The means of production consist of such materials as land, machines, or tools that people need to produce things. A group that controls the means of production can maintain or increase its wealth by taking advantage of the **surplus value of labor**.

The idea of the surplus value of labor works something like this: Take a product or commodity, such as bricks. Say that the labor value of bricks on the open market is $300 per 1,000 bricks; that is, people are willing to pay $300 above the cost of materials for each 1,000 bricks they purchase. If the same people make the bricks and sell 1,000 of them for $300 plus the cost of materials, they are getting a 100% return on their labor. But what if the person who owns or controls the means of production for bricks hires some people to make the bricks and pays them only $30 for every 1,000 bricks they make? The value of the labor to produce the bricks is still $300 per 1,000, but the laborers are getting only one-tenth ($30) of what their labor is worth, whereas the person who controls the means of production is getting the surplus value of labor—or the other nine-tenths of the labor value of the bricks ($270). In other words, the capitalist—the person who controls the means of production (the brickworks, in this case)—is expropriating $270 worth of labor from the worker who produced the bricks.

One of the trends of the past four decades is the decline in wages. Wage earners are getting proportionately less and less of this surplus value. Thus, while average incomes have increased in the United States, the share received by those toward the bottom of the income scale have decreased. Essentially, the rich have gotten richer, and the poor—that is, the wage earners—have gotten poorer. Table 7.4 provides a detailed look at the distribution of wealth and income in the U.S. over the past 20 years.

At least two things have produced this growing inequality: the movement of industry and jobs from richer countries to poorer countries—or **outsourcing**—and the systematic destruction of labor unions—trends associated with neoliberalism and globalization.

The jobs that have been most affected by outsourcing are those in such industries as fast food, agriculture, electronics, and, most notably, clothing, garment, and/or textile. Within these industries, there is intense competition, uncertain or changing demand, a lower profit margin, and a greater dependence on what gets termed *unskilled labor*. These industries are the least desirable for workers because to stay competitive, these companies must pay the lowest wages and yet maximize worker output. These are the industries most likely to expand operations to poorer countries, thus eliminating higher-paying jobs in one place and replacing them with lower-paying ones somewhere else. They are also the industries that are likely to hire the most vulnerable and the lowest-ranking members of a population. Traditionally, these people have been women, children, or members of subjugated groups.

The process of targeting the most vulnerable segment of the population for low-wage jobs also affects the meaning that societies give to specific tasks, systematically devaluing the work that people do. For example, the division between skilled and unskilled jobs is often not based on the nature of the work, as one would suppose; instead, it is based on who is doing the work. In other words, the work that women do in assembly factories is not necessarily less skilled than other work; it is considered unskilled because it is performed by women. In Brazil, women are hired to tend grapevines to produce the large, unblemished grape that consumers in industrial countries desire. The work is skilled (e.g., involving the grafting of vines), but because the work is done by women, it is described as requiring "manual dexterity, delicacy, and nimbleness of fingers" (Collins 2000:102). Thus, this work is defined as "unskilled" because it is done by women.

TABLE THE SIZE DISTRIBUTION OF WEALTH AND INCOME IN U.S. (WITH GINI COEFFICIENT), 1983–2007

Year	Gini Coefficient	Percentage Share of Wealth or Income Held by:								
		Top 1.0%	Next 4.0%	Next 5.0%	Next 10.0%	Top 20.0%	4th 20.0%	3rd 20.0%	Bottom 40.0%	All
A. Net Worth										
1983	0.799	33.8	22.3	12.1	13.1	81.3	12.6	5.2	0.9	100.0
1989	0.832	37.4	21.6	11.6	13.0	83.5	12.3	4.8	−0.7	100.0
1992	0.823	37.2	22.8	11.8	12.0	83.8	11.5	4.4	0.4	100.0
1995	0.828	38.5	21.8	11.5	12.1	83.9	11.4	4.5	0.2	100.0
1998	0.822	38.1	21.3	11.5	12.5	83.4	11.9	4.5	0.2	100.0
2001	0.826	33.4	25.8	12.3	12.9	84.4	11.3	3.9	0.3	100.0
2004	0.829	34.3	24.6	12.3	13.4	84.7	11.3	3.8	0.2	100.0
2007	0.834	34.6	27.3	11.2	12.0	85.0	10.9	4.0	0.2	100.0
B. Non-home Wealth										
1983	0.893	42.9	25.1	12.3	11.0	91.3	7.9	1.7	−0.9	100.0
1989	0.926	46.9	23.9	11.6	11.0	93.4	7.4	1.7	−2.5	100.0
1992	0.903	45.6	25.0	11.5	10.2	92.3	7.3	1.5	−1.1	100.0
1995	0.914	47.2	24.6	11.2	10.1	93.0	6.9	1.4	−1.3	100.0
1998	0.893	47.3	21.0	11.4	11.2	90.9	8.3	1.9	−1.1	100.0
2001	0.888	39.7	27.8	12.3	11.4	91.3	7.8	1.7	−0.7	100.0
2004	0.902	42.2	26.7	12.0	11.6	92.5	7.3	1.2	−1.1	100.0
2007	0.908	42.7	29.3	10.9	10.1	93.0	6.8	1.3	−1.0	100.0
C. Income (SCF)										
1982	0.480	12.8	13.3	10.3	15.5	51.9	21.6	14.2	12.3	100.0
1988	0.521	16.6	13.3	10.4	15.2	55.6	20.6	13.2	10.7	100.0
1991	0.528	15.7	14.8	10.6	15.3	56.4	20.4	12.8	10.5	100.0
1994	0.518	14.4	14.5	10.4	15.9	55.1	20.6	13.6	10.7	100.0
1997	0.531	16.6	14.4	10.2	15.0	56.2	20.5	12.8	10.5	100.0
2000	0.562	20.0	15.2	10.0	13.5	58.6	19.0	12.3	10.1	100.0
2003	0.540	17.0	15.0	10.9	14.9	57.9	19.9	12.1	10.2	100.0
2006	0.574	21.3	15.9	9.9	14.3	61.4	17.8	11.1	9.6	100.0

Reprinted with Permission from Wolff, Edward N. 2010. Recent Trends in Household Wealth in the United States: Rising Debt and the Middle-Class Squeeze—an Update to 2007. Levi Institute of Economics of Bard College, Working Paper No. 589. http://www.levyinstitute.org/pubs/wp_589.pdf.

A second reason for the devaluing of labor is declining union membership. In 1973, some 24% of all workers in the United States were members of unions.[1] The decline in union membership—more severe in the private sector than the

---

[1]See http://www.epi.org/page/-/old/datazone/05/union.pdf.

public—generally means less job protection and a declining ability to bargain collectively for wages. In addition, in order to attract business and investment, poorer countries often ban or severely weaken the ability of workers in these countries to form unions or to bargain collectively. Corporations and businesses as well as consumers benefit from this trend, but a consequence is persistent and growing inequality. Furthermore, there is a persistent effort as part of neoliberal philosophy to remove the bargaining rights of even public service unions.

Constructing a New Racism

In 2006, a soup kitchen in Paris discovered by chance that poor Muslims and Jews would not eat soup made with pork. So, they started making soup only with pork. The soup kitchen leader, Odile Bonnivard, declared that "European civilization and Christian culture is our choice," proclaiming the right to racial preference and initiating a campaign across France labeled "Ours Before the Others" (Goldberg, 2009, pp. 179–180).

The "identity soup" campaign, as it came to be called, is an example of what some have termed the *new racism*—based not on biological characteristics but instead on cultural differences that are assumed to be insurmountable. And it is just one bit of evidence, in spite of the claims by some that we have achieved a "raceless" society, that racism persists in one form or another. Quite simply, being "white"—however "whiteness" is defined—still matters. When Andrew Hacker in 1992 asked his students how much money they would demand if they were changed from white to black, they felt it was reasonable to ask for $50 million, or $1 million for each year they were black. This was the financial value they placed on being white (Hacker, 1992; Brown, 2003). While responses to similar surveys 10 and 15 years later seemed to indicate that students lowered the cost of being black, two-thirds of new immigrants to the United States—the majority from Latin America, Asia, and the Middle East—claim to be "white." We also find that rich Chinese immigrants to the United States are "lightened," while poor Cambodians are compared to African Americans. This is not unlike the pattern during colonial eras when descriptions of Pacific Islanders got darker as Western colonization increased.

Leith Mullings (2005, p. 684) says that **racism** is a "relational concept"—

> a set of practices, structures, beliefs and representations that transform certain forms of perceived differences, generally regarded as indelible and unchangeable, into inequality. It works through modes of dispossession, which have included subordination, stigmatization, exploitation, exclusion, various forms of physical violence, and sometimes genocide. Racism is maintained and perpetrated by both coercion and consent and is rationalized through paradigms of both biology and culture. It is, to varying degrees at specific temporal and special points, interwoven with other forms of inequality, particularly class, gender, sexuality, and nationality.

Modern forms of racism are a distinctly 17th- and 18th-century European phenomenon created to justify European economic expansion, slavery, and the killing and subjugation of hundreds of millions people. In the United States, it took its own unique form under slavery and, later, under legalized discrimination and segregation and was legitimized by "scientific" theories of race. The civil rights movement of the 1960s in the United States and the enactment of laws barring racial (as well as gender and age) discrimination are claimed, by many, to have ended racism, except for those isolated incidents of discrimination and violence dismissed as the acts of the few remaining racists. But a poll taken among Republican primary voters in 2011 had 46% in favor of banning interracial marriage.[2] And despite claims of progress, the real median income of black families at the start of the 21st century was 62% that of whites—only 10 points higher than it was in 1947, when the ratio was 52%.

The claim that racism is no longer a factor in inequality is part of the neoliberal philosophy that attributes a person's place in society solely to their own efforts. However, the claim that racism is dead ignores its accumulated historical effects and the extent that it is institutionalized in residential patterns, health care services, and the criminal justice system and how it has been reformulated in the debates in the United States and elsewhere over immigration.

For example, despite laws banning discrimination in housing, blacks are much more likely than Asian Americans or Latinos to live in segregated neighborhoods and less likely to obtain a mortgage, and when they do, they pay far higher interest rates.

Surveys of housing preferences reveal that white Americans prefer to live in communities that are at least 80% white, while blacks desire only 50% of residents to be black, leaving considerable room for the emergence of discriminatory patterns. These patterns of economic and personal discrimination create patterns of desirability in which white neighborhoods and schools are likely to be better.

Clearly, blackness is a disadvantage not only when shopping for a home or getting mortgage but for everyday consumer behavior. For example, one recent study of Los Angeles car dealerships found that salespeople offered lower sales prices to whites than to blacks and women, even when the economic status and bargaining strategies were held constant. Furthermore, blacks paid more for car loans arranged through dealers than whites.

The cost of being black is also imbedded in our health care system. The infant mortality rate for blacks remains twice that for whites and mortality rates for blacks are still 1.6 times that for whites—unchanged since 1950. Death rates from cancer are as much as 20 times higher for blacks, while black women are more likely to die of breast cancer, even though its incidence among black women is lower. Lung cancer deaths among blacks is higher—a result that cannot be attributable to smoking rates and is likely due to exposure to environmental toxins disproportionally located in poor neighborhoods. And blacks are 80% more likely to die as a result of a stroke than whites.

---

[2]See http://www.publicpolicypolling.com/pdf/PPP_Release_MS_0407915.pdf.

And racial discrimination continues to be a factor in law enforcement. Blacks in the United States are more likely to be targeted by the criminal justice system. Proportional to its population, the United States leads the world in prison incarceration, with some 2.3 million people in jail. Within that population, black men and women outnumber Hispanics by more than two to one and whites by nearly six to one. Because many states bar anyone who has served prison time from voting, some 13% of black men are politically disenfranchised.[3] The disproportional number of blacks who have gone through the criminal justice system is not a factor of increased criminal activity but, rather, the result of systematic discrimination in arrests and sentencing. For example, the arrest rate for marijuana offenses for blacks is 2.5 times the rate for whites—probably reflecting the degree of discretion allowed the police in making arrests. And African American youth under the age of 18 and tried as adults are 10 times more likely than white youth convicted of similar crimes to receive life sentences without the possibility of parole.

Claims that race is no longer responsible for inequality also ignores the cumulative historical impact of discrimination. Until slavery was abolished, the vast majority of black families were prohibited from owning property; immigrant families arriving largely from Europe in the late 19th century and early 20th century were able to accumulate monetary and educational capital—an opportunity denied to most blacks and Hispanics. While some criticize affirmative action programs for blacks and women, they forget that the United States practiced affirmative action for white males for over 300 years.

Finally, we have racist attitudes emerging in debates over immigration. There are estimated to be over 100 million migrants from developing countries seeking work in developed countries and sending some $4 billion back to families at home. This is a consequence of the vast inequalities in income found between the rich and poor nations. These workers not only face poverty at home but also discrimination when they travel abroad and sometimes even being linked to terrorist activities. As one U.S. Congressman said:

> Some of these people may be coming in here to get jobs washing dishes, but some of them are coming here to hijack airplanes. . . . I can't tell Jose Cuervo from the Al Qaeda operatives by looking at them, because they cut their beard [sic] off. . . . I mean, not a racist thing, but they're all brown with black hair and they don't speak English or Spanish and I don't speak Arabic. (quoted in Goldberg, 2009, p. 83)

Racism, of course, is not simply a U.S. problem; it emerged globally and remains global. In Europe, the seminal racial event was the Holocaust—the massacre of some six million Jews, Catholics, Roma, homosexuals, and others deemed a "threat" to the Nazi regime. After that horror, race was excised from the European context lest the horror be repeated, and for that reason, Europeans

---

[3]See http://www.nybooks.com/articles/archives/2008/sep/25/obama-the-price-of-being-black.

claim that racism is a thing of the past. But as we saw with the "identity soup" campaign in France, discrimination and the economic inequality that it produces remain directed largely at those driven from their home countries by poverty and seeking work. This includes Moroccans in the Netherlands, Algerians in France, Turks in Germany, Pakistanis and Bangladeshis in Britons—each attesting, in one way or another, to European colonial history and the institutionalization of discrimination based on skin color. One survey in 2005 found majorities in Germany and the Netherlands and significant minorities in Spain, France, Russia, and Poland expressing unfavorable views of Muslims. This phenomenon is not limited to Europe. For example, in Japan, the recent influx of Asian workers is perceived as a racial problem; in Hong Kong, racial discourse is used to link immigrant workers from the Philippines and India to crime; and even in Latin America, Bolivian, Chilean, and Peruvian migrants to Argentina face xenophobic campaigns (see Mullings, 2005, p. 675).

Thus, we see that race—however it is constructed in different countries—continues to play a significant role in maintaining economic and social inequalities.

QUESTION 7.3   *How Do People Come to Accept Social Hierarchies as Natural?*

Cultural anthropology is about seeing beyond the façade of everyday appearances to what lies behind those appearances. Understanding how societies construct rationales to justify and legitimize social discrimination is one of the most important and, to some extent, the most difficult tasks of anthropology. Franz Boas, one of the founders of anthropology, was among the first social scientists who worked to discredit racist and sexist theories and ideologies that sought to legitimize the marginalization of people based on race, religion, gender, and ethnicity. Part of the problem is that racist and sexist theories exist not only in popular culture but also in scientific ideology. It will be useful, then, to examine how such theories are constructed and often taken for granted and how they are used to justify the ranking of people within the social hierarchy.

Constructing the Ideology of Racism

In the United States, the ideology of class is based on the assumption that a person's position in the class hierarchy is determined largely by achievement or individual effort; that is, individuals who work hard and dedicate themselves to their work will succeed. But there is also the attempt to justify social position in terms of a person's biological makeup—largely by race, innate mental ability (intelligence), and gender. The hierarchical ordering of society is thus seen as an expression of a natural law that some people are born more fit to lead and succeed.

For centuries, European and American societies have been characterized by racial stratification. Traditionally, membership in certain racial or ethnic groups was enough to place people in particular positions in the status hierarchy that defined their social, political, and economic worth. For example, in the United States, position in the racial hierarchy often determined whether a person could vote, hold political office, pursue a particular occupation, live in a certain area, use certain public facilities, attend certain schools, or marry a particular person. Until the second half of the 20th century, racial stratification was written into the laws of many states.

Stratification by race and ethnicity has existed for a number of reasons. It was certainly economically profitable for people who could buy black slaves or obtain workers from among groups legally or socially barred from anything but low-paying jobs. It was also advantageous to those who did not have to compete for jobs with people who were socially or legally barred from them. But stratified societies frequently claim that the ranking of people by race and ethnicity is natural—that a social hierarchy is not socially constructed. In the case of racial stratification, some proponents claimed that it was God's will that some persons were inferior to others; others claimed that God created different races just as he created different species of animals, and the Bible says the species are to be kept apart. Others claimed that members of one race or another were intellectually or morally superior to members of other races. Generally, of course, it was the race of the person making reference to God or the Bible that was somehow superior.

Most people had little trouble constructing an ideology to justify racial stratification, especially because state and religious authorities reinforced it. Even the supposedly objective findings of scientists assisted in building a racist ideology. In the 19th century, reputable scientists devoted much time and energy to proving that the racial stratification of society was "in the nature of things." Their research findings supposedly proved that members of one race (usually whites or Europeans) were intellectually superior to members of another race (usually blacks or Asians).

Samuel George Morton was a respected scientist and physician who began in the 1820s to collect and measure skulls from all over the world. When he died in 1851, he left a collection of some 6,000 skulls. Like many in the 19th century, Morton believed that a person's intelligence was related to the size of his or her brain: the larger the brain, the more intelligent the person. Because the size of the brain could be determined by the size of the skull, he believed that a ranking of the races could be objectively achieved by a ranking of skull size.

Morton first measured the size—or, more specifically, the cranial capacity—of skulls by filling them with mustard seeds and then pouring the seeds into a container to measure the skull's volume in cubic inches. Dissatisfied with the inconsistency of measurements obtained with mustard seeds, he later used 1/8-inch-diameter lead shot. Morton concluded from his measurements that "white" skulls had a mean value of 92 cubic inches;

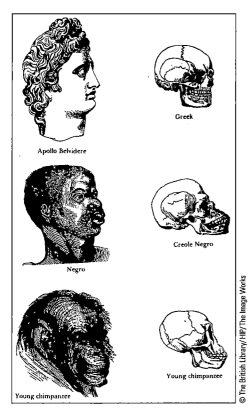

Greek

Apollo Belvidere

Creole Negro

Negro

Young chimpanzee

Young chimpanzee

Nineteenth-century scientists attempted to prove that whites were naturally superior to other races. In this illustration from an 1868 racist tract, the proportions of the skulls are distorted, giving the impression that blacks might even rank lower than the apes.

© The British Library/HIP/The Image Works

"American Indian" skulls, 79 cubic inches; and "black" skulls from America, Africa, and Australia, 83 cubic inches. Among "white" skulls, the largest were those of Germans and English people, in the middle were those of Jews, and at the bottom were those of Hindus. In other words, the evidence of brain size and intelligence was said to support the social hierarchy of whites at the top, with the English and Germans at the top of the top and blacks on the bottom.

Thus, "whites" (more specifically, northern European "whites") were not merely socially superior; they were also biologically superior. Morton believed he had provided objective evidence that the distribution of status and power in 19th-century America accurately reflected not merely social merit but also biological merit.

When Stephen Jay Gould, a Harvard biologist, re-examined Morton's published data in 1977, he concluded that Morton's summaries were a "patchwork of fudging and finagling" to reach conclusions that supported the socially constructed hierarchy. Gould found no evidence of conscious fraud. He concluded that Morton had simply selected or rejected certain data to ensure that the results confirmed what he and most other Americans "knew": that whites were naturally more intelligent than everyone else.

Working with the same skulls Morton had used more than 150 years earlier, Gould discovered that the sample of 144 Native American skulls included proportionally more small-brained Inca skulls from Peru and fewer large-brained Iroquois skulls. This naturally produced a lower mean cranial capacity for indigenous Americans than would have occurred had Morton correctly adjusted for this discrepancy. Moreover, Gould discovered that Morton's failure to include the small-brained Hindu skulls with his "white" skulls had produced a higher average cranial capacity for white skulls. When Gould corrected for Morton's sample biases, he discovered that there was no difference between Euro-American and indigenous American cranial capacity. As for comparisons between "white" and "black" skulls, Gould discovered that Morton had ignored the facts that brain size is related to body size and that male skulls are larger than female skulls. Examination of Morton's black skulls indicated that the group included proportionally more female skulls and fewer male skulls. When Gould remeasured the "black" and "white" skulls, he discovered that the mean cranial capacity of black males was slightly higher than the mean for white males, whereas the mean for white females was slightly higher than that for black females.

Gould does not believe that Morton consciously manipulated his skull measurements to prove that whites were intellectually superior to Native

Americans or blacks. Rather, he thinks Morton simply assumed that this is what his measurements would prove and set about achieving the results he expected. For example, Gould observed that when Morton used mustard seeds to measure cranial capacity, he obtained even greater differences between his "white" and "black" skulls than he obtained when using lead shot. Gould concludes that because mustard seeds are smaller and lighter than lead shot, Morton—probably unconsciously—packed more mustard seeds into "white" skulls to obtain a greater difference in cranial capacity between "blacks" and "whites." More importantly, although Morton's measurements were obviously in error—as was his assumption that cranial capacity reveals intelligence—and although his conclusions were dictated by the socially constructed hierarchy of his day, they were used well into the 20th century to support an ideology that the racial ranking of persons in society could be justified on natural rather than social grounds.

The Social Construction of "Intelligence"

Morton's experiments represent just one example of the efforts in America and Europe to show that people somehow deserve their ranking in society—that it is not the result of chance or family privilege but, rather, the result of some innate natural ability or talent. To believe otherwise would threaten a key assertion of American ideology: that all Americans enjoy an equal opportunity for success. Moreover, believing otherwise has serious political and economic consequences. If poverty and a low ranking in society are not the fault of the poor, then they must be the result of some failure of society. Such an admission provides a strong reason for reworking social, economic, and governmental policies (such as enacting laws barring racial and other forms of discrimination, programs of economic redistribution, or affirmative action). Because such changes might lead to a loss of privilege for those who benefit from present social, economic, and governmental policy, there is strong motivation to find some concept that legitimizes inherited privilege and lays the blame for poverty or lack of success on the poor themselves.

The concept of intelligence neatly solves this problem. If people accept the idea that intelligence can explain how well people do, then the fiction that people's rank in society depends solely on their own natural ability can be maintained. Moreover, if it can be shown that intelligence is inherited, then we can explain why it is that the children of successful people tend to be successful and why certain groups—notably people of color and certain immigrant groups—are disproportionately poor.

Consequently, the failure of the thesis that cranial capacity—and hence brain size—revealed intelligence did not end the attempts to link intelligence to success as well as to race and ethnicity. Instead, there has been a continuing effort on the part of some members of the scientific establishment to marshal evidence to prove that intelligence is inherited and that it differs according to racial groups. These efforts included the work of Arthur Jensen in the

1960s and 1970s and the publication in 1994 of *The Bell Curve* by Richard J. Herrnstein and Charles Murray. Missing from most of these accounts is any acknowledgment that the concept of intelligence itself is a social construct—an idea that is invented. Consequently, we need to look closely at our concept of intelligence. How did it evolve?

To begin, anthropologist Allan Hanson notes that the concept of intelligence contains a number of questionable assumptions. First, intelligence is assumed to be a single entity. Second, it is assumed to be measurable and unequally distributed in the population. Third, the amount people have is assumed to be relatively fixed throughout life. Fourth, the amount people have is assumed to largely explain their degree of success in life. Finally, it is assumed to be largely inherited.

Each of these assumptions is critical to the intelligence construct as most people think of it, and each has been the subject of enormous scientific attention and criticism. The first assumption requires that we accept the idea that someone who is intelligent in one way is also intelligent in other ways rather than believing that a person can be intelligent in some ways but not in others. The second assumption implies that we can somehow measure innate intelligence, as opposed to achievement, and the third presumes that we can show that whatever is measured does not vary throughout a person's life. The fourth is built on the idea that people who have more measurable intelligence are more likely to be successful, whereas the fifth assumption requires that we show that the children of people with high measurable intelligence also have high measurable intelligence.

Despite the many assumptions that lie behind the notion of intelligence and the studies that illustrate how questionable each of these assumptions really is, most Americans take the notion for granted. But it is a relatively unique idea that is not shared by many other societies. For example, indigenous maritime navigators of the South Pacific learned to read wave patterns, wind direction, celestial constellations, and other signs and find their way thousands of miles from one island to another. But others in the same society who are unable to duplicate this feat do not view the navigators as somehow being smarter; they see them as people who can navigate. The Japanese view what we call intelligence in much the same way as we view health—except for certain (and generally temporary) circumstances, we all have enough of it.

This book is not the place to summarize the works that call the concept of intelligence into question. But we might learn something about the social construction of ideologies of class by briefly looking at the early history of the intelligence construct and reviewing how reputable scientists proceeded to develop it. Three pioneers—Francis Galton, Karl Pearson, and Charles Spearman—supplied the basic ideas and experimental proofs for the classic concept of intelligence as a fixed "mental" entity that is differentially distributed in the population, is measurable, largely explains a person's educational and occupational success, and is inherited.

Galton was one of the leading intellectual figures of the late 19th century—the founder of modern statistics and the founder of eugenics, which is the attempt to identify the most desirable human traits, specify the individuals who possess them, and, through selective reproduction, enhance the number of people possessing the desired characteristics. In his best-known work—*Hereditary Genius*, published in 1869—Galton sought to demonstrate that the "genius" of selected eminent men was linked to the fact that they had eminent parents and, consequently, that their "genius" was largely inherited. In his sample of 997 eminent British men, he found that 31% had eminent fathers, 48% had eminent sons, and 41% had eminent brothers—far higher percentages than one would expect by chance. Galton concluded that these statistics illustrate the power of heredity in the distribution of "genius." He was, of course, rightly criticized for ignoring the impact of environment. But he did something else that is more interesting—something that went largely unchallenged: He selected the eminent men from the British upper and upper-middle classes, ignoring the "captains of industry and finance" and, of course, women; eminence was eminence only within a select range of activities and occupations. Galton, the nephew of Charles Darwin and of an upper-middle-class background, was faithfully reproducing the judgments of his own status as to what constituted intelligence.

Much of Galton's later research was devoted to arguing that those characteristics he called "genius," "mediocrity," and "imbecility" were analogous in their statistical distribution within a society to certain physical characteristics. He developed a number of tests for cranial capacity and for sensory capacities—for example, the ability to discriminate between colors or smells. Galton was not the only one trying to do this; in Germany, the United States, and England, other researchers were trying to measure intelligence—largely through the measurement of sensory and reflex activity, such as reading aloud rapidly, quickly giving the colors of named objects, naming and classifying plants, animals, and minerals, and other tests of memory and spatial judgment. However, around 1900, there was a move away from these kinds of measures—largely because they were not showing any correlation with each other and, more importantly, because they showed only a low correlation with teachers' estimates of the mental capability of their students. Regardless, by 1900, the classic intelligence construct had been laid out, although its proof was somewhat wanting.

The next person in our story is Karl Pearson, one of the most fascinating figures of the late 19th and early 20th centuries, whose published works included more than 400 articles on mathematical physics, statistics, and biology as well as poetry, a passion play, art history, studies of the Reformation and medieval Germany, and political essays. In 1901, Pearson published a study in the *Proceedings of the Royal Society of London* in which he concluded: "The mental characteristics in man are inherited in precisely the same manner as the physical. Our mental and moral nature is quite as much as our physical nature, the outcome of hereditary factors" (1901, p. 155).

It is instructive to look at how Pearson reached this conclusion. He took pairs of brothers and measured specific physical characteristics, such as stature, forearm length, hair color, eye color, and cephalic index. Not surprisingly, he found that there was a high correlation among brothers for these traits—a mean correlation of 0.5171. Then, he asked teachers, using another sample of brother pairs, to rank them on seven "mental characteristics": intelligence, vivacity, conscientiousness, popularity, temper, self-consciousness, and shyness. Teachers were asked to rate each child as "keen" or "dull" and to choose among six subdivisions of intelligence. When the teachers' evaluations of brother pairs were tabulated, Pearson found a strong correlation between brother ratings—a mean correlation of 0.5214—thereby proving the power of inheritance.

Much about this study is questionable, but of particular note is the role of teachers' judgments. Obviously, teachers were evaluating selected behavior patterns and personal characteristics—patterns and characteristics that they judged to be evidence of various "mental characteristics." In other words, the teachers' judgments were highly subjective and, at best, questionable. But Pearson's work marked an important development in the construction of our concept of intelligence. Whatever intelligence was, he claimed to show that it was inherited at least as much as physical characteristics.

Let us move forward a couple of years to the next important stage in the construction of the intelligence construct: Charles Spearman and "general intelligence." Spearman's research, published in the *American Journal of Psychology* in 1904, was designed to prove that there were different degrees of correspondence between an individual's performance on different types of tests. Thus, one would expect to find a high degree of correspondence between one's performance on geometrical tests and tests of spatial perception and a low degree of correspondence between one's performance on, say, tests of musical ability and tests of weight discrimination. If there were some degree of correlation among all the test results, this would indicate that there was some general factor, g, that would affect performance on all tests. Thus, tests that resulted in high correlation (e.g., geometrical ability and spatial perception) would be heavily saturated with g, whereas tests with little correlation would not be. To use an athletic analogy, if someone hits a baseball and a golf ball a long way, we might assume that some general factor for athletic ability could account for both skills.

Spearman suggested that the g factor underlies all mental operations and that if it could be ascertained, it would approximate true intelligence. This is a major claim, for to prove the existence of g would result in the dismissal of the idea—widely held up to that time—that different people could be intelligent in different ways and that each person had a unique contribution to make.

With *g*, people would be intellectually different in only one way, and people with lots of *g* would have more to contribute than people with only a little *g*.

To experimentally prove the existence of general intelligence, Spearman isolated four kinds of intelligence that, he claimed, when correlated would show a high degree of correspondence: "present efficiency," "native capacity," "general impression produced upon other people," and "common sense." "Present efficiency" referred to the "ordinary classification according to school order" in such subjects as Greek, Latin, or mathematics. "Native capacity" was arrived at by taking the difference between a child's rank in school and his age, whereas "general impression produced on other people" was obtained by asking the teacher of a class who was the brightest pupil, the next brightest, and so on. "Common sense" was arrived at by asking the oldest child in a class to rank her schoolfellows on the basis of "sharpness and common sense out of school." As Spearman said, she seemed "to have no great difficulty in forming her judgments concerning the others, having indeed known them all her life." As a check on the reliability of judgments, he also asked the rector's wife to rank the children, although as Spearman notes regretfully, she did not know some of them. Not surprisingly, Spearman found that children who ranked high on one kind of intelligence tended to rank high on others, thereby validating the existence of *g*.

Obviously, the methodology of these classic studies was seriously flawed, relying as they did on subjective judgments as to who was intelligent and who was not—judgments that were bound to be biased by such factors as the social class of teachers and students. From Galton's first major work—*Hereditary Genius*—through Spearman's work on general intelligence, members of the professional middle class were selecting as intelligent those people whose behavior patterns and appearance most conformed to their own. Moreover, little effort was made to conceal the fact; subjective judgments of members of the professional class were the major means by which intelligence was defined. Nonetheless, the intelligence construct as we know it was generally complete, and reputable scientists considered it to be experimentally validated: Intelligence is a singular trait, represented by *g*, that is inherited and is differentially distributed in the population.

Much more was to come, of course, in the social construction of intelligence—most notably the development of the Stanford-Binet IQ test and, later, the Scholastic Aptitude Test (SAT)—more recently renamed the Scholastic Assessment Test. Additional and more sophisticated experiments were performed that some claimed supported the conclusions of such early pioneers as Galton, Pearson, and Spearman. But the most interesting feature is the continued part played by social judgments—largely of teachers, psychologists, and school administrators—in determining what does or does not constitute intelligence. As late as the 1960s, results of intelligence tests were still being cross-checked with teachers' judgments and students' ranks in class; if the test scores failed to correlate with the teachers' judgments, the tests were changed.

But in spite of the obvious flaws in the concept of intelligence—flaws that most social scientists acknowledge—it continues to serve as a means of

Exercise 7.3 ▷

**DEVISING A MEASURE OF SENSITIVITY
TO OTHERS (SO)**

The National Space Settlement Agency (NSSA) has hired your research and consulting company, Testers, Inc., to develop a test to determine a person's sensitivity to others. NSSA will use the test as part of its national program for selecting candidates to participate in a program of space settlement. Because space settlers will be required to spend many months and years together in close quarters, NSSA has determined that settlers' sensitivity to others is critical for the success of its mission.

This is a pioneering effort, so you are free to approach the task in any way you see fit. However, there are some guidelines.

1. You must carefully *define* what constitutes sensitivity to others. This involves not only a straightforward definition but also a list of those behavioral or personality features that would characterize a person's degree of SO.
2. You must *devise a test* that could be given to a person that would allow you to measure the behavioral or personality features that characterize sensitivity as you have defined it.
3. The test needs to be *simple* enough to be graded by machines (e.g., multiple-choice or true/false questions). Your test should contain no more than 10 "questions."
4. The test that you devise must allow the tester to clearly *discriminate* differences among people in SO. That is, your questions must elicit a significant portion of "wrong" answers. (If everyone gets a question "right" or everyone gets it "wrong," then the question fails to discriminate between those high and low on the factor being tested.) NSSA requires that each person tested be assigned an SO score.
5. You must suggest how to *test the test*. That is, how can you determine that it does effectively measure the degree of a person's sensitivity to others?

legitimizing the social order, making it seem as if a person's place in it is "in the nature of things." Clarence J. Karier put it particularly well:

> The many varied tests, all the way from IQ to personality and scholastic achievement, periodically brought up-to-date, would serve a vital part in rationalizing the social class system. The tests also created the illusion of objectivity, which on the one side served the needs of the "professional" educators to be "scientific," and on the other side served the need of the system for a myth which would convince the lower classes that their station in life was part of the natural order of things. (1976, p. 136)

Constructing Stratification by Gender

Looking back at Morton's mismeasurements and the history of the social construction of intelligence, it is easy to condemn the biases that seemed to create a scientifically supported system of stratification by race and class. But the biases that falsely linked race to biology and intelligence to class also led to the linkage of gender stratification and biology—the belief that the superiority of men over women was not socially constructed but "natural." Many people believed that women's bodies defined their social position and their function, which was to reproduce, as men's bodies dictated that they manage, control, and defend. At the beginning of the 20th century, even the U.S. Supreme Court ruled that women should be prohibited from jobs that might endanger their reproductive function. The court concluded that a "woman's physical structure and the performance of maternal functions place her at a disadvantage in the struggle for subsistence. Since healthy mothers are essential to vigorous offspring, the physical well-being of women becomes an object of public interest and care in order to preserve the strength and vigor of the race."

The view that the biology of females makes them lesser persons than males remains embedded in American culture—sometimes in very subtle ways. An example is the language used by professionals to describe women's bodily processes of menstruation and menopause. Anthropologist Emily Martin says that during the 19th century, Americans regarded the female body as if it were a factory whose job was to "labor" to produce children. Menopause was viewed negatively because it marked the end of productive usefulness, and menstruation was described as a sign of the failure of the implantation of a fertilized egg. Medical writers of the time—such as Walter Heape, a Cambridge zoologist and militant antisuffragist—described how in menstruation, the entire epithelium (cellular tissue) is torn away, "leaving behind a ragged wreck of tissue, torn glands, ruptured vessels, jagged edges of stroma, and masses of blood corpuscles, which it would seem hardly possible to heal satisfactorily without the aid of surgical instruments."

Martin says that the same attitudes toward female reproductive functions that existed in the 19th century persist today—encoded in contemporary medical and biology textbooks. Menopause is described in some texts as a breakdown of communication between the brain and the reproductive parts of the female body. In menopause, says one college textbook, the ovaries become unresponsive to hormonal stimulation and, as a result, regress. The hypothalamus, which controls hormone production, has gotten estrogen addiction from years of menstruation. Because of the withdrawal of estrogen at menopause, the hypothalamus gives inappropriate orders. Menopause is described as a breakdown of authority: Functions fail and falter; organs wither and become senile. Our language still depicts the female body as a machine that in menopause is no longer able to fulfill its proper goal; it can no longer produce babies. In this view, at menopause, the female body becomes a broken-down factory.

Menstruation is likewise described even today as a breakdown in the reproductive process. When an egg is not implanted, the process is described in negative terms as a disintegration or shedding. One otherwise objective text says: "When fertilization fails to occur, the endometrium is shed, and a new cycle starts. This is why it used to be taught that 'menstruation is the uterus crying for lack of a baby.'" Menstruation is depicted as a sign of an idle factory, a failed production system, or a system producing "scrap" or "waste." Note the language used in this passage from another textbook:

> If fertilization and pregnancy do not occur, the corpus luteum degenerates and the levels of estrogen and progesterone decline. As the levels of these hormones decrease and their stimulatory effects are withdrawn, blood vessels of the endometrium undergo prolonged spasms (contractions) that reduce the blood flow to the area of the endometrium supplied by the vessels. The resulting lack of blood causes the tissue of the affected region to degenerate. After some time, the vessels relax, and allow blood to flow through them again. However, capillaries in the area have become so weakened that blood leaks through them. This blood and the deteriorating endometrial tissue are discharged from the uterus as the menstrual flow. As a new ovarian cycle begins and the level of estrogen rises, the functional layer of the endometrium undergoes repair and once again begins to proliferate. (Martin, 1987, p. 47)

Martin notes that very different language is used in the same textbooks to describe male reproductive functions. For example, the textbook from which the above description of menstruation is taken describes the production of sperm as follows:

> The mechanisms which guide the remarkable cellular transformation from spermatid to mature sperm remain uncertain. Perhaps the most amazing characteristic of spermatogenesis is its sheer magnitude: the normal human male may manufacture several hundred million sperm per day. (Martin, 1987, p. 48)

This text, which describes menstruation as "failed production," fails to mention that only about one of every 100 billion sperm ever makes it far enough to fertilize an egg. Moreover, other bodily processes that are similar to menstruation are not spoken of in terms of breakdown and deterioration. Seminal fluid picks up shredded cellular material as it passes through the male ducts, and the stomach lining is shed periodically. Why are these processes not also described in the same negative terms as menstruation? Martin says the reason is that men and women have stomachs, but only women have uteruses. The stomach falls on the positive side; the uterus on the negative.

Rather than describing menstruation as failed production, Martin suggests that it might be more accurate to describe it as the successful avoidance of an egg implant. If a couple has done anything to avoid the implantation of an egg, is it still appropriate to talk of the reproductive cycle in terms of production? The following description of menstruation offered by Martin represents it not as a failure to reproduce but as the successful avoidance of a pregnancy:

> A drop in the formerly high levels of progesterone and estrogen creates an appropriate environment for reducing the excess layers of endometrial tissue. Constriction of capillary blood vessels causes a lower level of oxygen and nutrients and paves the way for a vigorous production of menstrual fluids.

As a part of the renewal of the remaining endometrium, the capillaries begin to reopen, contributing some blood and serous fluid to the volume of
endometrial material already beginning to flow. (1987, p. 52)

Martin's analysis reveals that in contemporary American society, the
ideology of gender stratification remains embedded in our language and in
our scientific ideas about the bodily functions of males and females. Describing the bodily processes of women in negative terms makes women seem to
be lesser human beings. Moreover, describing menstruation and menopause
in negative terms leads women themselves to believe that their bodily functions are less clean and less worthy than those of men.

QUESTION 7.4   *How Do People Living in Poverty Adapt to Their Condition?*

The position in a social hierarchy occupied by each person is like a window
through which he or she sees the world: different windows; different worlds.
In order to survive in the impoverished conditions that exist in the lower tiers
of society, people adopt specific adaptive strategies. Anthropologist Oscar
Lewis coined the term **culture of poverty** to describe the lifestyle and worldview of people who inhabit urban and rural slums. Some anthropologists object to that term because it implies that poverty is somehow rooted in the
subcultural values passed on from one generation to another rather than in
the social and cultural values of the larger society—of which the poor are only
a part. The implication is that if it were not for the culture of poverty, the poor
would have no culture at all.

Modifying that view, some anthropologists maintain that the behavior of
people in poverty represents their adaptations to their socioeconomic condition:
no money and no jobs. These conditions are the result of inequality—usually
reinforced by racism and further buttressed by an economic system that
requires a source of cheap labor. Moreover, descriptions of poor families as
broken, fatherless, or female-centered are misleading. Many of the behaviors
of the poor that are viewed negatively by the dominant society are actually
resilient responses to the socioeconomic conditions of those living in poverty.

More recent views confirm that conditions of poverty and oppression that
exist in U.S. cities do require a cultural adaptation built on trying to compensate for living at the economic and social margins of society. This poverty and
marginalization of inner cities has spawned, says Philippe Bourgois, an "inner-
city street culture"—

a complex and conflictual web of beliefs, symbols, modes of interaction,
values, and ideologies that have emerged in opposition to exclusion from
mainstream society. . . . This "street culture of resistance" is not a coherent,
conscious universe of political opposition but, rather, a spontaneous set of
rebellious practices that in the long term have emerged as an oppositional
style. (1995, p. 8)

In fact, much of this culture has been commercialized by the mainstream U.S. culture through fashion, music, film, and television and adopted by middle- and upper-class youth.

Kinship as an Adaptation to Poverty

In the late 1960s, anthropologist Carol B. Stack conducted one of the classic studies of how families cope with poverty. She worked closely with a predominantly black community she called The Flats, a section of a small midwestern city of some 55,000 people. Unemployment in The Flats was higher than 20%, and 63% of the jobs held were in such low-paying service occupations as maids, cooks, and janitors. Although only 10% of whites in the city lived in housing classed as deteriorating, 26% of blacks did. Moreover, blacks had inadequate access to health care, and their infant mortality rate was twice that of whites.

Stack's interest was in how the residents responded to their impoverished conditions. She discovered that they fostered kinship ties and created fictive kinship links to form close, interlocking, cooperative groups that would ensure economic and social support in times of need. Few people earned enough to provide them or their families with enough to eat or a place to stay on a regular basis; even welfare payments could not always guarantee food and shelter for a family. Accordingly, people in The Flats regularly "swapped" food, shelter, child care, and personal possessions. In this respect, the community resembled societies such as the Ju/wasi, in which a person shares with others but expects them to reciprocate at some later time. Anthropologists call this type of sharing **generalized reciprocity**—as distinguished from **balanced reciprocity**, in which items are exchanged on the spot; a direct trade of items would be an example. **Negative reciprocity** is an attempt to get something for nothing or make a profit. The advantage of generalized reciprocity is that widespread sharing ensures that nobody lacks the basic needs for survival. People in The Flats cultivated diffuse kinship and friendship relations by giving when they could so others would give to them when they were in need. These networks were often framed in a kinship idiom—even though no biological kin tie existed.

Another adaptation to poverty in The Flats involved child care. Given the unpredictability of employment, the sometimes young age at which women had children, and the need to respond to unpredictable living conditions and substandard housing, a child might reside with three or four different adults. Often, different people performed the roles of provider, discipliner, trainer, curer, and groomer. Stack points out that those who provided child care did so because they considered it a privilege as well as a responsibility. Children were valued, and they were considered the responsibility of a wide network of kin and friends.

Male-female relations were most affected by the difficulty that men had in finding steady employment. Generally, a couple in The Flats would not

Anthropologists have found that people living in poverty find ways to adapt to their circumstances. For these children in a poor section of New York City, the street and sidewalk serve as a playground.

marry unless the man had a steady job. Men in The Flats had accepted the mainstream American model of the male provider, and being unable to find regular employment prevented their assumption of that role. Moreover, marriage removed people from the widespread sharing network because after marriage, their major obligations belonged to their husbands or wives. In addition, because a woman was cut off the welfare rolls if she married, kinship networks and welfare benefits offered a woman more security than a husband could. Nevertheless, men and women in The Flats did form intimate relationships—out of which children were born. Moreover, the fathers took considerable pride in their children, as did the paternal grandparents, to whom the children often went for help. However, the mothers often regarded the fathers as friends who had failed to fulfill their paternal obligations. Thus, the conditions of poverty drew people into kinship and friendship networks rather than the nuclear family patterns valued by the larger society.

In Search of Respect: Selling Crack in El Barrio

Although people do make creative adaptations to impoverished conditions, they also attempt to resist the patterns of oppression and discrimination that are the roots of the poverty. But the resistance itself can lead to self-destructive behavior. In his study of drug use on the Upper East Side of New York City, Bourgois portrays a culture that emerges out of people's personal search for dignity and their rejection of racism and marginalization. But because this culture centers on drugs, it leads people into lives of violence, substance abuse, and internalized rage.

There is a tendency in the United States, with its overdeveloped value of individualism and the willingness of people to blame the victims, to overlook the historical and economic conditions that give rise to impoverished ghettos amidst urban affluence. The questions with which we must then begin are "How do places such as El Barrio develop?" and "How do you create an impoverished ghetto?"

The Upper East Side of New York City, East Harlem, has long been home to poor minorities. After a period when it was the site of elite farms and country houses, the building of cheap transportation in the late 19th century turned it into the home of wave after wave of immigrant groups, creating what some called the most ethnically diverse area in the United States. In the mid-20th century, "slum clearance" programs destroyed functioning Italian working-class communities and replaced them with concentrated populations of poor Puerto Ricans. But what brought people—in this case, from Puerto Rico—to live in East Harlem?

El Barrio, says Bourgois, must be seen in the historical context of a colonized island: Puerto Rico. In the late 19th and early 20th centuries, the island was taken over by American multinational sugar growers who dispossessed thousands of rural farmers, forcing them to seek wage labor on coastal sugar plantations.

After World War II, hundreds of thousands of people migrated from Puerto Rico to the United States—many to New York City and East Harlem. Overall, some 1.5 million left the sugarcane fields, shantytowns, and highland villages for New York City. In two or three generations, these migrants were transformed from semisubsistence peasants on private plots or haciendas to agricultural laborers on foreign-owned, capital-intensive, agro-export plantations, to factory workers in export-platform shantytowns, to sweatshop workers in ghetto tenements, to service sector employees living in public high-rise housing.

By the 1970s, many of the new migrants were faring relatively well, having obtained employment in various manufacturing jobs in and around New York City. But once again, the global economy served to disrupt lives. The exodus of manufacturers from the United States to other countries to take advantage of cheap labor, tax breaks, and lax environmental standards left millions of workers without jobs. In New York City alone, from the 1960s to the early 1990s, some 800,000 manufacturing jobs were lost.

Thus, over the course of the past century, the global economy—combined with systematic racism and discrimination—has produced high rates of unemployment, substance abuse, broken families, and deteriorated health. No group in the United States other than Native Americans fares as badly statistically as Puerto Ricans. In 1993, the median household income for Puerto Ricans was $14,000 less than for whites and more than $4,000 less than for other Latino groups. But perhaps the greatest irony is that despite this history, most members of El Barrio see their violent actions and deteriorated lives as a result of their own actions and their own choices.

The area in East Harlem where Bourgois worked had a poverty rate of almost 40%, and more than half the population, given their incomes, should not have been able to meet subsistence requirements. That many do, says Bourgois, is a tribute to the underground economy that allows people to meet basic food and clothing needs. Underground economic activities for women include babysitting, working "off the books" as seamstresses, tending bar at social clubs, and taking in boarders. Men's jobs tend to be more visible: street-corner car repairs, working for unlicensed contractors, selling "numbers," or selling drugs. Drugs are the multibillion-dollar foundation of the underground economy, with cocaine, crack, and heroin the most prevalent drugs.

These drugs are easily accessible. Bourgois says that within a two-block radius of the tenement in which he lived with his family while doing field-work, he could obtain heroin, crack, powder cocaine, hypodermic needles, methadone, Valium, angel dust, marijuana, bootleg alcohol, and tobacco. Within 100 yards of his stoop were three competing crack houses selling vials at $2, $3, and $5. And just a few blocks away in what was called a *pill mill*, one doctor wrote $3.9 million worth of Medicaid prescriptions; 94% of these were on the NYC Department of Social Services' list of frequently abused prescription drugs.

Crack—a combination of cocaine and baking soda that can be smoked (unlike powdered cocaine) and that delivers an almost instantaneous high— was by far the most in demand in El Barrio. Selling crack enabled some mem-bers of El Barrio to amass wealth and prestige. One of the most important dealers that Bourgois came to know was Ray. Ray built his business, which required him to balance discipline and the threat of violence with respect, around the Game Room. Ray formed special ties with workers, serving as god-father to children of his workers and friends in much the same way as local landlords in Puerto Rico would use godfather or *compadrazgo* ties to ensure the loyalty of their farmworkers. Ray also bestowed special benefits on his employees, including bail money, lawyer fees, holiday bonuses, family gifts, and special dinners.

Some drug workers employed by Ray would earn hundreds of dollars a night running a crack house, and others earned considerable sums serving as lookouts. But Bourgois found that despite the amount of money they earned, most workers in the crack trade were almost always penniless. He discovered that whatever they earned they would spend on gifts, expensive radios, clothes, and other consumer items—consumption behavior that is mirrored by rapidly upward mobile persons in the legal economy.

Furthermore, says Bourgois, when you calculate the risks in crack work of getting shot, arrested, or beaten up, the time spent in jail or when the police shut down the crack house, and the poor working conditions, employ-ment in the crack economy is generally much worse than legal employment. For these reasons, most workers in the drug trade prefer legal employment. In fact, most drug workers have had legal work experience—often beginning at the age of 12, bagging or delivering groceries for tips or stocking groceries at the local *bodegas* (grocery stores) off the books. But by the time they reach the age of 21, few residents of El Barrio have fulfilled their dreams of find-ing stable, well-paying jobs. Instead, they settle for low-paying service sector jobs, nonunion jobs in fast-food restaurants, or jobs as unlicensed asbestos removers, street-corner distributors of flyers, night-shift security guards for the hospital for the criminally insane, errand runners, mailroom clerks, or photocopiers.

Many of the people involved in the crack house economy alternate between street-level crack dealing and minimum wage jobs in the legal econ-omy. But most, says Bourgois, either quit or are fired from these jobs because

Curbside auto repairs enliven a Sunday in the upper Broadway neighborhood of Hamilton Heights in New York City. Informal economic activities such as this represent people's attempts to cope with limited access to jobs in the formal economy.

of a refusal to be exploited or because of the racist or condescending attitudes of the largely white, middle-class employers and supervisors. Often, they view their return to the streets as a triumph of free will and resistance.

But, says Bourgois, there is much self-reproach at not being able to hold a steady legal job or being seen as lazy. Often, failure at legal employment or the inability to find a job (particularly during the economic recession of 1989–1991) drove them to more substance abuse. Furthermore, the older they got, the more difficult it was to get hired—particularly when job centers sent three or four people for the same job to allow employers to choose the person they wanted. It also became harder to explain to prospective employers the reasons for their periods of unemployment. They became what economists call "discouraged workers"—those who no longer seek employment and are no longer counted in the unemployment statistics. But this discouragement leads to a spiral of depression, increased substance abuse, evictions, and fractured social relations.

In this environment of little economic opportunity, drugs play economic, psychological, and social functions. They provide income; they provide a respite and escape from the conditions of El Barrio; and they constitute a form of symbolic resistance to the racism, discrimination, and subordination that users experience in the larger society. But, says Bourgois, this adaptation is self-destructive. Not only does drug use dissipate bodies, but because male drug users feel powerless as their role in households diminishes, they lash out at the women and children they can no longer control as their wage-earning fathers and grandfathers did.

Women in El Barrio face their own special problems. Many—particularly those involved in the drug economy—must be able to balance the demands of the two state agencies that dominate their lives: the penal system and the welfare system. Given the federal and state budget cuts of the past two decades, it is virtually impossible to support a family on welfare alone. Women had to supplement their welfare income with off-the-books jobs, maintain two or more social security cards, or sell drugs. Making matters worse, welfare rules required people to requalify every six months or be cut from the welfare rolls. As a result, 10 to 15% of New York recipients were cut each year.

The dilemma of women in El Barrio is exemplified by Maria, whose boyfriend, Primo, was one of Bourgois's closest friends. Maria, who shared an apartment with her 250-pound mother, became pregnant and was overjoyed. It was, writes Bourgois, precisely her terrible living conditions that made motherhood so attractive. It offered her, he says, a romantic escape from her difficult surroundings and cemented her love for Primo, who at the time faced the prospect of a four- to six-year jail sentence. For young women, the way to escape a troubled home is a romantic relationship with an idealized male and the embrace of motherhood.

Having a child also symbolized economic independence. Mothers are eligible for desired public housing, which for all but pregnant teenagers involves an 18-year waiting list. Once their romantic ideals disappear, as they often do when people lack the financial resources to enact this ideal, children become a woman's main focus in life.

However, for children, life in El Barrio is especially destructive. Given the poverty, the lack of day care support, the deteriorating schools, the prevalence of drugs, and a life centered on the streets, Bourgois witnessed the metamorphosis of cute, bright eight-year-old girls into pregnant, crack-using 13-year-old "teenagers" or bright, energetic nine-year-old boys into juvenile inmates accused of "assault with a deadly weapon." For many children, the crack house is the only space that is heated in the winter and air-conditioned in the summer. Children become socialized into the street culture and take it for granted.

In many ways, says Bourgois, East Harlem resembles the poverty of Third World countries, where infants and children die at a rate 10 to 100 times that of developed countries. But it is not a lack of calories and potable water that is killing them; instead, it is substance abuse, racism, a withdrawal of public services, and the exodus of factory jobs to other countries. The death and destruction of inner-city children, says Bourgois, occurs in adolescence rather than infancy. In the mid-1990s in East Harlem, 18- to 24-year-olds had a greater risk of violent death than soldiers on active duty in World War II.

But although crack dominates the economic, social, and psychological life of men, women, and children in El Barrio, it is not the root of the problem. As Bourgois puts it:

> Self-destructive addiction is merely the medium for desperate people to internalize their frustration, resistance, and powerlessness. In other words, we can safely ignore the drug hysteria that periodically sweeps through the United States. Instead we should focus our ethical concerns and political energies on the contradictions posed by the persistence of inner-city poverty in the midst of extraordinary opulence. In the same vein, we need to recognize and dismantle the class- and ethnic-based apartheids that riddle the U.S. landscape. (1995, p. 319)

The studies by Stack in The Flats of a midwestern city and by Bourgois in New York's East Harlem provide convincing evidence that people do not passively accept their position at the bottom of a stratified society; rather, like people in other environments and economic conditions, they adapt to their circumstances as best they can. They have the same social and economic aspirations as people higher up in the social hierarchy, who have greater income and opportunity. Although Stack, like others, emphasizes this, she concludes:

> Those living in poverty have little or no chance to escape from the economic situation into which they were born. Nor did they have the power to control the expansion or contraction of welfare benefits or of employment opportunities, both of which have enormous effect on their daily lives. In times of need, the only predictable resources that can be drawn upon are their own children and parents, and the fund of kin and friends obligated to them. (1974, p. 107)

QUESTION 7.5   *Can a Nonstratified Community Exist Within a Larger Hierarchical Society?*

Many people who are convinced of the harmful effects of social stratification nevertheless believe that although it may be possible for the Inuit or Ju/wasi to have a relatively egalitarian society, stratification is inevitable in a modern industrial state. But for thousands of years, some groups in stratified societies have attempted to create classless, egalitarian, utopian social settings. Christianity began as a utopian dream of universal equality, and the idea of a real-life utopia emerged with the idea that man, under God, has the power to create an earthly paradise. Among the earliest expressions of this idea was Christian communalism, which led to the founding of Catholic monastic orders—isolated, virtually self-sufficient communities in which the work was collective and egalitarian. In the 19th century, industrialists such as Robert Owen attempted to build utopian factory communities, and Karl Marx's goal was to build a national utopian society. In the middle of the 20th century, psychologist B. F. Skinner outlined a utopian society based on scientific technology in *Walden Two*, a controversial novel that inspired an attempt to translate his fiction into a real-life utopia at Twin Oaks in Virginia. All these attempts to construct utopian societies are evidence of the long history of the search for an egalitarian social order.

Anthropologist Charles Erasmus examined hundreds of utopian communities in an effort to discover why most failed but some succeeded. He concluded that the main problem for these communities is trying to motivate community members to work and contribute to the common good without the promise of individual material rewards, status, or prestige. Of the successful utopian communities in the United States, the most notable are those of the Hutterites, a Protestant sect that originated in Moravia in the 16th century. Why did the Hutterites succeed while so many others failed? Is it possible to use communities such as theirs as models for modern egalitarian communities?

The Hutterites and the Colony of Heaven

"If there will ever be a perfect culture it may not be exactly like the Hutterites—but it will be similar." These words of a member of a Hutterite colony express the feeling that the group has succeeded in building utopian communities. In fact, the Hutterite colonies are among the most successful products of the Christian communal movement, which includes the Mennonites and the more familiar Amish.

The Hutterites originated during the Protestant Reformation. In 1528, they began to establish colonies throughout what are now Germany, Austria, and Russia. Their pacifism and refusal to perform military service brought them into conflict with European governments, and in 1872, to avoid conscription, they immigrated to South Dakota and established colonies. During World War I, a confrontation over military conscription with state and federal authorities in the United States resulted in a Hutterite move to Canada. But their successful agricultural techniques were valued in the United States during the Great Depression of the 1930s, and state governments persuaded them to return and establish new colonies in the United States. In the early 1970s, there were more than 37,000 Hutterites distributed among 360 colonies in the United States and more than 9,000 in 246 colonies in Canada, and estimates today put their population in the United States and Canada at between 40,000 and 50,000 distributed among some 500 colonies.

Cooperation is valued in Hutterite society, where community members worship, work, and eat as a group. Here, women are shown preparing a meal for the entire community.

© Kryn Taconis/Magnum Photos

The goal of the Hutterites is to create a "colony of heaven." Drawing their inspiration from the Old and New Testaments, the Hutterites believe in the need for communal living and the proper observance of religious practice. They reject competition, violence, and war and believe that property is to be used and not possessed. They respect the need for government, but they do not believe they should involve themselves in it or hold public office. An elected board that includes the religious leaders and the community teacher govern a Hutterite colony, so authority is group centered. It is a family-based, agricultural community in which everyone is expected to contribute to the work and to share equally in the bounty. Unlike the Amish, whose beliefs they in essence share, the Hutterites accept and use modern technology; they are acknowledged to be among the most successful agriculturists in North America.

The Hutterites are not totally egalitarian. Their society is ranked by age and gender; members do not participate in the decision-making process until they are married, and women are considered intellectually and physically inferior to men. But they reject the unequal distribution of wealth and competition among members for status, prestige, or personal possessions. The Hutterites minimize competition by renouncing private adornment and ostentatious displays of wealth and by practicing collective consumption. There is little difference in dress, and adornment is usually frowned on. All the housing is plain and utilitarian. And as in most Christian communes, they are careful to indoctrinate their children against competition. Children are taught to avoid seeking honors or placing themselves above others. They are taught to never envy others.

One way the Hutterites build commitment to the group is through frequent face-to-face interaction. Members eat together in a communal dining hall, work together, and meet frequently to discuss the affairs of the community. Almost every evening, the entire community gathers for church service. Although the Hutterites have no formal means of punishing those who violate group rules, they do practice a form of ostracism called *den Frieden nehmen* ("taking away the individual's peace of mind"). An ostracized man is not allowed to talk to other members, including his own wife. He may also be assigned a special room in which to sleep and may be required to eat alone.

In addition, the practice of "branching," or community fission, functions not only to adjust community size, reduce friction, and settle other colonies but also to build internal commitment and reduce competition. Erasmus points out that social movements have difficulty maintaining long-range goals, especially as wealth accumulates. The Hutterites address this problem by dividing the communities, or branching, every 15 years. Each community saves a portion of its earnings to purchase additional land, build houses and barns, and accumulate necessary machines and livestock to start a new colony. When the new physical facilities are complete, members of the community draw lots to determine which families will relocate. Branching provides each Hutterite community with a tangible goal. "Wealthier" colonies that delay branching are often disrupted by internal quarrels and become examples of the danger of failing to branch on schedule. Branching also has a built-in renewal factor; new communities reproduce the founding enthusiasm and ideals. If there is competition, it is between colonies rather than individuals.

The Hutterites have resisted specialization, unlike other movements that have evolved into industries producing goods such as silverware in the Oneida community in New York and furniture and woolens in the Amana Society in Iowa. The Hutterites have also resisted hiring outside labor; instead, they exchange labor among colonies and use technology to further agricultural production.

In sum, the Hutterites, by a collective effort, have created within the larger society a community without poverty, without economic classes, and with little or no crime, where each person, without the promise of material reward, contributes to the common good. However, there are some negatives. Based on their interpretation of biblical scriptures, the Hutterites preach male supremacy and severely limit individual freedom. The question is whether

Exercise 7.5 ➤

Imagine for a moment that you have just been hired by NASA to plan the development of the first human extraterrestrial settlement. NASA wants you to use your knowledge of other societies to build an ideal community, avoiding the problems of modern society. How would you go about the task? What communities or societies that you know about might you choose as models? What would be the main values that you would build into your community? How would people be rewarded for the work they performed? How would you maintain order and settle conflicts? What kind of educational system would you propose? Finally, what are the most serious problems in modern society that you would want to avoid?

these negatives outweigh the benefits of creating nonstratified communities within the larger stratified society. There is also a question of whether cooperative communities such as the Hutterites can serve as a model for the poor in the larger society; that is, does the establishment of closed, collective communities offer a solution to the endemic poverty of those at the bottom level of modern society, and does the success of the Hutterites suggest that it is within our means to build societies without poverty?

CASE STUDY IN DOING ANTHROPOLOGY #7: HEALTH AND HUMAN RIGHTS

In Charles Dickens's *A Christmas Carol*, Marley, in his ghostly form, descends on Ebenezer Scrooge to tell him to expect a visit that night from three ghosts. As he disappears, he leaves Scrooge with the sound of wailing and lamentations coming from outside the window. When he looks out, Scrooge sees

> phantoms, wandering hither and thither in restless haste, and moaning as they went. Every one of them wore chains like Marley's Ghost; some few (they might be guilty governments) were linked together; none were free. Many had been personally known to Scrooge in their lives. He had been quite familiar with one old ghost, in a white waistcoat, with a monstrous iron safe attached to its ankle, who cried piteously at being unable to assist a wretched woman with an infant, whom it saw below, upon a door-step. *The misery with them all was, clearly, that they sought to interfere, for good, in human matters, and had lost the power for ever.* (Dickens, 1867, p. 33; emphasis added)

The phantoms' dilemma might very well serve as a metaphor for the wealthy in the world who seem resigned to helplessness when it comes to permanently alleviating poverty and oppression. Inequality, as we discussed earlier, is striking and is growing worse—within wealthy countries and between the rich and the poor countries of the world. Worse yet, inequality produces differential access to life's necessities: food, water, shelter, health care, and protection from torture and cruel punishment and from polluted environments. The question is, of course, what can be done to alleviate these problems, and what role might anthropology play in addressing them?

There are various ways that a background in anthropology is relevant for dealing with problems stemming from inequality. Anthropology prepares people for careers in the delivery of health services, the administration of treatment programs, the counseling of dysfunctional families, or finding the connections between old age and depression. In previous sections, we have already examined anthropological work in the areas of economic development, the development of HIV/AIDS prevention programs, and the counseling of adolescent girls. But perhaps some of the most significant contributions that can be made by people with a background in anthropology are in designing and implementing measures to protect people from human rights abuses.

Anthropology and Human Rights

The idea of individual rights comes to us from the 17th- and 18th-century Enlightenment—most notably codified by Thomas Jefferson in the U.S. Declaration of Independence:

> We hold these truths to be self evident: that all men are created equal; that they are endowed by their Creator with certain unalienable rights; that among these are life, liberty, and the pursuit of happiness.

The modern human rights movement originated, for the most part, with the Nuremberg trials of German officials accused of war crimes during World War II and in the Universal Declaration of Human Rights adopted on December 10, 1948, by the General Assembly of the United Nations. The rights outlined include, among others, the right to life, liberty, and security of person; the right to be free of the threat of torture or cruel, inhuman, or degrading treatment or punishment; and the right to freedom of opinion and expression. In addition to these legal rights, the UN declaration also includes the right to a standard of living adequate for health and well-being, including food, clothing, housing, medical care, and necessary social services, along with the right to security in the event of unemployment, sickness, disability, widowhood, old age, or another lack of livelihood in circumstances beyond the person's control.

Similar rights are incorporated into various other international treaties and conventions. Unfortunately, however, most of the rights outlined in these agreements are largely unenforceable or ignored. For example, although the United States and other member countries of the UN are signatories to the Convention on the Prevention and Punishment of the Crime of Genocide, all stood by in 1994 while more than 800,000 Rwandans were slaughtered by residents of their own country, avoiding taking action by simply refusing to define what was taking place as genocide until it was over. Amnesty International and Human Rights Watch— two of the major nongovernmental organizations addressing issues of human rights—have documented violations of individual rights in at least 150 countries

Anthropologist Carole Nagengast.

of the world, where nonviolent dissidents have been held without trial, imprisoned, tortured, killed, raped, or disappeared by police, military, or paramilitary forces. But when the UN instituted the post of High Commissioner for Human Rights, the position was allocated only $700,000—small even by nongovernmental organization standards. In his first year on the job, the High Commissioner did not criticize a single government anywhere in the world.

Furthermore, as we saw earlier in this chapter, the economic and social inequality that creates the conditions for human rights violations continues to grow as billions of people live in conditions of poverty and oppression while the top 358 global billionaires have a combined income equal to that of the 2.3 billion poorest people in the world.

Anthropologist Carole Nagengast, who coordinated the work of Amnesty International USA (AIUSA) for political prisoners in Turkey and served on and chaired the board of directors of AIUSA, and her coeditor Carlos G. Vélez-Ibáñez suggest that anthropologists are, of all social scientists, uniquely prepared for work on human rights. Anthropologists and those with anthropological training are most prepared to deal with cultural variation and to understand complex community struggles. They are trained to understand the workings of official bureaucracies and global processes, and as Nagengast and Vélez-Ibáñez put it, anthropologists have "a strong penchant for supporting the underdog." The issue, they say, is that although anthropologists often discover and reveal human rights abuses, they must also find a way to predict human rights abuses and, indirectly through participation in the design of public policy or directly in the delivery of services, do something about them.

In their edited book *Human Rights: The Scholar as Activist*, Nagengast and Vélez-Ibáñez suggest that the human rights agenda—in addition to addressing such individual and political abuses as land grabs, torture, murder, rape, and disappearances—must include collective and economic, social, and cultural rights. There are, they point out, no binding or enforceable laws or guidelines to constrain the power of corporations and their support agencies, such as the World Bank and International Monetary Fund, to set working conditions or wages or to impose development projects that displace persons or leave them worse off than before. Virtually all written and customary international laws leave it to nation-states to enforce the recognition of rights. But nation-states, which claim the right to self-determination, are also the major violators of human rights— either directly through the operation of military or police or indirectly by allowing extra-state or paramilitary groups to violate human rights.

Nagengast and Vélez-Ibáñez then ask "What can scholars do?" First, they say, anthropologists—who among all social scientists most often work with the poor—can publicize human rights abuses. The development of a global communication network, they say, allows human rights information to be quickly disseminated. When Augusto Pinochet, the former president of Chile, was arrested in London in 1998 following a request from Spain and Belgium for acts of genocide, torture, and "disappearances" committed during his presidency of 1973–1990, his defense of immunity because he was a head of state was rejected by the British High Court largely because of the widespread publicity that followed his case.

Anthropologists can also work with groups whose rights may be violated to help them develop the means to defend themselves. For example, Terence Turner has been working with the Kayapo of central Brazil since 1962. In addition to research and writing on Kayapo social organization, ritual, history, politics, and interethnic conflict, Turner has worked with the Kayapo to prevent development projects that threaten their land. Turner has been directing the Kayapo Video Project, in which Kayapo have been shooting and editing their own videos on their life and culture and on their relations with Brazilians. Turner is also a founding member of the American Anthropological Association's Committee on Human Rights.

Anthropologist Robert Hitchcock has worked with the San peoples in Botswana and Namibia to map their homelands, institute land claims, and stave off settler takeovers of their land. Hitchcock ensured that the San were active participants in these efforts. As a result, San communities have developed their own human rights development and development agencies.

People with anthropological training have worked to design policy and with service providers to alleviate the plight of refugees. In 2010, the number of internally displaced people worldwide reached 27.5 million.[4] These are defined as someone who,

> owing to a well-founded fear of being persecuted for reasons of race, religion, nationality, membership of a particular social group, or political opinion, is outside the country of his nationality, and is unable to or, owing to such fear, is unwilling to avail himself of the protection of that country.

In addition to these 17 million, more than 100 million people are displaced within their own country.

Angela Thieman-Dino and James A. Schechter describe how anthropologists can assist policymakers and expose biases in refugee policy. For example, why are some people (such as members of repressed religious minorities) granted asylum in the United States, whereas others (such as Haitians fleeing violence from a repressive regime) are intercepted and returned to the country from which they are fleeing? Anthropologists, they suggest, are better

---

[4]See http://www.reuters.com/article/2011/03/23/us-norway-displacement-idUSTRE72M3KE20110323.

positioned to document nonstate violations of human rights by paramilitary organizations or by corporations. Persons with an anthropological background can also serve as mediators between refugees and service providers, helping providers appreciate social or cultural concerns they might otherwise overlook. For example, Thieman-Dino discovered that some refugee service organizations were sometimes unaware that information they collected concerning abuses suffered by clients might pose security threats to either the refugees or themselves.

These are just a few of the examples of how anthropological skills and perspectives can contribute to the protection and restoration of human rights. But a description of such efforts would not be complete without the story of Paul Farmer and his efforts, according to one author, to "cure the world."

Anthropology and Medical Rights: The Work of Paul Farmer

In his book *Mountains Beyond Mountains*, about the work of anthropologist and physician Paul Farmer, Tracy Kidder describes how Farmer's background in anthropology and his experiences in Haiti molded his view of the connections between anthropology, medicine, and human rights. While studying anthropology as an undergraduate at Duke University, Farmer met and began visiting with Haitians working on tobacco farms. He soon becoming fascinated with Haitian history and culture, and as a consequence, he visited Haiti in 1983 when the country was still controlled by the U.S.-supported dictatorship of the Duvalier family. Haiti, a country of some 7.5 million people, is the poorest country in the Western Hemisphere, with 80% of the population living in poverty.

Farmer began to work with local and international agencies, delivering health and social services to the local population and conducting a health census on infant and juvenile mortality—the results of which he characterized as "horrific." He watched a young pregnant woman with malaria die because even after he helped to raise the $15 needed to purchase blood, he could not raise enough for the inexpensive equipment needed for the transfusion.

Among the lessons that Farmer drew from his initial experience in Haiti was that a knowledge of anthropology was necessary in addressing the health problems of the poor in Haiti. In one instance, a mother permitted a Voodoo priest to treat her child for malaria while also agreeing to let Farmer treat the patient with chloroquine. It was critical, Farmer says, to appreciate the role of Voodoo—a religion that combines traditional Catholicism with tradition African beliefs—in the life of most Haitians. A doctor who knew nothing about local beliefs might end up at war with Voodoo priests, mistaking patient complaints for bizarre superstitions. However, a doctor with a background in anthropology could find a way to work with the priest. For example, a female patient might complain of something Haitians call *move san, lét gate*. The condition is brought on by *sezisman*, a surprise of some sort or a frightening action. The result is "bad blood," in which a nursing mother's milk stops flowing. Although such a description might be dismissed by someone without knowledge of local culture, Farmer notes that, metaphorically, the explanation turns two vital fluids—blood and milk—into poison, thus serving as a symbolic warning about the abuse of pregnant women, particularly those who are nursing.

A second defining lesson that emerged from Haiti for Farmer was learning about liberation theology. In the 1960s in Latin America, during heightened periods of human rights abuses by often dictatorial states, Catholic priests organized communities for the defense of human rights and attacks against government repression. A few church leaders in Latin America attacked inequality and injustice and began to participate in forming organizations and social movements to give the poor a political and economic voice. It was an attempt, as some put it, to apply the Gospel to everyday life in the hope that these efforts would ultimately replace the old order of things. Farmer considered liberation theology to be, as he put it, "a powerful rebuke to the hiding away of poverty":

> Someone is witnessing this horror show? . . . I know it sounds shallow, the opiate thing, needing to believe, palliating pain, but it didn't feel shallow. It was more profound than other sentiments I'd known, and I was taken with the idea that in an ostensibly godless world that worshiped money and power or, more seductively, a sense of personal efficacy and advancement . . . there was still a place to look for God, and that was in the suffering of the poor. (Kidder, 2003, p. 85)

Farmer was attracted to the activism of liberation theology because it was driven by a need to accomplish something concrete in the lives of the poor and was characterized by what Farmer calls "pragmatic solidarity" with the communities that it sought to assist. Liberation theology argued for giving the poor not equal treatment but preferential treatment.

In addition to the role of anthropology and the pragmatism of liberation theology, Farmer also gained an appreciation for understanding the context in which poverty and oppression occurred. He understood that, as he put, "a minor error in one setting of power and privilege could have an enormous impact on the poor in another." For example, in the 1950s, with money from the U.S. Export-Import Bank, the U.S. Army Corps of Engineers built the Péligre Dam, which displaced thousands of Haitian farmers, who were forced to rebuild on the sides of mountains that were unsuited for growing crops or move to cities such as Port-au-Prince for jobs as housekeepers or as low-paid laborers in American-built assembly plants. The most valuable asset that remained for the remaining farmers were their Creole pigs, but an outbreak of swine fever in the Dominican Republic led the United States to destroy all the Haitian pigs in order to protect the American pork industry. The pigs were replaced with pigs purchased from Iowa farmers, but these were delicate and most died, leaving the peasants with little. These are examples of what Farmer refers to as "**structural violence**"—actions of remote government or international agencies that result in denial to the poor of basic rights of food, shelter, or livelihood.

After his initial experiences in Haiti, Farmer enrolled at Harvard in the Ph.D. program in anthropology and the medical school. He completed both programs while spending much of his time traveling back and forth to Haiti working to build, among other things, a public health program in the village of Cange that included vaccination programs, protected water supplies, and sanitation while also training people to administer medicines, treat minor ailments, and recognize symptoms of such serious ones as TB, malaria, and typhoid. He received his Ph.D. in anthropology and his M.D. in 1990, writing his Ph.D. thesis—*AIDS and Accusation*—on HIV/AIDS in Haiti. Since that time, Farmer has applied his expertise in the area of infectious disease to problems of drug-resistant tuberculosis in Russian prisons and in impoverished communities in Peru, and he has worked to help develop health services in Chiapas, Mexico, and Huhuetenango, Guatemala, while continuing to work in Haiti.

Health as a Human Right

Based on his experiences in Haiti, Farmer became convinced that health is a basic human right and that medical workers, along with social scientists, are uniquely situated—in temperament and profession—to address the problems of structural violence and to engage with the poor in the spirit of pragmatic solidarity. In his book *Pathologies of Power: Health, Human Rights, and the New War on the Poor*, Farmer outlines a rationale and a strategy for addressing human rights abuses, making concrete contributions to the life of the poor.

Farmer offers as an example the case of Russian prisons, where multi-drug-resistant tuberculosis (MDRTB) became a major problem. In Russia, prisoners are crowded together in cells whose air is thick with tubercle bacilli. Consequently, tuberculosis is the leading cause of death among Russian prisoners. Clearly, says Farmer, the situation is rife with human rights abuses. The first set of abuses begins with pretrial detention and the violation of the right to a speedy trial. The Russian court system is backlogged for months, and people who are being held for trial must live in deplorable conditions ripe for the contraction of TB—even before it is determined that they have committed a crime. The second set of abuses occurs if they are convicted and are held in a prison in conditions that guarantee exposure to MDRTB. Next, they are denied adequate food and medical care. As one Russian physician put it: "I have spent my entire medical career caring for prisoners with tuberculosis. And although we complained about shortages in the eighties, we had no idea how good we had it then. Now it's a daily struggle for food, drugs, lab supplies, even heat and electricity" (Farmer, 2003, p. 215).

Finally, then, prisoners are dying because of ineffective treatment—a clear violation of Article 25 of the Universal Declaration of Human Rights, which says that everyone has a right to "share in scientific advancement and its benefits." Farmer points out that people are dying not because there are no effective treatments—there are combinations of drugs that can cure MDRTB in the vast majority of cases—but because they or the agencies responsible for their care lack the money to pay for the medicine. "Untreatable" becomes a euphemism for "too expensive." And the case of MDRTB in Russia is mirrored in the cases of HIV/AIDS and malaria in Africa and HIV/AIDS and TB in Haiti as well as in most of Latin America. Worldwide, 32% of all deaths are caused by infectious disease, but in the poor countries, infectious disease is responsible for 42% of all deaths, compared to 1.2% in industrial countries.

Once we have defined health as a human right and recognize the structural violence that either creates conditions for disease or denies the afflicted access to medicine, what can anthropologists, other social scientists, or medical professionals accomplish?

First, says Farmer, they can put the human rights violations into the global contexts that identify the structural causes of the abuse. For example, Russian prison doctors lack the medicines to cure their patients because international financial agencies such as the International Monetary Fund require countries such as Russia—and most other countries around the world—to cut government services as a condition for receiving loans. Pharmaceutical companies, which often receive sizable government subsidies and support for research, refuse to waive patent rights to allow poor countries to supply generic forms of drugs that could help HIV/AIDS patients in poor countries. It is in placing violations in these broader perspectives that anthropologists can make a major contribution. As Farmer puts it: "Social inequalities based on race or ethnicity, gender, religious creed, and—above all—social class are the motor force behind most human rights violations. In other words, violence against individuals is usually embedded in entrenched structural violence" (2003, p. 219).

But understanding the context for the violation of health rights, says Farmer, is inadequate. Russian penal codes already prohibit overcrowding in prisons, long pretrial detentions, and the exposure of patients to malnutrition and disease. Prison officials already recognize the problem of MDRTB, which is why they sought Farmer's help. Physicians in Haiti already know that poverty generated by oppression and corruption drives people to become sex workers in Port-au-Prince, exposing them to HIV/AIDS, and people in Peru know that a lack of sanitation facilities exposes the population to various gastrointestinal disorders.

What is needed, says Farmer, is a strategy to confront structural violence. The problem, he says, is that traditional government agencies and nongovernmental organizations (NGOs) are unnecessarily restricted in addressing rights issues. International institutions such as the UN and organizations such as Amnesty International and Physicians for Human Rights are constrained by the fact that they must work through governments, and governments are often the major violators of rights. For this reason, Farmer suggests that while NGOs and other groups must work with and through governments when possible, NGOs and such independent groups as universities, hospitals, churches, and health care professionals should listen to the needs of and work in solidarity with the members of affected communities. If healing and health care can become the "symbolic core," as he puts it, of a new human rights agenda, we can tap into an almost universal concern for the sick while also involving persons in medicine, public health, and the natural and social sciences.

Farmer's own efforts provide a model for the approach to addressing human rights abuses that he is suggesting. On one of his trips back to Boston from Haiti, he tried to raise money to build a bread oven in Cange, the village in which he was working. He approached a local charity, which gave him the money and also put him into contact with one of their regular donors, Tom White, a local contractor who contributed money that helped establish Partners In Health and a corresponding organization in Haiti called Zamni Lasante, on which Farmer could draw for his work in Cange. Partners In Health has subsequently grown into a major provider of health care programs in Haiti, Peru, and Russia.

Summarizing his approach, Farmer (2003, p. 238) writes:

> We have a long way to go in the struggle for health and human rights. We cannot merely study this topic without proposing meaningful and pragmatic interventions; but to succeed, we must distinguish between our best analysis and our best strategies. The focus on health offers a critical new dimension to human rights work and is a largely untapped vein of resources passion, and good will.

CONCLUSIONS

The problem underlying this chapter is why extremes of poverty and wealth exist in modern societies. The criteria customarily used to rank people in social hierarchies include wealth or income, occupation, ethnic group membership, personal appearance, race, gender, and age. The consequences of such ranking, especially in the creation of poverty and the gap between the rich and poor, have raised some of the most challenging questions in modern societies.

Next, we examined the reasons that social and economic inequalities exist and suggested that our financial system—particularly the accumulation of debt, the tendency to devalue labor, and the persistence of old and new forms of racism—helps maintain and even increase economic and social divisions in society.

We also examined the reasons people come to accept social hierarchies as natural because they believe that hierarchy is a biological principle. Some people are thought to be naturally more or less intelligent or otherwise more or less worthy than others. For example, females' biological functions have been described in terms that make women seem less valuable than men.

People at the lowest level of the social hierarchy—those who live in poverty—adapt to their conditions in various ways. Blacks in The Flats of a midwestern city adapted by building kinship ties, and Puerto Ricans on the Upper East Side of New York City adapted by building an underground economic system centered on drugs.

A few groups have demonstrated that it is possible to build egalitarian, nonstratified communities within a larger industrial society. Perhaps the most successful in the United States have been the Hutterites, a religious group that emphasizes communal ownership of poverty and equal distribution of production while rejecting competition, violence, and war.

Finally, we examined various areas in which persons with a background in anthropology can contribute to addressing the poverty and oppression that often arises from inequality. We focused largely on the area of human rights abuses—most of which arise from differential access to wealth—describing the work of people such as Carole Nagengast and Paul Farmer.

REFERENCES AND SUGGESTED READINGS

Introduction: The Rationale for Social Inequality

The epigraph comes from Robert Hertz's *Death and the Right Hand*, translated and edited by Claudia and Rodney Needham (Free Press, 1960). The quote from Thomas Belmonte is from *The Broken Fountain* (Columbia University Press, 1989). You can find a wealth of information about inequality in the United States in Valdas Anelauskas's book *Discovering America As It Is* (Clarity Press, 1999). Information regarding income distribution can be found in David Harvey's *A Brief History of Neoliberalism* (Oxford University Press, 2005). Information on children's health and economic condition in the United States can be found in "Estimating the Risk of Food Stamp Use and Impoverishment During Childhood" by Mark R. Rank and Thomas A. Hirschl in the *Archives of Pediatric and Adolescent Medicine*, vol. 163 (2009), 994–9.

How Do Societies Rank People in Social Hierarchies?

One of the classic works on social hierarchy, especially as it relates to India's caste system, is Louis Dumont's Homo *Hierarchicus: An Essay on the Caste System* (University of Chicago Press, 1970). Pierre L. van den Berghe and his associates produced a series of books on class and ethnicity in Europe, Africa, and South America. These include *Inequality in the Peruvian Andes: Class and Ethnicity in Cuzco*, with George P. Primov (University of Missouri Press, 1977); *South Africa: A Study in Conflict* (Wesleyan University Press, 1965); and *Race and Ethnicity* (Basic Books, 1970). A review of anthropological studies of social class is Raymond T. Smith's "Anthropology and the Concept of Social Class" in the *Annual Review of Anthropology*, vol. 13 (1984), pp. 467–94. Studies on youth in Africa are contained in Alcinda Honwana and Filip de Boeck's *Makers and Breakers: Children and Youth in Postcolonial Africa* (Africa World Press, 2005). Jean and John L. Comaroff's observations about global youth are contained in *Millennial Capitalism and the Culture of Neoliberalism* (Duke University Press, 2001). William McCollum's statement, made during a floor debate in Congress in 1997, can be found at http://www.counterpunch.org/youth.html. Murray Milner Jr. describes the social structure of American high schools in *Freaks, Geeks, and Cool Kids: American Teenagers, Schools, and the Culture of Consumption* (Routledge, 2006). Paul Willis's classic study of working class youth is found in *Learning to Labor: How Working Class Kids Get Working Class Jobs* (Columbia University Press, 1977). An excellent review of the literature on women's status is "Anthropological Studies of Women's Status Revisited: 1977–1987" by Carol C. Mukhopadhyay and Patricia J. Higgins in the *Annual Review of Anthropology*, vol. 17 (1988), pp. 461–95.

Why Do Social and Economic Inequalities Persist?

Margrit and Declan Kennedy illustrate how debtors transfer wealth to creditors in *Interest and Inflation Free Money: Creating an Exchange Medium That Works for Everyone and Protects the Earth* (New Society Publishers, 1995). An excellent book on the role of debt in our society and how people are encouraged by banks and others to borrow is anthropologist Brett Williams's *Debt for Sale: A Social History of the Credit Trap* (University of Pennsylvania Press, 2004). A description of the role of outsourcing in our economy can be found in *Global Problems and the Culture of Capitalism* (5th edition) by Richard Robbins (Pearson, 2011), and the skills required for workers in the grape industry is described in Jane L. Collins's "Tracing Social Relations in Commodity Chains: The Case of Grapes in Brazil" in *Commodities and Globalization: Anthropological Perspectives*, edited by Angelique Haugerud, M. Priscilla Stone, and Peter D. Little (Rowman & Littlefield, 2000).

There is in anthropology a large body of work on race, racism and discrimination. A good place to start is *How Real Is Race? A Sourcebook On Race, Culture, and Biology* by Carol C. Mukhopadhyay, Rosemary Henze, and Yolanda T. Moses (Rowman & Littlefield, 2007). Leigh Mullings provides an excellent review of anthropological studies of race and racism in "Interrogating Racism: Toward an Antiracist Anthropology" in the *Annual Review of Anthropology*, vol. 34 (2005), 667–93. Andrew hacker provides an excellent account of racism and the attitudes of his students into the 1990s in *Two Nations: Black and White, Separate, Hostile, Unequal* (Ballantine Books, 1995). The extent to which we have tried to minimize the persistence of racism (and failed) is detailed in *Whitewashing Race: The Myth of a Color-Blind Society* by Michael K. Brown, Martin Carney, Elliott Currie, Troy Duster and David P. Oppenheimer (University of California Press, 2003), and the relationship between neoliberalism and race and how it is represented globally is described by David Theo Goldberg in *The Threat of Race: Reflections on Racial Neoliberalism* (Wiley-Blackwell, 2009).

How Do People Come to Accept Social Hierarchies as Natural?

Stephen Jay Gould's examination of Morton's experiments on cranial capacity and intelligence are described in *The Mismeasure of Man* (W. W. Norton, 1981). Francis Galton originally published his ideas about hereditary intelligence in *Hereditary Genius: An Inquiry into its Laws and* Consequences in 1869 (Prometheus Books, 2006). An excellent anthropological examination and critique of the concept of intelligence and the role of testing in American life can be found in Allan Hanson's *Testing Testing* (University of California Press, 1993). An examination of the attempts to legitimize social class through testing and education can be found in Paul Henderson's "Class Structure and the Concept of Intelligence" and Clarence J. Karier's "Testing for Order and Control in the Corporate Liberal State"—both in *Schooling and Capitalism: A Sociological Reader*, edited by Roger Dale, Geoff Esland, and Madeleine MacDonald (Routledge & Kegan Paul, in association with Open University Press, 1976). Karl Pearson's "On the Inheritance of Mental Characteristics in Man" appeared in *Proceedings of the Royal Society of London*, vol. 69 (1901), pp. 153–5, and Charles Spearman's first attempts to prove the existence of *g* appeared in his article "General Intelligence" in the *American Journal of Psychology*, vol. 115 (1904), pp. 201–92. The most recent and widely publicized attempt to legitimize the American class structure through the use of the concept of intelligence can be found in *The Bell Curve: Intelligence and Class Structure in American Life* by Richard J. Herrnstein and Charles Murray (Free Press, 1994). An evaluation of the literature on differences in IQ scores, contrasting the hereditarian and environmentalist positions, is provided by John F. Longres in *Human Behavior in the Social Environment* (F. E. Peacock, 1990). Emily Martin's *The Woman in the Body: A Cultural Analysis of Reproduction* (Beacon Press, 1987) describes her work on the social construction of female biology. Robert Hertz's analysis of the symbolic use of the human body to justify hierarchy can be found in *Death and the Right Hand,* cited earlier. A review of the ways in which reproductive biology affects the role of women is given in "The Politics of Reproduction" by Faye Ginsburg and Rayna Rapp in the *Annual Review of Anthropology,* vol. 20 (1991), pp. 311–43.

How Do People Living in Poverty Adapt to Their Condition?

Oscar Lewis's pioneering work on the lives of people in poverty is represented by *Five Families: Mexican Case Studies in the Culture of Poverty* (Basic Books, 1959). A critique of the culture-of-poverty concept can be found in Charles A. Valentine's *Culture and Poverty: Critique and Counter-Proposals* (University of Chicago Press, 1968). Carol Stack's account of The Flats appears in *All Our Kin: Strategies for Survival in a Black Community* (Harper & Row, 1974). The research on how Puerto Ricans on the Upper East Side of Manhattan adapted to their socioeconomic situation is reported in Philippe Bourgois's book *In Search of Respect: Selling Crack in El Barrio* (Cambridge University Press, 1995).

Can a Nonstratified Community Exist Within a Larger Hierarchical Society?

The examination of attempts to build egalitarian societies is based primarily on Charles Erasmus's *In Search of the Common Good* (Free Press, 1977). The description of the Hutterites relies on John Hostetler's *Hutterite Society* (Johns Hopkins University Press, 1974). For additional work, see Robert Moos and Robert Brownstein's *Environment and Utopia* (Plenum Press, 1977) and Kathleen Kinkade's *A Walden Two Experiment: The First Five Years of Twin Oaks Community* (William Morrow, 1973).

Case Study in Doing Anthropology #7: Health and Human Rights

The Universal Declaration of Human Rights is available at http://www.ohchr.org/en/udhr/pages/language.aspx?langid=eng. Descriptions of the human rights work of Carole Nagengast, Carlos G. Vélez-Ibáñez, Terence Turner, Robert Hitchcock, Angela Thieman-Dino, and James A. Schechter comes from the book edited by Nagengast and Vélez-Ibáñez: *Human Rights: The Scholar as Activist* (Society for Applied Anthropology, 2004). Information on refugees can be found on the website of the United Nations High Commission for Refugees at http://www.unhcr.org/cgi-bin/texis/vtx/home. A description of Paul Farmer's work is contained in Tracy Kidder's *Mountains Beyond Mountains* (Random House, 2004), and Farmer outlines his work and strategies for dealing with human rights abuses in *Pathologies of Power: Health, Human Rights, and the New War on the Poor* (University of California Press, 2003). You can find out more about Partners In Health at http://www.pih.org.

CHAPTER

8

THE CULTURAL CONSTRUCTION
OF VIOLENT CONFLICT

PROBLEM 8: HOW DO SOCIETIES GIVE MEANING TO AND JUSTIFY COLLECTIVE
VIOLENCE?

> *[R]osa had her breasts cut off. Then they cut into her chest and took out her heart. The men had their arms broken, their testicles cut off, and their eyes poked out. They were killed by slitting their throats, and pulling the tongue out through the slit.*
>
> **—Witness to the attack (1984)**

INTRODUCTION

The Justification of Violent Conflict

When the Spaniards invaded the New World in the 16th century, they met fierce resistance from the Carib. A warlike people, the Carib inhabited the northeast portion of South America around what is now Venezuela and Guyana. The neighbors of the Carib recognized their ferocity by calling them "sons of the tiger's teeth." Moreover, the Carib were cannibals. To prepare for war, a Carib chief would hold a feast at which women urged the dancing warriors to be fierce and avenge their dead. The dancing was intended to encourage the tiger spirit, Kaikusi-yuma, to take possession of the warriors, and when they went to war, it was the spirit of Kaikusi-yuma that killed, not them. A warrior could rid himself of the possession only after tasting the blood and flesh of a dead enemy.

From our perspective, the acts of the invading Spanish, like the acts of the Carib, were horrific. The Spanish invaders murdered and enslaved thousands of indigenous people, and the Carib devoured human flesh. But the Europeans and the Carib considered their acts to be moral and proper; the Spaniards justified their killing and enslavement as the work of God, and the Carib defined their killing as the act of an animal possessing a human body. Both peoples constructed meanings for their acts that distanced them from the consequences of their violence. Although we may condemn these acts, we live in a world in which governments construct systems of meaning that allow them to plan and contemplate the use of weapons that are much more deadly than the clubs, spears, crossbows, and primitive firearms of the Carib and Spaniards— weapons capable of incinerating millions of people.

Purposeful, organized, and socially sanctioned combat involving killing— what most people call **war** or **feud**—seems to be an intrinsic feature of human societies. In fact, it is difficult to find societies that do not sanction violence for one reason or another. Why is collective violence so universally sanctioned? Some suggest that human beings have an innate instinct toward aggression and that the roots of war and collective violence lie somewhere in the biological mechanisms that animals and humans have in common. Violent conflict is regarded as a part of human nature. Others reject this explanation as simplistic; collective violence, they say, is above all a cultural construction whose roots lie in the human mind, not in the genes. Although there may be some innate aggressive impulse, human beings can choose how that impulse is expressed.

The fact that human beings construct systems of meaning to justify violent conflict and distance themselves from its consequences suggests that it has little to do with a natural aggressive impulse. Acts of collective violence, such as those described in the epigraph, are rationalized as purposeful, noble, or inevitable acts, not as evidence of wanton cruelty. The problem is to discover how societies construct meanings for violent conflict that mask its consequences and convince people that it is right and proper.

To evaluate this issue, the first question to be addressed is how societies create a bias in favor of collective violence. That is, what kinds of meanings are constructed to encourage people to commit violence against others? Then, if there are societies without collective violence, how do they create a bias against it? If violent conflict is not simply natural and inevitable but is culturally constructed, it may be possible to learn from societies in which there is little if any violence. Are there significant social, economic, or political differences between violent and peaceful societies? Next, we examine the effects of violent conflict on societies to determine whether, as some maintain, engaging collectively in deadly quarrels might serve some useful purpose in the long run. Because collective violence is sanctioned in American society, it is instructive to ask how we have created a bias toward violent conflict and constructed meanings that allow us to contemplate, plan for, and pursue the destruction of millions of people in other nations. Finally, we examine how an anthropological perspective can better help us understand the rhetoric of war and violence.

QUESTIONS

8.1   How do societies create a bias in favor of collective violence?
8.2   How do societies create a bias against violent conflict?
8.3   What are the economic, political, or social differences between peaceful and violent societies?
8.4   What are the effects of war on societies?
8.5   How is it possible to justify the creation of weapons of mass destruction?

Case Study in Doing Anthropology #8: The Uses (and Misuses?) of Anthropology for Peace and War

QUESTION 8.1   *How Do Societies Create a Bias in Favor of Collective Violence?*

One way societies create a bias toward collective violence is to reward it. For example, among the Native Americans of the western plains, raiding other groups for horses was a means by which a man gained status. Horses symbolized wealth, and in many groups, the number of horses a man owned and gave to others as gifts measured his importance.

Horses, Rank, and Warfare Among the Kiowa

Horses were not indigenous to North America; the Spaniards brought them to the continent in the 1500s. Native American groups such as the Kiowa captured some horses and acquired others in trade with the Spaniards. The Kiowa also obtained horses by attacking other Native American groups with raiding parties of from six to 10 and occasionally as many as 30 men. The object of the raid was not only to secure as many of the enemy's horses as possible but also to demonstrate bravery. Among the Kiowa, rank was determined in two ways: by the number of horses a man possessed and by the honors accruing to him in warfare.

Kiowa society was divided into four ranks or grades. In the top rank were *ongop*—men who were generous, owned considerable wealth, and, most importantly, had distinguished themselves in war. In the second rank were *ondeigupa*—men who had property, especially horses, and were generous but had not yet distinguished themselves in war. The lower ranks of Kiowa society were occupied by *Keen* or *dupom*, people who were poor, propertyless, or helpless.

To rise in status, a young Kiowa male needed to acquire a horse. Often, he would begin his climb through the ranks of Kiowa society by borrowing a horse from a kinsperson to go on a raid, hoping to repay the loan with another horse he captured. With a horse of his own, he could participate in more raids, gradually obtaining enough horses to rise to the rank of *ondeigupa* or, as the Kiowa put it, "rise out of the bush of *keen*." Several years of raiding might bring him 20 or 30 horses, at which point people would begin speaking of him with respect.

To rise to the top rank of *ongop*, however, also required the accumulation of honors won in war. The Kiowa had a very elaborate system of battle honors divided into three groups of brave deeds, with group I being the most honorific (see Table 8.1). For example, counting first coup involved charging the

TABLE 8.1   KIOWA RANKING AND HONORS

Group I	Group II	Group III
1. Counting first coup	1. Killing an enemy	1. Dismounting, turning horse loose, and fighting on foot
2. Charging an enemy while the party is in retreat, thus covering the retreat	2. Counting second coup	2. Counting third and fourth coup
3. Rescuing a comrade while the party is retreating before the enemy	3. Receiving a wound in hand-to-hand combat	3. Serving as raid leader
4. Charging the leading man of the enemy alone before the parties have met		4. Success in stealing horses
		5. Efficiency in war camp life

Source: Information from Bernard Mishkin's *Rank and Warfare Among the Plains Indians* (Seattle: University of Washington Press, 1940).

enemy alone and striking one of them with a stick. The number of feathers a man wore in his headdress was a measure of his heroic exploits. Anthropologist Bernard Mishkin estimates that approximately 10% of the men would rise to the top rank of Kiowa society by obtaining a significant number of horses and accumulating sufficient battle honors. In this way, the Kiowa rewarded aggressive behavior and bravery in battle.

Good Hosts Among the Yanomamö

Another way societies create a bias in favor of collective violence is to make it necessary as a way of protecting valuable resources. A classic example is the Yanomamö of Venezuela. The Yanomamö live in villages of from 40 to 250 people and practice slash-and-burn (*swidden*) agriculture, living primarily on the crops they grow in their gardens.

Intervillage warfare is endemic to the Yanomamö. Anthropologist Napoleon Chagnon, who began to work with the Yanomamö in 1964, reports that one village of 200 people was attacked 25 times during a period of 15 months, and 10 people were killed, representing a loss of 5% of the village population. Chagnon estimates that some 20 to 25% of all male deaths are the result of warfare.

For the Yanomamö, women and children are valuable resources. The men believe that to protect themselves and their resources, they must be fierce, and raiding another village is one way they demonstrate their ferocity. Men may conduct raids to avenge the death of a village member at the hands of an enemy village or as the result of an act of sorcery by an enemy. They may also make raids to capture women or children. Violence can also take the form of inviting members of another village to a feast and, usually with the aid of allies from another village, killing the guests and abducting their women. Raiding by other villages also forces them to move fairly frequently, and they sometimes take refuge from their enemies in the villages of their allies. However, this practice is risky because host villages generally expect sexual access to the wives of their guests or expect unmarried female guests to marry men of their village. These expectations often lead to open hostilities between hosts and guests.

Expressions of ferocity may also be directed among village members. For example, men often vent anger and demonstrate their ferocity to others by beating their wives. A man who accuses another of cowardice or making excessive demands for goods or women may challenge his opponent to a chest-pounding duel, in which they take turns hitting each other in the chest as hard as they can. The duel generally ends when one of the contestants is too injured to continue. Fights with clubs are another form of settling disputes between men; these fights generally result in free-for-alls that can be deadly.

In this environment, where each man strives to acquire females from others, it is necessary to adopt an antagonistic stance toward others, encouraging the development of what the Yanomamö call *waiteri* (ferocity). The *waiteri* complex, as Chagnon calls it, is evidenced in ways other than direct conflict.

The Yanomamö express it in their origin myth, which tells how the original people were created from the blood of the moon, which had been shot with an arrow by beings who believed their children's souls were being devoured by the moon. The first Yanomamö born of the blood of the moon were exceptionally fierce and waged constant war on one another.

The Yanomamö also socialize male children to be aggressive and hostile. Boys are teased to strike tormentors and to bully girls. At one gathering of two villages attended by Chagnon, men were to satisfy their grievances against each other with a chest-pounding duel. Before the duel, the men gathered all the boys between the ages of eight and 15 and forced them to fight one another. At first, says Chagnon, the boys were reluctant and tried to run away, but their parents dragged them back and insisted that they hit each other. At the first blows, the boys cried, but as the fight progressed, fear became rage, and they ended up pounding each other while they screamed and rolled in the dirt amidst the cheers and admiration of their fathers.

Defending Honor in Kohistan

Another way societies create a bias toward collective violence is by making it part of a code of honor. Among the Kohistani in the mountains of northwest Pakistan, villagers follow a code that demands vengeance against any threat to a man's honor. When anthropologist Lincoln Keiser worked in the village of Thull in 1984, defense of honor continually led to relationships of *dushmani* or blood feud. The men of Thull view each other with guarded suspicion, and relationships of friendship can easily slip into *dushmani*. They believe that if another person wrongs them, they must retaliate, but the act of revenge should not exceed the original wrong. However, any unwarranted behavior toward a man's daughter, wife, or unmarried sister requires deadly retaliation. Even staring at these female relatives requires death for the offender.

One of Keiser's friends related how a neighbor killed his brother Omar while he was bringing a basket of food to the neighbor's family because Omar had heard the family had nothing to eat. "But why," asked Keiser, "would a man kill his neighbor who only tried to help him?" "Who knows?" the friend replied. "But I will take vengeance." Keiser says he had no doubt he would. Looking into the incident, Keiser heard gossip that Omar was killed because he really went to the house to stare at his neighbor's wife and brought the food only as a trick. Keiser himself was ultimately forced to leave Thull because of a rumor that in taking a photograph of a goatherd he was actually trying to photograph the herd owner's wife.

The people of Thull are mostly farmers and herders. As followers of Islam, a religion that emphasizes peace and harmony, they have constructed a system of meaning in which taking vengeance is considered a religious act. Central to the beliefs of the people of Thull is the idea of *ghrairat*—a man's personal worth, integrity, or character. *Ghrairat* is given to men by God and can be lost only if they fail to protect it. Women's behavior is also a matter of *ghrairat* because men must control their women; any act of a woman—or a person toward a woman—that threatens to bring shame is a direct attack on the man's *ghrairat* and must be avenged. Women must never walk outside their father's or husband's house without an escort, must never speak to an unrelated man, and must always comport themselves with modesty, hiding and minimizing their sexuality. Men who allow their women freedom are *baghrairatman*—"men without personal integrity."

However, defending *ghrairat* is more than simply the concern of an individual. Because of the webs of kinship, friendship, and political ties, it often involves whole groups within the community in violence against one another. Men in Thull constantly ally themselves with others in groups that may be based on kinship or may represent political factions. A man seeking vengeance for a wrong may enlist the help of others with whom he is allied. More importantly, an act of vengeance may be taken not only against the man who committed the wrong but also against a kinsperson or a member of his faction.

One case reported by Keiser illustrates the course of collective violence or feud. Two young men—Mamad Said and Amin—were herding their goats in the mountains. In response to a friendly shove, Mamad Said playfully swung a stick at Amin, hitting him in the face and drawing blood. Amin went to his uncle, Shah Hajji Khan, who gathered some of his friends to avenge the injury by beating Mamad Said. But friends and relatives of Mamad Said met them, and in the ensuing melee, Shah Hajji Khan's group suffered greater injuries; his son almost lost his life from an ax blow to the head. Now two insults needed to be avenged by Shah Hajji Khan: the original blow received by his nephew and the beating inflicted on his son by friends and relatives of Mamad Said. Some two years later, Shah Hajji Khan hatched a plot to ambush Mamad Said, who escaped by hiding in an irrigation ditch. Six months later, Mamad Said died from tuberculosis, which might be expected to bring an end to the feud begun by his accidental blow to Amin's face. But Mamad Said's brother, Qui Afsal, claimed that Mamad Said had died from sickness he contracted while hiding from Shah Hajji Khan in the irrigation ditch. In revenge, he allegedly killed the son of a friend of Shah Hajji Khan, who had helped avenge the injury to Amin. Qui Afsal was later shot in the stomach but survived.

As a consequence of such escalation of violence, the men of Thull habitually walk around armed, design their houses for defense against the gunfire of their neighbors, and spend most of their money on rifles and arms. A prized possession is a Russian-made AK-47 assault rifle.

Exercise 8.1 ➤

Examples of group-sanctioned conflict are readily available in newspaper reports. To examine the justifications for such conflict, follow a daily newspaper for a couple of days and document the instances you find of group-sanctioned violence and the reasons attributed for it.

François Dubois, *St. Bartholomew Day's Massacre*, 24 August 1572, is a vivid portrayal of religious violence. Musée d'Archéologie et d'Histoire, Lausanne, Switzerland.

Constructing Religious Justifications for Violence

Another way that violence is justified is to frame it as a cosmic struggle between good and evil. Most modern religions contain sacred texts metaphorically describing violent confrontations between the forces of good and the forces of evil. The book of Revelation of the New Testament, with its description of the forces of Satan and the final battle between good and evil, provides one of the best (and most violent) metaphors of war and redemption in Western literature. As Elaine Pagels notes, the characterization of one's enemies as "satanic" and oneself as God's people has long been a formula for justifying hatred and mass slaughter.

Therefore, it should not be surprising that people use religious rhetoric to justify violent acts. However, when devout adherents to Christianity, Judaism, Sikhism, Buddhism, or Islam commit violent acts in the name of God or some spiritual mission, they are also often using religious rhetoric to respond to social, political, or economic grievances. Reverend Michael Bray set fire to abortion clinics in the name of God, but he also claimed that the U.S. government was undermining individual freedoms and moral values. Osama bin Laden sought the establishment of an Islamic state, but he was also protesting the Israeli occupation of Palestinian territories, the stationing of U.S. troops in Saudi Arabia, and U.S. support for oppressive governments in the Middle East.

Virtually all major religions have their violent militants. The militant groups of Protestant fundamentalism include Operation Rescue and the Army of God—dedicated to, among other things, halting abortion. Operation Rescue was not the first group to use violence to protest abortion. The right-to-life movement goes back to the 1973 Supreme Court ruling in *Roe v. Wade* that recognized a woman's right to abortion. Some groups had already adopted confrontational tactics of blocking the entrances to clinics and harassing abortion providers. The National Abortion Federation keeps a record of violent incidents against abortion providers that includes invasions of clinics, vandalism, murders, death threats, bomb threats, bombings, assaults, arson attempts, arson, and kidnapping attempts. From 1977 through 2009, they documented a total of 6,263 such incidents, including eight murders, 41 bombings, 175 cases of arson, 97 cases of attempted arson or bombings, and 391 cases of invasion. They also documented 33,834 arrests of abortion protesters.

The Army of God is another example of a militant Protestant group. Its doctrine was outlined in an underground manual—*Army of God*—whose authorship is attributed to Bray. Bray was convicted in 1985 of setting fire to seven abortion clinics. He authored the book *A Time to Kill*, which defends the killing of abortion providers. According to Bray, Americans live in a state of "hidden warfare"—comparable to that of Nazi Germany—and a dramatic event, such as an economic collapse, would reveal the demonic role of the government. At that point, believers would take up a revolutionary struggle and establish a new moral order based on biblical law. Until then, he and others must have the moral courage to resist, particularly by defending unborn babies and killing those who threaten them. Jessica Stern asked one young member of the Army of God how he became involved with the group. "I am a Christian," he said, "and therefore opposed to abortion. Unborn babies are dying by the millions, and I feel compelled to help." For members of the group, killing abortion providers is "justifiable homicide."

Another example of religion being used to justify violence occurred on March 20, 1995, when five members of the Aum Shinrikyo movement—all with scientific training—walked into the Tokyo subway and, using sharpened umbrellas, punctured plastic bags filled with deadly sarin gas, killing 12 people and injuring more than 5,500. Group members explained to Mark Juergensmeyer that Aum Shinrikyo represented for them a critique of Japanese religion and the "hierarchical Japanese social system." The movement was founded by Shoko Asahara based on the idea that a world catastrophe would occur—a World War III or Armageddon in which the forces of good and evil would confront each other but members of Aum Shinrikyo would survive. Asahara justified his acts by reference to Tibetan Buddhism and the concept of *Phoa*. Rather than focusing on the effect that killing has on the killer's moral purity, this doctrine focuses on the one who is killed and the merit that comes after death. According to Asahara, if a person is a scoundrel or is part of an evil social system, he or she is accumulating negative karmic debt. Killing such people represents a mercy killing that allows their souls to move to a higher plane than if they continued to exist in sin.

Juergensmeyer asks under what conditions people are likely to use religious justifications for violence. He suggests that by locating a struggle on a cosmic scale, aggressors elevate its importance beyond local concerns and instead invoke legendary battles between good and evil. Bray defended the need to kill and, if necessary, die over the issue of abortion. There is a great cosmic war going on, he said—a confrontation between good and evil—but that is unseen because the enemy has imposed control. Bin Laden justified violence by projecting the struggle as that between the forces of Islam and those trying to destroy it. The rhetoric of wars of good versus evil has even entered the U.S. political mainstream with terms such as "axis of evil." There is real power, suggests Juergensmeyer, in elevating a political conflict to a cosmic war. To live in a state of war, he says,

> is to live in a world in which individuals know who they are, why they have suffered, by whose hand they have been humiliated, and at what expense they have persevered. The concept of war provides cosmology, history, and eschatology and offers the reins of political control. Perhaps most important, it holds out the hope of victory and the means to achieve it. In the images

of cosmic war this victorious triumph is a grand moment of social and personal transformation, transcending all worldly limitations. One does not easily abandon such expectations. To be without such images of war is almost to be without hope itself. (2000, pp. 154–55)

QUESTION 8.2   *How Do Societies Create a Bias Against Violent Conflict?*

Anthropologist Thomas Gregor suggests that because war is so widespread in human societies, the task of the social scientist is not so much to explain war as to explain peace. Peaceful societies, he says, are difficult to find. By peaceful, he means a society that is not involved in internal collective violence and in which there is little interpersonal violence. A peaceful society has no special roles for warriors and places a positive value on nonaggressive behavior and the peaceful resolution of conflict. Societies that have been characterized as relatively peaceful include the Ju/wasi, the Semai of West Malaysia, the Inuit, the Xinguano of the Amazon region in South America, and the Buid of the Philippines.

Characteristics of Peaceful Societies

Conflict over material resources is avoided in peaceful societies by a strong emphasis on sharing and cooperation. It is expected that everyone in the group has a legitimate claim to what the group possesses. Among the Ju/wasi, the person whose arrow kills an animal is considered to be the owner of the game, but he is obligated to distribute it. The Ju/wasi will share arrows with the understanding that if they kill an animal with an arrow given to them by someone else, they will give the owner the game to distribute. This also works to spread out the responsibility for meat sharing and the glory (and perhaps the hostility) that accompanies meat distribution.

The Semai of West Malaysia are known for their nonaggressiveness and avoidance of physical conflict. The approximately 15,000 Semai live in small hamlets of fewer than 100 people each. Understanding Semai nonviolence, says anthropologist Clayton Robarchek, requires understanding the Semai notion of *Pehunan*—a state of being in which a person is unsatisfied in regard to some need or want, such as food or sex. The Semai believe that to refuse a request and deny a person in need intensifies the danger to the individual and the group; for that reason, the group is obligated to help. The idea of *Pehunan* encompasses a depiction of the community as nurturant caregivers. Rather than saying that it is each person's obligation to meet his or her own needs, the Semai believe that it is the obligation of all members of the community to help and give nurturance to others. Thus, Semai values stress affiliation, mutual aid, and the belief that violence is not a viable option for settling disputes.

Another way people in peaceful societies create a bias against violence is by condemning those who boast or make claims that can be interpreted as a challenge to others. Among the Ju/wasi, for example, no one is praised for gathering food or making a kill, and people go out of their way to minimize their accomplishments. Those who make boastful claims are ridiculed. Anthropologist Richard Lee painfully learned this lesson himself when, to show his appreciation to the Ju/wasi for the help they had given him, he brought a fine ox to be slaughtered and distributed at a Christmas feast. The Ju/wasi, much to Lee's chagrin, ridiculed the ox, claiming it was thin and unappetizing. Lee later realized that they were acting toward him as they would have toward one of their own. They were letting him know that he was not as important as the gift made him think he was.

People in peaceful societies also avoid telling others what to do and carefully control their emotions in order to maintain goodwill. For example, the Inuit fear people who do not demonstrate their goodwill by smiling or laughing because someone who is unhappy may be hostile. The Inuit believe that strong thoughts can kill or cause illness, and they go to great pains to satisfy other people so resentment does not build up. Anthropologist Jean Briggs, who lived among a group of Inuit, describes them as people who emphasize kindness and concern and never, under any circumstances, demonstrate anger or resentment. So great is their fear of causing conflict that they make requests indirectly to avoid being refused or to avoid embarrassing someone by making them refuse a request. So great is the crime of losing one's temper that someone who does so may be ostracized from the group. Briggs herself was virtually ignored for months by her adopted family after she lost her temper with some Canadian sports fishermen who she thought were taking advantage of them.

Gregor says that villagers in the Xingu basin of the Amazon maintain harmony by purposely sanctioning village monopolies in the production of such certain goods as shell belts, stone axes, salt, cotton, fish spears, and ceramic pots. In this way, each village has something that other villages need. The villages therefore maintain good relations because to alienate another village might deprive one's own village members of a desired good. Moreover, trade is positively valued in itself. When villagers are asked why they do not make the goods they need themselves, they reply that this might anger those who do make them. Or they may claim that they do not have the knowledge to produce the items, although when they are temporarily cut off from a supply, they seem to learn how to make or acquire them very quickly. Gregor says it is unlikely that any village could not produce the goods desired because marriage between groups is common, and each village contains people with the skills of other villages.

Xinguanos place a strong negative value on aggression and things that symbolize aggression. Killing is wrong because it produces blood; even animal blood is considered defiling. Most game animals are considered inedible, and even fish must be well cooked so there is no blood. The Xinguanos also hold strong negative stereotypes of aggressive groups. They consider non–Xingu Indians to be "wild Indians" who are violent; they beat their children, rape their women, and shoot arrows at white people's planes. The wild Indian has almost the status of an animal and represents everything a Xinguano does not want to be. When Xingu villages have been the object of aggression by others, they have defended themselves, but successful warriors take no trophies and are given no special honor. In fact, they have to take special medicine to cleanse themselves of the defilement of the blood of their victims.

The Buid of the Philippines are also known for their nonviolence. For them, says anthropologist Thomas Gibson, violence is an expression of all that is disliked. For example, they have no word for courage, and one of their most prestigious activities is the creation of poetry. The Buid believe that the outside world is filled with threatening spirits that prey on people and that any intragroup hostility might weaken the group and expose them to these spirits.

Peaceful societies also minimize violence and conflict through ceremony. The Ju/wasi believe that everyone has what they term their "medicine," or power. In the same way that nearby Bantu tribes have witchcraft and sorcery and Europeans have pills and syringes, the Ju/wasi have *n/um*, a substance they say lies in the pit of the stomach. *N/um* has the capacity to keep people healthy and to help cure people who are sick. Most importantly, *n/um* can be transferred from someone who is acting as a healer to others through the medium of the trance dance—their most common ceremony. The idea of the dance is for a person to "heat up" his or her *n/um* by dancing; as the person dances, the *n/um* in the stomach is vaporized and travels up the spinal cord into the brain, which causes the dancer to go into a trance. The dancer then goes from person to person, laying on hands and transferring power to those who are touched, thereby enabling them to ward off sickness and death. Anyone can be a healer among the Ju/wasi; in a lifetime, each person is likely to serve as a healer at one time or another.

The trance dance has meanings that go beyond the power to heal, however. Some Ju/wasi are thought to have special powers that allow them to see the ghosts of dead ancestors who hover around the fires, the ability to see distant scenes, to see through things, and, in special cases, to change themselves into lions and stalk the veldt in search of human prey. Trance dances are most frequent when large numbers of people come together (from about once a month in small groups to four times a week in large camps) and during such certain occasions as the arrival of visitors to a camp, the presence of meat, or sickness. The congregation of large numbers of people, the presence of meat, and the arrival of new people are all occasions that in one way or another create the potential for interpersonal conflict. The fact that trance dances are more frequent during such times seems to indicate that they may serve to heal social conflict as well as individual maladies. By bringing people together in the ceremony, through the sharing of *n/um* and the ritual recognition of common threats, the trance dance unites people and serves to symbolize the relationship between group harmony and individual well-being.

In sum, peaceful societies create a bias against violence by sharing, valuing nonaggressive behavior, building relations of dependence between individuals and groups, and engaging in collective behaviors that promote harmony. They are not always successful; even among some so-called peaceful societies, there is violence. For example, Lee collected accounts of 22 homicides among Ju/wasi groups during a 35-year period from 1920 to 1955 but found little if any sanctioned group violence.

QUESTION 8.3   *What Are the Economic, Political, or Social Differences Between Peaceful and Violent Societies?*

Thomas Hobbes, a 17th-century philosopher, proposed that human beings in their natural state, without government or laws, are driven by greed and the quest for gain. Without some common power to keep them in awe, Hobbes said, they live in a state of war, with every person against every other person. Here is one of the more famous passages from *Leviathan*, in which Hobbes describes his vision of life before civilization:

> Whatsoever therefore is consequent to a time of warre, where every man is enemy to every man; the same is consequent to a time, wherein men live without other security, than what their own strength and their own invention shall furnish them withall. In such a condition there is no place for Industry; because the fruit thereof is uncertain; and consequently no Culture of the Earth [agriculture]; no navigation, nor use of the commodities that may be imported by sea; no commodious Building; no Instruments of moving, and removing such things as require much force; no Knowledge of the face of the Earth; no account of Time; no Arts; no Letters; no Society; and which is worst of all, continual feare, and danger of violent death; And the life of man, solitary, poore, nasty, brutish, and short. (Hobbes, 1651/1881, pp. 94–6)

Hobbes saw human beings as having a natural inclination to be violent—an inclination that can be controlled only by some form of centralized authority. However, as anthropologists have discovered, societies with little formal government, such as the Ju/wasi, Inuit, Buid, and Semai, are among the most peaceful in the world (see Question 8.2). These peaceful societies are small in scale and make their living primarily by hunting and gathering or by slash-and-burn agriculture. Most are relatively isolated and lack formal mechanisms for resolving conflict once it begins. There are no courts, no police, no jails, and no formally sanctioned threats of violence, even against wrongdoers. Because there is little that people in these societies can do once violence begins, they go to great lengths to avoid it.

However, had Hobbes known the Yanomamö, he might have found that his vision of a stateless society—"where every man is enemy to every man"— had been verified. Their social and economic life closely resembles that of the Semai, and they live in virtually the same environment and are neighbors of the peaceful Xinguano. But the Yanomamö society creates attitudes favoring collective violence in order to protect its women and children (see Question 8.1), which suggests that Hobbes may have been correct—at least in part. In this case, the lack of any centralized control or formal mechanisms for putting an end to conflict results in unrestrained violence rather than the avoidance of conflict.

The Need to Protect Resources and Honor

In societies without any form of centralized control and a bias favoring collective violence, such as those of the Yanomamö and the Kohistani (whose code of honor demands vengeance for any threat), individuals must protect their own resources through force. For example, because the Yanomamö do not effectively control intravillage conflict, men of their own as well as other villages are constantly seeking to seduce others' wives. Consequently, the men—individually or in groups—must build a reputation for fierceness in order to protect themselves and their families. Thus, failure to control conflict, along with the need for men to build a reputation for aggressiveness to protect their resources, combine to produce a society that places a positive value on violent behavior.

The conditions that give rise to violent conflict among the Yanomamö are not unlike those that promote violence among street gangs in the United States. When Lincoln Keiser worked in the 1960s with the Vice Lords, a Chicago street gang (or club, as they preferred to call themselves), he concluded that boys joined gangs because alone they could not protect themselves from shakedowns or safeguard their interests in girls. Whereas the Yanomamö encouraged *waiteri*—fierceness—the Vice Lords valued "heart"—a willingness to follow any suggestion regardless of personal risk. Whereas a Yanomamö demonstrated fierceness in chest-pounding duels, ax fights, and raids against enemy villages, members of street gangs in Chicago confirmed heart in gang fights, or "gangbangs." Street gangs even formed alliances with each other against other gangs, as do Yanomamö villages with each other. The similarities in the dynamics and values of violent conflict among the Yanomamö and among street gangs in the United States illustrate how under certain conditions, individuals form groups to protect themselves against other groups. To discourage attacks from others in the absence of protection from other agencies, these groups cultivate a reputation for violence.

The gang violence that Keiser observed in Chicago during the late 1960s has escalated since, and weapons more typical of Thull are now being used. Alex Kotlowitz, in *There Are No Children Here*, reports how the Vice Lords—one of three gang factions in Chicago in the early 1990s—were making use of an arsenal that included Uzis and grenades. The purpose was the same, although the stakes were higher. Drugs have become the major source of contention among Chicago gangs (the head of one Vice Lord faction grossed some $50,000 to $100,000 a week). When drug wars erupt over territory, the violence reflects the increased stakes and more massive firepower. Some years ago, four members of the Vice Lords came upon a rival gang member in the lobby of a housing project and shot him five times with an Uzi, two sawed-off shotguns, and a .25-caliber automatic handgun to establish their dominance in the neighborhood.

The social and political conditions that characterize the societies of the Vice Lords and the Yanomamö are such that in each of them, individuals must mobilize and use force to protect or acquire desired resources. In neither case is there any effective centralized authority to guarantee the safety of resources or stop violence once it begins. There is a centralized force in Chicago—the police—but they rarely intervene in gang violence because they are unwilling or do not have the resources to do so or because local residents are afraid or reluctant to report violence.

The idea that violence may erupt because of a lack of centralized control to protect valued resources is also evident among the Kohistani in Thull. Good land is scarce, and ownership of land is often questioned because there is no central system of land recording or registration. Land is usually acquired by inheritance, but there is little to stop anyone from saying that some relative was wrongfully denied ownership of a particular piece of land in the past and claiming the land on that basis. Whether such a claim is won or lost may depend on which of the claimants has the greater influence or firepower. Even Keiser was suspected of potential land grabbing while he was conducting fieldwork. He was accused of burying papers in the woods that he would later dig up and claim were old documents giving him title to the land. Because he must have had political connections, he would win. In other words, in Thull too, an ideology that encourages collective violence may be attributable to a need to protect resources in the absence of any effective centralized authority.

Creating the Conditions for Violence

Napoleon Chagnon characterized Yanomamö warfare as a "truly primitive cultural adaptation before it was altered or destroyed by our culture." It was, he said, the normal state of affairs before it was suppressed by colonial governments. However, there is considerable evidence that Yanomamö warfare and aggression were less a product of their "primitive" existence or nature than a consequence of Western contact.

Brian Ferguson maintains that the period of Chagnon's fieldwork (1964–1972), on which he based his best-selling ethnography *The Fierce People*, was one of the most turbulent periods in Yanomamö history. Violence and aggression, says Ferguson, were a product of three major changes: (1) the presence of new outpost settlements of government agents, missionaries, and researchers; (2) competition for Western manufactured goods, particularly steel cutting tools; and (3) a breakdown of social relations brought about by epidemics and depletion of game and other food resources.

The Yanomamö, Ferguson points out, had been in contact with outsiders for centuries. Europeans raided the Yanomamö for slaves from the mid-17th century until around 1850. In the late 19th century, the rubber boom in the Amazon—a horrendous period for indigenous groups who were forced into collecting rubber under the threat of torture and death—brought the Yanomamö into increased contact and conflict with other indigenous groups. After the Amazonian rubber boom collapsed in the 1920s as a result of competition from Asian rubber plantations, the area in which the Yanomamö lived was relatively peaceful until the 1950s and 1960s, when influenza and measles epidemics swept the area, leaving only one-quarter of the children with both parents. But even more disruptive was the presence of new Western outposts.

The new outposts made available manufactured items (such as steel knives, machetes, aluminum pots, and shotguns) desired by the Yanomamö. For example, steel-cutting tools were 10 times more efficient than the stone cutting tools used by the Yanomamö. Shotguns were effective both for hunting and raiding. The Yanomamö could obtain these items in various ways. They could relocate their villages near the outposts, they could send trading parties on long voyages to get them, or they could raid other groups for them. The greatest advantage went to what Ferguson called "anchor villages"—those that relocated near outposts. The result was a hierarchy of settlements, ranging from anchor villages whose members were able to monopolize the new desired goods to more isolated settlements whose members had fewer and lower-quality goods.

Yanomamö in anchor settlements traded Western items to distant groups for local such handicrafts as cotton hammocks, spear points, or manioc flour. But trading parties were also targets of raids by groups desiring Western goods. To protect themselves and their monopoly on Western trade goods and to discourage raiding, Yanomamö groups found it advantageous to cultivate reputations for violence and aggression. A reputation for fierceness was also an advantage in negotiating for desired goods. Thus, one man told of the number of people he had killed on raids just before demanding a machete.

In addition to access to desired goods, proximity to Western outposts incited violence in other ways. For example, once people relocated their village near an outpost settlement, they were reluctant to move. One way that small-scale, mobile societies such as the Yanomamö avoid conflict is by moving villages away from enemies when conflict is threatened. But because moving would mean giving up access to and a monopoly on Western goods, members of anchor villages were reluctant to move and hence needed to protect themselves and the goods that they obtained from Westerners. In addition, more permanent settlements quickly depleted game resources—resources that had been used in reciprocal exchanges with other people and groups. Thus, sharing patterns, which we noted in Question 8.2, are crucial for maintaining peaceful relations, began to break down, leading to more conflict.

Thus, deaths from disease and war disrupted traditional social relations, the depletion of game weakened traditional patterns of sharing and cooperation, and access to Western technology provided new sources of conflict. Furthermore, the new technology introduced a new way of ordering society and enhanced the ability of people in anchor villages to make war.

In addition to creating situations that promoted violence and aggression, access to Western goods also helps explain the aggressive attitudes of Yanomamö men to women. Traditionally, the Yanomamö practiced brideservice: A groom was obligated to work for his bride's family for one to four years. But families of grooms in anchor villages were able to substitute Western goods for brideservice, and one result was a movement of wives to villages with greater access to Western goods. Combined with the Yanomamö practice of female infanticide and polygamy, this resulted in a shortage of and greater competition for females and more frequent raiding of other villages for women. In addition, Yanomamö wives go to live in their husband's family village, particularly where Western goods take the place of brideservice. The result is that women are removed from the protective influence of their families and are more likely to be victims of abuse.

In sum, many of the patterns of Yanomamö warfare, violence, and aggression cannot be understood without knowledge of their history of contact with Western society and the contact conditions that increased the likelihood of violence and war. Even the power of chiefs, whose feast giving played such an important role in Chagnon's descriptions of alliance formation and aggression, was largely a function of Western contact. Following traditional customs, outsiders brought gifts to local leaders. But the gifts that outsiders brought were far more valuable. For example, Chagnon gave one chief a gift of 25 machetes, providing him with items that he could use to enhance his power. Ferguson summarizes:

> If villages were not anchored to outposts but were able to move freely, if long-established marital alliances were not disturbed by massive mortality, if communal sharing of meat were still the norm, and, above all, if necessary technology were widely and equally available, my theoretical expectation is that there would be little collective violence among the Yanomami. (1992, p. 225)

Sexism and Violent Conflict

Another difference between peaceful and violent societies that has been suggested has to do with gender roles. Among the Ju/wasi, Buid, Xinguano, and Semai, men and women are relatively equal, and there is little institutionalized violence against women. In contrast, the Yanomamö and Kohistani (and the Vice Lords) are characterized by male dominance, and they all sanction violence against women. Several reasons have been advanced to support the link between sexist values and violent conflict. A number of things are suggestive about this connection. First, it is men that make war, although women may fill certain positions in the armed forces. Although there have been societies where women engage in armed combat, such instances are the exception rather than the rule. Even in a war of liberation, such as during the Sandinista rebellion in Nicaragua in the 1980s, where women took an active role in combat, they were banned from active combat once the Sandinistas gained power. Second, there is a strong cross-cultural link between patriarchy and violent conflict. After examining information on more than 1,000 societies, William Tulio Divale and Marvin Harris concluded that the intensity of collective violence is significantly higher in societies characterized by a strong male bias—patrilocal residence, patrilineal descent, polygyny, postmarital sex restrictions on females, male secret societies, and men's houses. Finally, there is evidence that societies characterized by sexual violence against women tend to be more warlike and prone to collective violence. Peggy Sanday's study of 95 societies in which there was evidence of frequency of rape supports this conclusion. The question is, "Does a sexist ideology promote violent conflict or does the incident of violent conflict promote sexism?"

Those who claim that sexism promotes violent conflict make that connection in various ways. Betty Reardon and Leslie Cagan suggest that societies that relegate women to an inferior position explicitly or implicitly sanction violence against women. Moreover, violence toward women serves as what they call a "primal" paradigm for violent warfare against other peoples. That is, once violence is allowed as a means of domination of one group, such as women, it can serve as a model for dominance and violence against other groups.

For Sanday as well as many others, sexism and violent conflict have their roots in competition over scarce resources. She says women are generally associated with fertility and growth, whereas men are associated with aggression and destruction. During periods in which resources are not scarce, males and females are valued equally. When there is an imbalance between food supply or distribution and needs or when groups are competing for resources, males become of greater value, females become objects to be controlled, and sexual violence becomes one way that men demonstrate their dominance. For example, among cattle-herding people in East Africa, raiding for cattle was common and sometimes led to violent conflict between groups. Violence was defined as a manly activity, leading East African societies to place great emphasis on masculinity and manliness. However, manliness was tested not only in battle but also in male-female relations because sex was a way of demonstrating strength. For example, among the Acoli, a boy could demonstrate his strength against girls. Girls would frequently visit their boyfriends in their huts, but it took a strong boy to get a girl to lie on the bed and yield. A weak one had to *keng ki nqwece*, or "be content with the smell."

In sum, factors such as a lack of centralized control, competition over scarce resources, private property, and sexism may lead societies to construct an ideological bias toward violence. Examining the effects of violent conflict to see if some of them could be beneficial may provide further insights into the factors that promote violent conflict.

QUESTION 8.4   *What Are the Effects of War on Societies?*

Are there any beneficial effects of violent conflict? For example, biologists studying animal populations suggest that predators help the species they prey on by limiting population growth and eliminating the weak from the breeding population. Some anthropologists suggest that war may play a similar function for the human species by limiting populations or by influencing the biological composition of the human species through the process of natural selection.

The Impact of War on Population

In a fascinating book entitled *The Statistics of Deadly Quarrels*, mathematician Lewis F. Richardson statistically examined the causes and effects of violent conflict between the years 1821 and 1945. During that period, there were 282 wars that had battle fatalities of from 300 to 20 million people. If Richardson's estimate of the number of murders committed during that period and the number of deaths from disease caused or spread because of war are included, deaths from deadly quarrels would account for about 10% of all deaths that occurred between 1821 and 1945.

However, anthropologist Frank Livingstone has concluded that in spite of the enormous number of deaths inflicted by modern war, it seems to have had little appreciable effect on population growth. About 51 million people died as a result of World War II, including 9% of the Russian population and 5% of the German population. But this had almost no effect on their rates of population growth because these two populations had recovered within a decade to the level at which they would have been had there been no war. In the United States, the effect of World War II on population was almost negligible; only about 0.2% was lost.

Violent conflict in small-scale societies may have had a much greater impact on their population, as Livingstone points out. Among the Murngin of Australia, about 28% of male deaths were due to war; among the Enga and the Dani of New Guinea, about 25% of all male deaths came from violent conflict. Chagnon estimates a death rate due to fighting of 20 to 25% among the Yanomamö. Among the Blackfoot Indians of the American plains, there was a 50% deficit for males in the male/female ratio in 1805 and a 33% deficit in 1858, when horse raiding was still common. But during the reservation period, after horse raiding was banned, the sex ratio approached 50/50. However, Livingstone notes that it is hard to see where any of this has affected the biology of the species. The killing seems to have been more or less random. Moreover, because males are the most frequent victims and because the incidence of polygyny (marriage to multiple wives) increases in societies that suffer losses, the number of children born should remain more or less constant.

Divale and Harris address the problems posed by Livingstone by proposing that violent conflict does indeed regulate population growth; it does so not by killing grown men but by encouraging the killing of infant girls. The incidence of violent conflict, they reason, is strongly associated with a strong preference for male children, along with female infanticide or the benign neglect of female infants. This is evidenced in either direct reports of female infanticide or the skewed sex ratios of children under the age of 14 in societies characterized by violent conflict. Violent societies average 128 boys to 100 girls under 14—far higher than the normal ratio of 105 boys to 100 girls.

If war or violent conflict is frequent in a society, Divale and Harris reason, the society or group that raises the largest number of fierce, aggressive warriors will be at an advantage. Consequently, the existence of violent conflict encourages a strong preference for rearing male children, supports the ideological restrictions on the rearing of female children, and, in general, creates an ideology of male supremacy. Moreover, restricting the number of childbearing females in a population is a far more effective means of population control that killing adult males. Thus, they conclude, war and violent conflict do encourage sexism but only because they serve to promote selective population control.

The Evolution of the Nation-State

Anthropologists also suggest that violent conflict may encourage certain forms of political organization. For example, Robert Carneiro argues that in the course of human history, violent conflict has been the primary agent that has transformed human societies from small-scale, autonomous communities into vast, complex nation-states. Carneiro reasons that war has served to promote the consolidation of isolated, politically autonomous villages into chiefdoms of united villages and into states. At first, war pits village against village, resulting in chiefdoms; then it pits chiefdom against chiefdom, resulting in states; and then it pits state against state. War, he says, began as the effort to oust a rival from a territory but soon evolved into an effort to subjugate and control an enemy. As the process continued, warfare became the mechanism by which the number of political units in the world began to decline. Carneiro predicts that if the number of political states continues to decline as it has in the past, by the year 2300, there should be only a single world state.

The rise of the Zulu state in Africa illustrates Carneiro's theory of how a group of largely separate political units is transformed into larger forms of state organization through violent conflict. The Zulu state took form in southeast Africa in the early 19th century. Prior to that time, the region was inhabited by small, sometimes warring groups. About 100,000 people lived in an area of about 80,000 square miles, practicing agriculture and cattle herding. While there were separate entities labeled tribes by Westerners, the largest political unit was the clan. Warriors from these clans raided each other for cattle, but there was no conquest of land.

Warfare increased between 1775 and 1800 as the population of southeast Africa increased. The strongest groups were those that could muster the most warriors and organize and discipline them effectively. The process of state formation, whereby these separate groups combined into a larger political unit, was begun by a leader of the Mtetwa tribe named Dingiswayo. He developed new ways to organize his troops and began to take control of the land of those he defeated. When he conquered an area, he would appoint a person from the head family of the group he conquered to rule for him. Using new techniques of war and political control, he achieved dominance over a wide area. His reason for extending his control, according to one 19th-century writer, was to make peace among warring groups; Dingiswayo, it was said, "wished to do away with the incessant quarrels that occurred amongst the tribes, because no supreme head was over them to say who was right or who was wrong" (Service, 1975, pp. 108–9).

By the early 1800s, Dingiswayo had conquered and united some 30 different groups. He was aided by a young officer named Shaka Zulu, the son of the chief of the Zulu clan. When the Zulu chief died, Dingiswayo installed Shaka as the head of the clan, and when Dingiswayo was killed by a rival, Shaka took over the army and established his Zulus as the dominant clan. By 1822, Shaka had defeated every rival and was master of all the present South African province of Kwa-Zulu Natal.

Violence and Male Solidarity

In addition to controlling population and uniting tribal societies into large-scale states, violent conflict may also be valued as a means of promoting group solidarity. For example, male solidarity seems to be enhanced by collective violence. Societies in which there is frequent violence often have more men's clubs, men's sports teams, or special men's houses. Some people assume that male solidarity and the resulting domination of women lead to increased collective violence, whereas others assume that increased male solidarity is itself the result of conflict. Anthropologist Ralph L. Holloway suggests that the psychological attributes that allow human beings to create sentimental bonds between members of a group are the same attributes that, when turned outward, promote violent conflict against nongroup members. That is, collective violence is simply the other side of group togetherness.

There is evidence to support the idea that societies that engage in war place a greater emphasis on male solidarity. There are all-male clubs or organizations among the Plains Indians and men's houses among tribes in New Guinea. In Frederic Thrasher's classic study of boys' gangs in Chicago in 1927, he concluded that fighting, encountering other gangs, outwitting enemies, raiding, robbing, defending the hangout, and attacking enemies were the types of activities that produced male solidarity. In fact, the gang does not solidify as a group unless there is conflict.

Exercise 8.4 ➤

There is some suggestion of a link between militarism and competitive sports; that is, societies that are prone to collective violence are more likely to value games in which men aggressively compete against other men. How does this apply to American society? Which sports in America most closely resemble or promote the values of militarism and war? Does the language of these sports reflect militaristic values? Do gender roles reflect these values?

QUESTION 8.5   *How Is It Possible to Justify the Creation of Weapons of Mass Destruction?*

Because the ability to mask the consequences of violent conflict may be one of the reasons for its frequency, it is useful to examine how people manage to mask for themselves the consequences of planning what now would be the ultimate form of violence—the unleashing of nuclear weapons.

When people participate in a social setting, they begin to adopt the culture—the system of meanings, the language, the physical environment, the institutional rules, the rituals, and the character of social interactions—of that setting. In other words, the social setting produces in each participant a characteristic view of the world. For example, Mary Douglas and Aaron B. Wildavsky note that the strength of the boundaries members of a group construct between themselves and others—combined with the degree that each member's role in the group is proscribed—determines which dangers members of a group fear most. That is, people's social setting will determine what they feel most at risk from—whether economic collapse, disease, moral decay, foreign invasion, or environmental devastation.

The Anthropology of a Nuclear Weapons Laboratory

Anthropologist Hugh Gusterson, who had been an antinuclear activist, wanted to know how nuclear weapons scientists could justify conducting research on and testing weapons of mass destruction. That is, what could create a view of the world that would enable people to justify to themselves performing that kind of work? What would they have to fear to justify creating the means to destroy everyone? To answer that question, he set out to study the culture of a nuclear weapons laboratory: the Lawrence Livermore National Laboratory in Livermore, California.

Gusterson suggests that "nuclear realists" who justify the manufacture and use of nuclear weapons and who question the wisdom of nuclear disarmament make four assumptions about the world. First, unlike national systems where a monopoly on the use of force guarantees stability, they claim that anarchy characterizes international relations; they see the international system existing in a state of nature. Second, they assume that states must rely on self-help to protect themselves because no one else is going to help them. Third, nuclear realists assume that nuclear weapons are the ultimate form of self-help because they vastly increase the cost of aggression against them. And fourth, they assume that relatively little can be done in the short term to change the anarchistic nature of the international system.

Critics of nuclear weapons and those who argue for nuclear disarmament make very different assumptions. They argue that international relations are not as anarchistic as they are made out; they claim that there are rules and norms that control aggression—many of them centering on the institution of trade. Marxists argue

How is it possible to justify the manufacture of weapons capable of destroying everyone on earth? For those who work in a nuclear weapons laboratory, the manufacture of such weapons is both justified and necessary. For others, such as these nuclear weapons protesters, it is madness.

that proponents of nuclear weapons overlook the power of the military-industrial complex and the international class system, whereas feminists argue that the pronuclear prospective is dominated by male notions of power. Many critics see the nuclear arms race as "objective social madness." People who work in the area, they assume, must be in denial and must demonize the other to justify their work. Gusterson wanted to find out not so much who was "right" but rather how people came to hold such divergent opinions and, particularly, how nuclear weapons scientists came to their views.

When he began his research at the laboratory, Gusterson was surprised to find the variety of political and religious viewpoints of people working at Livermore. Although white males did dominate, political views ran the gamut from social and political conservatives to active environmentalists, civil rights supporters, and women's rights advocates. Two-thirds of the workers were active churchgoers. How, he asked, could such a diverse population all agree on the value of nuclear weapons development—an agreement so profound that "they often asked me in puzzlement to explain why antinuclear activists were so afraid of nuclear weapons"?

Nuclear weapons scientists did not, says Gusterson, avoid the ethical concerns of nuclear weapons research. However, most accept the central axiom that nuclear research is necessary to make the world safe by developing a deterrent to the use of nuclear force. To some, working on nuclear weapons is more ethical than working on conventional weapons because conventional weapons are more likely to be used. Nuclear weapons, the scientists assume, are simply symbolic chips in a game whose goal is to avoid using them. When asked if he would ever foresee a circumstance in which nuclear weapons would be used, one scientist said, "No, even if we were under attack." The only reason you have nuclear weapons is for deterrence; once you are being attacked, the whole thing has failed. Others rationalize it more baldly by saying they are not responsible for how what they design is used. "Are automobile designers," they ask, "responsible for deaths caused by drunk drivers?"

The construction of a nuclear weapons scientist, says Gusterson, begins with the recruitment process. For scientists leaving the university, particularly in physics, there are few places to go aside from government-funded weapons research. Two-thirds of U.S. government research funding goes to military research (compared to 12.5% in Germany and 4.5% in Japan). Livermore and Los Alamos—the other major government-run nuclear weapons laboratory—together employ 6% of all physicists in the country.

When Gusterson asked people why they chose to work at Livermore, most cited the intellectual freedom they enjoyed working in a weapons laboratory. Almost all compared Livermore favorably to working in universities (which they characterized as "stodgy," "cutthroat," or "high-pressure") or in private organizations. One compared university work with being in the military! Some also cited the challenge of weapons research and the opportunity to work with state-of-the-art equipment. Livermore also paid about twice as much as a university position, although a little less than what most could have earned in industry.

Once a person was hired, secrecy played a major role in forging a person's identity as a nuclear weapons scientist. Livermore employees are investigated before being given security clearance to gain access to laboratory facilities. Personnel are divided into different security categories and given colored badges to denote their level of clearance. Q clearance (a green badge) is necessary for classified research; L clearance (yellow badge) allows access to classified areas but not to classified information. The labs themselves are divided into areas of lesser (e.g., cafeterias = white area) and greater security (classified research = green area; research on foreign capabilities = blue area). As Gusterson puts it, the laboratory is "an enormous grid of tabooed spaces and tabooed topics."

Without a green badge, says Gusterson, a weapons scientist is not considered a full adult in the lab. But the process involved in getting Q clearance is elaborate and may take from six months to two years. Virtually every aspect of a person's life is subject to investigation in search of clues that might make the person unfit to handle classified material. But most people pass, and because secrecy is not that well guarded in practice, it suggests that the security clearance process functions more as a rite of passage to add mystique to the process of weapons research and to discipline the initiate.

Secrecy, says Gusterson, is one of the main ways that the diverse population of the lab is brought together. Knowing secrets, regardless of how mundane they might be, serves to mark a person as a member of a special group and lends an air of dramatic importance to one's work. Secrecy also serves to limit discussion that could change a people's view of the work that they do. As Gusterson (1995, p. 68) puts it,

> [T]he laboratory's culture of secrecy does tend to produce certain effects in its scientists: it segregates laboratory scientists as a privileged but somewhat isolated elite; it inculcates a sense of group loyalty; and it thrusts on laboratory scientists an amorphous surveillance, which can become internalized.

The process of testing nuclear weapons, says Gusterson, is in many ways the critical step in creating the nuclear scientist. Any Livermore scientist can propose a weapons test, but reviewers (senior scientists at the laboratory) select only about one out of 20 ideas for testing. Approval of an idea for testing further reaffirms the scientist's membership in the group. Nuclear tests, says Gusterson, have elements of myth and ritual. Rarely in narratives that he collected on testing did anyone note the importance of testing nuclear reliability. Instead, people spoke of the fulfillment of personal ambition, the struggle to master a new technology, the drama of creating something new, and the experience of community that each test created.

Thus, testing, says Gusterson, produces not only weapons, but it also produces weapons' designers. It is a way of producing the elite—those with special knowledge and power. The more tests one participates in, the greater the prestige and power that accrues. A successful test validates status and credentials and brings forth congratulatory support and reinforcement. The test provides what Gusterson calls a symbolic simulation of the reliability of the whole system of deterrence:

> Each time a nuclear test is successfully carried off, the scientists' faith in human control over nuclear technology is further reinforced. Seen in this light, the "reliability" the tests demonstrate has an expandable meaning, extending out from the reliability of the particular device being tested to the entire regime of nuclear deterrence. (1995, p. 161)

The Language of Nuclear Destruction

Carol Cohn spent one year studying the culture of a strategic studies institute, or "think tank," for government defense analysts who plan nuclear strategy. Like Gusterson, she began her study with the questions "How are people

This sketch of the effects of the U.S. bombing of Hiroshima was drawn by eyewitness Sawami Katagiri, who recalled, "I was walking among many dead people. . . . It was like hell. . . . This picture shows only a part of Hiroshima. The whole city was just like this at that time." Sawami Katagiri, from *The Unforgettable Fire*, NHK Publishing (Japan Broadcasting Corp.), 1981.

Sawami Katagiri, from *The Unforgettable Fire*, NHK Publishing (Japan Broadcast Publishing Co., Ltd.). Courtesy Hiroshima Peace Memorial Museum, Hiroshima, Japan.

whose job it is to plan nuclear destruction able to do it? How can they think that way?" One of her conclusions is that language is used to distance the planners from the consequences of the actions they are planning. The language they use obfuscates and reassembles reality in such a way that what is really being talked about—the fundamental business of war, which is destroying human creations and injuring and killing human beings—is somehow hidden from view behind metaphors and euphemisms.

During her first weeks at the center, as she listened to the participants (all men) talking matter-of-factly about nuclear destruction, she heard language that she labeled *technostrategic*. This language includes such expressions as *clean bombs* (fusion bombs that release more energy than fission bombs—not as radiation but as explosive power); *penetration aids* (technology that helps missiles get through enemy defenses); *collateral damage* (human deaths); and *surgical strikes* (bombing that takes out only weapons or command centers). Domestic metaphors are common in the technostrategic language: Missiles are based in *silos*; piles of nuclear weapons in a nuclear submarine are *Christmas tree farms*; bombs and missiles are *re-entry vehicles* or *RVs*; massive bombing becomes *carpet bombing*. Cohn says that the domestic images must be more than simply a way to distance speakers from the grisly reality they are discussing. Calling the pattern in which a bomb falls a *footprint* seems to remove the speakers from any position of accountability for the acts they are contemplating.

Cohn's experience was similar to that of anthropologists who find themselves immersed in the reality of another culture. For example, she discovered that the language and metaphors of those working at the institute seemed incapable of expressing certain realities. The aftermath of a nuclear attack is described in the language of technostrategic as "a situation bound to include EMP blackout, brute force damage to systems, a heavy jamming environment, and so on" (Cohn, 1987, p. 707). Cohn contrasts this with a description of the aftermath from the perspective of Hisako Matsubara, a survivor of the nuclear bombing of Hiroshima, in *Cranes at Dusk:*

> Everything was black, had vanished into the black dust, was destroyed. Only the flames that were beginning to lick their way up had any color. From the dust that was like fog, figures began to loom up, black, hairless, faceless. They screamed with voices that were no longer human. Their screams drowned out the groans rising everywhere from the rubble, groans that seemed to rise from the very earth itself. (Cohn, 1987, p. 708)

There is, says Cohn, no way of describing this experience with the language of technostrategic. This speaker is a victim; the speaker in the first instance is preparing for the deployment of nuclear weapons. One of the consequences of technostrategic is that it removes the speakers from having to think about themselves as victims of nuclear war. This does not mean that defense analysts convince themselves that they would not be victims, but the language removes them from the viewpoint of a victim and provides them with that of the planner—the initiator of nuclear war.

Cohn also discovered that she could not use ordinary language to speak to the defense analysts. If she tried, they acted as if she were ignorant or simple minded. To communicate at all, she had to use such terms as *subholocaust engagement* and *pre-emptive strikes*. The word *peace* was not a legitimate part of the vocabulary; to use it was to brand oneself as a softheaded activist. The closest she could come to *peace* in the language of technostrategic was *strategic stability*.

Cohn encountered descriptions of nuclear situations that made little sense until she realized that different realities were being discussed. For example, the following passage describes a nuclear exchange in a situation in which missiles with more than one warhead are mutually banned:

> The strategic stability of regime A (a scenario) is based on the fact that both sides are deprived of any incentive ever to strike first. Since it takes roughly two warheads to destroy the enemy silo, an attacker must expend two of his missiles to destroy one of the enemy's. A first strike disarms the attacker. The aggressor ends up worse off than the aggressed. (Cohn, 1987, p. 710)

By what type of reasoning, asks Cohn, can a country that has dropped a thousand nuclear bombs 10 to 100 times more powerful than the one dropped on Hiroshima end up "worse off" than the country it dropped the bombs on? This would be possible only if winning depends on who has the greatest number of weapons left. In other words, nuclear war would be a kind of game in which the object is to have more weapons at the end than the enemy has.

To an anthropologist, the fact that people are limited by their culture, their language, and their viewpoint is, of course, no surprise. All cultures give a characteristic meaning to violent conflict—whether it be viewed as the act of an animal in possession of a human body (like the tiger spirit of the Carib), the will of God, or a kind of game to determine winners and losers. The more serious implication of Cohn's observations is that the roles of nuclear planners as scientists and academics lend weight to their claim that their perspective is "objective" and therefore has greater truth value than other perspectives. Moreover, says Cohn, if one can speak to defense analysts only in the language of technostrategic and if the language is constructed in such a way as to be incapable of expressing different realities, then there is no way for these analysts to appreciate or understand the other realities involved in the use of nuclear weapons.

Each Christmas outside a now closed Air Force base in northern New York State, Santa is shown mounted on a bomber. Displays such as this mask the violence for which the bomber was constructed, gain acceptance for military action, and make clear whose side Santa is on.

© Richard Robbins

CASE STUDY IN DOING ANTHROPOLOGY #8:
THE USES (AND MISUSES?) OF ANTHROPOLOGY
FOR PEACE AND WAR

We have examined the value of anthropological perspective in business, in cultural development, for public policy deliberations, for political consulting, for disease prevention, for adolescent counseling, and for the protection of human rights. The perspective is also valuable when it comes to conflict and conflict resolution. For example, anthropologists are prominent in the area of peace studies. Peace studies focus on factors that promote peace and the peaceful resolution of conflict and address a range of issues, including inter- and intragroup conflict, the dehumanizing effects of prejudice and discrimination, rape, and even schoolyard bullying. The need for peace education is even built specifically into the United Nations' Declaration of Human Rights, the Convention on the Discrimination Against Women, the Convention on the Rights of the Child (CRC), the World Declaration on Education for All, and many other international compacts.[1]

Anthropologist Leslie Sponsel, who teaches a course on war and aggression[2] and is affiliated with the Spark M. Matsunaga Institute for Peace at the University of Hawaii, notes that most participants in peace studies place an emphasis on nonviolence, peace, life, creativity, and cooperation, as opposed to violence, death, destruction, and competition. Most peace-education practitioners also feel that the current level of global military expenditures is excessive and is destructive to the quality of life. The United States spends by far the most on military weapons, accounting for almost half of all arms expenditures in the world (see Table 8.2). The United States is also the largest supplier of weapons to the rest of the world and has by far the most far-ranging global military presence, with some 725 military bases distributed among 132 countries.

Some suggest that anthropologists can play a prominent role in helping bring peace to Iraq and Afghanistan. Unlike so-called conventional wars, those conflicts involve local insurgencies. In the so-called "war on terror," there are no state enemies with whom to fight—only local groups with specific local or sometimes global grievances. In 2004, retired Major General Robert H. Scales Jr. wrote an article questioning whether technical superiority could defeat insurgents in Iraq or Afghanistan, suggesting instead that these new conflicts require "an exceptional ability to understand people, their culture, and their motivation." The "war on terror," said one retired general, is a "social scientist's war," in which culture itself will become a critical weapon. It was this thinking that led to the development of the Human Terrain System program.

---

[1] See http://www.un.org/cyberschoolbus/peace/frame2.htm.
[2] His course syllabus is available at http://www.soc.hawaii.edu/sponsel/Courses/345.html/Syllabi/Syllalbus06.html.

TABLE 8.2 **MILITARY SPENDING, PERCENT OF WORLD SHARE, SPENDING PER CAPITA, SHARE OF GDP AND CHANGE FROM 1999–2008 OF 15 COUNTRIES WITH THE HIGHEST MILITARY SPENDING**

Country Rank	Country	Spending (billions $)	World Share (%)	Spending per Capita ($)	Share of GDP 2007 (%)[a]	Change from 1999–2008 (%)
1	USA	607	41.5	1967	4.0	66.5
2	China	[84.9]	[5.8]	[63]	[2.0]	194
3	France	65.7	4.5	1061	2.3	3.5
4	UK	65.3	4.5	1070	2.4	20.7
5	Russia	[58.6]	[4.0]	[413]	[3.5]	173
6	Germany	46.8	3.2	568	1.3	−11.0
7	Japan	46.3	3.2	361	0.9	−1.7
8	Italy	40.6	2.8	689	1.8	0.4
9	Saudi Arabia[b]	38.2	2.6	1511	9.3	81.5
10	India	30.0	2.1	25	2.5	44.1
11	South Korea	24.2	1.7	501	2.7	51.5
12	Brazil	23.3	1.6	120	1.5	29.9
13	Canada	19.3	1.3	581	1.2	37.4
14	Spain	19.2	1.3	430	1.2	37.7
15	Australia	18.4	1.3	876	1.9	38.6
	World	1.464	100	217	2.4	44.7

[ ] = estimated figure; GDP = gross domestic product
[a]The figures for national military expenditure as a share of GDP are for 2007, the most recent year for which GDP data is available.
[b]The figures for Saudi Arabia include expenditure for public order and safety and might be slight overestimates.
Data Source: Military expenditure: *SIPRI Yearbook 2008: Armaments, Disarmament and International Security* (Oxford: Oxford University Press, 2008), Appendix 5A.

The Human Terrain Concept and the Human Terrain Systems (HTS)

In 2001, Montgomery McFate contemplated what to do with her life. She was an Army wife with a Harvard Law degree and a Ph.D. in anthropology from Yale. Her academic interest was in warfare—particularly insurgencies—but, she said, that was not an area that anthropology was interested in at the time. Building on the growing sentiment in the military that "shock and awe" military tactics could not work to defeat an insurgency, McFate (2005a) published an article in the *Military Review* applying her background in anthropology and arguing that there is a "culture gap" that inhibits our understanding of the conflict in Iraq—a gap, she says, whose cause is "the almost total absence of anthropology within the national-security establishment."

In her article, McFate traces the history of the use of anthropology by governments in military and colonial situations and argued that successful counterinsurgency requires a total understanding of local culture, including its history, tribal/family/social structure, values, religions, customs, and needs. To defeat the insurgency in Iraq, she said, the U.S. military must exploit the tribal structure of the country and understand the traditional authority structure and the divisions and competing interests of different groups, such as the Shia, Sunni, and Kurds. In a second article in *Military Review* (2005b) written with Andrea Jackson, McFate outlined a proposal to establish in the military an Office for Operational Cultural Knowledge that would train teams to provide battlefield commanders with knowledge of local society and culture—or, as it was being called, the "human terrain," as opposed to the "geographic terrain."

The new emphasis on cultural knowledge was consistent with a re-evaluation of military strategy and policy on counterinsurgency contained in a new Army field manual—*Field Manual (FM) 3-24*—published in December 2006. The manual was an expression of the military philosophy on counterinsurgency of General David Petraeus and General James N. Mattis and emphasized the importance of cultural knowledge in fighting insurgents. Petraeus, who has a Ph.D. in international relations from Princeton, described the use of cultural knowledge in this way:

> Knowledge of the cultural terrain can be as important as, and sometimes even more important than, the knowledge of the geographical terrain. This observation acknowledges that the people are, in many respects, the decisive terrain, and that we must study that terrain in the same way that we have always studied the geographical terrain.

When *FM 3-24* was released, it was highly praised. It was described as "radical" and "revolutionary" by *Time* magazine and got rave reviews from the *New York Times*. It was called a "rare work of applied scholarship" and "probably the most important piece of doctrine written in the past 20 years."

One outcome of this new interest by the military in cultural knowledge is the development of Human Terrain Systems (HTS). First outlined by McFate in her proposal for an Office for Operational Cultural Knowledge, the centerpiece of the $250 million program is the creation of Human Terrain Teams (HTTs). Trained at Fort Leavenworth, Kansas, each HTT consists of five people:

- The HTT leader, holding the military rank of major or lieutenant colonel
- A cultural analyst, who is a civilian with an MA or Ph.D. in anthropology or sociology
- A regional studies analyst with an MA or Ph.D. in regional studies and fluency in the language of the area
- A Human Terrain (HT) research manager with a military background in tactical intelligence
- An HT analyst with a military background in tactical intelligence

Each team would be attached to a battalion commander, to whom each HTT reports the results of its information gathering. Initially, five HTTs were sent to Iraq and one to Afghanistan. By the end of 2009, nearly 30 teams had been deployed.

US civilian anthropologist and HTT (Human Terrain Team) Social Scientist, talk to local resident to investigate a tribal dispute on August 12, 2009 in the village of Wum Kalay, Paktya Province, Afghanistan.

Anthropologists who have joined the HTS project explain their volunteering as an attempt to do something meaningful; one said from the field that "I came here to save lives, to make friends out of enemies." Cultural anthropologist Marcus Griffin wrote on his website that "[t]here is an obligation to give back to society in the form of new knowledge. . . . I have an obligation to use my skills to learn about people and to share what I learn." Working as a member of an HTT in Iraq, Griffin sees his job as finding out what Iraqis need and helping them fulfill those needs (see Hunter, 2008). Journalists embedded with military units describe the work of HTTs in humanitarian terms, describing how the teams help to build job training programs, create health clinics, and rebuild mosques. And while the pay is good (up to $300,000 for nine months), the work is not without risk: Three team members—Nicole Suveges, Paula Loyd, and Michael Bhatia—have been killed in action.

The Anthropological Reaction to HTS

However, not everyone viewed these developments favorably. After reviewing the work anthropologists and others were doing in aiding the military in counterinsurgency programs, the American Anthropological Association issued a formal statement in 2007 condemning specifically the Human Terrain System Project. Reiterating that there are valuable ways that anthropology can contribute to policy discussions in a wide range of areas, the association concluded:

> (i) that the HTS program creates conditions which are likely to place anthropologists in positions in which their work will be in violation of the AAA Code of Ethics and (ii) that its use of anthropologists poses a danger to both other anthropologists and persons other anthropologists study.

In 2008, the Society for Applied Anthropology[3] expressed a similar sentiment, and a group—the Network of Concerned Anthropologists[4]—was formed in 2007 to allow anthropologists to pledge not to engage in counterinsurgency operations. And in December 2008, a special commission formed by the American Anthropological Association to examine the relationship between anthropology and U.S. security and intelligence communities[5]

---

[3]*Society of Applied Anthropology Newsletter, 19*(2), p. 4

[4]Network of Concerned Anthropologists at http://sites.google.com/site/concernedanthropologists.

[5]See http://www.aaanet.org/issues/policy-advocacy/CEAUSSIC-Releases-Final-Report-on-Army-HTS-Program.cfm.

Anthropologists Roberto Gonzalez has questioned the ethics and efficacy of HTS.

concluded that "while we stress that constructive engagement between anthropology and the military is possible, [the commission] suggests that the AAA emphasize the incompatibility of HTS with disciplinary ethics and practice for job seekers and that it further recognize the problem of allowing HTS to define the meaning of 'anthropology' within DoD."

Professor Roberto Gonzalez has been one of the foremost critics of HTS. After examining the history of U.S. counterinsurgency operations, particularly those that attempted to use information gathered by social scientists, Gonzalez concludes that there are a number of dangers inherent in HTS: First, is it possible for informants to give genuine informed consent as to whether they participate? Second, what type of information will be gathered by anthropologists and how will it be used? Third, how well will those who provide information to the military be protected from retaliation from hostile groups or political rivals? As Gonzalez demonstrates, the answers to these questions are not reassuring.

One of the major rules of anthropological research regarding the collecting of information is that informants must consent to be questioned and sign a form to that effect. However, there is a problem: whether informants talking to anthropologists attached to military combat groups in a war zone are really free to refuse to provide information. As one of Gonzalez's students asked, "How would you feel if you were an Iraqi being interviewed by some tall American guy with a soldier's uniform and a gun? Something just doesn't seem right about it." Another notes after seeing a photo of an embedded anthropologist wearing camouflage fatigues with a sidearm strapped to his leg, "Is he *really* doing social science? Seems to me he's doing something else" (Gonzalez, 2009, p. 99).

Another issue is what is the purpose of gathering the information and how will it be used? Proponents of the program claim that the purpose of collecting cultural knowledge is to win "hearts and minds" and, in the end, save lives. The problem is that history says otherwise.

One of the more elaborate counterinsurgency programs developed by the U.S. military was the Civil Operations and Revolutionary Development Support (CORD) program implemented in Vietnam in the 1960s. The program, which bears enough of a resemblance to HTS that one military official was able to declare HTS a "CORDS for the Twenty-First Century," was also designed to gather cultural knowledge to win "hearts and minds" by discovering what people desired and helping them to get it. The program distributed millions of dollars for medical agricultural and educational programs. But it also spawned the Phoenix Program, a CIA-led initiative that led to the capture, torture, and assassination (or "neutralization") of suspected insurgents, resulting in at least 26,000 deaths.

In his book *The Phoenix Program*, Douglas Valentine describes how counterterrorism teams were given information about Vietnam superstitions, myths, and religious beliefs to be used to manipulate, frighten, or terrorize civilians. For example, because Buddhists believe that a person cannot enter heaven unless his or her liver is intact, operatives would kill and cut out the liver of suspected insurgents as a message to others. One of the operatives described how they terrorized uncommitted civilians:

> We left our calling card nailed to the forehead of the corpses we left behind. They were playing card size with a light green skull with red eyes and red teeth dripping blood, set against a black background. We hammered them into the third eye, the pituitary gland, with our pistol butts. The third eye is the seat of consciousness for Buddhists, and this was a form of mutilation that had a powerful psychological effect. (quoted in Valentine, 1990, p. 61)

The Phoenix program was not the only counterinsurgency program to result in the death of thousands. As Gonzalez (2009, p. 12) notes, virtually all modern counterinsurgency programs, such as those in Guatemala, Algeria, Vietnam, Northern Ireland, Chile, and Argentina, have resulted in torture, mass murder, and state terror and thousands—if not hundreds of thousands—of civilian deaths. Given what we already know about torture at Abu Ghraib in Iraq, forced renditions around the world, and the conditions at the military prison at Guantanamo, it is naïve to think that counterinsurgency efforts involving the gathering of intelligence by social scientists would not have similar results.

Regardless of the efforts of the military and others to put a humanitarian face on the counterinsurgency contributions of social scientists, military officers are clear that the information gathered will be used to attain whatever ends are desired. Thus, in an article entitled "The Human Terrain of Urban Operations," Lieutenant Colonel Ralph Peters (U.S. Army) suggests that the role of the armed forces is, as he puts it, "to keep the world safe for our economy and open to our cultural assault. To those ends, we will do a fair amount of killing." The military art, he continues, "will consist in knowing more about the enemy than he knows about himself, manipulating data for effectiveness and efficiency, and denying similar advantages to our opponents" (quoted in Gonzalez, 2009, p. 32).

Major O. Kent Strader of the U.S. Army Command and General Staff College at Fort Leavenworth, Kansas, advocates using human terrain to exploit weakness and vulnerabilities, such as religious shrines, which have the potential, as he puts it, to be "weaponized." Weaponizing culture, he says, is to use it as an instrument of attack or defense.

And as Gonzalez points out, the job descriptions, such as this one, for positions with HTS do not sound humanitarian:

> . . . to improve the gathering, interpretation, understanding, operational application and sharing of local population knowledge. . . . Human Terrain Analysts apply a thorough understanding of the ops/intelligence fusion process to compile, collate, analyze and evaluate data sources and unevaluated intelligence to develop a coherent picture of the human terrain in which the BCT/RCTs (brigade combat team/regimental combat team) operate. (quoted in Gonzalez, 2009, p. 54)

Another problem with HTS, according to Gonzalez, is that, as with the Phoenix Program, there is little effort to limit the use of information collected by social scientists. In fact, supporters of HTS advocate making whatever information collected widely available to other government agencies as well as the governments of Iraq and Afghanistan to "enable them to more fully exercise sovereignty over their country" (Gonzalez, 2009, p. 74). When Phoenix data was given to the South Vietnamese government, it was used to target political opponents and dissidents. What sort of precaution is being taken to ensure that the Iraqi and Afghan government does not use HTT information to target political rivals, such political dissidents as union organizers or students, or create a blacklist for personal vendettas, particularly when anthropologists provide data on social networks, kinship relations, and so on?

In fact, there seems to be a general insensitivity to how information collected from civilians by anthropologists will be protected. One former HTT employee claimed that during four months of training, no one discussed the dangers to Iraqis or Afghans of cooperating with HTTs or any discussion of ethical issues, such as obtaining consent from people to be interviewed. And there are other ethical oversights in the program, such as the alleged plagiarism in *FM 3-24* on counterinsurgency that contained many passages from anthropological works that were unattributed (see Price, 2007).

Participants in and supporters of the HTS initiative have responded to criticism in various ways. For example, Sheila Miyoshi Jager (2007) asks whether anthropologists could really deny commanders in Iraq and Afghanistan the knowledge they need to wage a war political leaders have charged them with fighting? Is it ethically correct, she asks, for them to "retreat from the world and leave others do the fighting"?

One veteran of the war in Iraq, in response to the claims by one HTT anthropologist that he is working to help Iraqis, wrote that HTTs do in fact contribute to the targeting and killing of the enemy. But he concludes by saying:

> I am in favor of this program of HTTs and see great utility in it for combat commanders. I understand the debate too between these field anthropologists who are part of the HTTs and academia. I think academia is wrong to chastise these people for being a part of the HTTs. But I think also that people like you should call a spade a spade and accept the reality of the effects that these HTTs produce. (quoted in Gonzalez, 2009, p. 68)

However, McFate insists that the role of anthropology in HTT is to provide information that will result in fewer deaths and that anthropological critics of the program, such as Gonzalez, fail to understand the military's need to understand local populations. Without such understanding, she says, the military is more likely to make mistakes that result in property destruction and the loss of human life (see McFate & Fondacaro, 2008).

Limiting the Application of the Technologies

The use of social scientists for HTTs in Iraq and Afghanistan raises the larger issue of the responsibility of anthropologists and other social scientists to be aware of how their research and data may be used. For example, the Pentagon is developing computer programs by using data that include those collected by social scientists to tell users of the program which neighborhoods in some distant city, such as Baghdad, Kabul, or Islamabad, are dangerous. It would predict which neighborhoods are at risk for riots, gun violence, or bombings—often providing the names of possible participants, along with their addresses, fingerprints, ID photos, relatives, friends, and associates.

Perhaps more ominous is the number of grants that have been awarded to social scientists and engineers by the military to forecast human behavior. The Department of Defense has a budget item dated February 2007 called the Human Social and Culture Behavior Modeling (HSCB) project scheduled for development between 2008 and 2013.

Much of this work will be contracted out to private corporations eager to secure lucrative government contracts. One corporation, Aptima, boasts working with the military. On its webpage, it says: "[T]he enemy of today derives its power not from the size and strength of its military, but from its diffuse structure, elusiveness, and adaptability" and that "countering this new enemy requires a shift in strategy and tactics to focus on the 'human terrain'—the territory that Aptima knows best."[6]

Among Aptima's current products is its Social Network Analysis (SNA) software, developed in conjunction with Carnegie Mellon University. SNA, as Aptima describes it, "draws on state of the art social science, psychology and economic theories of human behavior" and has been used by the U.S. military "to predict a state's potential for instability of civil unrest in terms of nine key factors," ranging from "lack of essential services" to "corruption level" to "tension."

One danger, of course, is that the philosophy of HTS and the development of elaborate surveillance technologies by using vast quantities of information now available on citizens will move from military applications in such places as Iraq and Afghanistan to domestic uses that seriously undermine democratic freedoms.

---

[6]See http://www.aptima.com/domains.php?domain_id=1.

Gonzalez concludes his critique of HTS as follows:

What comes across from the accounts of many social scientists supporting counterinsurgency initiatives in Iraq and Afghanistan is a fundamental acceptance of modern warfare in general and the US-led occupations in particular. Furthermore, they generally accept the false notion that counterinsurgency— the "graduate level of war" to quote one military enthusiast—is more antiseptic, more humane, less damaging than conventional warfare. As technicians of power, some adhere to Machiavellian principles: do not question the prince or his war, but instead use the most efficient means to help him achieve victory. War's inevitability is taken for granted. Basic assumptions are left unquestioned. Missing from these accounts is the question of whether war is appropriate at all today. (Gonzalez, 2009, pp. 123–4)

CONCLUSIONS

To examine how people give meaning to and justify collective violence, our first question had to do with how societies create a bias in favor of collective violence. Violent conflict is justified in some societies as a way of achieving status or acquiring or protecting possessions, as a means of revenge, or as a necessary defense of personal honor or integrity. In peaceful societies, violence is avoided by sharing resources, building relations of dependence among groups, devaluing or discouraging aggressive behavior, and emphasizing collective behaviors that promote intragroup and intergroup harmony.

There are economic, political, and social differences between peaceful and violent societies. One difference is the encouragement in violent societies of competition over resources, leading to a situation in which individuals are required because of a lack of central authority to protect their own property by violent means. The conversion of communal property to private property, which resulted in the disenfranchisement of peasant farmers, has been linked to revolution, and sexist ideologies in violent societies may promote violent behavior against other groups.

A question in examining the effects of war on society is whether there have been any beneficial effects that might explain the occurrence of violent conflict. Population does decline in war, especially in small-scale societies, but apparently not enough to exercise any control on population growth or to have any impact on the human species through biological selection. According to some, war has served throughout human history to promote the centralization of authority and the growth of state-level political structures. While violent conflict may increase male solidarity, it also can promote greater violence against women.

We find that people can easily justify even the manufacture and testing of weapons of mass destruction. The language of defense analysts masks some of the realities of nuclear destruction, keeps them from viewing themselves as potential victims, and turns nuclear planning into a game.

Finally, we examined the uses of anthropology for peace and war, specifically the use of anthropology in counterinsurgency programs—particularly the Human Terrain Systems Project—and the dangers involved with the use of data collected by anthropologists and other social scientists.

REFERENCES AND SUGGESTED READINGS

Introduction: The Justification of Violent Conflict

The opening quote is from an account of a witness to a Contra attack on a Nicaraguan village in 1984, as cited in Noam Chomsky's book *Turning the Tide: U.S. Intervention in Central America and the Struggle for Peace* (South End Press, 1985). The account of Carib warfare is from Neil Lancelot Whitehead's article "The Snake Warriors—Sons of the Tiger's Teeth: A Descriptive Analysis of Carib Warfare, ca. 1500–1820," in *The Anthropology of War*, edited by Jonathan Hass (Cambridge University Press, 1990). The definition of war relies on Clark McCauley's article "Conference Overview," in *The Anthropology of War*. McCauley draws his definition from a book compiled from a symposium on war held in 1966, *War: The Anthropology of Armed Conflict and Aggression*, edited by Morton Fried, Marvin Harris, and Robert Murphy (Natural History Press, 1967). Different views on the cultural or biological roots of war can be found in *Societies at Peace: An Anthropological Perspective*, edited by Signe Howell and Roy Willis (Routledge, 1989), and Carol Greenhouse's "Cultural Perspectives on War," in *The Quest for Peace: Transcending Collective Violence and War Among Societies, Cultures and States*, edited by R. Varynen (Sage, 1987).

How Do Societies Create a Bias in Favor of Collective Violence?

The account of Kiowa warfare and horse raiding is from Bernard Mishkin's *Rank and Warfare Among the Plains Indians* (University of Washington Press, 1940). The account of the Yanomamö is based on Napoleon Chagnon's article "Reproductive and Somatic Conflicts of Interest in the Genesis of Violence and Warfare Among Tribesmen," in *The Anthropology of War*, cited previously, and Chagnon's book *The Fierce People* (3rd ed., Holt, Rinehart and Winston, 1983). The feud in Kohistan is described by Lincoln Keiser in *Friend by Day, Enemy by Night: Organized Vengeance in a Kohistani Community* (Holt, Rinehart and Winston, 1991). A classic work on violent protest is Eric Hobsbaum's *Primitive Rebels: Studies in Archaic Forms of Social Movement in the 19th and 20th Centuries* (Praeger, 1959).

How Do Societies Create a Bias Against Violent Conflict?

Thomas Gregor discusses peaceful societies in "Uneasy Peace: Intertribal Relations in Brazil's Upper Xingu," in *The Anthropology of War*, cited previously. The discussion of the Ju/wasi relies on Elizabeth Thomas's *The Harmless People* (Knopf, 1959) and Richard Lee's *The Dobe !Kung* (Holt, Rinehart and Winston, 1984). The description of the Semai is based on Clayton Robarchek's "Motivations and Material Causes: On the Explanation of Conflict and War," in *The Anthropology of War*, cited previously. Robarchek also discusses the Hobbesian image of man as it relates to the Semai in "Hobbesian and Rousseauan Images of Man: Autonomy and Individualism in a Peaceful Society," in *Societies at Peace: An Anthropological Perspective*, cited previously. The material on the Xinguanos comes from Thomas Gregor's article cited previously. The description of the Inuit is derived from Jean Briggs's

Never in Anger (Harvard University Press, 1970), and an account of the Buid can be found in Thomas Gibson's "Raiding, Trading and Tribal Autonomy in Insular Southeast Asia," in *The Anthropology of War*, cited previously. Mark Juergensmeyer provides an extensive study of religious violence in his book *Terror in the Mind of God: The Global Rise of Religious Violence* (University of California Press, 2000), as does Jessica Stern in *Terror in the Name of God: Why Religious Militants Kill* (HarperCollins, 2003). Elaine Pagels discusses the uses of the devil in *The Origin of Satan* (Vintage Books, 1995). Statistics on attacks on abortion providers can be found in the National Abortion Federation's 2003 publication *Incidents of Violence and Disruption Against Abortion Providers* (http://www.prochoice.org). The full text of Osama bin Laden's "Letter to America," which details his grievances against the United States, is available at the *Guardian-Observer*'s website: http://observer. guardian.co.uk/worldview/story/0,11581,845725,00.html.

What Are the Economic, Political, or Social Differences Between Peaceful and Violent Societies?

Two works cited previously deal extensively with debates about the reasons for war: *War: The Anthropology of Armed Conflict and Aggression*, edited by Morton Fried, Marvin Harris, and Robert Murphy, and *The Anthropology of War*, edited by Jonathan Hass. The views of Thomas Hobbes are taken from *Leviathan*, first published in 1651 (Oxford University Press, 1881). *The Vice Lords: Warriors of the Streets* (Holt, Rinehart and Winston, 1969) contains Lincoln Keiser's account of Chicago street gangs in the 1960s. Alex Kotlowitz gives an account of the lives of two Chicago children growing up amid the violence of Chicago housing projects in *There Are No Children Here* (Anchor Books, 1991). The analysis of Yanomamö violence and the reasons for it can be found in R. Brian Ferguson's article "A Savage Encounter: Western Contact and the Yanomami War Complex," in *War in the Tribal Zone: Expanding States and Indigenous Warfare*, edited by R. Brian Ferguson and Neil L. Whitehead (School of American Research Press, 1992). For a more detailed account, see *Yanomami Warfare: A Political History* by R. Brian Ferguson (School of American Research Press, 1995). William Tulio Divale and Marvin Harris discuss the connection between male dominance and war in "Population, Warfare, and the Male Supremacist Complex," in *American Anthropologist*, vol. 78 (1976), pp. 521–38. The feminist analysis of war is represented by Leslie Cagan's "Feminism and Militarism," in *Beyond Survival: New Directions for the Disarmament Movement*, edited by M. Albert and D. Dellinger (South End Press, 1983); Riane Eisler's *The Chalice and the Blade* (Harper & Row, 1987); and Betty Reardon's *Sexism and the War System* (Columbia University Teachers College Press, 1985). Peggy Sanday's study of rape and war was reported in "The Socio-Cultural Context of Rape: A Cross-Cultural Study," in *Journal of Social Issues*, vol. 37 (1981), pp. 5–27. A description of the Acoli appears in Dent Ocaya-Lakidi's "Manhood, Warriorhood and Sex in Eastern Africa," in *Journal of Asian and African Studies*, vol. 12 (1979), pp. 134–65.

What Are the Effects of War on Societies?

The figures on the number of people killed in modern war come from Lewis Richardson's classic work *The Statistics of Deadly Quarrels* (Boxwood Press, 1960) and Quincy Wright's extensive work *A Study of War* (University of Chicago Press, 1965). Frank B. Livingstone discusses "The Effects of Warfare on the Biology of the Human Species," in *War: The Anthropology of Armed Conflict and Aggression*, cited previously. The connection between war and female infanticide is made in Divale and Harris's article "Population, Warfare, and the Male Supremacist Complex," cited previously. Robert Carneiro's theories about the relationship between war and the development of the state can be found in his article "Political Expansion as an Expression of the Principle of Competitive Exclusion," in *Origins of the State*, edited by Ronald Cohn and Elman Service (Institute for the Study of Human Issues, 1978), and more recently in his article "Chiefdom-Level Warfare as Exemplified in Fiji and Cauca Valley," in *The Anthropology of War*, cited previously. The description of the rise of the Zulu state comes from Elman Service's book *Origins of the State and Civilization* (W. W. Norton, 1975). A discussion of war and human bonding can be found in Ralph Holloway Jr.'s "Human Aggression: The Need for a Species-Specific Framework," in *War: The Anthropology of Armed Conflict and Aggression*, cited previously. Frederic Thrasher's study of Chicago gangs is reported in *The Gang*, originally published in 1927 (University of Chicago Press, 1963). An excellent article on the relationship between sports and war is Richard G. Sipes's "War, Sports, and Aggression: An Empirical Test of Two Rival Theories," in *American Anthropologist*, vol. 74 (1973), pp. 64–86.

How Is It Possible to Justify the Creation of Weapons of Mass Destruction?

The connection between social settings and worldviews is elaborated by Mary Douglas and Aaron Wildavsky in *Risk and Culture: An Essay on the Selection of Technological and Environmental Dangers* (University of California Press, 1983). Hugh Gusterson's research in a nuclear weapons laboratory is described in *Nuclear Rites: A Weapons Laboratory at the End of the Cold War* (University of California Press, 1995). Carol Cohn's article "Sex and Death in the Rational World of Defense Intellectuals" appeared in *Signs*, vol. 12 (1987), pp. 687–718. For more on what Cohn calls "newspeak," see her article "Decoding Military Newspeak," in *Ms.*, March/April 1991, p. 88. The description of the aftermath of the atomic bombing of Hiroshima comes from Hisako Matsubara's *Cranes at Dusk* (Dial Press, 1985).

Case Study in Doing Anthropology #8: The Uses (and Misuses?) of Anthropology for Peace and War

On the United Nations and peace education, see http://www.un.org/cyberschoolbus/peace/frame2.htm. Leslie Sponsel's article "The Mutual Relevance of Anthropology and Peace Studies" is contained in *The Anthropology of Peace and Nonviolence*, edited by Leslie E. Sponsel and Thomas Gregor (Lynne Rienner, 1994). His course syllabus is available at http://www.soc.hawaii.edu/sponsel/Courses/345.html/Syllabi/Syllalbus06.html. Excellent works about the expansion of American Empire include Noam Chomsky's book *Hegemony or Survival: America's Quest for Global Dominance* (Metropolitan Books, 2003) and Chalmers Johnson's work *The Sorrows of Empire: Militarism, Secrecy, and the End of the Republic* (Metropolitan Books, 2004).

For information on the origins of Human Terrain Systems, see Montgomery McFate's original article "Anthropology and Counterinsurgency: The Strange Story of Their Curious Relationship," in *Military Review* (March–April 2005a) and her and Andrea Jackson's proposal in "An Organizational Solution for DOD's Cultural Knowledge Needs," also in *Military Review* (2005b). Sheila Miyoshi Jager's monograph *On the Uses of Cultural Knowledge* (Strategic Studies, 2007) provides another positive assessment of HTS. On the military side, you can find justifications for the use of cultural knowledge in *Field Guide 24-3 on Counter Insurgency* (University of Chicago Press, 2006); Jacob Kipp, Lester Grau, Karl Prinslow, and Don Smith's article "The Human Terrain System: A CORDS for the 21st Century," in *Military Review* (Sept.–Oct., 2006); and Ralph Peters's "The Human Terrain of Urban Operations," in *The Eurasian Politician* (issue 2, October 2000). The American

Anthropological Association statement on the Human Terrain Systems Project can be found at http://dev.aaanet.org/issues/policy-advocacy/Statement-on-HTS.cfm. For a humanitarian defense of HTS, see James P. Hunter's article "Anthropologist Helps Soldiers Understand Iraqis' Needs" (American Forces Press Service, 2008; http://www.defense.gov/news/newsarticle.aspx?id=48766).

Roberto Gonzalez's book on HTS is *American Counterinsurgency: Human Science and the Human Terrain* (Prickly Paradigm Press, 2009) and offers the most extensive critique of HTS. The most complete work on the Phoenix Program is Douglas Valentine's *The Phoenix Program* (William Morrow and Company, 1990). And for the details of the plagiarism in the U.S. Army's *Field Manual 3-24* on counterinsurgency, see David Price's article "Pilfered Scholarship Devastates General Petraeus's Counterinsurgency Manual," in *Counterpunch* (October 30, 2007; http://www.counterpunch.org/price10302007.html). Montgomery McFate and HTS program manager Steve Fondacaro respond to criticisms of the program in "Cultural Knowledge and Common Sense," in *Anthropology Today* (24, p. 37).

GLOSSARY

agroecological approach   Agricultural methods that incorporate indigenous practices of food production that preserve the environment along with contemporary agricultural research.

anthropological fieldwork   Firsthand or direct immersion and observation of the people or culture a researcher is trying to understand.

balanced reciprocity   A form of exchange in which items of equal or near-equal value are exchanged on the spot.

bilateral kinship   A system in which individuals trace their descent through both parents.

brideservice   The requirement that when a couple marries, the groom must work for the bride's parents for some specified period of time.

bridewealth (brideprice)   The valuables that a groom or his family are expected or obligated to present to the bride's family.

capital conversion   The transformation of something that has no monetary value into something that can be bought and sold in the market.

caste   A system of social stratification based on assignment at birth to the ranked social or occupational groups of parents. There is no mobility from one caste to another, and intermarriage may be forbidden.

clan   A unilineal descent group whose members claim descent from a common ancestor.

commodities   Goods that carry little personal meaning. (Compare with *possessions*.)

commodity money   Money that is backed by something of worth, such as gold or silver.

credit money   Money that is created by loans.

cultural anthropology   One of the four major subfields of anthropology, with the others being physical or biological anthropology, archaeology, and linguistics.

cultural text   A way of thinking about culture as a text of significant symbols—words, gestures, drawings, natural objects—that carries meaning.

culture   The system of meanings about the nature of experience that are shared by a people and passed on from one generation to another.

culture change   The change in meanings that a people ascribe to experience and changes in their way of life.

culture of poverty   A phrase coined by Oscar Lewis to describe the lifestyle and worldview of people who inhabit urban and rural slums.

domain of experience   An area of human experience (e.g., business, war, science, family life) from which people borrow meaning to apply to other areas.

dowry   The goods and valuables a bride's family supplies to the groom's family or to the couple.

economic development   The term used to identify an increase in the level of technology and, by some, the standard of living of a population. Others view it as an ideology based on three key assumptions: (1) that economic growth and development are the solution to national as well as global problems; (2) that global economic integration will contribute to solving global ecological and social problems; and (3) that foreign assistance to undeveloped countries will make things better.

egocentric   A view of the self that defines each person as a replica of all humanity—the locus of motivations and drives—capable of acting independently from others.

ethnocentric fallacy   The mistaken notion that the beliefs and behaviors of other cultures can be judged from the perspective of one's own culture.

ethnocentrism   The tendency to judge the beliefs and behaviors of other cultures from the perspective of one's own culture.

ethnographic method   The immersion of researchers in the lives and cultures of the peoples they are trying to understand in order to comprehend the meanings these people ascribe to their existence.

ethnographic present   Use of the present tense to describe a culture, although the description may refer to situations that existed in the past.

exogamy   A rule that requires a person to marry someone outside one's own group.

exploitative theory of social stratification   A theory based on the assumption that social stratification and hierarchy exist because one group of individuals seeks to take advantage of another group for economic purposes.

extended family   A family group based on blood relations of three or more generations.

factory model (of agriculture)   An energy-intensive, ecologically damaging form of agriculture intended to grow or raise as many crops or livestock as possible in the shortest period of time.

factory system   A system of production characterized by the concentration of labor and machines in specific places. It is associated with the industrial revolution.

family of orientation   The family group that consists of ego and ego's father, mother, and siblings.

family of procreation   The family group that consists of a husband, a wife, and their children.

feud   Purposeful, organized, and socially sanctioned combat involving killing.

fiat money   Money that is backed by nothing other than a government decree that it be accepted for the sale of goods or services or the settlement of debt.

frames   Mental structures that shape the way we see the world.

free trade   The removal of barriers to the free flow of goods and capital between nations by eliminating import or export taxes or subsidies paid to farmers and businessmen. It may also mean reducing environmental or social laws when they restrict the flow of goods and capital.

generalized reciprocity   A form of exchange in which persons share what they have with others but expect them to reciprocate later.

Gini coefficient   A measure of variability, developed by Italian statistician and demographer Corrado Gini, used to measure income distribution.

globalization   A process that can best be described as the continuing imposition on global economies of policies that accelerate economic growth. These policies generally correspond to what has been termed the "Washington consensus."

gross domestic product (GDP)   The total of all goods and services bought and sold in a given year.

holistic   A view of the self in which the individual cannot be conceived of as existing separately from society or apart from his or her status or role.

identity struggles   A term coined by Wallace and Fogelson to characterize interaction in which there is a discrepancy between the identity a person claims to possess and the identity attributed to that person by others.

identity toolbox   Features of a person's identity (such as gender, age, or personal appearance) that he or she chooses to emphasize in constructing a social self.

ideology of class   A set of beliefs characteristic of stratified societies that justifies the division of a society into groups with differential rights and privileges as being natural and right.

impartible inheritance   A form of inheritance in which family property is passed undivided to one heir.

incest taboo   A rule that prohibits sexual relations within certain categories of kin, such as brothers or sisters, parents and children, or, in some cases, cousins.

individualistic   A view of the self in which the individual is primarily responsible for his or her own actions.

Industrial Revolution   A period of European history, generally identified as occurring in the late 18th century, marked by a shift in production from agriculture to industrial goods, urbanization, and the factory system.

integrative theory of social stratification   A theory based on the assumption that social hierarchy is necessary for the smooth functioning of society.

International Monetary Fund (IMF)   Formed in 1944 at the Bretton Woods Conference to regulate currency transactions between countries, the IMF now makes loans and regulates the economies of recipient countries.

interpersonal theory of disease   A view of disease in which it is assumed that illness is caused by tensions or conflicts in social relations.

interpretive drift   The slow, often unacknowledged shift in someone's manner of interpreting events as he or she becomes involved with a particular activity.

irrigation agriculture   A form of cultivation in which water is used to deliver nutrients to growing plants.

key metaphors   A term coined by Sherry Ortner to identify metaphors that dominate the meanings that people in a specific culture attribute to their experience.

key scenarios   Dominant stories or myths that portray the values and beliefs of a specific society.

market externalities   Costs or benefits of economic transactions that are not included in prices. These may include the environmental, social, or political consequences of market transactions.

matrilineage   A lineage that is formed by tracing descent in the female line.

matrilineal kinship   A system of descent in which persons are related to their kin through the mother only.

means of production   The materials, such as land, machines, or tools, that people need to produce things.

metaphor   A figure of speech in which linguistic expressions are taken from one area of experience and applied to another.

myth   A story or narrative that portrays the meanings people give to their experience.

negative identity   The attribution of personal characteristics believed to be undesirable.

negative reciprocity   A form of exchange in which the object is to get something for nothing or to make a profit.

neoliberalism   An economic philosophy that argues for minimal government involvement in the economy and greatly accelerated economic growth. Well-being, neoliberals argued, is best served by liberating individual entrepreneurs to operate in a framework of strong property rights, free markets, and free trade.

nuclear family   The family group consisting of a father, a mother, and their biological or adopted children.

outsourcing   The process whereby corporations and businesses move all or some of their operations from rich countries to poorer ones to reduce their labor costs and escape environmental and labor laws.

partible inheritance   A form of inheritance in which the goods or property of a family is divided among the heirs.

participant observation   The active participation of a researcher or observer in the lives of those being studied.

pathogen   An infectious agent, such as a bacterium or a virus, that can cause disease.

patrilineage   A lineage that is formed by tracing descent in the male line.

patrilineal kinship   A system of descent in which persons are related to their kin through the father only.

phallocentrism   A term coined by Peggy Sanday that refers to the deployment of the penis as a symbol of masculine social power and dominance.

plow agriculture   A form of cultivation in which fields must be plowed to remove weeds and grasses prior to planting.

political capital   The freedom we have to regulate our own lives and the access we have to societal leaders and decision-makers.

political or social repression   The use of force by a ruling group to maintain political, economic, or social control over other groups.

polyandry   A form of marriage in which a woman is permitted to have more than one husband.

polygamy   A form of marriage in which a person is permitted to have more than one spouse.

polygyny   A form of marriage in which a man is permitted to have more than one wife.

population density   The number of people in a given geographic area.

positive identity   The attribution to people of personal characteristics believed to be desirable.

possessions   Goods that are associated in some personal way with their producer and/or distributor. (Compare with *commodities*.)

principle of reciprocity   The social principle that giving a gift creates social ties with the person receiving it, who is obliged to eventually reciprocate.

progress   The idea that human history is the story of a steady advance from a life that depends on the whims of nature to a life of control and domination over natural forces.

"putting out" system   A means of production, common in the 16th and 17th centuries and surviving today, in which a manufacturer or merchant supplies the materials and sometimes the tools to workers, who produce the goods in their own homes.

racism   A set of beliefs, behaviors, and symbolic representations that turn perceived or constructed differences among people thought to be indelible into inequality.

relativism   The attempt to understand the beliefs and behaviors of other cultures in terms of the culture in which they are found.

relativistic fallacy   The mistaken idea that it is impossible to make moral judgments about the beliefs and behaviors of members of other cultures.

revitalization movements   The term suggested by Anthony F. C. Wallace for attempts by a people to construct a more satisfying culture.

rites of passage   The term suggested by Arnold van Gennep for rituals that mark a person's passage from one identity or status to another.

ritual   A dramatic rendering or social portrayal of meanings shared by a specific body of people in a way that makes them seem correct and proper. (See *symbolic actions*.)

Sapir-Whorf hypothesis   The idea that there is an explicit link between the grammar of a language and the culture of the people who speak that language.

secondary elaboration   A term suggested by E. E. Evans-Pritchard for people's attempts to explain away inconsistencies or contradictions in their beliefs.

sedentary   A style of living characterized by permanent or semipermanent settlements.

selective perception   The tendency of people to see and recognize only those things they expect to see or those that confirm their view of the world.

slash-and-burn (swidden) agriculture   A form of agriculture in which forests are cleared by burning trees and brush and then crops are planted among the ashes of the cleared ground.

social capital   Relations of reciprocity and trust that enable people collectively to solve their problems.

social classes   A system of social stratification based on income or possession of wealth and resources. Individual social mobility is possible in a class system.

social identities   Views that people have of their own and others' positions in society. Individuals seek confirmation from others that they occupy the positions on the social landscape that they claim to occupy.

sociocentric   A view of the self that is context-dependent; there is no intrinsic self that can possess enduring qualities.

state   A form of society characterized by a hierarchical ranking of people and centralized political control.

Structural Adjustment Program (SAP)   Agreements between the International Monetary Fund and indebted countries in which countries agree, in exchange for a new repayment schedule, to reduce their government workforce, lower remaining government salaries, sell and/or privatize state-owned businesses and services (e.g., utility companies, railroads, health facilities, etc.), end government subsidies (e.g., help to farmers, food programs for the poor, etc.), reduce taxes on foreign investors, weaken state environmental and labor regulations, and devalue local currency.

structural violence   The actions or policies of governments or multilateral organizations that result in denial to the poor of basic rights of food, shelter, or livelihood.

suppressing evidence   The tendency to reject or ignore evidence that challenges an accepted belief.

surplus value of labor   The term suggested by Karl Marx and Friedrich Engels for the portion of a person's labor that is retained as profit by those who control the means of production.

symbolic actions   The activities—including ritual, myth, art, dance, and music—that dramatically depict the meanings shared by a specific body of people.

totemism   The use of a symbol, generally an animal or a plant, as a physical representation for a group, generally a clan.

vector   When referring to disease, an organism—such as a mosquito, tick, flea, or snail—that can transmit disease to another animal.

violent revolution   The term suggested by Karl Marx and Friedrich Engels for the necessary response of workers to their repression by the ruling class.

war   See *feud*.

World Bank   One of the institutions created at the Bretton Woods, New Hampshire, meeting in 1944 of Allied nations. The World Bank (or the Bank for Reconstruction and Development) functions as a lending institution to nations largely for projects related to economic development.

REFERENCES

Adams, John W. 1973. *The Gitksan Potlatch: Population Flux, Resource Ownership and Reciprocity.* Toronto: Holt, Rinehart and Winston of Canada.

Alford, Richard D. 1988. *Naming and Identity: A Cross-Cultural Study of Personal Naming Practices.* New Haven, CT: HRAF Press.

American Anthropological Association. 2007. Executive Board Statement on the Human Terrain System Project. http://dev.aaanet.org/issues/policy-advocacy/Statement-on-HTS.cfm.

Anelauskas, Valdas. 1999. *Discovering America As It Is.* Atlanta: Clarity Press.

Angeloni, Elvio. 1990. *Anthropology 90/91.* Guilford, CT: Dushkin Publishing.

Arens, William. 1976. "Professional Football: An American Symbol and Ritual." In *The American Dimension: Cultural Myths and Social Realities.* Edited by William Arens and Susan P. Montague. Port Washington, NY: Alfred Publishing.

Baker, Dean, and Mark Weisbrot. 2001. *Social Security: The Phony Crisis.* Chicago: University of Chicago Press.

Barlow, Maude. 2001. *Blue Gold: The Global Water Crisis and the Commodification of the World's Water Supply.* International Forum on Globalization. Available online at http://www.thirdworldtraveler.com/Water/Blue_Gold.html.

Barnes, Barry. 1974. *Scientific Knowledge and Sociological Theory.* London: Routledge & Kegan Paul.

Beaud, Michel. 1983. *A History of Capitalism, 1500–1980.* New York: Monthly Review Press.

Bellah, Robert, Richard Madsen, William M. Sullivan, Ann Swidler, and Steven M. Tipton. 1984. *Habits of the Heart.* Berkeley, CA: University of California Press.

Belmonte, Thomas. 1989. *The Broken Fountain.* New York: Columbia University Press.

Benedict, Ruth. 1934. *Patterns of Culture.* New York: Houghton Mifflin.

Blankenburg, Stephanie, and José Gabriel Palma. 2009. "Introduction: The Global Financial Crisis." *Cambridge Journal of Economics*, 33, 531–38.

Boas, Franz, and George Hunt. 1905. "Kwakiutl Texts." *Memoir of the American Museum of Natural History*, 5.

Boas, Franz. 1966. *Kwakiutl Ethnography.* Edited by Helen Codere. Chicago: University of Chicago Press.

Bodley, John. 1985. *Anthropology and Contemporary Problems* (2nd edition). Palo Alto, CA: Mayfield Publishing.

Bodley, John. 1994. *Cultural Anthropology: Tribes, States, and the Global System.* Mountain View, CA: Mayfield Publishing.

Bodley, John. 1999. *The Victims of Progress*. Mountain View, CA: Mayfield Publishing.

Bohannan, Laura. 1966. "Shakespeare in the Bush." *Natural History Magazine*, August/September.

Bohannan, Paul (editor). 1970. *Divorce and After.* New York: Doubleday.

Bourdieu, Pierre. 1986. "The Forms of Capital." In *Handbook of Theory and Research for the Sociology of Education.* Edited by John G. Richardson. New York: Greenwood Press.

Bourgois, Philippe. 1995. *In Search of Respect: Selling Crack in El Barrio.* Cambridge, UK: Cambridge University Press.

Braudel, Fernand. 1982. *Civilization and Capitalism 15th–18th Century: Vol. II. The Wheels of Commerce.* New York: Harper & Row.

Briggs, Jean. 1970. *Never in Anger.* Cambridge, MA: Harvard University Press.

Brown, Michael K., Martin Carney, Elliott Currie, Troy Duster, and David P. Oppenheimer. 2003. *Whitewashing Race: The Myth of a Color-Blind Society.* University of California Press.

Burton, Thomas. 1993. *Serpent-Handling Believers.* Knoxville: University of Tennessee Press.

Cagan, Leslie. 1983. "Feminism and Militarism." In *Beyond Survival: New Directions for the Disarmament Movement.* Edited by M. Albert and D. Dellinger. Boston: South End Press.

Cairns, Ed. 1982. "Intergroup Conflict in Northern Ireland." In *Social Identity and Intergroup Relations.* Edited by Henri Tajfel. New York: Cambridge University Press.

Campbell, Joseph. 1949. *The Hero With a Thousand Faces.* Princeton, NJ: Princeton University Press.

Campion, Nardi Reeder. 1990. *Mother Ann Lee: Morning Star of the Shakers.* Hanover, NH: University Press of New England.

Carneiro, Robert. 1978. "Political Expansion as an Expression of the Principle of Competitive Exclusion." In *Origins of the State.* Edited by Ronald Cohn and Elman Service. Philadelphia: Institute for the Study of Human Issues.

Carneiro, Robert. 1979. "Slash-and-Burn Cultivation Among the Kuikuru and Its Implications for Cultural Development in the Amazon Basin." In *The Evolution of Horticultural Systems in Native South America: Causes and Consequences. Anthropologica* (supplement 2). Edited by J. Wilbert. Caracas, Venezuela.

Carneiro, Robert. 1990. "Chiefdom-Level Warfare as Exemplified in Fiji and Cauca Valley." In *The Anthropology of War.* Edited by Jonathan Hass. New York: Cambridge University Press.

Carrier, James G. 1993. "The Rituals of Christmas Giving." In *Unwrapping Christmas.* Edited by Daniel Miller. Oxford, UK: Clarendon Press.

Carrier, James G. 1995. *Gifts and Commodities: Exchange and Western Capitalism Since 1700.* London: Routledge.

Carrillo, Hector. 2002. *The Night Is Young: Sexuality in Mexico in the Time of AIDS.* Chicago: University of Chicago Press.

Carsten, Janet E. 1989. "Cooking Money: Gender and the Symbolic Transformation of Means of Exchange in a Malay Fishing Village." In *Money and the Morality of Exchange*. Edited by J. Parry and M. Bloch. Cambridge, UK: Cambridge University Press.

Cathcart, Dolores, and Robert Cathcart. 1985. "Japanese Social Experience and Concept of Groups." In *Intercultural Communication: A Reader* (4th edition). Edited by Larry A. Samovar and Richard E. Porter. Belmont, CA: Wadsworth Publishing.

Chagnon, Napoleon. 1983. *The Fierce People* (3rd edition). New York: Holt, Rinehart and Winston.

Chagnon, Napoleon. 1990. "Reproductive and Somatic Conflicts of Interest in the Genesis of Violence and Warfare Among Tribesmen." In *The Anthropology of War.* Edited by Jonathan Hass. New York: Cambridge University Press.

Chomsky, Noam. 2003. *Hegemony or Survival: America's Quest for Global Dominance.* New York: Metropolitan Books.

Churchill, Ward. 1994. *Indians Are Us?* Monroe, ME: Common Courage Press.

Clay, Jason W. 1984. "Yahgan and Ona—The Road to Extinction." *Cultural Survival Quarterly, 8,* 5–8.

Cohen, Mark. 1977. *The Food Crisis in Prehistory.* New Haven, CT: Yale University Press.

Cohen, Mark. 1989. *Health and the Rise of Civilization.* New Haven, CT: Yale University Press.

Cohn, Carol. 1987. "Sex and Death in the Rational World of Defense Intellectuals." *Signs, 12,* 687–718.

Cohn, Carol. 1991. "Decoding Military Newspeak." *Ms,* March/April, 88.

Collier, Jane E., and Michelle Rosaldo. 1981. "Politics and Gender in Simple Societies." In *Sexual Meanings: The Cultural Construction of Gender and Sexuality.* Edited by Sherry B. Ortner and Harriet Whitehead. New York: Cambridge University Press.

Collins, Jane L. 2000. "Tracing Social Relations in Commodity Chains: The Case of Grapes in Brazil." In *Commodities and Globalization: Anthropological Perspectives.* Edited by Angelique Haugerud, M. Priscilla Stone, and Peter D. Little. Lanham, MD: Rowman & Littlefield.

Comaroff, Jean, and John L. Comaroff. 2001. *Millennial Capitalism and the Culture of Neoliberalism.* Durham, NC: Duke University Press.

Conklin, Beth. 2001. *Consuming Grief: Compassionate Cannibalism in an Amazonian Society.* Austin: University of Texas Press.

Covington, Dennis. 1995. *Salvation on Sand Mountain: Snake Handling and Redemption in Southern Appalachia.* New York: Addison-Wesley.

Cowell, Daniel David. 1985/86. "Funerals, Family, and Forefathers: A View of Italian-American Funeral Practices." *Omega, 16,* 69–85.

Crick, Malcolm R. 1982. "Anthropology of Knowledge." *Annual Review of Anthropology,* vol. 11, pp. 287–313. Palo Alto, CA: Annual Reviews.

Crotty, James. 2009. "Structural Causes of the Global Financial Crisis: A Critical Assessment of the 'New Financial Architecture.'" *Cambridge Journal of Economics, 33,* 563–80.

Crowley, Aleister. 1985. *The Book of Thoth.* Stamford, CT: U.S. Games Systems.

Culler, Jonathan. 1977. "In Pursuit of Signs." *Daedalus*, *106*, 95–112.

D'Andrade, Roy. 1995. "Moral Models in Anthropology." *Current Anthropology*, *36*, 399–408.

Davis, D. L., and R. G. Whitten. 1987. "The Cross-Cultural Study of Human Sexuality." *Annual Review of Anthropology*, vol. 16, pp. 69–98. Palo Alto, CA: Annual Reviews.

de Vries, Jan, and Ad van der Woude. 1997. *The First Modern Economy: Success, Failure, and Perseverance of the Dutch Economy, 1500–1815*. Cambridge, UK: Cambridge University Press.

Delaney, Carol. 1991. *The Seed and the Soil: Gender and Cosmology in a Turkish Village Society*. Berkeley, CA: University of California Press.

DeLind, Laura B. 1998. "Parma: A Story of Hog Hotels and Local Resistance." In *Pigs, Profits, and Rural Communities* (pp. 23–38). Edited by Kendall Thu and E. Paul Durrenberger. Albany: State University of New York Press.

Desai, Ashok V. 1972. "Population and Standards of Living in Akbar's Time." *Indian Economic and Social History Review*, 9, 42–62.

Divale, William Tulio, and Marvin Harris. 1976. "Population, Warfare, and the Male Supremacist Complex." *American Anthropologist*, 78, 521–38.

Douglas, Mary. 1966. *Purity and Danger*. New York: Frederick A. Praeger.

Douglas, Mary. 1970. *Natural Symbols: Explorations in Cosmology*. London: Barrie and Rockliff.

Douglas, Mary. 1978. *Cultural Bias*. Royal Anthropological Institute, Occasional Paper No. 35.

Douglas, Mary. 1982. *Essays in the Sociology of Perception*. London: Routledge and Kegan Paul.

Douglas, Mary. 1986. *How Institutions Think*. Syracuse, NY: Syracuse University Press.

Douglas, Mary, and Aaron Wildavsky. 1983. *Risk and Culture: An Essay on the Selection of Technological and Environmental Dangers*. Berkeley, CA: University of California Press.

Dowty, Rachel, Peter May, William Wallace and Colin Beech. 2011. "Organizational Culture and the Katrina Response in Louisiana." In *Dynamics of Disaster: Lessons on Risk, Response, and Recovery*. Edited by Rachel Dowty and Barbara Allen. Oxford, UK: Earthscan.

Drèze, Jean, and Amartya Sen. 1991. *Hunger and Public Action*. New York: Cambridge University Press.

Dumont, Louis. 1970. *Homo Hierarchicus: An Essay on the Caste System*. Chicago: University of Chicago Press.

Durham, William H. 1990. "Advances in Evolutionary Culture Theory." *Annual Review of Anthropology*, vol. 19, pp. 187–210. Palo Alto, CA: Annual Reviews.

Durkheim, Emile. 1961. *The Elementary Forms of the Religious Life*. New York: Collier. (Originally published in 1912.)

Eckert, Penelope, and Sally McConnell-Ginet. 2003. *Language and Gender*. Cambridge, UK: Cambridge University Press.

The Economist. 2009. "Sharia Calling: A Political Row About Muslim Law." Nov. 12. http://www.economist.com/world/europe/displaystory.cfm?story_id=14859353.

Eisler, Riane. 1987. *The Chalice and the Blade*. New York: Harper & Row.

Erasmus, Charles. 1977. *In Search of the Common Good.* Glencoe, IL: Free Press.

Ervin, Alexander M. 2005. *Applied Anthropology: Tools and Perspectives for Contemporary Practice.* Boston: Allyn & Bacon.

Escobar, Arturo. 1995. *Encountering Development: The Making and Unmaking of the Third World.* Princeton, NJ: Princeton University Press.

Evans-Pritchard, E. E. 1937. *Witchcraft, Oracles and Magic Among the Azande.* London: Oxford University Press.

Evans-Pritchard, E. E. 1940. *The Nuer: A Description of the Modes of Livelihood and Political Institutions of a Nilotic People.* Oxford, UK: Clarendon Press.

Evans-Pritchard, E. E. 1985. *Theories of Primitive Religion.* San Francisco: Greenwood Press.

Ewen, Stuart. 1996. *PR: A Social History of Spin.* New York: Basic Books.

Farmer, Paul. 2003. *Pathologies of Power: Health, Human Rights, and the New War on the Poor.* Berkeley, CA: University of California Press.

Fausto-Sterling, Anne. 1993. "The Five Sexes: Why Male and Female Are Not Enough," *The Sciences*, 33(March/April), 20–4.

Fei, Hsiao-Tung. 1939. *Peasant Life in China: A Field Study of Country Life in the Yangtze Valley.* London: Routledge & Kegan Paul.

Ferguson, Niall. 2008. *The Ascent of Money.* New York: Penguin Press.

Ferguson, R. Brian. 1992. "A Savage Encounter: Western Contact and the Yanomami War Complex." In *War in the Tribal Zone: Expanding States and Indigenous Warfare.* Edited by R. Brian Ferguson and Neil L. Whitehead. Santa Fe, NM: School of American Research Press.

Ferguson, R. Brian. 1995. *Yanomami Warfare: A Political History.* Santa Fe, NM: School of American Research Press.

Fernandez, James W. 1978. "African Religious Movements." *Annual Review of Anthropology*, vol. 7, pp. 195–234. Palo Alto, CA: Annual Reviews.

Foley, Douglas E. 1990. *Learning Capitalist Culture: Deep in the Heart of Tejas.* Philadelphia: University of Pennsylvania Press.

Foley, Ellen E. 2010. *Your Pocket Is What Cures You: The Politics of Health in Senegal.* New Brunswick, NJ: Rutgers University Press.

Foucault, Michel. 1979. *Discipline and Punishment: The Birth of the Prison.* New York: Vintage Books.

Fraser, Steve. 2005. *Every Man a Speculator.* New York City: Harper Perennial.

Fried, Morton, Marvin Harris, and Robert Murphy (editors). 1967. *War: The Anthropology of Armed Conflict and Aggression.* Garden City, NY: Natural History Press.

Geertz, Clifford. 1972. "Deep Play: Notes on the Balinese Cockfight." *Daedalus, 101*, 1–37.

Geertz, Clifford. 1973. "The Impact of Culture on the Concept of Man." In *The Interpretation of Cultures.* New York: Basic Books.

George, Susan, and Fabrizo Sabelli. 1994. *Faith and Credit: The World Bank's Secular Empire.* Boulder, CO: Westview Press.

Gibson, Thomas. 1990. "Raiding, Trading and Tribal Autonomy in Insular Southeast Asia." In *The Anthropology of War.* Edited by Jonathan Hass. New York: Cambridge University Press.

Gilmore, David D. 1990. *Manhood in the Making: Cultural Concepts of Masculinity.* New Haven, CT: Yale University Press.

Ginsburg, Faye, and Rayna Rapp. 1991. "The Politics of Reproduction." *Annual Review of Anthropology*, vol. 20, pp. 311–43. Palo Alto, CA: Annual Reviews.

Glanz, James. 2007. "Iraqi Factories, Aging and Shut, Now Give Hope." *New York Times.* January 18. http://www.nytimes.com/2007/01/18/world/middleeast/18factory.html.

Goffman, Erving. 1959. *The Presentation of Self in Everyday Life.* New York: Doubleday.

Goldberg, David Theo. 2009. *The Threat of Race: Reflections on Racial Neoliberalism.* Hoboken, NJ: Wiley-Blackwell.

Goldschmidt, Walter. 1978. *As You Sow: Three Studies in the Social Consequences of Agribusiness.* Montclair, NJ: Allanheld & Osmun.

Gonzalez, Roberto J. 2009. *American Counterinsurgency: Human Science and the Human Terrain.* Chicago: Prickly Paradigm Press.

Gould, Stephen Jay. 1981. *The Mismeasure of Man.* New York: W. W. Norton.

Green, Nancy. 1995. "Living in a State of Fear." In *Fieldwork Under Fire: Contemporary Studies of Violence and Survival.* Edited by Carolyn Nordstrom and Antonius C. G. Robben. Berkeley, CA: University of California Press.

Greenhouse, Carol. 1987. "Cultural Perspectives on War." In *The Quest for Peace: Transcending Collective Violence and War Among Societies, Cultures and States.* Edited by R. Varynen. Beverly Hills, CA: Sage Publications.

Gregor, Thomas. 1990. "Uneasy Peace: Intertribal Relations in Brazil's Upper Xingu." In *The Anthropology of War.* Edited by Jonathan Hass. New York: Cambridge University Press.

Gusterson, Hugh. 1995. *Nuclear Rites: A Weapons Laboratory at the End of the Cold War.* Berkeley, CA: University of California Press.

Guttmann, Robert. 1994. *How Credit-Money Shapes the Economy: The United States in a Global System.* London: M. E. Sharpe.

Gwynne, Margaret A. 2003. *Applied Anthropology: A Career-Oriented Approach.* Boston: Allyn & Bacon.

Hacker, Andrew. 1995. *Two Nations: Black and White, Separate, Hostile, Unequal.* New York: Ballantine Books.

Hall, Edgar T. 1966. *The Hidden Dimension.* Garden City, NY: Doubleday.

Hanson, Allan. 1993. *Testing Testing.* Berkeley, CA: University of California Press.

Harris, Marvin, and Eric Ross. 1987. *Food and Evolution: Toward a Theory of Human Food Habits.* Philadelphia: Temple University Press.

Harris, Marvin. 1977. *Cannibals and Kings: The Origins of Culture.* New York: Vintage Books.

Hart, Keith. 2000. *Money in an Unequal World: Keith Hart and His Memory Bank.* New York: Texere.

Hartwick, Elaine, and Richard Peet. 2003. "Neoliberalism and Nature: The Case of the WTO." *Annals of the American Academy of Political and Social Science, 590,* 188–211.

Harvey, David. 2005. *A Brief History of Neoliberalism.* London: Oxford University Press.

Hayden, Dolores. 1981. *Seven American Utopias: The Architecture of Communitarian Socialism, 1790–1975.* Cambridge, MA: MIT Press.

Henderson, Paul. 1976. "Class Structure and the Concept of Intelligence." In *Schooling and Capitalism: A Sociological Reader.* Edited by Roger Dale, Geoff Esland, and Madeleine MacDonald. London: Routledge & Kegan Paul in association with Open University Press.

Henle, Paul. 1958. *Language, Thought and Experience.* Ann Arbor: University of Michigan Press.

Hernandez-Giron, C.A., A. Cruz-Valdez, M. Quiterio-Trenado, F. Uribe-Salas, A. Peruga, and M. Hernandez-Avila. 1999. "Factors Associated With Condom Use in the Male Population of Mexico City." *International Journal of STD & AIDS, 10*(2), 112–17.

Herrnstein, Richard J., and Charles Murray. 1994. *The Bell Curve: Intelligence and Class Structure in American Life.* New York: Free Press.

Hertz, Robert. 1960. *Death and the Right Hand.* Translated and edited by Claudia and Rodney Needham. Glencoe, IL: Free Press. (Originally published in 1909.)

Ho, Karen. 2009. *Liquidated: An Ethnography of Wall Street.* Durham, NC: Duke University Press.

Hobbes, Thomas. 1881. *Leviathan.* London: Oxford University Press. (Originally published in 1651.)

Hobsbaum, Eric. 1959. *Primitive Rebels: Studies in Archaic Forms of Social Movement in the 19th and 20th Centuries.* New York: Frederick A. Praeger.

Holloway Jr., Ralph. 1968. "Human Aggression: The Need for a Species-Specific Framework." In *War: The Anthropology of Armed Conflict and Aggression.* Edited by Morton Fried, Marvin Harris, and Robert Murphy. Garden City, NY: Natural History Press.

Honigmann, John J. 1976. *The Development of Anthropological Ideas.* Homewood, IL: Dorsey Press.

Honwana, Alcinda, and Filip de Boeck, 2005. *Makers and Breakers: Children and Youth in Postcolonial Africa.* Trenton, NJ: Africa World Press.

Hostetler, John. 1974. *Hutterite Society.* Baltimore: Johns Hopkins University Press.

House, James S., Karl R. Landis, and Debra Umberson. 1988. "Social Relationships and Health." *Science, 241,* 540–45.

Howell, Signe, and Roy Willis (editors). 1989. *Societies at Peace: An Anthropological Perspective.* London: Routledge.

Hsu, Francis L. K. 1967. *Under the Ancestor's Shadow.* New York: Anchor Books.

Hunter, James P. 2008. "Anthropologist Helps Soldiers Understand Iraqis' Needs." American Forces Press Service. http://www.defense.gov/news/newsarticle. aspx?id=48766.

Ikerd, John E. 1998. "Sustainable Agriculture, Rural Economic Development, and Large-Scale Swine Production." In *Pigs, Profits, and Rural Communities* (pp. 157–69). Edited by Kendall Thu and E. Paul Durrenberger. Albany: State University of New York Press.

Illich, Ivan. 1975. *Tools for Conviviality.* London: Marion Boyars.

Inhorn, Marcia C., and Peter J. Brown. 1990. "The Anthropology of Infectious Disease." *Annual Review of Anthropology,* vol. 19, pp. 89–117. Palo Alto, CA: Annual Reviews.

Jager, Sheila Miyoshi. 2007. "On the Uses of Cultural Knowledge." Strategic Studies Institute. http://www.strategicstudiesinstitute.army.mil/pdffiles/pub817.pdf.

Janes, Craig, and Oyuntsetseg Chuluundorj. 2004. "Free Markets and Dead Mothers: The Social Ecology of Maternal Mortality in Post-Socialist Mongolia." *Medical Anthropological Quarterly, 18*, 230–57.

Johnson, Chalmers. 2004. *The Sorrows of Empire: Militarism, Secrecy, and the End of the Republic.* New York: Metropolitan Books.

Johnson, Norris Brock. 1985. *Westhaven: Classroom Culture and Society in a Rural Elementary School.* Chapel Hill: University of North Carolina Press.

Juergensmeyer, Mark. 2000. *Terror in the Mind of God: The Global Rise of Religious Violence.* Berkeley, CA: University of California Press.

Karier, Clarence J. 1976. "Testing for Order and Control in the Corporate Liberal State." In *Schooling and Capitalism: A Sociological Reader.* Edited by Roger Dale, Geoff Esland, and Madeleine MacDonald. London: Routledge & Kegan Paul in association with Open University Press.

Kearney, Michael. 1991. "A Very Bad Disease of the Arms." In *The Naked Anthropologist: Tales From Around the World.* Edited by Philip Devita. Belmont, CA: Wadsworth Publishing.

Keesing, Roger. 1991. "Not a Real Fish: The Ethnographer as Inside Outsider." In *The Naked Anthropologist: Tales From Around the World.* Edited by Philip Devita. Belmont, CA: Wadsworth Publishing.

Kehoe, Alice. 1989. *The Ghost Dance: Ethnohistory and Revitalization.* New York: Holt, Rinehart and Winston.

Keiser, Lincoln. 1969. *The Vice Lords: Warriors of the Streets.* New York: Holt, Rinehart and Winston.

Keiser, Lincoln. 1991. *Friend by Day, Enemy by Night: Organized Vengeance in a Kohistani Community.* New York: Holt, Rinehart and Winston.

Kelly, John D., and Martha Kaplan. 1990. "History, Structure, and Ritual." *Annual Review of Anthropology*, vol. 19, pp. 119–50. Palo Alto, CA: Annual Reviews.

Kennedy, Margrit 1995. *Interest and Inflation Free Money Gabriola Island.* BC, Canada: New Society Publishers.

Kennedy, Paul. 1993. *Preparing for the Twenty-First Century.* New York: Random House.

Kets de Vries, Manfred, and Danny Miller. 1987. "Interpreting Organizational Texts." *Journal of Management Studies, 24*, 233–47.

Kidder, Tracy. 2003. *Mountains Beyond Mountains.* New York. Random House.

Kiefer, Christie. 1977. "Psychological Anthropology." *Annual Review of Anthropology*, vol. 6, pp. 103–19. Palo Alto, CA: Annual Reviews.

Kindleberger, Charles P. 1978. *Manias, Panics and Crashes: A History of Financial Crisis* (4th edition). Hoboken, NJ: John Wiley and Sons.

Kinkade, Kathleen. 1973. *A Walden Two Experiment: The First Five Years of Twin Oaks Community.* New York: William Morrow.

Kipp, Jacob, Lester Grau, Karl Prinslow, and Don Smith. 2006. "The Human Terrain System: A CORDS for the 21st Century." *Military Review*, September/October. http://www.army.mil/professionalWriting/volumes/volume4/december_2006/12_06_2.html.

Klein, Naomi, 2004. "Baghdad Year Zero: Pillaging Iraq in Pursuit of a Neocon Utopia." *Harper's Magazine*, September. http://harpers.org/archive/2004/09/0080197.

Kopytoff, Igor. 1986. "The Cultural Biography of Things." In *The Social Life of Things: Commodities in Cultural Perspective*. Edited by Arjun Appadurai. Cambridge, UK: Cambridge University Press.

Kotlowitz, Alex. 1991. *There Are No Children Here*. New York: Anchor Books.

Kottak, Conrad Phillip. 1990. *Prime Time Society: An Anthropological Analysis of Television and Culture*. Belmont, CA: Wadsworth Publishing.

Kroeber, Alfred L. 1948. *Anthropology*. New York: Harcourt, Brace.

Kuhn, Thomas. 1957. *The Copernican Revolution: Planetary Astronomy in the Development of Western Thought*. Cambridge, MA: Harvard University Press.

La Barre, Weston. 1962. *They Shall Take Up Serpents: Psychology of the Southern Snakehandling Cult*. Minneapolis: University of Minnesota Press.

Lakoff, George, and Mark Johnson. 1980. *Metaphors We Live By*. Chicago: University of Chicago Press.

Lakoff, George. 1996. *Moral Politics: What Conservatives Know That Liberals Don't*. Chicago: University of Chicago Press.

Lakoff, George. 2004. *Don't Think of an Elephant: Know Your Values and Frame the Debate*. White River Junction, VT: Chelsea Green Publishing.

Lakoff, Robin. 1975. *Language and Woman's Place*. New York: Harper & Row.

Lappé, Frances Moore, and Joseph Collins. 1977. *Food First: Beyond the Myth of Scarcity*. New York: Random House.

Layard, Richard. 2005. *Happiness: Lessons From a New Science*. New York: Penguin Books.

Lear, Jonathan. 2006. *Radical Hope: Ethics in the Face of Cultural Devastation*. Cambridge, MA: Harvard University Press.

Lee, Richard. 1969. "Eating Christmas in the Kalihari." *Natural History Magazine*, December.

Lee, Richard. 1984. *The Dobe !Kung*. New York: Holt, Rinehart and Winston.

Levi-Strauss, Claude. 1974. *Tristes Tropiques*. New York: Atheneum Publishers.

Lewis, Oscar. 1959. *Five Families: Mexican Case Studies in the Culture of Poverty*. New York: Basic Books.

Linderman, Frank B. 1962. *Plenty Coups: Chief of the Crows*. Lincoln: University of Nebraska Press.

Livingstone, Frank B. 1968. "The Effects of Warfare on the Biology of the Human Species." In *War: The Anthropology of Armed Conflict and Aggression*. Edited by Morton Fried, Marvin Harris, and Robert Murphy. Garden City, NY: Natural History Press.

Longres, John F. 1990. *Human Behavior in the Social Environment*. Itasca, IL: F. E. Peacock Publishers.

Lorber, Judith. 1995. *Paradoxes of Gender*. New Haven, CT: Yale University Press.

Lowie, Robert H. 1983. *The Crow Indians*. Lincoln: University of Nebraska Press.

Luhrmann, Tanya M. 1989. *Persuasions of the Witch's Craft: Ritual Magic in Contemporary England*. Cambridge, MA: Harvard University Press.

Lutz, Catherine, and Anne Lutz Fernandez. 2010. *Carjacked: The Culture of the Automobile and Its Effects on Our Lives*. Hampshire, UK: Palgrave Macmillan.

Maddison, Angus. 2003. *The World Economy: A Millennial Perspective*. Paris: Development Centre of the Organisation for Economic Co-Operation and Development.

Malinowski, Bronislaw. 1929. *The Sexual Life of Savages in North-Western Melanesia*. New York: Halcyon House.

Malinowski, Bronislaw. 1961. *Argonauts of the Western Pacific*. New York: E. P. Dutton. (Originally published in 1922.)

Mandelbaum, David G. 1949. *Selected Writings of Edward Sapir in Language, Culture, and Personality*. Berkeley, CA: University of California Press.

Marshall, Lorna. 1976. *The !Kung of Nyae Nyae*. Cambridge, MA: Harvard University Press.

Martin, Emily. 1987. *The Woman in the Body: A Cultural Analysis of Reproduction*. Boston: Beacon Press.

Marwick, Max. 1965. *Sorcery in Its Social Setting*. Manchester, UK: University of Manchester Press.

Matsubara, Hisako. 1985. *Cranes at Dusk*. New York: Dial Press.

Maurer, Bill. 2005. *Mutual Life, Limited: Islamic Banking, Alternative Currencies, Literal Reason*. Princeton, NJ: Princeton University Press.

Mauss, Marcel. 1967. *The Gift: Forms and Functions of Exchange in Archaic Societies*. Translated by Ian Cunnison. New York: W. W. Norton. (Originally published in 1925.)

Maybury-Lewis, David. 1997. *Indigenous Peoples, Ethnic Groups, and the State*. Boston: Allyn & Bacon.

McCauley, Clark. 1990. "Conference Overview." In *The Anthropology of War*. Edited by Jonathan Hass. New York: Cambridge University Press.

McElroy, Ann, and Patricia Townsend. 1979. *Medical Anthropology*. North Scituate, MA: Duxbury Press.

McFate, Montgomery, and Andrea Jackson. 2005. "An Organizational Solution for DOD's Cultural Knowledge Needs." *Military Review*, July/August. http://www.au.af.mil/au/awc/awcgate/milreview/mcfate2.pdf.

McFate, Montgomery 2005. "Anthropology and Counterinsurgency: The Strange Story of Their Curious Relationship." *Military Review*, March/April. http://www.au.af.mil/au/awc/awcgate/milreview/mcfate.pdf.

McFate, Montgomery, and Steve Fondacaro. 2008. "Cultural Knowledge and Common Sense." *Anthropology Today*, 24, 27.

McKibben, Bill. 2007. *Deep Economy: The Wealth of Communities and the Durable Future*. New York: Times Books.

Milner Jr., Murray. 2006. *Freaks, Geeks, and Cool Kids: American Teenagers, Schools, and the Culture of Consumption*. New York: Routledge.

Mintz, Sidney W. 1985. *Sweetness and Power: The Place of Sugar in World History*. New York: Viking Press.

Mishkin, Bernard. 1940. *Rank and Warfare Among the Plains Indians*. Monograph No. 3, American Ethnological Society. Seattle: University of Washington Press.

Moffatt, Michael. 1989. *Coming of Age in New Jersey: College and American Culture.* New Brunswick, NJ: Rutgers University Press.

Montague, Susan P., and William Morais. 1976. "Football Games and Rock Concerts: The Ritual Enactment of American Success Models." In *The American Dimension: Cultural Myths and Social Realities.* Edited by William Arens and Susan P. Montague. Port Washington, NY: Alfred Publishing.

Mooney, James. 1965. *The Ghost Dance Religion and the Sioux Outbreak of 1890.* Chicago: University of Chicago Press.

Moore, Robert B. 1976. *Racism in the English Language.* New York: Council on Interracial Books for Children.

Moos, Robert, and Robert Brownstein. 1977. *Environment and Utopia.* New York: Plenum Press.

Morgan, Lewis Henry. 1964. *Ancient Society.* Cambridge, MA: Belknap Press. (Originally published in 1877.)

Mukhopadhyay, Carol C., and Patricia J. Higgins. 1988. "Anthropological Studies of Women's Status Revisited: 1977–1987." *Annual Review of Anthropology*, vol. 17, pp. 461–95. Palo Alto, CA: Annual Reviews.

Mukhopadhyay, Carol C., Rosemary Henze, and Yolanda T. Moses. 2007. *How Real Is Race?: A Sourcebook On Race, Culture, and Biology.* Lanham, MD: Rowman & Littlefield Education.

Mullings, Leigh. 2005. "Interrogating Racism: Toward an Antiracist Anthropology." *Annual Review of Anthropology, 34,* 667–93. Palo Alto, CA: Annual Reviews.

Munoz-Laboy, Miguel, Vagner de Almeida, Luis Felip Rios do Nascimento, and Richard Parker. 2004. "Promoting Sexual Health Through Action Research Among Young Male Sex Workers in Rio de Janeiro, Brazil." *Practicing Anthropology, 26(2),* 30–4.

Myers, Fred R. 1988. "Critical Trends in the Study of Hunters-Gatherers." *Annual Review of Anthropology,* vol. 17, pp. 261–82. Palo Alto, CA: Annual Reviews.

Nagengast Carole. 1994. "Violence, Terror, and the Crisis of the State." *Annual Review of Anthropology, 23,* 109–36. Palo Alto, CA: Annual Reviews.

Nagengast, Carole, and Carlos G. Vélez-Ibáñez (editors). 2004. *Human Rights: The Scholar as Activist.* Oklahoma City: Society for Applied Anthropology.

Needleman, Jacob. 1991. *Money and the Meaning of Life.* New York: Doubleday.

Nichter, Mimi. 2000. *Fat Talk: What Girls and Their Parents Say About Dieting.* Cambridge, MA: Harvard University Press.

Nigh, Ronald. 1995. "Animal Agriculture for the Reforestation of Degraded Tropical Rainforests." *Culture and Agriculture, 51/52,* 2–5.

Nordhoff, Charles. 1966. *The Communistic Societies of the United States.* New York: Dover Publications. (Originally published in 1875.)

Ocaya-Lakidi, Dent. 1979. "Manhood, Warriorhood and Sex in Eastern Africa." *Journal of Asian and African Studies, 12,* 134–65.

Oldfield-Hayes, Rose. 1975. "Female Genital Mutilation, Fertility Control, Women's Roles, and the Patrilineage in Modern Sudan: A Functional Analysis." *American Ethnologist, 2,* 617–33.

Omohundro, John T. 2001. *Careers in Anthropology.* Mountain View, CA: Mayfield Publishing.

Ortner, Sherry B. 1973. "On Key Symbols." *American Anthropologist*, 75, 1338–46.

Pagels, Elaine. 1995. *The Origin of Satan*. New York: Vintage Books.

Palgi, Phyllis, and Henry Abramovitch. 1984. "Death: A Cross-Cultural Perspective." *Annual Review of Anthropology*, vol. 13, pp. 385–417. Palo Alto, CA: Annual Reviews.

Parry, J., and M. Bloch (editors). 1989. *Money and the Morality of Exchange*. Cambridge, UK: Cambridge University Press.

Pasternak, Burton. 1976. *Introduction to Kinship and Social Organization*. Englewood Cliffs, NJ: Prentice Hall.

Payne, David. 1989. "The Wizard of Oz: Therapeutic Rhetoric in a Contemporary Media Ritual." *Quarterly Journal of Speech*, 75, 25–39.

Pearson, Karl. 1901. "On the Inheritance of Mental Characteristics in Man." *Proceedings of the Royal Society of London*, 69, 153–55.

Peters, Ralph. 2000. "The Human Terrain of Urban Operations." *The Eurasian Politician* (Issue 2), October. http://www.carlisle.army.mil/usawc/parameters/Articles/00spring/peters.htm.

Petraus, David, and James N. Mattis. 2006. *The U.S. Army/Marine Corps Counterinsurgency Field Manual*. http://www.fas.org/irp/doddir/army/fm3-24fd.pdf.

Pfeiffer, James, and Rachel Chapman. 2010. "Anthropological Perspectives on Structural Adjustment and Public Health." *Annual Review of Anthropology*, 39, 19–65. Palo Alto, CA: Annual Reviews.

Philips, Susan U. 1980. "Sex Differences and Language." *Annual Review of Anthropology*, vol. 9, pp. 523–44. Palo Alto, CA: Annual Reviews.

Polanyi, Karl. 1957. *The Great Transformation*. Beacon Press: Boston. (Originally published in 1944.)

Price, David, 2007. "Pilfered Scholarship Devastates General Petraeus's *Counterinsurgency Manual*." *Counterpunch*. October 30. http://www.counterpunch.org/price10302007.html.

Putnam, Robert D. 2000. *Bowling Alone: The Collapse and Revival of American Community*. New York: Simon & Schuster.

Rank, Mark R., and Thomas A. Hirschl. 2009. "Estimating the Risk of Food Stamp Use and Impoverishment During Childhood." *Archives of Pediatric and Adolescent Medicine*, 163, 994–99.

Read, Kenneth E. 1965. *The High Valley*. New York: Columbia University Press.

Reardon, Betty. 1985. *Sexism and the War System*. New York: Columbia University Teachers College Press.

Reinhart, Carmen M., and Kenneth S. Rogoff. 2009. *This Time Is Different: Eight Centuries of Financial Folly*. Princeton, NJ: Princeton University Press.

Rich, Bruce. 1994. *Mortgaging the Earth: The World Bank, Environmental Impoverishment, and the Crisis of Development*. New York: Beacon Press.

Richardson, Lewis. 1960. *The Statistics of Deadly Quarrels*. Pacific Grove, CA: Boxwood Press.

Ridington, Robin. 1968. "The Medicine Fight: An Instrument of Political Process Among the Beaver Indians." *American Anthropologist*, 70, 1152–60.

Rindos, David. 1984. *The Origins of Agriculture*. New York: Academic Press.

Rivoli, Pietra. 2005. *The Travels of a T-Shirt in the Global Economy: An Economist Examines the Markets, Power, and Politics of World Trade*. Hoboken, NJ: John Wiley.

Robarchek, Clayton. 1989. "Hobbesian and Rousseauan Images of Man: Autonomy and Individualism in a Peaceful Society." In *Societies at Peace: An Anthropological Perspective*. Edited by Signe Howell and Roy Willis. London: Routledge.

Robarchek, Clayton. 1990. "Motivations and Material Causes: On the Explanation of Conflict and War." In *The Anthropology of War*. Edited by Jonathan Hass. New York: Cambridge University Press.

Robbins, Richard H. 2011. *Global Problems and the Culture of Capitalism* (5th edition). Upper Saddle River, NJ: Pearson.

Rosaldo, Michelle, and Jane Monnig Atkinson. 1975. "Man the Hunter and Woman: Metaphors for the Sexes in Ilongot Magical Spells." In *The Interpretation of Symbolism*. Edited by Roy Willis. New York: John Wiley & Sons.

Rosaldo, Renato. 1989. *Culture and Truth: The Remaking of Social Analysis*. Boston: Beacon Press.

Roy, Ramashray. 1985. *Self and Society: A Study in Gandhian Thought*. Beverly Hills, CA: Sage Publications.

Rubel, Arthur. 1964. "The Epidemiology of a Folk Illness: Susto in Hispanic America." *Ethnology*, 3, 268–83.

Rummel, R. J. 1994. *Death by Government*. New Brunswick, NJ: Transaction Press.

Saitoti, Tepilit Ole. 1986. *The Worlds of a Maasai Warrior*. New York: Random House.

Sanday, Peggy Reeves. 1981. "The Socio-Cultural Context of Rape: A Cross-Cultural Study." *Journal of Social Issues*, 37, 5–27.

Sanday, Peggy Reeves. 1990. *Fraternity Gang Rape: Sex, Brotherhood, and Privilege on Campus*. New York: New York University Press.

Scaglion, Richard. 1990. "Ethnocentrism and the Abelam." In *The Humbled Anthropologist: Tales From the Pacific*. Edited by Philip Devita. Belmont, CA: Wadsworth Publishing.

Scheper-Hughes, Nancy. 1992. *Death Without Weeping: The Violence of Everyday Life in Brazil*. Berkeley, CA: University of California Press.

Scheper-Hughes, Nancy. 1995. "The Primacy of the Ethical: Propositions for a Militant Anthropology." *Current Anthropology*, 36, 409–20.

Schieffelin, Bambi B., and Elinor Ochs. 1986. "Language Socialization." *Annual Review of Anthropology*, vol. 15, pp. 163–91. Palo Alto, CA: Annual Reviews.

Schrire, Carmel. 1984. "Wild Surmises on Savage Thoughts." In *Past and Present in Hunter Gatherer Studies*. Edited by Carmel Schrire. New York: Academic Press.

Schwartz, Gary, and Don Merten. 1968. "Social Identity and Expressive Symbols." *American Anthropologist*, 70, 1117–31.

Scott, James C. 1998. *Seeing Like a State: How Human Schemes to Improve the Human Condition Have Failed*. New Haven, CT: Yale University Press.

Shipton, Parker. 1990. "African Famines and Food Security." *Annual Review of Anthropology*, vol. 19, pp. 353–94. Palo Alto, CA: Annual Reviews.

Shore, Chris, and Susan Wright. 1997. *Anthropology of Policy: Critical Perspectives on Governance and Power*. London: Routledge.

Shostak, Marjorie. 1983. *Nisa: The Life and Words of a Ju/wasi Woman*. New York: Vintage Books.

Shweder, Richard A., and Edmund J. Bourne. 1984. "Does the Concept of the Person Vary Cross-Culturally?" In *Cultural Conceptions of Mental Health and Therapy*. Edited by A. J. Marsella and G. M. White. Boston: D. Reidel Publishing.

Sipes, Richard G. 1973. "War, Sports, and Aggression: An Empirical Test of Two Rival Theories." *American Anthropologist*, *74*, 64–86.

Smith, Adam. 1994. *The Wealth of Nations*. Edited by Edwin Cannan. New York: Modern Library. (Originally published in 1776.)

Smith, Arthur H. 1970. *Village Life in China*. Boston: Little, Brown.

Smith, Raymond T. 1984. "Anthropology and the Concept of Social Class." *Annual Review of Anthropology*, vol. 13, pp. 467–94. Palo Alto, CA: Annual Reviews.

Smith, Robert J. 1983. *Japanese Society: Tradition, Self and the Social Order*. New York: Cambridge University Press.

Solomon, Robert C. 1981. *Love: Emotion, Myth, and Metaphor*. New York: Anchor Press/Doubleday.

Spearman, Charles. 1904. "General Intelligence." *American Journal of Psychology*, *115*, 201–92.

Spindler, George, and Louise Spindler. 1983. "Anthropologists View American Culture." *Annual Review of Anthropology*, vol. 12, pp. 49–78. Palo Alto, CA: Annual Reviews.

Sponsel, Leslie. 1994. "The Mutual Relevance of Anthropology and Peace Studies." In *The Anthropology of Peace and Nonviolence*. Edited by Leslie E. Sponsel and Thomas Gregor. Boulder, CO: Lynne Rienner Publishers.

Stack, Carol. 1974. *All Our Kin: Strategies for Survival in a Black Community*. New York: Harper & Row.

Stein, Stephen J. 1992. *The Shaker Experience in America: A History of the United Societies of Believers*. New Haven, CT: Yale University Press.

Stern, Jessica. 2003. *Terror in the Name of God: Why Religious Militants Kill*. New York: HarperCollins.

Stiglitz, Joseph. 2002. *Globalization and Its Discontents*. New York: Norton.

Stone, Lawrence. 1977. *The Family, Sex and Marriage in England, 1500–1800*. New York: Harper & Row.

Strathern, Andrew. 1971. *The Rope of Moka: Big Men and Ceremonial Exchange in Mount Hagen, New Guinea*. London: Cambridge University Press.

Tett, Gillian. 2009. *Fool's Gold: How the Bold Dream of a Small Tribe at J. P. Morgan Was Corrupted by Wall Street Greed and Unleashed a Catastrophe*. New York: Free Press.

Thomas, Elizabeth. 1959. *The Harmless People*. New York: Alfred A. Knopf.

Thompson, E. P. 1967. "Time, Work-Discipline and Industrial Capitalism." *Past and Present*, *38*, 56–97.

Thompson, Michael, Richard Ellis, and Aaron Wildavsky. 1990. *Cultural Theory*. Boulder, CO: Westview Press.

Thrasher, Frederic. 1963. *The Gang*. Chicago: University of Chicago Press. (Originally published in 1927.)

Thu, Kendall, and E. Paul Durrenberger (editors). 1998. *Pigs, Profits, and Rural Communities.* Albany: State University of New York Press.

Trice, Harrison M., and Janice M. Beyer. 1984. "Studying Organizational Cultures Through Rites and Ceremonials." *Academy of Management Review,* 9, 653–69.

Turner, Victor. 1967. *The Forest of Symbols: Aspects of Ndembu Ritual.* Ithaca, NY: Cornell University Press.

Tylor, Edward. 1871. *Primitive Culture.* London: Murray Publishers.

Underhill, Paco. 1999. *Why We Shop: The Science of Shopping.* New York: Simon & Schuster.

Underhill, Paco. 2004. *Call of the Mall.* New York: Simon & Schuster.

Valentine, Charles A. 1968. *Culture and Poverty: Critique and Counter-Proposals.* Chicago: University of Chicago Press.

Valentine, Douglas. 1990. *The Phoenix Program.* New York: William Morrow.

van den Berghe, Pierre L. 1965. *South Africa: A Study in Conflict.* Middletown, CT: Wesleyan University Press.

van den Berghe, Pierre L. 1970. *Race and Ethnicity.* New York: Basic Books.

van den Berghe, Pierre L., and George P. Primov. 1977. *Inequality in the Peruvian Andes: Class and Ethnicity in Cuzco.* Columbia: University of Missouri Press.

van Gennep, Arnold. 1960. *The Rites of Passage.* Translated by Monica B. Vizedom and Gabrielle L. Chaffe. Chicago: University of Chicago Press. (Originally published in 1906.)

Wagner, Roy. 1984. "Ritual as Communication: Order, Meaning, and Secrecy in Melanesian Initiation Rites." *Annual Review of Anthropology,* vol. 13, pp. 143–55. Palo Alto, CA: Annual Reviews.

Walens, Stanley. 1981. *Feasting With Cannibals: An Essay on Kwakiutl Cosmology.* Princeton, NJ: Princeton University Press.

Wallace, Anthony F. C. 1966. *Religion: An Anthropological View.* New York: Random House.

Wallace, Anthony F. C., and Raymond D. Fogelson. 1965. "The Identity Struggle." In *Intensive Family Therapy.* Edited by I. Boszormenyi-Nagy and J. L. Framo. New York: Harper & Row.

Wallerstein, Immanuel. 1989. *The Modern World-System III: The Second Era of Great Expansion of the Capitalist World-Economy, 1730–1840s.* New York: Academic Press.

Warde, Ibrahim. 2001. "The Prophet and the Profits." *Le Monde Diplomatique.* September. http://mondediplo.com/2001/09/09islamicbanking.

Weatherford, Jack. 1997. *The History of Money: From Sandstone to Cyberspace.* New York: Crown.

Weiner, Annette B. 1988. *The Trobrianders of Papua New Guinea.* New York: Holt, Rinehart and Winston.

White, Leslie. 1949. *The Science of Culture.* New York: Farrar, Straus and Giroux.

White, Leslie. 1959. *The Evolution of Culture.* New York: McGraw-Hill.

Whitehead, Harriet. 1981. "The Bow and the Burden Strap: A New Look at Institution-alized Homosexuality in Native North America." In *Sexual Meanings: The Cultural*

Construction of Gender and Sexuality. Edited by Sherry B. Ortner and Harriet Whitehead. New York: Cambridge University Press.

Whitehead, Neil Lancelot. 1990. "The Snake Warriors—Sons of the Tiger's Teeth: A Descriptive Analysis of Carib Warfare, ca. 1500–1820." In *The Anthropology of War*. Edited by Jonathan Hass. New York: Cambridge University Press.

Williams, Brett. 2004. *Debt for Sale: A Social History of the Credit Trap*. Philadelphia, PA: University of Pennsylvania Press.

Williams, Walter L. 1986. *The Spirit and the Flesh: Sexual Diversity in American Indian Culture*. Boston: Beacon Press.

Willis, Paul. 1977. *Learning to Labor: How Working Class Kids Get Working Class Jobs*. New York: Columbia University Press.

Wilmsen, Edwin N., and James R. Denbow. 1990. "Paradigmatic History of San-speaking Peoples and Current Attempts at Revision." *Current Anthropology*, 31, 489–512.

Wolf, Eric. 1966. *Peasants*. Englewood Cliffs, NJ: Prentice Hall.

Wolf, Eric. 1982. *Europe and the People Without History*. Berkeley, CA: University of California Press.

Wolf, Margery. 1968. *The House of Lim*. Englewood Cliffs, NJ: Prentice Hall.

Wolff, Edward N. 2010. Recent Trends in Household Wealth in the United States: Rising Debt and the Middle-Class Squeeze—an Update to 2007. Levi Institute of Economics of Bard College, Working Paper No. 589. http://www.levyinstitute.org/pubs/wp_589.pdf.

Woodburn, James. 1968. "An Introduction to Hadza Ecology." In *Man the Hunter*. Edited by Richard Lee and Irven DeVore, with the assistance of Jill Nash. Chicago: Aldine Publishing.

World Commission on Environment and Development. 1987. *Our Common Future*. Oxford, UK: Oxford University Press.

Worsley, Peter. 1982. "Non-Western Medical Systems." *Annual Review of Anthropology*, vol. 11, pp. 315–48. Palo Alto, CA: Annual Reviews.

Wright, Quincy. 1965. *A Study of War*. Chicago: University of Chicago Press.

Yanagisako, Sylvia Junko. 1979. "Family and Household: The Analysis of Domestic Groups." *Annual Review of Anthropology*, vol. 8, pp. 161–205. Palo Alto, CA: Annual Reviews.

Young, Allan. 1982. "The Anthropologies of Illness and Sickness." *Annual Review of Anthropology*, vol. 11, pp. 257–85. Palo Alto, CA: Annual Reviews.

Zechenter, Elizabeth. 1997. "In the Name of Culture: Cultural Relativism and the Abuse of the Individual." *Journal of Anthropological Research*, 53, 319–48.

INDEX